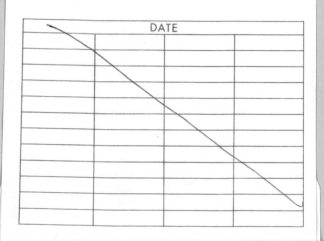

DAVID LLOYD GEORGE AND THE BRITISH LABOUR MOVEMENT

Peace and War

David Lloyd George
and the
British Labour Movement

PEACE AND WAR

CHRIS WRIGLEY
Lecturer in Economic History,
Loughborough University

THE HARVESTER PRESS . HASSOCKS
BARNES AND NOBLE BOOKS . NEW YORK

First published in 1976 by
THE HARVESTER PRESS LIMITED
Publisher: John Spiers
2 Stanford Terrace
Hassocks, Nr. Brighton
Sussex, England
and published in the U.S.A. by
HARPER & ROW PUBLISHERS, INC.
BARNES & NOBLE IMPORT DIVISION
10 East 53rd Street, New York 10022

The Harvester Press Limited
ISBN 0 85527 254 6

Barnes & Noble Books
ISBN 0-06-497910-5

Printed in Great Britain by
Latimer Trend & Company Ltd, Plymouth

Acknowledgments

The greater part of the research upon which this book is based was done by 1970. I was the very grateful recipient of a D.E.S. major award which enabled me to carry it out. I enjoyed the considerable privilege of having Professor Eric Hobsbawm as my supervisor for the thesis. I am also grateful to Professors Royden Harrison and James Joll, its examiners, for their useful and kind comments. The research material has been revised gradually into its present shape whilst I have been a lecturer at Queen's University, Belfast, and at Loughborough University. In teaching I have learnt a lot.

I have enjoyed many pleasant hours of research in the Beaverbrook Library between 1968 and its closure in March 1975. I am very grateful to all its staff for making it such a splendid place in which to work; particularly (during the time the research for this book was done) to A. J. P. Taylor, W. Igoe, and the late Rosemary Brooks. I am also grateful to all the librarians and archivists who so ably look after the collections of documents listed at the back of the book; and to those of Battersea Public Library, Birkbeck College Library, the Queen's University Library, Belfast, and Loughborough University Library.

I am also indebted to the copyright holders of material I have used in this book. I am especially grateful to the First Beaverbrook Foundation, Mrs K. Idwal Jones, Mrs J. Simon, Evelyn, Lady Mottistone, Mrs P. Dower, the Hon G. Samuel and the House of Lords Record Office, the University of Newcastle Library, and the British Library of Political and Economic Science. Transcripts from Crown copyright records in the Public Record Office appear by permission of the Controller of H.M. Stationery Office. If I have failed to contact any copyright holders I sincerely apologise to them. I am very grateful to Viscount Simon and Viscount Harcourt for allowing me to visit their homes in order to inspect their fathers' papers when they were located there.

I would like also to thank A. J. P. Taylor and Dr Mary Cumpston for their kind and useful advice when I embarked on research; Professor Michael Fry for inspecting documents in North America on my behalf; Dr Geoffrey Searle, Geoffrey Hinds and Rodney Lowe for commenting on drafts of various sections of this book; Mrs Sylvia Wrigley, Mrs Maureen Thompson and Mrs Joyce Tuson for patiently typing it; and to John Spiers and the Harvester Press for the helpful and considerate manner in which they deal with their authors. Finally, I am delighted to acknowledge how deeply indebted I am to my family and family friends for their invaluable help and kindness over the years: to Viola and Harold Keat; to my aunt, Joan Hepple; and, above all, to my parents, Sylvia and Arthur Wrigley. This book is dedicated to them.

C. W.

The author and publisher are honoured and grateful to acknowledge an award from the Isabel Thornley Bequest towards publication expenses.

Contents

Introduction

On the whole Lloyd George's biographers have ignored his relationship with the Labour Movement.[1] This is surprising as the years of his premiership were years when economic problems and industrial unrest were at the forefront of public affairs. Indeed throughout the seventeen continuous years he was in the Cabinet there was a transformation in the role of the state in industrial relations and in the economy generally. This was particularly marked in the war and immediate post-war periods.

Lloyd George's relationship with organised Labour was a central strand of his career. His pragmatic interventionist kind of radicalism was a marked contrast to the individualist type of many of the great Victorian radicals. His policy of piecemeal social reform and his fierce verbal assaults on the landed interest before the First World War often overshadowed the nascent parliamentary Labour Party. In these years his well publicised handling of industrial disputes also helped to establish his reputation in Government, and displayed him as the man who could brilliantly negotiate with the trade unions and settle disputes which threatened the economy. His relationship with the Labour Movement between 1914–22 was the major cause of his political isolation after his fall from the premiership. During the First World War his part in the drafting and later the enforcement of the Munitions Acts, his role in the introduction of conscription, and his apparent opposition to 'democratic' war aims, alienated sections of the Labour Movement. At the end of the war his continuance in office under the sponsorship of the Tories, his frequent misrepresentations of the Labour Party's aims, his dealings with the Triple Alliance (especially the Sankey Commission) along with the failure to provide the promised major social reconstruction destroyed his political credibility with large sections of the working class. The distrust organised Labour came to have for him prevented him forming a Centre Party or later successfully moving to the Left.

The concept of the Labour Movement is fundamental to an

understanding of British history of the last hundred years.[2] The
movement has stemmed from the various responses of large
sections of the working class to their economic and social environment. These have had a variety of aspects – such as a cultural
response to urban living, a co-operative response to certain consumer problems, the creation of trade unions in response to
industrial work-place conditions, and a political response to the
problems, and eventually to the whole nature, of the state and
economy. It has been an inclusive movement, a coming together
of sometimes very disparate working-class endeavours, and so has
naturally had some sections more politically advanced than others.
Despite contradictory sectional interests and major ideological
differences many of those in the parts of it have felt themselves to
be in a wider movement. The British Labour Movement has
gained its strength and its fundamental character from the shop
floor and the urban working-class areas, with their pubs, working
men's clubs, co-ops and general way of life.

In the years before the war the Labour Movement generally
was coming to reject the view that labour should bear the brunt of
cyclical down-swings in the economy. Flexible wage rates and
unemployment were increasingly deemed to be unacceptable.
Labour expected a 'living wage' if not a good guaranteed wage,
as a matter of natural justice. To meet this Labour inevitably came
to demand that the Government's activities should go further
than helping those made needy by natural causes (the old, the
sick, etc.) and intervene and manage whole sectors of the economy
in order to safeguard the interests of the working class as a whole.
The war economy, with full employment and with labour recognised as an essential ingredient for victory, gave the Labour
Movement an unprecedented chance to press its demands.

This study deals with Lloyd George's relationship with the
Labour Movement up to the end of the First World War. It
focuses on the First World War as this was a period in which
there was a dramatic change in the relationship between the State
and the British Trade Union Movement. In trying to meet the
needs of 'a war of production' the Government came to attempt
to legislate good industrial relations in war industries. Lloyd
George played a central role in these and subsequent developments. His activities in regulating labour had wide political
repercussions. They were a major contribution to the growth of
his image as the man who could win the war. However, in the
long term, these activities were a major element in the deep
distrust which much of the British Labour Movement came to
have of him.

PART I

Before the First World War

I

The Welsh Radical

During the opening years of the twentieth century Lloyd George was close to Labour's leaders on many of the issues of the day. The Labour Representation Committee (L.R.C.), formed in 1900 and transformed into the Labour Party after its success in the 1906 general election, was an alliance of trade unionists and socialists. The L.R.C. supported the radical crusades against the Boer War and the Balfour Government's Education Bill; and in these crusades Lloyd George was considered by many to be the foremost protagonist. His background was different from those of the leading trade unionists, whose particular industrial concerns he had little experience of in North Wales. And his ideological position was different from socialism – though many of the L.R.C. socialists still shared some of his Gladstonian notions. As a leading non-individualist radical and a noted opponent of issues that the L.R.C. opposed, it is not surprising that when Keir Hardie appealed for a strong progressive alliance to realign the forces in Parliament, it was to Lloyd George that he turned to lead it.

Lloyd George's early career was an integral part of the Welsh nationalist revival of the last decades of the nineteenth century. This was a different social environment from that of the spontaneous revolt from liberalism of industrial workers in the north of England during the same period, which was the background to such men as Philip Snowden's and Fred Jowett's early socialism. The conflict in Wales, particularly in North Wales, in this period was between a largely rural and nonconformist native population and alien English Anglican landlords, many of whom oppressed the farmers and labourers in a truly feudal manner. Thus the conflict was social and economic – against the alien's privileges (including their privileged Church) and against the unjust land system.

Lloyd George from 1890 to 1945 represented Carnarvon boroughs, the area in which he grew up; which, apart from quarrymen and some railwaymen, was virtually devoid of collective groups of workers. His supporters were more likely to be nonconformist small businessmen, shopkeepers, artisans, quarrymen, smallholders and labourers. Indeed the area's characteristics closely resemble the typical background of advanced rural radicalism in France, rather than most English constituencies.

Lloyd George's own plaintive allusions to a starving childhood – which he often made when faced with obdurate trade unionists or shop-floor militants – exaggerate his background somewhat. Richard Lloyd, his lay-preacher uncle, was *a*, if not *the*, leading figure in the village community; and in such a community his background was far from mean. The *Welsh News* obituary commented,

> Like his father, Mr Richard Lloyd had a large shoe trade and employed several hands – It may be pointed out that it is a mistake to say that Mr Lloyd was of humble origin. His ancestry is a fine stock on his mother's side, and equally good on the side of his father, whose forebears were highly respected farmers, the family being still well known in South Pembrokeshire. His pedigree on both sides is of the best agricultural breed in *E. fiondyll*.[1]

Lloyd George recollected times of dining luxuriously on half an egg, but this was untypical of his childhood, as his brother recollected many years later.[2] He himself observed to Frances Stevenson,

> The people in the village where I lived were poor, but there was no real want or privation . . . There was no *wretchedness* in our district . . . I never saw there any of the privation and suffering which is depicted in *Les Miserables*. It was not until I grew up and left Wales that I realized what poverty really meant and what a need the poor have of someone to fight for them.[3]

Despite the particularist Welsh background, his early political consciousness was of high Victorian politics and many high Victorian stock notions underlined his evolving political views. Thus, for example, in his early political career, and to a large extent throughout his life, he was a firm believer in the efficiency and moral values of individualism and democracy.

He revelled in the nonconformist tradition which he publicly extolled as stretching back from the Wales of his youth to Cromwell and beyond; and this conconformity to him was remarkable for its development of a rugged individualism. Thus in 1895 he declared:

One of the great principles of the Puritans was to teach personal responsibility, to confer honour upon the country, upon the man and not upon the official, upon the man rather than the squire, upon the man more than upon the priest. The man was, according to Cromwell, greater than the King, and also greater than property. That briefly sums up the Puritan faith . . . There never has been a time in the history of Nonconformist Wales when it was more necessary to expound those principles than the present.[4]

He was a life-long democrat, from early on in favour of universal suffrage.[5] His early speeches argued the case of democracy not only in order to bring all the people into participation in the shaping of their future but also as being valuable morally in the actual use of the vote:

And how beneficient soever in intent and conception may be the measures we design for the workman, they will not obtain their full object unless he has a part in fighting for them himself. The noblest effect of good legislation is the influence it has upon character, and the best part of that influence of good laws is derived from the struggle to obtain them.[6]

And he saw the purpose of Liberalism, especially in these early years, as providing the *opportunity* of even the poorest to be a self-respecting citizen and a 'whole man'. 'Toryism', he said, in November 1890, 'has a different mode of appealing to the people whom it coaxes with promises of an occasional blanket or a quantity of coal. To Toryism the life of a workman is only a matter of charity. Liberalism, however, raises a man from the ditch and enables him to face the highest in the land to demand what is right for his labour.'[7]

To differing extents, Lloyd George kept these and similar high Victorian radical attitudes. Of course these were a common heritage he shared with the majority of the trade unionists and, indeed, with many of the socialists – most notably with provincial nonconformists such as Hardie and Snowden.

But the difference in outlook between Lloyd George's views and the socialists', though occasionally blurred by his fiercer language and their continued attachment to many old radical panaceas, was marked – especially on land, industry and profit.

Whereas for the Independent Labour Party (I.L.P.) urban socialists the essential question (despite hang-overs of Henry George and obsessions with land) was the struggle for justice of the industrial working class, Lloyd George's early experience was of agrarian conflict. Instead of postulating the socialist view of the class struggle, Lloyd George saw the conflict in the rural radical light of landlord and parson (backed by the brewer) against the small farmer, urban tenant and labourer; and the Welsh situation of the alien Tory landlords and Church often in conflict with nonconformist Welsh tenant farmers and labourers gave force to his position.

Though a section of advanced radicals, influenced by Henry George, accepted land nationalisation, Lloyd George never advocated this much. Indeed, following Welsh radical precedents, his early remedies were very far from drastic. In urging that 'the Welsh farmers should have greater fixity of tenure, that the allowances for unexhausted improvements should be upon a more liberal scale, and that leaseholders should be enfranchised' he followed Thomas Gee's policies, as he did in advocating the appropriation of tithes for secular purposes.[8] By the turn of the century he was urging another old radical remedy – the taxing of the 'unearned increment'. Already he had turned to these aspects of the land system as a source of raising revenue to pay for social reform; thus in 1895 he was suggesting appropriating the tithe, increasing death duties, taxing urban ground rents or taking mineral royalties as a way of paying for old age pensions.[9]

Indeed Lloyd George often attacked more vigorously the social aspects of the land system than the economic basis of it. Thus in a speech, which is all but a parody of assumptions often implicit in his land speeches, he makes the moral case for land reform: 'We do not object to the present land system because it produces poverty and engenders ill-feeling, but because it makes for servility and encourages greed, and we wish to bring up men who are strong and self-reliant on their own resources.'[10] He also made out the characteristic advanced radical case why land alone should be a special case for State intervention and breaking laissez-faire economics:

> The question is asked: 'Why should you invoke legislative inter-ference for the purpose of fixing the price of land more than that of any other commodity?' The answer is a simple one, and I think a very conclusive one. Competition affects the price of land in a very different manner from that in which it affects goods in general. The general effect of competition is to reduce the price of an article, but with land its only influence is to increase the price. This is not the full statement of the case, because whilst competition increases the value of the land, it decreases the value of the produce out of which the farmer is enabled to pay the rent, so that it becomes necessary that the farmer should be protected against extortionate rents.[11]

For Lloyd George the basis of his economic attack on landlords was that they were an idle class who reaped the benefits of the work of others and their exhorbitant rents oppressed the farmer into working beneath a reasonable profit margin. Thus in 1896 in opposing the Agricultural Land Rating Bill he attacked the Tory argument 'that it was unfair to rate land on a different standard from that applied to personalty' in these very clear terms – 'There was this difference between the two kinds of property – personalty was the creation of the industry of its owner; land was not so. Land had not been improved materially by the owners of the soil.'[12] He also deplored in this Bill, the aid to the landlords whilst the farmers were not making sufficient profit – 'They were not suffering in the actual and real sense of the word, the same as the farmers who had got their sons working hard like labourers on a farm, and who yet were receiving no wages . . . it was a simple act of justice to come to the rescue of these farmers.'[13]

In general Lloyd George advocated a degree of redistribution of wealth. He recognised the fact that greater national wealth did not necessarily help all classes.[14] And he could succinctly state the case for achieving social justice by redistribution of existing wealth.

> It is a matter which is notorious to all of you that there is not one of the horses of these high born gentlemen that is not better fed, better housed, and less worked than thousands of working men in this very Union. Things must be equalized. This deplorable state of things cannot go on forever . . . The countries in which the worker has attained the greatest share of comfort and competence are not the very rich and prosperous, but the comparatively poor countries like Switzerland. It is not in the creation of wealth that England lacks, but in its distribution.[15]

However, his proposals of redistribution usually centred on the land – he saw the idle landlord at one extreme and the impoverished farmer and overworked labourer at the other, but very little in between.

His comments on Harcourt's famous 1894 Budget indicate his tendency to attack the landlords' return on their assets, but not the industrialists'. 'The Budget Bill', he said, 'is the most important reform placed upon the Statute Book during the last half century. Here you have a Bill which contains the principle that you should tax the landlord as you tax the merchant, that you should place the man who does nothing to earn his livelihood at any rate on the same basis as the man who earns his fortune by his own skill and industry.'[16] Characteristically he overlooked the fact that the day of the entrepreneur was largely past, and that many of the fruits of industrialisation were taken by shareholders who, like the 'idle landlord' did not participate in the business. Thus Bernard Shaw's comment whilst upbraiding delegates at the I.L.P. Inaugural Conference in 1893 could have applied to Lloyd George. Shaw said that they made the 'very undesirable distinction between income arising out of Rent and those coming from Interest which, he thought, they ought to have grown out of by now'.[17]

Even when monopolies and trust became an issue for speeches at the time of Chamberlain's tariff reform campaign, Lloyd George remained blinkered to 'the great land trust'[18] which was indeed a social hindrance, but the changing pattern of British industry was surely also worth a mention! Lloyd George would attack the agrarian system with great gusto, but he avoided any major questioning of the industrial system (at least until the profiteering of the First World War forced it to his attention).

If the difference between the socialists and Lloyd George was ideology, the differences between L.R.C. trade unionists and Lloyd George were just as marked, even if their outlooks shared many nonconformist and Gladstonian traits. The bulk of the trade unionists' particular interests were measures to improve the conditions of the urban working class, both at work and at home. Lloyd George's rural background caused him to have a very different emphasis. During the 1890s, and with slowly diminishing emphasis thereafter, his attention was largely fixed on the issues of home rule, Welsh disestablishment (and later education) and temperance.

Welsh home rule was posed by Lloyd George in these years as the way whereby all social evils in Wales would be cured.[19] In his more progressive advocacies of it, he posed it as a means to the solution of the real social evils (though characteristically the implicit enemy was the landlord): 'If Wales has the management of her own affairs, will she punish the poor labourer who covets the luxuries of nature for his half starving children, while at the same time showering honour and dignity upon those who have plundered the people of whole estates?' And whilst speaking to miners at Merthyr he argued that Welsh home rule would protect them from low wages during trade recessions: 'When the depression comes – as come it must – the whole resources of the country will be marshalled around the grim monster of hunger to find a home for it in the places of idlers and thriftless.'[20] But just as often Welsh home rule was advocated as a further extension of democracy – the old Liberal panacea that whatever faults there were in the system all would come better with truer and more efficient democracy. And Lloyd George's arguments pushed beyond the old Liberal concept of democracy being both a duty and a moral lesson to the citizen to advocating Welsh home rule as the means of achieving 'the nation's collective salvation'.[21]

The issue of Welsh disestablishment was a question of privileges at the heart of Welsh liberalism. The Anglican Church in Wales was an alien Church in a privileged position, which catered for a minority of the population. The exactions of the Church were not great, but they fell on nonconformist and Churchmen alike and were an especial irritant to Welsh farmers in this period of agricultural depression. In Wales, though probably not as much as in Ireland, to strike at the established Church, which was very closely linked to the ascendant English aristocracy, was also to strike a blow at the social structure as a whole. As Lloyd George put it, 'It is a fight of the people against the aristocracy – a fight of Nonconformists for their rights against Churchmen for their privileges.'[22] When Irish home rule was damaged as an election issue by the Parnell tragedy, Lloyd George felt that in Wales Liberals should 'fight the next election on Disestablishment and practically ignore the Irish question'.[23]

Though Lloyd George at first took the extreme temperance position that temperance reform must come *before* any other reforms he soon came to argue that as well as temperance legislation there must be social reform.

> Temperance reform is not altogether a question of removing the public houses; there are other incentives to drink which need attention. Poverty, misery, the sense of wrong, ill treatment by our social system, squalor, dinginess, the lack of proper nourishment, and the environment which surround the poorest classes were all incentives to the people to forget their miseries in drink. To effect legislation on the temperance question all the misery which surrounds the people must be removed . . .[24]

When he put the case as vigorously as this his position was very close indeed to Keir Hardie's, which was that society should control drink (it should be municipalised) and that the rapid cure of social evils would get at the causes of drunkenness (the reverse view of the temperance fanatics).[25] But usually Lloyd George concentrated on denouncing the drink trade and pressing for local option rather than primarily emphasising the social causes encouraging drunkenness.

However Lloyd George's recognition of the need for the collective conscience of the community to act on drink helped save him from individualistic laissez-faire; and he would recognise the need for State intervention on other social problems (such as advocating old age pensions in the 1892 and 1895 elections). He said on more than one occasion, 'The State now, like the individual, recognises that it is possessed of a conscience, the combined consciences of all, and the State now, therefore, meddles with everything . . .'[26]

Whilst these issues, which were central to Lloyd George's position in Wales, were low on the list for the L.R.C. trade unionists, their particular interests were matters he scarcely came across in North Wales. Indeed before he entered office his contact with the trade unions was small. In this he was not exceptional among M.P.s.

Up until the 1890s the State very largely avoided intervening in industrial relations. The various Arbitration Acts of the nineteenth century were ineffective.[27] Where Parliament did intervene was in working conditions. From the early years of the Industrial Revolution it had regulated various conditions of work – including safety regulations, the maximum hours which children could work, and the form of payment for work. There had seemed to be no pressing need for State intervention in industrial relations in mid-Victorian England when strikes were generally confined to districts, and the overall number of days lost tended to be small. Such strikes did not threaten the framework of society nor – before German and American competition became vigorous in foreign markets – did they threaten the national economy to any great extent.[28] There was no pressing need for governments to abandon laissez-faire in this direction.

During the 1890s, as prosperity returned, trade union rank and file members became increasingly restless with the joint conciliation and arbitration boards and, in certain industries, with the sliding scales which together had helped to reduce the number of disputes during the great depression (1873–96) when selling prices and consequently wages had fallen.[29] Gladstone was forced to act in 1893 when the coal miners in Yorkshire, Lancashire and the Midlands were locked out from August until November, this stoppage threatening to harm other industries, and to reduce severely domestic supplies that winter. He intervened by inviting both sides to accept Lord Rosebery as conciliator; and Rosebery successfully brought them to agreement.[30] M.P.s and the Speaker had acted as conciliators before – but on the initiative of one side or the other of the dispute, not as a member of the Government on the instigation of the Government.

Pressure from Lloyd George in Parliament led to a precedent being set of a 'private' dispute between employers and employees being discussed in the House of Commons. The occasion for this was the arbitrary sacking of fifty workmen, who spoke only Welsh, by the London and North-Western Railway Company in the autumn of 1894. Lloyd George at first wished to move a direct censure of the company, and Balfour asked the Speaker if it was in order 'to bring forward . . . a Resolution directed against the management of a private enterprise in respect of matters with regard to which it is not suggested that the managers of that enterprise have, directly or indirectly, broken either the letter or spirit of the law'. Lloyd George explained that he was going to amend the resolution to one moving that a select committee should look into the matter, and the Speaker allowed a discussion on these terms to take place.[31]

In the ensuing discussion Lloyd George justified his raising of the subject by arguing that a railway company had its monopoly granted by Parliament, that various improvements in its assets had been paid for by Parliament, and that Parliament already intervened in fixing the rates the company charged.[32] The Government front bench hesitantly supported him in raising the issue, Bryce (President of the Board of Trade) saying that the Welsh members were right to bring up an issue about which the Welsh felt strongly, and weakly commenting that he 'did not at all admit that there might not be cases in which it might be proper for the House to enquire into the management and rules of a great statutory company'.[33]

The Opposition protested vigorously at such an intrusion into the affairs of companies. Plunket, a director of the company, protested that 'in future it would be the right and established practice, should the House establish this Resolution . . . to call for an enquiry into the conduct of the private business of any private company or private employer as to whom he shall engage, the laws which shall govern him, and the circumstances in which he shall be at liberty to dismiss his servants'.[34] Balfour concluded the discussion by commenting that the House would never have the time 'to interfere with every controversy that may arise between a company and its employees', that a committee appointed by the House would have no powers to gather evidence or to enforce its decision, and concluded by hoping 'that we may never again be asked to occupy our time by constituting ourselves an amateur Board of Conciliation'.[35]

During the 1895 general election campaign Lloyd George was not dilatory in claiming the credit for this parliamentary innovation in industrial relations and indeed magnified the scope of his precedent. Thus at Carnarvon he said 'It is the first time in the history of the House that a direct motion has been proposed for the purpose of instituting an enquiry into an act of oppression committed by a company of employers against their servants. Up to this point is has not been considered to be a part of the functions of the House of Commons to protect workingmen against the tyrannical acts of employers', and he proudly added 'Mr John Burns afterwards told me that he considers the discussion marks one of the most important epochs in the Parliamentary history of labour during the last 30 years, because it establishes the right of the House of Commons for the first time to protect working-men against every act of tyranny and oppression in every part of the Kingdom.'[36]

However, in taking up the issue his prime motive was to bang the nationalist drum, not establish such a precedent. Thus he wrote in a letter to his uncle the day before he put his motion to the Speaker, 'I think we will make a good show and gain something. No harm in proving that Nationalism means something more immediate and substantial than ideals.'[37] And this is further revealed by his remarks at Holywell in November 1894 that a similar case had occurred two or three years before, but that as he had no evidence of the linguistic cause of dismissal and the company denied it, he had had to let the matter drop.[38] The fact is that the issue arose in the midst of his vigorous Cymru Fydd campaigning – and for this purpose it was a godsend to him. In his speeches he characterised it as 'the greatest scandal which has been perpetrated in Wales within living recollection'.[39] It fitted into the pattern of his nationalist expositions. 'The Welsh language', he declaimed at Rhyl,

is still a badge of servitude . . . In political warfare we ought to be fighting for the national honour. The contempt with which Welsh-men are treated in legislative matters as if they are of no account, permeates the whole dealings of a certain class of men towards them, and it is time that Welshmen stand up to them. The shameful treat-ment of our countrymen by a couple of railway pashas is only another instance of it. The officials cannot talk the language of the country in which they dwell but, instead of their being sent about their business for linguistic incompetence, the livelihood of hundreds of Welsh workmen and their families are to be sacrificed for their ignorance. In India, knowledge of the native language is essential to railway officials; in Wales it seems to be a disqualification. Welshmen are held of less account than niggers. Well, all that we have to say is 'If we stand this treatment we deserve it'. The remedy rests with us Welsh-men. We must combine for our own protection. Whether dealing

face to face with monopolists who despise our language, our tradi-
tions, our aspirations, or extracting legislation out of indifferent or
hostile Parliaments, that is the only sure means of success.[40]

It also provided him with yet another nationalist issue he could
press on his colleagues in the Welsh parliamentary party.[41]

The case that industrial disputes were not just private matters
but concerned the State was strengthened in the last years of the
century by the national engineering strike and lock-out of 1897
and the notorious conduct of Lord Penrhyn to his quarrymen in
1899–1903. In the latter case, Lloyd George was again prominent,
both as a local M.P. and as the men's lawyer. In this dispute
Lloyd George was a strong supporter of the quarrymen and made
the case for better conditions for labour; but once again his
approach was more of the nationalist and radical than of a Labour
man.

Penrhyn's authoritarian control of his quarries led to bitter
strikes in 1896–7 and 1899–1903 over wages and conditions.
Penrhyn refused to recognise the men's union, though his father
had recognised it earlier.[42] He refused to allow the disputes to go
to arbitration, even by the Board of Trade, which had been given
authority by the Conciliation Act of 1896 to intervene in trade
disputes if both sides agreed. Ritchie, the President of the Board
of Trade, intervened and communicated personally with Penrhyn,
but to no avail. His rebuff discouraged his successors from such
a forward personal role until Lloyd George's accession to the
post.[43]

In these strikes Lloyd George spoke up for the workmen's
rights. Before the Conciliation Act, Lloyd George in 1893 had
supported moves to send such disputes to arbitration; at a
demonstration in support of 500 Llechwedd quarrymen, when
their strike had lasted three months, he backed the motion, 'that
it is of the utmost importance for the good of the slate industry
and the community at large that such Boards [joint boards of
arbitration] in labour matters should be established by law, with
the necessary compulsory powers, and calls upon the Party in
power to take the matter in hand without delay'.[44] In his speeches
Lloyd George emphasised that such disputes were matters of
public concern; thus in 1897 he asserted, 'Lord Penrhyn . . . says,
"This is my private affair, it is my business". The Board of Trade
says that it is not his business alone, where the rights of three
thousand men are concerned. It is not his business when there is
nothing between ten thousand people and famine, but the charity
of their sympathetic countrymen.'[45] And he was forthright in his

support of 'the right of workmen to combine to obtain their rights', commenting 'Lord Penrhyn has refused to acknowledge the right of the men to combine. I know very well that an isolated individual, especially if he is half starved and has a large family dependent on him, can easily be cowed, but it is different when he has to deal with a committee entrusted to act for the isolated individual.'[46] During the 1896–7 dispute he saw the significance of the dispute for workmen elsewhere, commenting at the beginning of 1897, 'The Bethesda men are really fighting the battle of the workingmen throughout the country, and if they are supported by their fellow workmen in the struggle, I venture to prophesy that the employers will eventually have to change their tune to the producers of wealth.'[47] And when the 1899–1903 strike became a national issue, he successfully appealed at the 1902 T.U.C. that the unions should support the quarrymen against Penrhyn (who was 'not only a great capitalist, he was a feudal lord') so that 'while they were fighting their children should be placed beyond the reach of starvation'.[48]

But in his speeches on these strikes he more often emphasised the radical rather than the trade union points of the dispute. This was probably the most acceptable approach in the area, and with the quarrymen themselves, who were a very untypical group of workmen. The quarrymen formed a distinct community of their own, which was almost wholly Welsh in nationality and language, and nonconformist in religion; and apparently many of them had small plots of land which they cultivated to help maintain their families during hard times.[49]

The arbitrary power of such an individual as Penrhyn over thousands of others was taken by Lloyd George as a grave threat to the existing order as well as being unjust; whereas to a socialist critic it would have been used as evidence of the iniquity of the whole capitalist system. Thus at the Queen's Hall, London, in 1903 Lloyd George said of Penrhyn, 'He has been offered any amount of alternatives, but he has rejected them all, and it is for the State to deal with him. Men of this sort are a danger even to property.'[50] On one occasion only did he question the whole economic system, and then in a phrase: 'Since this is a battle between the masses and the capitalists it behoves every Welshman and every quarryman who cherishes the principle of union to stand by the Llechwedd men in this conflict.'[51] But this was the mere use of the phrase – it had no significance in ideological terms for him, as can be seen by the combination of the call to 'every Welshman' with the statement of class struggle. Quite possibly Lloyd George picked up this kind of expression from Keir Hardie's recent visit to the local miners' second May Day demonstration. More characteristic is the rest of the speech where he used the old radical phraseology and fiery speech to call for mild remedies; thus his peroration: 'Messrs Greaves ought to be proud of their men, for have they not materially aided in placing them in a position of wealth and comfort? Mr Greaves has three mansions which have been maintained by the sweat of quarrymen. These men work in the bowels of the earth, in the midst of sufferings and toil, endangering their lives and limbs, and all this goes to increase the wealth of the quarry owners.' His conclusion to this was not a demand for nationalisation or profit sharing, however, but, 'Against this I say nothing further than that in return for all this wealth the employers should treat their men with some consideration.'

Similarly, he took the key of the dispute to be the land system. In dealing with minerals and land generally, as has already been indicated, he wanted to see reasonable rents; thus speaking on Crown lands on one occasion, he argued that, 'The Crown ought to set a good example to private owners by charging only such an amount as would enable the lessees of quarries to make reasonable profits and pay reasonable wages.'[52] In the case of Penrhyn he was confronted with an English landlord, whose lands were believed to be lapsed Crown lands, and who blatantly tyrannised his workmen. At the May Day carnival at Carnarvon in 1897 (where John Burns was also on the platform), Lloyd George was quite explicit in his emphasis, 'Apart from the principle of labour, there is involved in the dispute a principle of a greater importance, in which workmen in general are interested – namely the right of the people to the land, to the mountains, and to the resources of the earth.'[53] And generally on the quarry strikes, his was much more the voice of rural radicalism and of Welsh nationalism than of Labour. In one characteristic speech he spoke of the land before the Penrhyns stole it, on which 'there *dwelt* a *simple, honest community* of *small cotters*, farmers and shepherds', but in time

The *free mountain* has become Lord Penrhyn's quarry, and three thousand *Welshmen*, the *descendants*, many of them, of the *simple folk* who knew not how to *rob in legal fashion*, have become his *hewers of wood* and *drawers of water* . . . One of our *Welsh proverbs* says, '*Stronger a weak lord than a strong servant*' but another is equally true '*Better a country than a lord*'. Yes a *united people* is stronger than *many lords*. I trust the farmers of South Wales will unite and band themselves together, not only as farmers, but as *Welshmen*, to resist the *forces of oppression and tyranny*.[54]

Lloyd George, like many other radicals, stood firmly for fair wages (no lower than the district rate) in municipal and Government contracts as an example to private employers. In 1889–90 a committee of the House of Lords condemned sweating, and in 1891 the Commons passed a resolution that the Government should 'make every effort to secure the payment of the rate of wages generally accepted as current for a competent workman in his trade'.[55] On the Carnarvon County Council Lloyd George followed the L.C.C. Progressives' lead in supporting fair wages in municipal contracts. When a Tory Councillor argued the remedy should only be 'that individuals should not purchase goods which were the product of sweating', Lloyd George gave a collectivist reply:

> let the Council do what the individual was recommended to do . . . What London has done, what the Government has done, what large towns like Wolverhampton have done, I think Carnarvon County Council may safely follow, not only in the interests of labour, but also in the interests of the best employers and the whole community. The best interests of the ratepayers lies in the protection of the workmen. I do not agree . . . that it is the Council's business to get the cheapest goods at the lowest prices.[56]

During these years before Lloyd George gained office, he consistently supported the rights of trade unions. During the sweating debate on the Council he asserted he was 'a believer in trade unions'. On one occasion he showed he was better aware of overall trade union interests than his local railwaymen. The London and North Western railwaymen had made very favourable arrangements with the company on employer's liability for accidents occurring at work, and called Lloyd George to account for not supporting a contracting out amendment to the 1894 Employer's Liability Bill. Though the meeting was hostile to him, Lloyd George stood by his principles against the men's sectionalism:

> Railwaymen are one class of workmen whilst the Employer's Liability Bill deals with the whole country and with men in every description of trade. It must be said of the London and North-Western Railway Company that, as a rule, they treat their men with considerable liberality, but they are an exception, and the Bill . . . is to be applied to the whole country. Therefore Asquith . . . has to take into account what is best for the majority of the working classes.

He was clearcut in his views on contracting out – 'As a rule I believe that contracting out is a bad principle inasmuch as it is the right of every man to have full compensation for every injury received in the course of employment.'[57] In a similar vein he pressed the Government of the day to see that firms undertaking War Office contracts did not force their employees 'to sign agreements to belong to no trade union society'.[58]

Overall, in the years before he went to the Board of Trade Lloyd George did support trade unionism. He fairly commented in May 1905, when supporting a Liberal who was faced with socialist opposition, 'There has never been a working class question brought before the House of Commons in which I have not supported the claims – the legitimate claims – of the working classes.'[59] He did not go out of his way to champion trade union matters – but as the representative of an area with few groups of trade unionists in it, this is hardly surprising.

II

Lloyd George, Labour and social reform

In the first fourteen years of the century Lloyd George's type of radicalism frequently complemented and often outshone the political activities of the Labour leaders. This chapter surveys three aspects of this. Firstly, there is the attitude of the L.R.C. leaders to Lloyd George and his attitude to independent Labour representation. Secondly, there is his response to the critical problem of unemployment. Thirdly, there is the related matter of Lloyd George's ability, by his policies and his fiery oratory, to hold the limelight amongst those urging reform on the Left of British politics.

The tide of radical fortune, largely in abeyance since 1886, turned with the turn of the century. Radicals and Labour men campaigned in unison on the three issues which were at the fore-front – the Boer War, Balfour's Education Bill and Joseph Chamberlain's tariff proposals. In the 1890s the I.L.P. were at pains to take an independent line from the Liberals – emphasising unemployment and other defects of capitalism. But on these three issues the difference in outlook between a radical such as Lloyd George and a socialist such as Keir Hardie was small.

Lloyd George's attitude to the Boer War was fairly consistent and clear-cut. Where his views did change during the course of the war was on the practicality of returning independence to the Boers. Naturally his point of attack moved from the incompetence of the Government generally to the vile nature of the concentration camps, and from the implausibility of the Ministry's initial war aims to the continuance of operations after the capture of Pretoria (these he deemed to be a 'second' war which was designed as a means of acquiring territory and gold mines). Basically Lloyd George felt it was an unjustified and aggressive war. He was not a pacifist; nor was he totally against the Empire, as he made abundantly clear during the tariff controversy. He viewed the issue largely as a question of nationalism. 'The truest patriot', he said, 'is the man who reverences patriotism wherever it is found.'[1] In the past he had opposed imperialist ventures in Gladstonian terms,[2] and a large part of his political career to this time had centred on championing the rights of his small nation against a larger nation. He easily transferred his recurring theme of nationalism being a divine gift for the good of mankind from the Welsh situation to the Boer situation.

His arguments were little different than those of the Labour and socialist opponents of the war, although few Labour men put so much emphasis on nationalist arguments as Lloyd George did; and he did not go as far as some radicals (notably J. A. Hobson) and socialists in condemning it as a profiteering war. Lloyd George did not develop, as Marxists did, an analysis of capitalism which revealed it as leading to imperialism. Keir Hardie from early on was characterising it as '. . . a capitalist war. The British merchant hopes to secure markets for his goods, the investor an outlay for his capital, the speculator more fools out of whom to make money, and the mining companies cheaper labour and increased dividends.'[3] But Lloyd George did denounce the war as one intended to gain goldfields and enhance the value of South African mining shareholders, and he pointed to the unprincipled and unpatriotic nature of the Stock Exchange.[4]

He denounced the war as vigorously as Labour and socialist speakers for hindering social reform. In particular he pointed out that the war would set back the giving of old age pensions, which the Tories had promised in the 1895 general election. Thus in his first speech in Wales during the war he warned, 'There is not a lyddite shell which bursts on the African hills that does not carry away an old age pension.'[5] And like the Labour and socialist opponents of the war he argued that it would be the poorest sections of the community who would be most affected by its large cost. On several occasions he drew his conclusions from the effects of the Napoleonic Wars, conscious of the threat they had posed to the social order. Thus at Oswestry he urged, 'After the Napoleonic Wars, what happened in this country? Black bread for the people, and little of it; starvation and riot! We can not go to war and spend hundreds of millions without bringing want and misery and suffering to the lot of the poor.'[6]

With the issues of Balfour's Education Bill and Chamberlain's tariff proposals the nonconformist elements of the Labour Representation Committee again brought their new organisation into line with the radical wing of the Liberal Party. This overshadowed the L.R.C.'s claim of independence. Bernard Shaw observed,

> A Socialist Society cannot take the Free Trade point of view. We are necessarily anti-Free Trade, anti-Manchester, anti-laissez-faire, anti-Cobden and Bright, anti all the Liberal Gods. Twice already within a few years the Socialists and Labour men have bolted into the Liberal camp; first on the war, second on the Education Bill. In both cases there was room for differences of opinion. But now it seems that there is going to be a third bolt over Free Trade . . .[7]

For the Liberals the Education Bill was virtually an unmixed political blessing – uniting all sections of the Liberal Party after the sharp divisions on the Boer War. And for Lloyd George it was the right issue at the right time. 'This is the fight which has appealed to me most', he told a reporter, 'it has been in my blood.'[8] Even during his campaign against the Boer War he had made speeches arguing that freeing the people from the priesthood was a major political issue.[9] With the end of the war, the Education Bill, which was largely a religious controversy (though in pre-dominantly nonconformist Wales, with its exceptional pride in its education system, it had strong nationalist overtones), gave him an issue which not only helped Party unity but also allowed him to move to the centre of the Party. Lloyd George consolidated his reputation and gained recognition from the Liberal leadership by in effect leading the Liberal opposition to the Bill.[10]

He attacked the Tory Bill on the broad issue that 'Under the Bill, public money will be used to teach doctrines which the vast majority of the people do not believe in.'[11] And though now and then he played up to sectarian prejudices[12] he centred his arguments on civil and religious equality, and urged that education reform should be a means to industrial and national efficiency. The L.R.C. took much the same line. At their 1902 Conference they discussed the issue at some length. They passed resolutions in favour of a coherent education system from primary to technical school with adequate scholarships to give every child educational opportunities; and apart from particularly emphasising the need for feeding needy children they argued in much the same way as did radicals and Liberals.

Much the same was true of the tariffs controversy. For the radicals and Liberals it was a campaign on the pure milk of their gospel. Thus the aged Lord Ripon felt that this controversy – 'The abandonment of Free Trade, the taxation of foods, if not of raw materials, to which whatever J.C. may say, his policy leads, the disorganisation of industry and the war of tariffs, which are inevitable features of this policy' – 'is the greatest political struggle of my long political life'. The Liberal leaders hardly needed his prompting that they 'ought to unite against this vulgar clap-trap the intelligence and the knowledge of the country as well as the self-interest of the masses'.[13]

Lloyd George joined Asquith and the other Liberal leaders in campaigning round Britain against Chamberlain's proposals. He had spoken before of Protection being a measure at the expense of the poor. In 1892 he had asked an audience, '. . . the old Tory cry of Protection . . . what does it mean? It means increasing the inequalities that exist at the present moment. Protection in America means increasing the wealth of millionaires and the impoverishment of the working men there . . .'[14] This theme he kept up – and, very characteristically, he persistently argued that remedying the land system would solve Britain's social and economic problems. Thus at Oldham in 1903 he argued for better wages and housing for farm labourers – 'It will not inter- fere with trade; on the contrary it will improve trade. Instead of crowding to the towns to bring down the price of labour, the men will stick at and develop the soil.' Land reform was his alternative to tariff reform. He explained to his Oldham audience, 'The land is the real problem that any statesman should try to solve. If a man is given fixity of tenure, things will improve, produce will be increased, and the population will go back to the land. Then drooping agriculture will revive, blossom and bring fruit, in which we will all participate.'[15] L.R.C. speakers had little to add on the subject; speakers such as Snowden joined Lloyd George in pressing land reform as a major part of their alternative to tariffs.[16]

By becoming shadows of the Liberals in their opposition to these 'Tory iniquities' the L.R.C. did themselves little good in the country. Probably they had little choice if they intended speaking on the major issue of the day. Attempts to arouse enthusiasm for other issues, such as industrial reform, did not get them far in these circumstances. As their Executive noted of the by-election in December 1903 (where the Liberal candidate won and theirs came third), 'The contest almost exclusively turned upon Mr Chamberlain's fiscal proposals, and labour issues were altogether obscured.'[17]

With few supporters in the House of Commons, Keir Hardie and MacDonald considered gaining more immediate parliamentary impact by arranging an alignment with the radicals and Irish. They appealed to John Morley (though a laissez-faire radical he

was approached as an opponent of the Boer War), then Lloyd
George, and, later, to John Burns to lead such a group.

In an open letter in the *Labour Leader* of 3rd March 1903,
Hardie appealed to Lloyd George not to be tempted by the flesh-
pots of office 'but to lead a Progressive Alliance of Radicals, Irish
and Labour with the battle-cry of, "People versus Privilege"'.
Keir Hardie warned him of being 'muzzled and manacled' by
minor office in a Liberal Government led by 'its Mammon wor-
shipping Roseberys, Haldanes, Fowlers, Asquiths and their like';
and, recalling the frustration of the Welsh group during the dis-
mal 1892–5 Liberal Government, and Lloyd George's stand on
the Boer War and Education Bill, he urged him to lead such an
Alliance for 'genuine reform . . . before you . . . sink into the bog
of political turpitude into which the will-of-the-wisp of office
will seek to allure you'.[18]

Keir Hardie and MacDonald believed at this time that co-
operation with the 'other forces of Progress' on social reform was
quite legitimate, arguing that 'independence is not isolation'.[19]
The more advanced socialists expected that, as the 'new politics'
would be on class lines, there would be an inevitable realignment
and the radicals would come to them. As 'Marxian' of the *Labour
Leader* put it, 'As soon as Liberalism sheds its rich weaklings the
Radical rump is bound to come over to Socialism'.[20]

Lloyd George was frequently one of the radicals mentioned by
Hardie in his plans for new alignments. In May 1899 he called for
the creation of a real radical party and named Lloyd George along
with Dilke, Logan and Atherley Jones as men who might
organise it. Once this was done they could have 'Socialist and
Socialist-Radical working side by side to overthrow the common
enemy', the 'Rosebery–Chamberlain' supporters.[21] Later Hardie
followed Glasier's suggestion that a 'White List' should be made
of radicals whom the L.R.C. should support in the forthcoming
general election. He recognised that the opponents of the war
'held mixed opinions on many matters and include such unbending
individualists as John Morley and Leonard Courtney, together
with some Socialists like Dr Clarke and Lloyd George', but
argued that, 'It might . . . be the means of adding one more
element to the slowly uniting forces of Democracy, by bringing
into line those Radicals who are with us in all but name . . .'[22]
Naturally Labour men of Lib-Lab inclination such as Richard Bell
welcomed the suggestion. Moderate socialists such as George
Barnes protested at 'the War being made the test'. Fred Bramley
acidly observed,

Do we not as Socialists look upon this War and all wars as part of an inevitable outcome of the present economic condition, and that war is, after all an effect and not a cause? What then are we going to say to those individualists who oppose the war with all their might, but still do all they can to support the present competitive system? Are we going to give men our support because they oppose an effect but still do nothing to remove the cause?[23]

No national 'White List' was prepared. But though Hardie had his knuckles rapped on ideological grounds on this occasion, he and MacDonald still pursued a progressive alliance. Such a move was to the taste of many who attended the L.R.C. annual conferences, as is suggested by the fact that they regularly voted down attempts by the socialists to get 'ultimate aims' motions passed at them.

It was hardly surprising that Lloyd George made no response to Hardie's approach. Many representatives of organised Labour, notably the miners' M.P.s, had no desire to be independent from the Liberals. The number of supporters the L.R.C. had in Parliament was negligible at this time; and of these a man such as Richard Bell was virtually indistinguishable from the Lib-Labs.[24] Lloyd George, who knew full well the importance of a party machine, was not going to throw aside his position in the Liberal Party for such a Labour grouping, especially when Liberal fortunes were rapidly improving. At last he was receiving recognition from the Liberal leadership. He had demonstrated his parliamentary skills in organising the Welsh group in the 1892–5 Parliament, in his vigorous opposition to the Tories' Agricultural Rating Bill of 1896, and in his efforts on behalf of the Penrhyn quarrymen. Herbert Samuel testified to these skills in a letter to his wife: 'I have had an excellent lesson in Parliamentary tactics in Lloyd George's class.'[25] Lloyd George had made a name for himself throughout Britain by his campaigns against the Boer War and Balfour's Education Act. By mid-1904 the Liberal leaders were frequently consulting him.[26] As he later commented, 'It is a terrible struggle, the struggle to secure recognition.'[27] He was not going to break away from the Liberal Party when success seemed at hand.

In addition, Lloyd George had hitherto always been dubious of Labour forming a separate party rather than existing as an 'interest' within the Liberal Party. From the beginning of his political career he had spoken up for working-class unity in elections. Thus in one very early speech he observed,

A philosopher has said that the way to make a man happy was by

B

whipping him until he felt he was happy. The Tory workingmen do not exactly believe in that, but they vote for the Tories because they want something from the Tories – to rent a piece of land which the Tories possess, or are afraid of being turned out of their cottages which are the property of the Tories. Let the workingmen unite, and then all the forces of the enemy cannot overcome the stern sons of Eryi.[28]

But the unity he wanted was within the Liberal Party – Liberal principles would uplift the workingman[29] and the Party would 'relieve labour by replacing the burden upon the right shoulders', by which he meant those of the idle landlords.[30] With the appearance of the I.L.P. in 1892 he was most emphatic that the working class should organise within the Liberal machinery. Thus amongst the quarrymen at Bethesda he said:

I cannot understand why there should be any necessity for a separate Labour Party at all. When it is a case of a small nationality like Wales or Ireland forcing its views upon the great majority of the electors of the United Kingdom, then undoubtedly a separate party is justifiable and highly desirable; but inasmuch as those interested in Labour questions compose the overwhelming majority of the electorate of the United Kingdom, they have only to express their views clearly, and to take the simple course of joining Liberal Associations and then select candidates who fairly represent their views. The demand for a Labour Party will therefore be unnecessary. ... The danger of the labour movement at the present moment seems to be to confine itself to one or two questions of what I cannot but help thinking to be of secondary importance. The great subjects which have been inscribed on the Liberal programme are none the less of interest to labour that they are championed by *an officially recognized Party in the State*. I consider the land question, the temperance question and the question of Disestablishment to be equally matters of interest to labourers as an Eight Hours Bill. These questions invoke the emancipation of labour from its trammels, the elevation of the working man by educating him, by removing from his path temptations to the formation of habits which degrade and enslave him; and as far as the land question is concerned, by providing a source of productive employment which will enrich the country and make him more independent.[31]

Apart from the very condescending attitude to the workingman exhibited in this last passage, his comments on the party the working class should support emphasise a basic divergence between the L.R.C. outlook and his. The majority of the L.R.C.'s supporters accepted the ideal (if not, sometimes, the practice) of the unity of labour, whatever trade, whether skilled or unskilled. This idea was emphasised in the L.R.C.'s Executive's Second Annual Report: 'There is some danger . . . in action which makes the Labour member the representative of one trade rather than of the general interest of wage earners. It is the wage earner, and not only the miner, the engineer or the railway servant who needs representation . . .'[32] Whereas the politics of Liberalism were much more ostensibly bound up with varying 'interests' vying for attention within the Party's programme (the Newcastle programme being the obvious example).

In the period before the 1906 election Lloyd George earned himself the reputation of being the leading Liberal most favourable to Labour. During the election campaign he spoke for Labour candidates where they were not opposing Free Trade Liberals. At Newcastle in 1903 he said, 'I hope to see Liberal and Labour returned at the next election. For my own part I have never been able to see the distinction. Once in the House of Commons there is none: Liberal and Labour always work together. I have never seen a Labour resolution for which I have not voted, and there has not been a Liberal resolution which Labour has not supported. The distinction is purely nominal.'[33] But he remained quite explicit in his doubts about the need for a Labour Party. Thus at Carnarvon he commented, 'Liberals are against anything in the nature of class representation, and I think that it was a mistake for the Labour Party to go in for anything like independent class representation. They will realise that sooner or later.'[34] Other prominent Liberals made comments favourable to Labour, notably Campbell-Bannerman and Grey, the latter on one occasion urging Herbert Gladstone (himself notably favourable to Labour): 'Labour should have more direct representation in the House of Commons and every Liberal should not only admit this but wish it.'[35] But Lloyd George's particularly strong reputation for being a friend of Labour stemmed from his radical utterances and his promises of social reform.

Those reforms he gave details of remained his familiar catalogue of Welsh grievances, including the matters arising from his criticism of the land system. In addition he made unspecific promises of reform; for example at Falkirk in 1902, when speaking of election issues, he said, 'It is the part of every reformer and part of the principles on which I form my policy that if there is anything wrong, any misery or any injustice in the country, it has got to be righted.'[36] He made it clear that he felt a wide-based party of social reform could prevent the appearance of socialism. Thus in a speech in late 1904:

We have a great Labour Party sprung up. Unless we can prove, as I think we can, that there is no necessity for a separate Party to press forward the legitimate claims of labour, you will find the same thing will happen in England as has happened in Belgium and Germany – that the Liberal Party will be practically wiped out, and that, in its place, you will get a more extreme and revolutionary Party, which will sail under the colours of socialism or Independent Labour.

I don't think that will be necessary. I think that it would be a disaster for progress. I think that it is better that you should have a Party which combines every section and shade of opinion, taken from all classes of the community, rather than a party which represents one shade of opinion alone and one class of the community alone. Progress will suffer, I am sure, by a policy of that kind, and it rests with the Liberal Administration which we can see on the horizon, to prevent such a state of things from coming about.[37]

As well as being opposed to politics on a class basis, he even spoke of various reforms ending the class war. Thus of education reform, he predicted: 'How many problems will be solved? Capital may get a better remuneration without reducing wages. Wages might be increased, and still get better returns for capital. Above all the improved conditions of Labour will bring the end of civil war between capital and labour, which destroys industry and creates bitterness and strife.'[38]

The Liberal Government took office in December 1905, and during its tenure Lloyd George was closely associated with many of the social reforms that it did implement. The advent of the Labour Party and the growing impact of the Labour Movement, not just in industrial action but also in organising pressure for social reform, considerably influenced Lloyd George. The emergence of Labour gave strength to his wing of the Liberal Party; and he was quite adept at using the presence of Labour M.P.s to reinforce his arguments with his colleagues, in a similar way to Asquith's use of the Irish Nationalists.

After the 1906 election Lloyd George frequently urged substantial radical reforms as the alternative to socialism. He opposed 'socialism' not Labour representation. In Wales he spoke of the British variety as 'the wretched, pitiful socialism which was below even the socialism of the Continent', and commented that 'He objected to that Socialism, not because it called attention to real social evils and tried to remedy them, but because its remedy was worse than the disease.'[39] During the 1906 election campaign, when mentioning Labour, he had made his usual comments about them working together, preferably in the Liberal Party;[40] but after it, with a thirty-strong parliamentary Labour Party in the Commons, he urged the need for major reforms. Much of this was to put pressure on his more conservative colleagues, and to give leadership to radicals. Thus his most famous utterance came at Cardiff in the autumn of 1906 just before the Lords considered the Government's Education Bill. After a speech outlining his old favourite Welsh national policies (disestablishment, devolution, and education, land and temperance reform), he called for no division in the forces of progress, for Labour to give 'its assistance to give direction to the policy of Liberalism'; and warned fellow Liberals that if they 'tamely allowed the House of Lords to extract all the virtue out of their Bills, so that the Liberal statute book remained simply a bundle of sapless legislative faggots fit only for the fire; then would a real cry arise in this land for a new party, and many of us here in this room would join in that cry.'[41]

A year later at the time he settled the threatened railway strike, he made an even more radical utterance when talking about socialism:

> It was the feeling that there was something wrong where one man had wealth, and spent his whole day in trying to find out how he could consume it, and another spent the whole day in trying to find enough to keep misery, poverty and wretchedness from the door. That was wrong. The earth was made for the children of men. They were entitled to a fair share – all those who really made a good use of it. A great, wealthy country like this . . . this great palace, this imperial mansion . . . ought not to have a single toiler, however poor, living in its meanest attic. There were indications of some terrible unrest beneath the surface of our national affairs, and unless something were done, the rapids would sweep everything to destruction.[42]

Agitation over unemployment put pressure on the Liberal leadership to come up with positive social policies. The numbers of unemployed rose markedly at the end of the Boer War – and in the ensuing months S.D.F. agitation over this and over school feeding had more effect on the Liberal leaders than any Fabian permeation. In November 1904, after the S.D.F. had sent Campbell-Bannerman a resolution on school feeding, Gladstone observed, 'I would keep the S.D.F. courteously at arm's length. At the same time I think that this children's breakfast question ought to be looked into by someone like S. Buxton or Bryce, for we none of us know how far we can go in the matter.'[43] Campbell-Bannerman agreed and suggested the setting up of policy committees to look into this, other issues such as education, and possibly unemployment.[44] Campbell-Bannerman's interest in these committees was reinforced by the unemployed demonstrating; as he told Gladstone, 'I had the unemployed on hand at Manchester and did not know what the mischief to say.'[45]

Lloyd George's references to unemployment in the 1906 election campaign were not notably constructive. Indeed he accepted it like the weather: 'It is almost impossible to prevent unemployment. Business is as difficult to understand and appreciate in its fluctuations as the weather. All you know is that it is like the tide; one moment it surges up and seems as if it would cover the land with prosperity; the next moment it recedes, leaving a high and vast muddy bank. You can hardly tell why.' His conclusion was to alleviate the harmful consequences but not to search out the cause: 'The only thing you can do is to mitigate the distressful consequences or provide against them, and the business of a sensible Government is not to try to regulate matters by empirical methods, but to provide against unemployment when it comes.'[46] It is possible, though unlikely, he might have been more constructive in public if there had not been a Cabinet Committee just appointed 'to examine and advise the Cabinet'.[47] The level of unemployment fell after February 1906, and in July Campbell-Bannerman informed the King (who in February had expressed anxieties on the subject[48]) that the Cabinet had 'decided not to attempt to amend the very imperfect Act of last year, pending the Report of the Royal Commission on Poor Law administration but to propose a vote of a sum not exceeding £200,000 to meet next winter's requirements and to take the plan of H.M.'s Relief Fund and of a local rate.'[49]

Lloyd George was more thoughtful about the matter when unemployment rose markedly again in 1908. On 11 March the Cabinet considered the Labour Party's Right to Work Bill; of which Asquith observed to the King, 'The Bill imposes on Local Authorities the obligation to provide work for all applicants at public expense, and at the standard rate of wages – an obviously inadmissable proposal.'[50] However, there appears to have been division of opinion in the Cabinet as to what line to take on it; Lloyd George being one who was more favourably disposed to it,[51] though it is doubtful if he fully approved. Certainly by late April he was saying, 'It was a bad Bill. The worst service that you can render to any cause is to suggest wild, stupid, silly, impracticable remedies.'[52] It is doubtful that he would have said this much simply out of loyalty to a collective Cabinet decision or because he was particularly concerned about the cost of schemes as he was now Chancellor of the Exchequer.

However, his fertile mind was soon looking into alternative remedies. He argued 'it is not a question of one remedy; you will have to have several remedies'. He suggested that one such measure was his Patents Act, and that 'an improved land system, which would develop the resources of the country' would be another major contribution. Even with such improvements he felt 'there would be a margin left, but I believe that by a superior state of municipal organisation it would be possible to deal afterwards even with that surplus'.[53]

In the early autumn of 1908 Lloyd George tried to work out further measures which would contribute to the reduction of unemployment. After his return on 26 August from his trip to Germany with Harold Spender he was full of enthusiasm for social insurance in general. As early as 8 September he told Herbert Lewis of his projected unemployment scheme:

> After deducting such people as railway workers whom fluctuations did not affect, domestic servants for whom there was always a demand etc., he estimated there were 5 millions of workers who could be dealt with – the average of unemployment would be 3 or 4 per cent. If they had 10/- a week that would require 5 millions (?), three of which would be provided by the trades unions by contributions from the employers and men and two million by the State. That would mean the complete organisation of the trades and would of course immensely strengthen the position of the trades unions.[54]

He amplified how he felt the scheme would be administered in a conversation with Riddell in October. Riddell recorded: 'His idea is to form a board in each trade which will make a levy in prosperous times upon employers and workmen, and apply the sums contributed to alleviate distress in times of depression. His suggestion is that the Board should be formed of employees and workmen with an independent chairman.'[55] It is interesting to see that from his first thoughts on the matter Lloyd George was quite clear that such a policy would strengthen the unions. Also he hoped the State would provide 40 per cent of the contributions; in the event it provided 25 per cent. However, the planning of unemployment insurance passed from his hands. After Lloyd George enthused to Churchill on the topic, the latter took it up and the Board of Trade became responsible for the legislation.[56] In April 1911 Lloyd George tried to get unemployment insurance under his control as well as health insurance. He argued that the Board of Trade's Bill was weak, and in particular observed, 'The Engineers and a few other trades who are included in its scope will derive less benefit from it than they are now enjoying from their own trade union organisations against unemployment. Not merely will they receive nothing from the State contribution, but a part of their own employers' subscription, which is really earned by their labour, will be devoted to subsidising other trades which are not kindred to their own.'[57] He asked Elibank to press on Asquith the case for his being in charge of both, but in the event Sydney Buxton managed unemployment insurance through the Commons.

As well as raising the question of unemployment insurance in 1908, Lloyd George also pressed the possibility of reorganising Government naval contracts. In early September he discussed with McKenna the 'possibilities of allowing a few ships from next year's programme to be laid down at once so as to maintain a more even level of construction up to the end of March without increased unrest'. In doing so he expressed considerable concern at the level of unemployment 'in the engineering and ship-building trades which Churchill tells me is acute and increasing, especially on the Clyde and Tyne'.[58] McKenna, however, felt he had already done what he could.[59] An even stronger letter from Churchill, who apparently was behind the idea in the first place,[60] failed to alter his verdict until the Cabinet decided to do this in October.[61] Another proposal which Lloyd George aired was a major scheme of afforestation.[62] This was a proposal of which even Burns appears to have approved.[63]

The unemployment issue came to the fore again in mid-October 1908. On 14 October Churchill spoke passionately on unemployment and a Cabinet Committee was set up, which included Lloyd George and Churchill as well as Burns and McKenna.[64] However, although the setting up of the Committee was a blow to Burns' position, he managed to block a radical proposal that local authorities should be empowered to levy a 1d rate to pay wages.[65] This proposal stemmed from Henderson and the Labour Party, and was backed by Churchill and Buxton, and less warmly by Lloyd George.[66] The Cabinet was probably impressed by Burns' argument in the Cabinet Paper that such a rate 'would only yield in the areas of England and Wales having Distress Committees some £230,000. But the principle of paying wages out of rates would have been admitted, and this . . . would lead straight to the Right to Work Bill.' But the Cabinet did agree to increase the parliamentary grant to £300,000 to enable more people to be eligible for work, and to grant further loans to distress areas.[67] Eight days later the Cabinet called on Burns to furnish a weekly report.[68]

The numbers unemployed fell from December 1908, and from

1911 to the outbreak of the war usually less than 3 per cent of members of trade unions who made returns to the Board of Trade were unemployed. In this situation Lloyd George gave little more thought to the problem of unemployment, other than seeing it as one of the ills which would be lessened by land reform.

Pressure from the Labour Movement also played a part in prompting the Liberal Government to put social reform at the front of its programme. It stirred the Cabinet from expressions of general sympathy into taking action on the issues of feeding necessitous school children and providing old age pensions, as well as dealing with unemployment.

It cannot be said that at the outset of Campbell-Bannerman's Government Lloyd George was an advanced social reformer. The limitations of his outlook at this time are well revealed in the speech he made on poverty to the Society for Social Service of the North Wales Wesleyans on 25 September 1906.[69] In it he declared that the Poor Law system was inadequate to deal with the state of poverty which had been revealed by the investigations of men such as Charles Booth and Rowntree. He told his audience, 'There are ten millions in this country enduring year after year the tortures of living while lacking a sufficiency of the bare necessities of life; and all this amidst a splendid plenty . . .' His analysis of the immediate causes of poverty was a mixture of the old and new radicalism. 'There is', he said, 'the fact that a man's earnings are not adequate to maintain himself and his family; there is the inability of men to pursue their avocation owing to sickness, old age or inherent lack of stamina or vitality. Then there is the most fertile cause of all – a man's own improvident habits, such as drinking and gambling. That is supposed to account for 60 per cent of the poverty in this land.' In developing these points he fell back onto his old favourite causes of temperance and land reform. He declared, 'Drink and the land laws between them are responsible for nine tenths of the slumminess of our towns, and our system of land ownership is responsible for labour conditions in the country, which drive men in thousands from the villages into the towns.' On this occasion, as on many others, he advocated a limited redistribution of wealth:

I do not suggest that there should be a compulsory equal distribution of the wealth of this country amongst its inhabitants, but I do say that the law which protects those men in the enjoyment of their great possessions should, first of all, see that those whose labour alone produce that wealth are amply protected, with their families, from actual need, where they are unable to purchase necessaries owing to circumstances over which they have no control. By that I mean not that they should be referred to the scanty and humiliating fare of the pauper, but that the spare wealth of the country should, as a condition of its enjoyment by its possessors, be forced to contribute first towards the honourable maintenance of those who have ceased to be able to maintain themselves.

In this Lloyd George appears to accept the Labour theory of value but did not develop from it ideas of socialist redistribution.

Lloyd George's motivation for social reform was a mixture of deep feelings and considerable political sagacity. He frequently expressed concern for the efficiency of the nation, yet he also had a genuine concern for the sufferings of the poor. He had become aware of the lot of the urban poor through reading such books as Victor Hugo's *Les Miserables* and from walking around the East End of London at the time of the Jack the Ripper murders. His policies were a mixture of old radical panaceas and of a growing recognition that the State should intervene in a major way on behalf of the less fortunate members of the community.

Before taking office in December 1905, he usually appeared as an advanced radical of the Victorian type. Thus during the Boer War period, for example, he promised that under a future Liberal Government there would be a return to the old radical trinity of 'peace, honest finance and social reform'.[70] In this style he appeared as the spokesman of nonconformity, temperance and nationalist radicalism; and advocated education reform, temperance measures, Welsh disestablishment and land reform. In the Liberal Government he continued to press the nonconformist interests hard at times.

But mixed with this, and increasingly important, he showed he had no qualms about State intervention to meet what he felt to be a proven wrong. Thus just before the Liberal Government took office he commented, 'The old idea was the less legislation the better . . . Unfortunately – probably I ought to say fortunately – the vast majority of the people of this country have come to the conclusion that when they find a man hopeless and trodden underfoot in the terrible struggle for existence, and when that man is too weak to struggle for himself, it is the business of the community to give him a helping hand.'[71] Even so, as this statement shows, he still intimated that reform should only follow public opinion and that the sphere of the State was to help only the most depressed persons. Nevertheless, Lloyd George revealed from early on a great flexibility of approach to social problems, a willingness to feel his way to new pragmatic solutions. His approach was not ideological, stemming from clearly thought out first principles. But his solutions, though piecemeal, were collectivist in tendency. And so his actions justify his inclusion amongst the leading figures in the rethinking of Liberalism (the 'New Liberalism') which took place before the First World War.

The provision of old age pensions as a measure to remedy poverty stemming from old age was something Lloyd George had long supported, albeit intermittently. His former hero, Joe Chamberlain, brought forward a contributory pension plan in April 1891, and in the 1892 general election Lloyd George spoke up for pensions but denounced Chamberlain's contributory scheme. Lloyd George proclaimed the need for a fund to be formed to pay for them, and urged, 'let ground rents be taxed, let excessive pensions and salaries be reduced, and let the Royal Family be allowed just enough to keep up their dignity while they are with us'.[72] He returned to old age pensions in the 1895 election when the Tories again made promises to introduce them. In this election he proposed to pay for them by increasing the newly introduced death duties, using the tithe, and by introducing various taxes on the land.[73] Lloyd George next took an active interest in pensions when he became a member of the Select Committee of the House of Commons on 'The Aged Deserving Poor', which the Salisbury Government appointed in March 1899 after a national campaign for old age pensions had got underway. Lloyd George successfully widened the Committee's proposals considerably, partly out of altruism and partly to embarrass the Government ('They can neither carry out these recommendations nor drop them – not without discredit').[74] Subsequently he used the Tory Government's failure to implement this election promise as a stick with which to beat them – in particular whilst he was opposing the Agricultural Rating Bills and the Boer War.

However, on taking office Lloyd George himself was at first timid on pensions. During his 1906 election campaign he argued that the country could not afford a very ambitious scheme in view of the cost of the Boer War. He observed that the difference between giving a pension at sixty or at sixty-five meant 12 to 20 million pounds, and that 'at the present time it would be impossible to get the people of this country to face an expenditure of 20 million pounds for anything'. He concluded, 'They must first of all put the national finances in spick and span order, and then see that every man too old to pursue his ordinary avocation should be saved from the humiliation of the workhouse or parish relief.'[75] In this he was in line with the other Liberal leaders. One former Cabinet Minister even expressed a preference 'in giving precedence to the repeal of the Sugar Duties over a pension scheme' if there was any problem of financing pensions.[76]

Members of the Liberal Cabinet remained somewhat reluctant to make pensions a priority until they were pressurised by Labour and certain radical M.P.s. As with feeding of school children and proposals to deal with unemployment, it was pressure from these quarters which stirred the Liberal Cabinet from expressions of general sympathy for these measures into action. The question of pensions became even more pressing as the House of Lords mutilated the Government's Education Bill, and in 1907 when the Liberals lost by-elections in Jarrow and the Colne Valley to Labour and socialist candidates. These election defeats indicated to many Liberals that the Government should be more radical in its measures. Emmott observed that the Colne Valley result indicated 'that the country if tired of the Government is tired of its moderation'.[77] Lloyd George, writing of the 1908 Budget which contained the details of the Government's old age pension scheme, observed, 'It is time we did something that appealed straight to the people – it will, I think, help to stop this electoral rot, and that is most necessary.'[78]

Nevertheless concern at the cost overshadowed the nature of the Liberals' old age pension scheme. The scheme was non-contributory, though as Lloyd George was at pains to point out, 'You tax tea, coffee, sugar, beer and tobacco, and you get a contribution from practically every family in the land one way or another.'[79] In the House of Commons Lloyd George blocked extending the scheme by emphasising that in the form presented to the Commons it would cost at least £6 million and most probably more.[80] During its passage Lloyd George reluctantly agreed to cut out the proposal to reduce the amount of pension payable to couples living in one household. He also removed the flat rate of 10s per week, and allowed a sliding scale of benefits from 3s to 8s. This was opposed unsuccessfully by the Labour Party who wanted 5s as an absolute minimum and at least 10s as a maximum.[81]

One cannot help but feel that Lloyd George and Asquith were too attached to 'prudent finance' at this time. In presenting his financial policy to his colleagues soon after taking office as Chancellor Lloyd George was fervent in calling for economy. In his Cabinet memorandum, *The Financial Situation: This Year and Next*, he urged, 'I need hardly remind my colleagues that we have repeatedly pledged ourselves, both before we took office and since, to a substantial reduction of the national expenditure, and particularly that which depends upon the two combatant services.'[82] In reporting the Cabinet meeting of 1 May, which settled the Government's proposals, Asquith observed to the King, 'the general reorganisation of the Poor Law System which must follow the forthcoming Report of the Royal Commission may be expected to lead to substantial economies'.[83] Lloyd George wrote to his brother on 12 May, '. . . I am not going to increase taxation to pay old age pensions until I have exhausted all means of reducing expenditure'; though this reflects his determination to cut armaments expenditure as much as a devotion to economy.[84] Other than the provision of money for old age pensions, he proclaimed the main feature of the 1908 measures to be the very orthodox one of 'a very considerable reduction of the sugar duty'.[85] In doing this he was removing revenue which could have been used to make a more generous provision of pensions or for other social reforms.

However, during the pension debates he made an assessment of the Government's mandate which was quite contrary to 'economy'. He told the M.P.s: 'We certainly contemplated old age pensions, an improved educational system, and social reform generally, and we could not possibly have given pledges for a reduced expenditure when we contemplated social reform which involved increased expenditure.'[86] From this time onwards he appears determined to find money not only for pensions but also for wider social welfare policies. After failing to bring about major reductions in armament expenditure Lloyd George turned to bringing in greater revenue.

In drawing up his famous 1909 Budget, 'The People's Budget', Lloyd George needed to draw in an extra £16 million. This was needed to meet an estimated £8 million for old age pensions, over £3 million extra for the Navy, and an anticipated shrinkage of revenue from existing sources.[87] It was natural, given his record of supporting temperance and land reform, that he should have raised some of this by increasing licensing duties and bringing in land tax proposals, as well as increasing the higher grades of income tax and introducing supertax. Despite opposition from many of his colleagues in the Cabinet to land taxes, on 19 March 1909 he got them to accept taxes on 'the increment of value since the last valuation due to social causes when land is transferred or devolves by death' and on vacant land which would be valuable for building; though they rejected a proposal to tax ground rents of land already built on.[88] Lloyd George did not expect to get a large revenue from these land proposals. Speaking to Riddell he observed, 'I knew the land taxes would not produce much. I only

put them in the budget because I could not get a valuation without them.'[89]

A politically successful Budget was crucial at this time as the
Government's fortunes were flagging badly. Lloyd George intended the electoral appeal of his Budget to be centred on his
making a start on the land issue. In September 1908 he had been
talking of raising as much as £4¼ million from the land.[90] But
even the reduced proposals that the Cabinet adopted represented
a major challenge to the Opposition as they were so clearly the
thin end of the wedge. In addition Lloyd George intended to
cheer the Liberal rank and file by dealing with issues which the
House of Lords had hitherto emasculated. In a letter to J. A.
Spender he observed, 'I think it is this kind of running away at
the first menace of danger which has weakened us so much. On education and temperance, on Scottish land and on valuation we have
taken our defeat at the hands of the Lords with a meekness that
has brought on us much merited contempt.' In the 1910 campaigns
he carefully identified the budget as merely the first instalment of
a wide range of social reform. Thus at Cardiff he declared, 'The
budget will go through, and the whole flock will follow . . .
Security for the workman against unemployment, against
starving in the dark hours of sickness, security against old age,
security for the tenant farmers against capricious eviction,
security for the worker – it is all coming.'[91] The Budget as a whole
was a challenge to the Opposition as it undermined much of the
tariff reform case; it demonstrated the viability of Free Trade
finance in proposing to raise what was at that time a huge sum in
peacetime from new radical sources of taxation.

It is very unlikely that Lloyd George drew up the Budget with
the clear intention of getting the House of Lords to reject it. He
must have realised at the outset, however, that such a budget
would set the House of Lords the dilemma of either accepting it
and thereby experiencing some degree of humiliation or of
rejecting it and so facing the charge of being anti-democratic by
blocking a measure of more than sectional appeal. As soon as the
Budget was revealed some Liberal M.P.s were reported to 'think
it necessarily means a dissolution in the autumn, as it must be
guillotined and then the Lords will reject it. Some think we could
never have anything better to fight the Lords.'[92] Most probably
at the outset Lloyd George had no clear-cut determination to
bait the Lords into rejecting it. In the Commons, as Herbert
Samuel observed, 'Lloyd George [was] exerting all the arts of
conciliation.'[93] It seems he felt his way through the situation; just
as he did with industrial relations.

The rejection of the Budget led to the two 1910 elections, and greatly enhanced the Liberals' chances of another majority in the Commons. Lloyd George was well aware of the advances that Labour was making in many areas. From the early days of the Campbell-Bannerman Government leading politicians at West-minster received reports of the strong challenge to the Liberal Party from socialists in the industrial centres.[94] In 1910 Lloyd George pitched his appeal to the working-class voter, and pro-vided a national democratic drama. In a series of speeches, the most famous being at Limehouse on 30 July 1909, he denounced the landed aristocracy 'with a violence which would have done credit to a communist agitator'.[95] In doing this he was successful in reviving the Liberal Party's fortunes amongst the working class, though he may well have accelerated the movement of the middle class in the south of England to support of the Tories. Samuel ruefully observed after the first election, 'It is the abiding problem of Liberal statesmanship to rouse the enthusiasm of the working classes without frightening the middle classes. It can be done; but it has not been done this time.'[96]

The provision of old age pensions made Lloyd George not only propose new sources of revenue, but also think of measures to meet poverty stemming from other causes. During the debates on old age pensions he agreed with the Opposition that through sickness there were 'many cases of young people who have broken down with family cares, which are much harder than even cases of old people', and he concluded his remarks on the Bill during its second reading by saying that it was 'only a beginning' and that:

> These problems of the sick and of the infirm, of the men who cannot find means of earning a livelihood, though they seek it as if they were seeking for alms, who are out of work through no fault of their own, and who cannot even guess the reason why, are problems with which it is the business of the State to deal; they are problems which the State has neglected too long.[97]

In earlier speeches he had been explicit on the State being responsible for the very poor. Thus in April 1908, whilst speaking for Churchill in a by-election, he stated, 'If these poor people are to be redeemed it must be not by themselves, because nothing strikes you more than the stupor or despair into which they have sunk – they must be redeemed by others outside, and the appeal ought to be to every class of the community to see that in this great land all misery and wretchedness should be put to an end.'[98] But it was not until the summer of 1908 that he seriously began to think about measures to meet poverty stemming from sickness.[99]

He began to make his plans for a contributory national health insurance scheme shortly after his famous trip to Germany in August 1908. He had long viewed German developments with interest. Almost as soon as he went to the Board of Trade an official wrote that Lloyd George was 'desirous of initiating a comprehensive inquiry in Germany and certain other foreign countries with respect to conditions of industry and labour, especially as regards such matters as cost of living, prices, rents, wages, irregularity of employment etc.'. Lloyd George was impressed by the German national health insurance scheme, and later he frequently spoke very warmly of 'the magnificent system that looks after the sick and poor in Germany'.[100] On 1 October, in a major speech at Swansea, he reaffirmed that it was the State's duty to help the blameless poor,[101] and soon after started negotiating with the Friendly Societies. From the beginning he was anxious to consult the trade unions and any other knowledgeable parties.[102]

During his negotiations with the industrial insurance companies Lloyd George appears to have realised that passing national insurance would entail a gigantic political struggle. In view of this and other national problems he proposed to do a deal with the Tories. He proposed a coalition government in a memorandum he drew up on 17 August, in the period of the constitutional conference.[103] He was not alone amongst leading Liberal Cabinet ministers in his despondency. On seeing Lloyd George's memorandum, Crewe wrote to Asquith that he felt 'we have got not far from the end of our tether as regards the carrying of large reforms' and Grey wrote that if the constitutional conference was unsuccessful he foresaw 'the break up of the Liberal Party and a time of political instability, perhaps of chaos'.[104] Lloyd George even spoke publicly of the need for the parties to deal with poverty together. 'The presence of a mass of remediable poverty is common ground to both parties', he said on 17 October, '. . . there is no section of any consequence who will contend that the State cannot assist effectively in putting things right'.[105] However, nothing came of the coalition proposals; although when the health insurance scheme was before the Cabinet in April 1911 Lloyd George was still advocating that Balfour should be seen privately by Asquith 'in order to help it through'.[106]

After the 1910 general election Lloyd George went ahead with his Bill at full speed and continued to try and gain the co-operation of all interested groups. In view of the strong opposition of the insurance companies to state provision of widows' and orphans' benefits, he had the civil servants remove these from the drafts of the Bill.[107] The draft Bill came before his colleagues on 5 April; when, apparently, 'the P.M. was at first rather frightened by . . . [it], but the Cabinet were greatly pleased by it'.[108] When Lloyd George introduced it on 4 May the Bill was very well received by leading politicians on both sides. Lloyd George pressed to get it through the Commons as fast as possible, wanting to clear it before Home Rule legislation took everyone's attention.[109]

However, during the summer of 1911 opposition to national insurance grew, and Lloyd George now came to do a deal with the Labour Party. In July Snowden and Lansbury had led a group of Labour M.P.s in attacking the Bill in committee, and a meeting on 12 July between Lloyd George and a group of Labour M.P.s failed to stop this.[110] With the Bill still not through the committee stage in August Lloyd George had to press a reluctant Asquith to agree to an autumn sitting. During the summer the Master of Elibank, on Lloyd George's behalf, arranged with Ramsay MacDonald that 'after the passage of payment to Members . . . he and his friends should give general support to the Insurance Bill'.[111] In October, at Lloyd George's urgent request, MacDonald had a talk with him about the passage of the Bill, and MacDonald urged Elibank not to use the guillotine on it. MacDonald was not overimpressed by arguments that the run of bad by-election results for the Government were due to the National Insurance Bill alone, but rightly observed, '. . . the Bill is not popular. It will be still less popular when you begin to work it'.[112] In the autumn session the Labour Party leaders restrained all but a few of their colleagues, and despite Tory opposition the Bill passed its third reading on 6 December.

The National Insurance Act proved to be far from popular with a large section of the electorate. In January 1912 Arthur Murray noted of Lloyd George,

> It is evident that he realises that his future political career is largely staked upon its success. A.O.M. [Elibank] and he accordingly decided today to set on foot an immense educative campaign throughout the country. Such a campaign will also have the effect of concentrating public attention on the Insurance Act, and of allowing Home Rule and Welsh Disestablishment to ride through on its back. This, at least, is Lloyd George's hope. 'The Insurance Act', he says, 'touches every voter's pocket – they care comparatively little for the other two. If Insurance is successful, they will accept the others.'[113]

In fact the Insurance Act undermined the *morale* of back-bench Liberal M.P.s and appeared to threaten the Government's existence. But as Clifford Sharp observed in March 1912, 'But of course there is plenty of time for a turn in the political wheel – as long as Lloyd George is in the Cabinet it would be rash to prophesy. He may contrive at any moment to create a diversion and recreate Liberal enthusiasm.'[114]

Lloyd George very soon focused his attention on the land. The land campaign was to be his policy for regenerating Liberal enthusiasm. Whilst on his national insurance educational campaign he indicated that the next step in social reform was land reform, which he saw as the main obstacle to major housing schemes. Thus in November 1911 he said:

> ... the [National Insurance] Bill does not profess to do everything to mitigate the social evils of the day; it is merely a contribution to that end . . . For instance, it penalises the slums. That is not enough; after all the slum affords a better shelter than the roadside, and you have no right to clear out the slums unless you are prepared to put up better houses. And you cannot do that without imposing a crushing burden of taxation, nor until you reform our land system.
>
> In both town and country the land system hinders everything now – hinders small holdings, hinders allotments, hinders workmen's dwellings, hinders every attempt at social amelioration. It thwarts every enterprise, commercial, industrial, social and economic, including municipal enterprise. You will do no good until you recast the system.[115]

In June 1912, with Asquith's permission, Lloyd George set up an unofficial committee to investigate the land system. As this included several of the radical single-tax-on-land-values group it disconcerted moderate Liberals many of whom feared 'that the Government has in view land legislation of a revolutionary and confiscatory character'.[116] Lloyd George himself was never a single taxer, and apparently had little time for E. G. Hemmerde and the other extreme land reformers.[117] But he was determined 'to put fresh life into the dry bones' of radicalism, as he felt (mixing his metaphors) that 'the Radical cause has fallen into the abyss of respectability and conventionality'. The setting up of the committee meant both that the Cabinet could avoid coming to a decision immediately and that he was spared the necessity of following Joe Chamberlain's example and campaigning outside of the Cabinet.[118]

Two major themes in the land campaign were the provision of housing and the raising of the farm labourers' wages. Despite the fierceness of his denunciations of landlords once the campaign got underway in October 1913, Lloyd George's proposals to deal with housing were moderate. He spoke out against subsidised rents, stating: 'He was in favour of giving the working class a living wage. But he was against giving them charity rents.'[119] He did not believe it necessary to abolish the leasehold system in urban areas, though in November 1913 he promised security to lessees of houses.[120] Lloyd George favoured compulsory purchase of 'land at its value', 'not land under its value': 'The first condition of land reform in towns is the setting up of a procedure, cheap, expeditious, effective and reliable, by which municipalities can acquire land for public purposes at its fair market value.'[121] In speaking to C. P. Scott he adopted a strong nonconformist tone in arguing that housing was a priority because 'present conditions . . . make decency and morality practically impossible'.[122]

The other theme of the land campaign of particular importance to this study was the need for the farm labourer to be paid more. '14/– to 18/– a week', he observed, 'was not a living wage.'[123] He wanted tribunals to be created to fix agricultural wages for the various areas of the country.[124] He felt that better wages for farm workers could be afforded throughout the country as they were paid already to those in areas close to alternative work. He argued that better wages would lead to more efficient farm labour, and also that larger farms, if organised efficiently, would encourage higher labour productivity.[125] He recognised that the farm labourers' position was weakened by their failure to combine – and he spoke of the Insurance Act as encouraging them to organise.[126]

Lloyd George's land campaign had many radical elements to it but ultimately it was based on a belief that the land system was a monopoly and that there should be a return (with State assistance) to a free market. He argued that if there was a return to the land, encouraged by a reformed land system and higher wages, there would then be less labour in urban areas, and consequently wages would rise there and strikes would be unnecessary. 'The question of wages, then', he argued at Middlesborough, 'will be settled by the old inexorable law of supply and demand.' Of employers he stated, 'No great employer of labour – that is my experience of the business man – objects to pay the market price for any commodity, whether it is material or labour.' From this he argued that an effective free market would change employers' attitudes to their men:

Owing to the fact that you have always had, on the whole, an abundant supply of labour, taking good years and bad years together, employers have not considered it necessary, as part of their business to keep up the efficiency of labour. Do not misunderstand me. I am not attacking employers of labour or capitalists. As humane men, as philanthropists, as good citizens, they have concerned themselves for the well being of the workmen. But they have never been driven to do so as a business necessity.[127]

As in the 1890s Lloyd George made favourable comments about the urban capitalist, yet vigorously denounced the landlord and continued to champion the farmers' interests.[128] He summed up his attitude in his Middlesborough speech: 'Raising class against class – I have no interest in that . . . There are plenty of men to look after the top dog; I am here to look after the underdog.'

If the land campaign was a programme less advanced in many respects than it first appears, Lloyd George did at least advocate full employment in several of these speeches. The return to the land would remove the surplus labour. 'Instead of workmen seeking labour with heavy hearts, you will have work seeking workmen.'[129]

The land campaign may have had some impact on the rural voter but it did not rouse enthusiasm in urban areas.[130] The Labour leaders might express a belief in private that it was a key issue, but in fact the issue was not central to the Labour Movement's struggles before the war.[131] Questions of wages, conditions of work, union recognition and social reform more immediately affecting the workingmen had greater priority.

On the other side of politics, the Unionists were more concerned with Ireland, and many saw the land campaign as a deliberate attempt to divert attention from it.[132] Lloyd George himself appears still to have been hankering for a party truce. In more or less seriousness he suggested to Churchill, 'I have two alternatives to propose – the first to form a coalition, settle the old outstanding questions, including Home Rule, and govern the country on middle lines acceptable to both parties but providing measures of moderate social reform. The other to formulate and carry through an advanced land and social reform policy.'[133] Lloyd George continued to talk of some cross party agreement with F. E. Smith and spoke publicly along these lines at least twice in 1913. In January at a dinner for the Liberal Insurance Committee he stated, 'There are many grave social problems which men of all parties feel acutely the need for dealing with, which men of all parties realise should be dealt with in the interests of national health, national prosperity, national greatness, and the national existence of this country.'[134] Serious cross party talks were not to come until those on Ireland on the eve of the First

World War, and it was not until after the war that Lloyd George tried to bring forward social reform through a coalition government.

Local studies published in recent years have made it clear that the Liberal Party was not close to a state of collapse before the First World War – whether its strength was based on traditional policies, as in Wales, or a newer, more progressive Liberalism, as in Lancashire.[135] Nevertheless, the Liberals would have suffered considerably from a rift with Labour as it would have divided the 'progressive' vote sufficiently in many urban areas to exclude them from Government. The fact that Labour's parliamentary representation outside of the mining strongholds was generally dependent on Liberal goodwill greatly helped the Liberals contain the Labour Party in the 1910 general elections.[136] However, the growing strength of the Labour Movement as a whole made it increasingly difficult for such containment to take place in some areas in the pre-war years.[137]

Lloyd George's style of radicalism made him effectively the focus of the radical alternative to the early emergence of the Labour Party as the political party whom the bulk of the working class supported. In an article in early 1906 Masterman had suggested that both Liberals and Labour supported reform but the former gave priority to such matters as 'the Education Bill, Temperance Reform, One Man One Vote, Reform of the House of Lords, Disestablishment of the Welsh Church, Retrenchment on Naval and Military Expenditure', whilst the latter gave priority to such issues as 'Feeding of School Children, Old Age Pensions, Graduation of Income Tax, National Work for the Unemployed, Land Nationalisation'.[138] Lloyd George's pragmatic piecemeal approach to social reform bridged the gap. Action preceded ideology. By 1912 he was expressing a New Liberalism which fully recognised that the State should intervene to secure the social welfare of the people. Thus in a speech in the autumn of 1912 he observed, 'Investigators have proved that you have in Great Britain and Ireland millions of people not earning enough to build and sustain sufficient strength to discharge their daily task adequately – millions!' And he forthrightly declared: 'Liberalism has a good deal to do with the gigantic problems of preventible poverty. . . . I do not mean the poverty that is due to slothfulness, to wastefulness, to the misconduct of the individual. I mean the poverty that is due to conditions which the State can control and the individual cannot.'[139]

Lloyd George's achievement in largely eclipsing the Labour

Party before 1914 did not only rest on his policies. His oratory
and the fierceness of his denunciations of the landed interest kept
public attention on him. He was usually more aware of popular
sentiments than his colleagues; Asquith apparently felt him to be
'an excellent foolometer' of these.[140] Beatrice Webb observed in
1910 that since 1908 'Lloyd George and Winston Churchill have
practically taken the *limelight*, not merely from their own colleagues,
but from the Labour Party'.[141]

He was well aware of the challenge Labour represented to
radicalism. In July 1912 Riddell noted in his diary, 'It is evident
from what L.G. said today that the fight between the Liberal and
Labour Parties is pretty bitter. It is quite clear that the Liberals
would like to wipe out the Labour Party, and that failing this,
they are anxious to keep it "in its place".' In this context, in discussing two pending by-elections, Lloyd George observed, 'I
would rather see the Conservative get in than the Labour man.'[142]
Lloyd George's style of politics was in the radical tradition of
appealing to morality and high ideals, and he felt this would be
more effective in gaining support than the bread-and-butter
issues which the Labour M.P.s concentrated on. Thus, at the time
of the 1912 coal crisis he observed,

> In politics you must have an horizon. A policy which deals only
> with immediate benefits never succeeds. When you examine the
> landscape which is close at hand you see the greenfly . . . The Labour
> Party have never made any real progress. They have never made an
> appeal to the imagination. You can never run a great political
> campaign on wages. Your 5/- and 2/- is all very well but the appeal
> is too close at hand. It is too sordid. Individually people are selfish.
> In the mass they are prepared to look to the future and support
> measures which will benefit coming generations.[143]

Lloyd George and Ramsay MacDonald were on good terms at
this time. In the pre-war period their children often played together. MacDonald's friendship with Lloyd George was seen by
some as a threat to the parliamentary Labour Party's independence.[144] Periodically MacDonald appears to have been attracted
to a coalition with the Liberals. Thus in February 1910 he wrote
in an article, 'If there was a coalition it must be clearly understood
that it was for a specific piece of work, and that when the work
was accomplished, the situation was subject to change.'[145] Beatrice
Webb wrote to a friend of 'MacDonald's somewhat tortuous
policy with regard to the Liberal Party. None of his party seem to
know whether he really intends to play for some eventual fusion
with Cabinet office for himself, or whether he is going to

maintain his independence . . . I doubt whether he knows himself.'[146] In March 1913 Lloyd George actually approached Ramsay MacDonald about such possibilities.[147] In June 1913 MacDonald discussed the possibility with Wedgwood and Morrell, two radical back-benchers who after the war went over to Labour. Wedgwood wrote to MacDonald, 'To L. George I did hint that you might possibly be in a frame of mind to meet advances. He said it was "most, most, most important" and I could see floating through his mind a George-MacDonald combination . . . which should at the same time bury the Whigs and change people's thoughts.'[148] Such a development probably appealed to MacDonald even more strongly than usual because of the poor performance in Parliament of the Labour M.P.s. After 1910 the majority of the parliamentary Party was paralysed by the Government's dependence in the Commons on their and the Nationalist's support. It seemed as if they could only assert their independence at the expense of risking putting out the Liberals in favour of the Tories and by jettisoning the electoral agreement with the Liberals, on which so many of their seats depended. They also suffered from an inability to take a common line on major issues of policy (a notable example being the Insurance Act), and so frequently failed to be an effective pressure group.

Lloyd George was especially interested in good relations with the Labour M.P.s at this time because it would strengthen his hand in getting the land campaign going. He often used the presence of a Labour group in Parliament as a lever on his less radical colleagues. Reports of his leading a new left-wing grouping often occurred when he was making a radical stand in the Cabinet. Thus at the time Lloyd George was starting to prepare for the land campaign such a report appeared in the *Observer*.[149] There were similar rumours during the January 1914 Cabinet crisis over the naval estimates. In his opposition to Churchill's naval estimates he was undoubtedly hoping for support from the hundred Liberal and Labour M.P.s who abhorred such increased expenditure. As on other occasions his intention was the natural one of putting pressure on his Cabinet colleagues; it is excessive to see his aim as being to oust Asquith.[150]

Before the First World War Lloyd George exhibited strong sympathies for labour. Lucy Masterman recalled his description of one conference: 'There were the employers on the one hand, plump, full-fed men, well-dressed – men who had never known what it was to go short in their lives. On the other side were the men, great gaunt fellows, pale with working underground, their faces all torn . . . with anxiety and hard work . . . I know which side I am on when I see that sort of thing.' At the time of the 1912 London dock strike he was irritated by the Cabinet's action and observed, 'They make me wonder . . . whether I am really a Liberal at all.'[151] Similarly he was against imprisoning Larkin when the Ulstermen were blatantly flouting the law. He observed, 'No amount of argument could persuade the British workman that the difference in treatment accorded to Larkin as compared with that meted out to Carson is anything but pure class distinction.'[152] But despite his sympathies with labour and his frequent championing of the underdog, his career before 1914 does not suggest that there was any real likelihood of his breaking away from the Liberals to form a new grouping with Labour.

III

Trade and Industrial relations

During his time at the Board of Trade and Exchequer Lloyd George acquired a notable reputation for successfully intervening in industrial disputes. This surprised many of his opponents who had experienced his flair at raising passions on radical issues, and had not expected to find him a skilled conciliator.

Throughout his career his violent denunciations had been mostly confined to the landowning class, not businessmen. He went to the Board of Trade in a very unpartisan spirit. His speeches in Wales immediately after his appointment reveal pride at a Welshman attaining such a national post.[1] And at the Board of Trade he went out of his way to consult carefully the various interest groups affected by his department. His desire to be aloof from partisan strife on occasion disappointed his radical friends. Thus on the L.C.C. Electricity Bill, Herbert Lewis noted:

> L.G. is taking a very high line on this question, one that is bound to bring him into sharp and violent collision with the London Members. The present L.C.C. are introducing a Bill which contains a clause identically the same as that contained in the Bill of last year enabling the L.C.C. to lease their powers to private companies. The London Liberal Members want that clause out of the Bill, but Lloyd George on the ground that no change has taken place except an election, and that the expressed wishes of the electorate of London must be respected, refuses to consent to the excision of the clause. He would regard it as a negation of every Liberal principle to do so. This line is all the more virtuous when one considers that the Parliaments of 1895 and 1900 consistently spoiled all the L.C.C. progressive legislation.[2]

Soon he was receiving compliments from unusual quarters: the *Westminster Gazette* in mid-1907 commented, '. . . at the end of eighteen months we find one business man after another getting up in the House of Commons to testify that he is the best man of business they had had to deal with for many a long day'.[3]

For Lloyd George improving national trade and making British industry more efficient was a national issue not a party one. In November 1906 he told shipowners, 'Personally I do not believe in introducing party politics into business . . . My predecessors have kept party politics out of the administration of trade and business of the nation. That is the only way to succeed.'[4] He took the foreign competition in world markets very seriously. In speaking of the need for education reform during his campaign against Balfour's Education Bill, he became strongly Jingoistic: thus as a meeting in late 1902, he warned his audience: 'We need not be reminded that we are engaged in a series of wars more dangerous to our supremacy than the South African War. War with the United States! War with Germany! What kind of war? An industrial war, a war for commercial supremacy!'[5] He took this fervour for bettering British business enterprise with him to the Board of Trade. The *Manchester Courier* observed in August 1907, '. . . on more than one occasion he has displayed a patriotism which in a Conservative Minister would certainly have been denounced as "Jingoism" '.[6]

The main measures Lloyd George introduced during his time at the Board of Trade were designed to increase the efficiency of British trade and industry. His approach to the problems was pragmatic not doctrinaire; a point seized on by the Tories, where they could claim he was acting with protectionist aims.

He pressed ahead with plans to analyse the state of industry in Britain by means of a census of production. This was a considerable innovation. As Hubert Llewellyn Smith of the Board of Trade told him, 'The task is quite a new one, and we have absolutely nothing to guide us in solving the numerous difficult statistical problems that it presents.'[7] In arranging the details of the Bill, he saw the interested parties and coaxed them into cooperation, stressing, 'It is no use without the good-will of the trades concerned.' He saw manufacturers, and undertook to remove many of their apprehensions by amendments to his Bill. He stressed that his purpose was not to pry into minute details or company secrets but to gather aggregate statistics. On the crucial question of wages he frankly left the matter to the inclinations of the manufacturers, and avoided the political controversy of coercing them into divulging these details. At a meeting in October 1906 he told M.P.s particularly interested in his measure that, 'We are going to have a Wages Census next year but that will be purely voluntary, and if you do not want to give them you need not.'[8] Similarly his Port of London Act of 1909 was aimed both at making the docks more efficient and meeting the desires of the dock-owners.[9]

His Merchant Shipping Act, Patents and Designs Act and Companies Act were all aimed, in part at least, at removing unfair foreign competition. The Merchant Shipping Bill arose from the reports of two committees appointed by Balfour's Government to investigate ship-owners' grievances concerning the increasing number of foreign seamen and pilots employed on British ships and the question of subjecting foreign vessels to the same regulations on load and life-saving apparatus as were applied to British vessels. Lloyd George implemented the committees' main proposals and, as he himself said, it grew 'through consultation with those who are primarily interested'.[10] These were of value to the men in that better conditions were guaranteed for crews (the aim was to aid recruitment in Britain), and went some way to meet the owners' complaint that there was 'an undue charge placed on British shipping to the prejudice of the country's position as the sea carrier of the world'.[11] This 1906 Act included the raising of the Plimsoll Line, which was a retrogressive step, laying Lloyd George open to charges that he was responsible for the loss of any ships which had their load line raised.[12] Lloyd George undoubtedly felt the Bill did much for sailors and was impressed by the argument that since 1876 the structure of ships had become much safer.[13]

The Patents and Designs Act of 1907, as well as consolidating and simplifying previous measures, also prevented foreign firms registering patents in Britain and then preventing their use for more than three years within the country. Lloyd George brushed aside Tory jeers that he was breaching Liberal principles and vigorously asserted that 'he should object to any monopoly conferred by British Law being used to the detriment of British industries'.[14] Similarly part of the Companies' Act of 1907, whilst giving the State further control over private companies, also added conditions on foreign firms operating in Britain.[15] These policies did constitute 'economic nationalism' but as Sir John Clapham has fairly commented, they were 'a sensible dose of it'.[16]

These measures established a reputation for Lloyd George in business circles as a reasonable man to deal with. His radical career and his real sympathy for the under-dog gave him, at this stage of his career, the confidence of many sections of organised labour. In the years before the war he greatly enhanced his political reputation by using this position to intervene in industrial disputes as no President of the Board of Trade or Chancellor of the Exchequer had done before. Such intervention by the Government was increasingly necessary as strikes in major industries threatened the national economy. For Lloyd George they also tempted his flair as a political showman. He could try to reconcile the irreconcilable – and moreover do it in the limelight of the national, and occasionally even the international, press. It was fitting that his first attempt at intervention should be at the beginning of 1907 in a strike of music hall artists, which inevitably gained widespread press coverage. Lloyd George unsuccessfully tried to get T. P. O'Connor, a colourful politician of literary standing, to act as arbitrator.[17] Later G. R. Askwith successfully acted in this capacity.

However in the autumn of 1907 Lloyd George intervened in a major dispute concerning the railwaymen. This deserves to be considered in some detail as it marked the full recognition of the justification of State intervention in major disputes.[18] It was Lloyd George's first major intervention and success, and his conduct during the dispute well illustrates his style of negotiation.

Gladstone's Government in 1893 intervened in the coal lockout because it threatened widespread disruption of the economy. Similarly in 1907 disruption of rail services posed a threat to the country's major industries. In the autumn of 1907 parts of the press, which usually propounded the employers' side of disputes, demanded State intervention. *The Economist*, which before September had been hostile to the railwaymen's claims, in October propounded the rule, 'Railway strikes and railway lockouts cannot be permitted. They are contrary to public policy.' It was dramatic in its description of the effects of a disruption in this service: 'A stoppage of the railways, if only for a few weeks, would produce starvation, ruin, and revolution.' British industry had no interest in a stonewall stand by the railway companies, which would have crippling effects on their own interests. *The Economist* was reflecting popular opinion in industry when it stated, 'It is . . . our deliberate opinion that the Board of Trade will be justified in taking very strong measures to avert the threatened strike,' and urged that if their efforts failed then Parliament should arrange compulsory arbitration for the railways.[19]

The railwaymen had a very strong case to put to the companies. They worked long hours, their wages were failing to keep up with rising prices, and they were rapidly losing their wage differential to other groups of workers – over twenty years their weekly wage rates increased by only 5 per cent whilst those in the building, cotton manufacturing and engineering industries enjoyed increases of 18, 23 and 26 per cent respectively.[20] Yet the use of larger engines and trucks and other labour saving improvements meant that productivity per man was increasing.

However the railway companies on the whole were in the doldrums. Not only did they have the problems of an industry which had ceased to expand, but they also suffered from the freezing of their rates by Parliament. In the first decade of the century this hit them especially hard as the prices of commodities they needed, especially coal, were rapidly rising without any restriction. Largely for these reasons railway dividends were in a weak position; in ten years they had declined by 2·5 per cent down to an average 3·5 per cent dividend.[21] The companies replied to the men's demands by saying that they enjoyed special advantages over other workmen, such as regular employment, a pension, free travel and clothing. But this reply was clearly not relevant to the railwaymen's worsening position in regard to prices and relative wage rates.

The railway directors and certain sections of the press delighted to paint the Amalgamated Society of Railway Servants as agitators. In fact the A.S.R.S. had a remarkably mild leader, Richard Bell, who as a Member of Parliament refused to join the Labour Party. Bell personally wished to postpone the All Grades Movement until amalgamation schemes with other railmen's unions were successful.[22] However, pressure from the rank and file in the A.S.R.S. grew during 1905 for a national all grades programme; a programme which entailed a settlement nationally and not with each company individually, and improvements in terms of employment right across the board and not by negotiations on each grade. A.S.L.E.F. in April 1905 made the first call for major concessions. In November 1906 the A.S.R.S. formulated their programme of an eight-hour day for the traffic grades and a ten-hour day for the rest, time and a quarter for overtime, time and a half on Sundays, plus a guaranteed week and a 2s advance for the non-traffic grades. On top of this Bell and the A.S.R.S. demanded recognition of their union by the companies.[23]

The economic improvement of 1905–7 and the removal of the inhibition of the Taff Vale verdict by the Trades Disputes Act 1906 gave impetus to this programme. Nonetheless, Bell acted as a paragon of moderation, approaching the companies three times between January and June 1907 to enter discussions. In September a strike ballot was organised, which, when the result was declared in early November, showed 76,925 members in favour of strike action with only 8,773 against.

The circumstances for a popular intervention were ideal. The strike severely threatened the interests of other industries. The railways were a special class of service – they ran by right of a virtual monopoly granted by Parliament (the parliamentary restrictions on rates ensuring competition was minimal) and were an essential form of communication for the whole nation. This special position was urged by the railway directors when it suited them. They denied recognition of the union on the ground that as a public service there should be quasi-military discipline amongst employees. The press, apart from *The Times*, were appalled by the intransigent attitude of the railway managers – with first Cosmo Bonsor, Chairman of the South Eastern Railway, then Lord Claud Hamilton, Chairman of the Great Eastern Railway, making inflammatory statements against trade unionism as a whole. The position of trade unions as an essential part of industry at this time was less and less being denied; even *The Economist* spoke in their favour – declaring 'on the whole trade unions have operated rather beneficially than otherwise in our industrial development, to the advantage of the capitalist and employer as well as of the workmen'.[24] The Liberal Government soon after taking office had recognised the Postal Clerks' Union, reversing the Tory Government's decision to deny recognition. Public opinion was very sympathetic to the railwaymen, especially after the A.S.R.S. published their Green Book, which revealed the appalling terms and conditions of employment under which many of their members worked.

Lloyd George already had doubts about the private enterprise system of running the railways in Britain before the 1907 railway crisis began – and, most probably, these doubts were increased during his handling of the problem. He himself was favourable to railway nationalisation; not out of socialist belief, but because he believed it was desirable for the efficiency of British industry. In late December 1906 Herbert Lewis and others held a discussion with Lloyd George on the subject: 'Lloyd George has sent three men to Germany and is having enquiries conducted in other countries . . . Lloyd George's agents report that Germany is now very prosperous, that there is an immense boom in trade. One reason he assigned for the prosperity of the country was the system of State Railways on which they make a profit of £16,000,000 a year.'[25] In a debate in the Commons on railway nationalisation in February 1908 shortly after his successful arbitration, he barely disguised his sympathy for nationalisation. He pointed out that nationalisation by Bismarck had not been a socialist measure and stated with admiration, 'In Germany the railways had been used as an instrument for the development of

German industry and for fighting against foreign industry; and a very formidable weapon it was – more formidable . . . than tariffs.' He foresaw no probable improvement in British railways under the current system; whereas Italian national railways '. . . with State credit behind them, they were able to find capital, and they were really undertaking great works of improvement'.[26] As in many of his other actions at the Board of Trade, his concern was with national industrial efficiency in the face of foreign competition.

He also had other reasons for seeing the railways as a special case. In his defence of the sacked monoglot railway workers in 1896 he had made much of the special position of the railway companies in having both their monopoly conferred on them and their rates limited by Parliament.[27] In 1907 he presented a Cabinet paper deploring the donations given by railway companies to election funds. Many M.P.s were worried that 'the money power of great corporations should be used to corrupt politics as in America', his paper stated; and their remedy, with which he agreed, was that 'while private individuals – and possibly ordinary limited companies with the approval of their shareholders – can hardly be interfered with, corporations, specially constituted by statute, exercising special powers and enjoying monopolies conferred directly by Parliament, ought not to be allowed, even with the approval of their shareholders, to use their funds to influence elections.'[28] In his parliamentary speech after the 1907 dispute had been settled, he emphasised the changing nature of the companies' mode of operating: 'Not only was competition being stopped but . . . the railway companies were beginning to make arrangements which were not far short of amalgamation.'[29] This he found natural as the railway companies were being squeezed between the demands of industry and those of the men.

He saw the claims of the men as legitimate, and at least by the end of the dispute realised that these were irreconcilable with profit-making railway companies which could provide the necessary cheap transport for British industry to meet foreign competition. He told the Commons,

The railway companies themselves are beginning to realise that the present system is impossible. They are pressed for increased wages, shorter hours, cheap workmen's trains, whether or not they will pay as a commercial undertaking, for lower rates and for greater facilities. The companies cannot face all these demands under the present system. Unless the investor gets a fair return for his money the railways will not get the capital necessary for essential developments . . .

In addition to that there is the demand of the trader, which is after all the demand of the industries of the country.[30]

Soon after taking office Lloyd George had pressed the need for cheap workmen's trains on the railway companies, and in February 1906 had told a deputation of trade unionists that 'unless the railway companies could see their way to comply with what public opinion pretty generally regarded as the exigency of the situation, he could promise them there would be legislation in this direction'.[31] When a T.U.C. deputation again raised this matter in early 1908 he emphasised the difficulties he found of acting within the existing framework: 'I drafted a Bill last year but did not press it in Parliament. I do not intend to threaten the railways or to threaten the small investors. I think it is possible to introduce legislation which will be of great use to the traders, which will be useful to the workmen, and which will be a considerable guarantee to the investor for the security of his capital.'[32]

Lloyd George actively intervened as soon as he knew the way the strike ballot was going, and met representatives of both sides separately at the Board of Trade in October. Parliament had passed by this time a resolution of concern at the excessive hours, calling for enforcement of existing regulations and the creation of new statutes if necessary. And Lloyd George in May had indicated his interest in the railway position by using an 1889 Act to get returns from the companies of the hours worked in excess of twelve.

Lloyd George intervened on his own initiative, writing and calling the railway companies' chairmen to meet him on the 25th despite the contrary advice of his civil servants.[33] He was determined to enforce arbitration on the railways, and at the same time saw a political opportunity for himself. Thus he wrote home on 21 October, 'The Railway Strike is demanding all my attention. Things are going well so far. Whatever happens I am coming out on top of this business. I can see my way clear right to the station. Conciliation at first but, failing that, the steam roller. The companies must give way on that point. I am definite.'[34] He prepared the way for such action by writing to Campbell-Bannerman, 'We must, when Parliament meets, at once introduce a measure making arbitration in railway disputes compulsory in all cases where the Board of Trade consider the nature and magnitude of the dispute warrants such a course being adopted . . . The Conciliation Act itself is a poor thing. It is only the knowledge that there is something behind it that will induce the directors to pay any attention to it.'[35]

In his separate talks with the employers and the men he exercised his remarkable skill as a negotiator for the first time in an industrial dispute. His approach was typical of later negotiations. In facing the employers he knew that they realised public opinion would enable him to introduce compulsory arbitration in the industry if they proved demonstrably intransigent. He reinforced this during the negotiations by getting the *Daily Mail* to publish an article demanding compulsory arbitration for railway disputes.[36]

In his approach to the railway managers he displayed his characteristic mixture of sweet reasonableness and understanding, followed by a threat of the stick if a satisfactory compromise was not rapidly achieved. In his initial speech to the directors he reviewed their particular problems; moderately pointed out that the men's claims were a 'natural desire to improve conditions' and that they were merely a part of a 'movement everywhere in all trades and in all countries'; and diplomatically said that he had no desire to express an opinion on the rightness of the men's claims, that they were better settled directly by the companies and representatives of their own men, and to leave them to an independent enquiry would be to prolong the discontent and allow it to accumulate. He warned them that a national railway strike would be the 'most disastrous blow aimed within living memory at our trade' and warned that it would precipitate a trade depression in Britain and postpone it in Germany and the United States. He further warned them that the disruption of employment and food distribution would result in 'hundreds of thousands idle and angry' and 'perilous disturbances [would be] inescapable'.[37] The railway managers responded to his appeal and agreed to appoint a committee of six to meet him and consider his proposals and to issue no further manifestoes. He wrote home, 'I have won their confidence and that is almost everything. You never saw anything like the change in their demeanour.'[38] After the meeting one of those present, a Tory M.P., Herbert Maxwell, wrote to him expressing 'my sense of the tactful and considerate manner' in which he had dealt with the issue – 'There could not have been expressed a more comprehensive *aperçu* of the situation than you gave in your address.'[39] The measure of his success in swaying people to his policy in negotiations is colourfully captured by Maxwell by the account of the meeting he wrote in his memoirs:

On the morning of the day arranged for our meeting with Lloyd George, we held a preliminary meeting at Euston Station, where it was unanimously resolved that we would not yield in the slightest

C

degree to any proposal that he might put forward inconsistent with our determination to deal direct with our men, without intervention by the unions.

Down we went to the Board of Trade and were received by the President, affable in manner, slight in person, and, as we thought, amateurish in expression. Before any one spoke on our side, Lloyd George addressed us at length. He displayed such a thorough acquaintance with all the ins and outs of the subject; such a reasonable sympathy with the aspirations of the men; dwelt so forcibly on the disastrous consequence to the country of a prolonged strike on the railways, pointing out how, without compromising our authority, he thought we might set up machinery for settling domestic difficulties, that our opposition melted away and we left the conference having consented to the appointment of conciliation boards or committees.[40]

In fact, contrary to Maxwell's recollection, the agreement was not reached until several meetings had taken place. In these Lloyd George was stern. He wrote home of his meeting on 31 October, 'In the morning I had to threaten them. Told them that there must not be a strike on any account.'[41] The negotiations centred around recognition of the union. The employers refused to allow union officials to be on the companies' conciliation boards, but eventually agreed to include independent arbitration in the final stage in the conciliation system.[42] Even at the final stage on 1 November, Lloyd George had to be firm. Herbert Lewis was told by Lloyd George that,

> . . . the directors were at the last very timid, and he had to take them by the scruff of the neck and push them through the door. They wanted to refer the matter back to their shareholders and declined to sign the agreement until they had time for consideration but Lloyd George pointed out that Bell would have to refer to *his* shareholders [the men] and that delay probably makes an agreement impossible. He insisted upon having the terms ratified there and then and offered to accept the signatures of six of the directors elected by themselves.[43]

He next had to press the settlement on the unions. He had been able to make much impact on the employers by offering to withhold outright recognition of the unions: this he could do as he had prior knowledge that Bell was 'not going to press for recognition if he obtained a satisfactory method of dealing with grievances, consideration of the programme, and more opportunity for the men to deal with the conditions of their lives'.[44] And to facilitate the union's agreement to the conditions he had secured, which did not include their major aim of recognition, he again resorted to pressing a snap decision on them in order to forestall further thought.[45] He invited Bell and his colleagues to see him on the 6th. Beforehand he told Lord Stallbridge 'he is exceedingly anxious to bring matters to a conclusion tonight, and not to allow Bell and his friends to leave the Board of Trade before he has done so'.[46] This kind of time ultimatum was characteristic of many of Lloyd George's negotiations, notably with the Irish settlement.

The conciliation scheme was complex, and proved unsatisfactory,[47] but it did bring the companies towards collective bargaining with the unions. The scheme agreed on was to be operated nationally, not just in a district.[48] *The Economist*, amongst other commentators, felt 'it is a double victory, a victory for conciliation and a victory for arbitration; for while a settlement has been reached through the intervention of Mr Lloyd George, an independent conciliator, its terms provide . . . that future disputes which cannot be settled by diplomatic intercourse, shall also be referred without reservation or appeal, to an arbitrator'.[49] Lloyd George hoped that this seven-year settlement would in itself help railway development. In a speech he expressed the hope,

> From the point of view of the railways the important thing is that for seven years, at any rate, you are guaranteed that you will have no great labour trouble. It gives what is above all important to capital and through capital to industry – a sense of security. It is insecurity that disturbs a market, and when you have that sense of security, railway companies will be able to make their plans and to appeal to their markets to back them up with their plans.[50]

And immediately after the agreement, Lloyd George set about organising an 'enquiry by means of an informal committee as to the possibility of arriving at a general agreement with regard to such modifications of the existing law and of the relations existing both among railway companies and between the companies, traders and the general public, as may conduce to economy and elasticity of railway working, and also provide for the equitable discussion of any advantage accruing from these among the various parties interested'.[51]

The settlement was a political triumph for Lloyd George. Even if the conditions were ideal for intervention, it was no small success to get a rapid agreement. The final scheme may well have stemmed from Sam Fay, General Manager of the Great Central Railway;[52] but this in no way detracts from Lloyd George's success in bringing the two sides to agreement. He was lauded by his colleagues, the King and the press. He himself proudly reported home *The Times* leading article of 12 November 'Greatest asset of Government with commercial classes'.[53]

With this success he adopted the role of a general conciliator. He told one audience his object was to 'obtain peace with honour to both parties' and to another, he expressed the hope 'that the method of conference – conciliation and arbitration – which has proved to be successful in labour disputes may be extended to international disputes. There can be nothing more wasteful than wars, whether they are labour wars or military wars or tariff wars.'[54]

His further interventions in disputes during the remainder of his time at the Board of Trade were less dramatic, but none the less they widened the accepted sphere of intervention by the President of the Board of Trade.

The first was an intervention in a local dispute concerning the spinning unions in Oldham.[55] The unions had been growing increasingly dissatisfied with the 1893 Brooklands Agreement, which had set up joint procedures for adjusting wages and settling disputes, and they secured several modifications to it. In Oldham about 840 fine spinners felt they had been unduly left behind in wage advances in the industry, and their union threatened to sound their members as to a strike. Their claim was for a 12 to 24 per cent advance; whereas the Brookland Agreement only provided for a 5 per cent adjustment per year. The employers refused to budge from the 1893 Agreement. Lloyd George travelled to Manchester and successfully brought the two sides together in negotiations. The employers and unions reached a complex settlement, which according to *The Economist* worked out at about a 9 per cent rise.[56] This intervention earned the praise of the *Cotton Factory Times*, which observed, 'such . . . concern for peace has created a new interest in the work of the Board of Trade, and has indicated the possibilities of greater usefulness of this department to the industries of the country. After all, one cannot overlook the fact that much depends on the policy of the man at the top.'[57]

The Board of Trade was less successful in a further intervention in this industry later in the month. This time the ring spinners in Oldham demanded a $7\frac{1}{2}$ per cent advance and stopped work. The employers threatened a lock-out.[58] Whilst Lloyd George was away his officials contacted each side, as a preliminary to intervention.[59] The replies of both sides showed no hope of successful mediation.[60] In the event the parties reached a settlement by themselves. Llewellyn Smith felt consolation in the fact 'our letters do not seem to have been interpreted as official intervention, so much as preliminary enquiries to ascertain the attitude of the parties towards certain proposals if put forward', though he admitted, 'the distinction is of course a little thin'.[61]

However his third and final successful intervention during his time at the Board of Trade was in a strike of engineers on the Tyne.[62] In view of the 1908 depression other districts accepted a reduction in wages, but the men on the Tyne claimed their 36s was a minimum. After a district ballot which rejected the employers' proposals on 20 February, 12,000 men went on strike. Lloyd George, after consulting two leading employers, Sir Benjamin Browne and Sir Andrew Noble, and the union leaders, got the employers and union representatives to agree to a formula that the 36s skilled rate should remain until Easter, when a referee should decide whether or not there should be a reduction. These terms were twice rejected by the men, and the strike dragged on until long after Lloyd George had left the Board of Trade. In this strike Lloyd George's intervention gained widespread praise, even though the men threw over terms acceptable to their leaders.

Lloyd George's handling of disputes at the Board of Trade was in tune with his legislative activity there and the social concern soon evidenced by the social reform associated with his name. Both legislation and industrial interventions were aimed at national efficiency and social harmony; he told one audience, he considered his role in industrial disputes to be 'far more important than even those legislative matters that we have been trying to settle [at the Board of Trade]'.[63] His belief in social harmony came in part from his experience that it was the weakest who went to the wall in industrial struggles. This speech of March 1908 is his most explicit utterance on industrial disputes, and is worthy of lengthy quotation:

> . . . in my judgement, the era of strikes and lockouts is – or, at any rate, ought to be – over. They really do not settle the justice or injustice of any point in dispute. They settle probably the strength of the parties who engage in them, exactly as any other war would. They settle which Party is the stronger, which has the more resources at his back. The weak goes to the wall whether he has justice at his back or not. There is a kind of blind brutality about strikes and lockouts.
>
> Who suffers from them? Not the combatants. Take the workmen; as a rule, when they engage in these great controversies, they are well organised and have great funds. They get their strike pay. It

does not supply them with a superabundance of luxury; but there is a frugal plenty, in which they are kept during the period of the strike. But who suffers? The trades that depend upon that particular trade. There is no trade in which, if you get a dispute, you will not find a whole link of other industries involved, which suffer in consequence. I was amazed, when I went to try to settle the cotton dispute in Manchester, to find the innumerable trades, great and small, which would suffer. In a dispute of this kind, who suffers? Unskilled labour, very often unorganised, with no great funds, where a week out of work means poverty and privation!

Who suffers above all? Women and children, the weak, the feeble, the aged! No strike ever took place in any district that has not been followed by a rising death rate. Really it is time, in a civilised country where there is the reign of law, where there is a sense of justice, that there should be something better than the brute machinery of either strikes or lockouts to settle disputes. The little that I have ever seen of strikes has given me a horror of them, and that entered into the administration of my office.

From early 1908 until 1911 Lloyd George did not personally intervene in industrial disputes. There were basically three reasons for this. Firstly, the scale of strikes before this date were not sufficiently damaging to warrant intervention by the Chancellor of the Exchequer, a man whose standing in the country was second only to Asquith's. Secondly, Lloyd George's successor at the Board of Trade, Winston Churchill, was too strong a figure to welcome outside assistance. Thirdly, Lloyd George was too pre-occupied with taking over the old age pension scheme from Asquith, framing and then propagating 'the People's Budget' to take an active interest in industrial relations.

But the major industrial unrest of 1911–12 brought Lloyd George back into the field of industrial relations.[64] Since 1895 most workers had experienced a fall in real wages, whilst most employers enjoyed a greater return on their capital.[65] The upturn in trade in 1911 created more favourable conditions for strike action. In this situation the lower paid workers, who could barely keep their families above the bread line at the best of times, spontaneously revolted in an attempt to redress the specific grievances of their industries. The strikes were notable for the amount of support given to strikers by other groups of workers as well as for the strength of local feeling.

In February 1910 Charles Buxton succeeded Churchill at the Board of Trade. Buxton was a radical who represented the working-class constituency of Poplar and who had long worked for progressive social reforms; but he was not a heavyweight in national politics. Asquith and Lloyd George were to intervene when industrial relations came to the forefront of national politics in 1911 and 1912. Unlike Lloyd George, Buxton did not put pressure on to employers and unions to settle disputes. Lloyd George rather unkindly observed at the time of the 1912 coal strike, 'Poor Sydney Buxton was no good at all. He was in a cage with a lion and a tiger crouching down and afraid of both, instead of taking each by the throat.'[66] This lack of push was partly due to Buxton's belief that Government intervention in industrial relations should be carried out as unobtrusively as possible. Thus in 1911 at the time of the creation of the Industrial Council he said,

> One disadvantage of the existing system is undoubtedly that it brings into action and prominence the Parliamentary Head of the Board of Trade, who is necessarily a politician . . . and a member of the Government, in disputes and conciliations which ought to be purely industrial. It has been my policy, and, I hope, my action, during my two years at the Board of Trade to efface as far as possible my personality as a political President.[67]

Lloyd George, of course, did not hesitate through such worries.

Lloyd George as Chancellor of the Exchequer still retained his sympathy for workmen, especially those in trades which were weakly organised. Thus, speaking to Herbert Lewis about socialism in 1908, he said:

> Take the man who works at the Llechwedd Quarry. He risks his life. Our servant, Sarah, received a telegram to say that her father had been killed at the quarry. He was a fine old boy. The death rate of the quarry is very high. What does he get for his work? 25 shillings a week, often having to live away from home in uncomfortable lodgings or barracks. When there is no work it means starvation. And what about the owner of the quarry, the man who does not work? He has a beautiful house with gardens and ornamental grounds that extend for miles. Even that is not enough for him. He must have another house at Carnarvon – 20 miles away. There is no justice in it. It is not divine justice, it is not human justice.[68]

As A. J. P. Taylor has observed 'he remained closer to the people than any other Liberal Minister, including John Burns'.[69] But Lloyd George's concern was not so much with the man in a union but with the underdog, the man in an unorganised trade or in a weak union. As he observed to Herbert Lewis on another occasion, in a discussion on trade unions, '. . . they are very cruel to the workman below and outside them. Keir Hardie never forgot that class. He sympathised with them whereas Burns had no sympathy for them. He belonged to the aristocracy of labour. He had no feeling for the man driven to the wall; he assumed that it was his own fault. He declared that there were no deserving unemployed.'[70]

Whilst Lloyd George might denounce landed aristocrats vigorously, his hatred was of the idle rich and of certain aspects of capitalism only. Thus speaking after Campbell-Bannerman's death, he said the Liberal Government's reforms were 'challenging the most powerful interests and appealed to all but a selfish few'. 'We have [against us] the worst form of capitalism – the greedy side of it. I am glad to say that it is not the only side. But we have the hardest and greediest and most selfish side of capitalism arrayed against us, and we can only appeal to the sense of the community, to the human sympathy which, after all, is deep down in the hearts of the people, to enable us to carry through the great measures of reform to which we are pledged.'[71] So Lloyd George had deep sympathies with those in poor positions and no sympathy with those who did nothing for their wealth. He was the right man to get moderate settlements.

Lloyd George was not personally involved in the settlement of the seamen's and the dockers' strikes in the summer of 1911. The dramatic spread of violent strikes was raised vigorously by Churchill at the Cabinet on 21 July.

> Mr Churchill called attention to the disquieting condition of the industrial world and the almost daily outbreak of strikes, direct and sympathetic, accompanied by a growing readiness to resort to violence, and imposing heavy labour and responsibility both on the police and military. He suggested that the time had come for a careful inquiry, perhaps presided over by the Prime Minister, into the causes of and remedies for these menacing developments of industrial unrest. The Cabinet recognised the importance of the matter.

However it did not consider the industrial unrest again until 11 August.[72] The unrest in the docks spread naturally to the railwaymen, many of whom worked in the strike-bound port areas.[73]

On 15 August the railway unions' executive committees, finding that their members were taking industrial action without their lead, called on the railway companies to meet union officials to negotiate a settlement of the matters causing the unrest, and gave the companies twenty-four hours to come to a decision or 'there will be no alternative but to respond to the demand now being made for a national stoppage'.[74] Asquith and Buxton intervened, seeing both sides on the 16th and 17th. After a meeting on the

16th the Chairman of the Midland Railway asserted that the Government had 'undertaken to put at the service of the railway companies every available soldier in the country'.[75]

Lloyd George from early on in the dispute appeared conciliatory. That night in the Commons, he denied that the Government was backing the companies, and asserted '. . . it is so important that the Government's position of strict impartiality should be preserved'.[76] However, Asquith was not so conciliatory when he saw the unions' executive committees on the morning of the 17th. Asquith met them on the suggestion of the Cabinet. He 'announced to them the willingness of the Government to appoint a small commission to investigate promptly their grounds of complaint, and at the same time the resolve of the Government not to allow a general paralysis of the railway system of the country'.[77] But he gave no details of the nature of the Royal Commission, and the railwaymen apparently 'took his words as a threat and his tone as "take it or leave it".'[78] In the afternoon the union leaders returned and rejected his proposals. As Askwith has commented, 'Matters were not improved when he muttered "Then your blood be on your own head" as he left the room, the members at once going off to call out the railwaymen all over the country.'[79]

Why did Asquith take such a far from conciliatory line? It was probably partly because this sudden industrial threat on top of the dock disputes was too much for him. Asquith was concerned at the unrest in Liverpool and London; Samuel even wrote to his wife that, 'Liverpool is verging on a state of revolution.'[80] Asquith was also considerably irritated at the shortness of the railway union's ultimatum; he informed the King on the 16th, 'There is no doubt that the men have real grievances, but the threat of a strike after 24 hours deprives them for the moment of all claims to public sympathy, and of this they would be clearly notified.'[81] Other Cabinet ministers shared this feeling; Crewe reported, 'My colleagues are full of fight against these dangerous elements . . .'[82] Asquith might even have underestimated the seriousness of the situation. Samuel certainly did; on the 16th he wrote, 'If there is a railway strike I don't expect the main line express traffic will be stopped.'[83] If Asquith did underestimate the seriousness of the situation, he was very soon disillusioned. The response to the strike call exceeded the hopes of the union executives; the strike was almost fully effective in the industrial districts of South Wales, the Midlands and the North. Churchill urged use of police rather than troops up to the 17th, but afterwards allowed commanding officers to use troops at their discretion, suspending the army regulation requiring a requisition from a civil authority.

At Llanelly, after the strike ended a crowd rioted when troops arrived, and the soldiers opened fire killing two people; two more were killed when detonators in a wagon which was set on fire blew up.[84]

Whilst other members of the Cabinet favoured confrontation, Lloyd George remained conciliatory. After Asquith had seen the men, Lloyd George exclaimed, 'They are going to strike . . . and I could have stopped it if I had been there.'[85] Lloyd George re-opened negotiations through the Master of Elibank and Ramsay MacDonald.[86] The latter had been taken into the counsels of the railwaymen's leaders, and had put down a motion of censure on the Government in the Commons. In the Commons, as Samuel noted the next day, 'Lloyd George reviewed the situation last night, and arranged to keep a door open.'[87] Lloyd George stated that the commission was not intended to be a shelving commission, that it would consist of three members, and would work quickly 'with a view to administrative, and if necessary legislative, action being taken by the Government in order to see a fair state of things established'.[88] Ramsay MacDonald had spoken in the Commons before him in a similarly conciliatory manner.

Negotiations on a settlement were deadlocked by the 19th, when Lloyd George made his famous patriotic appeal to the railway authorities to see the unions.[89] At lunch time Lloyd George was complaining, 'The men are the damnedest fools . . . I have got them everything they want and yet they are now sticking out for Recognition before the strike ends. It is not possible.'[90] Lloyd George pressed on them that, in view of the Moroccan crisis, the national railway strike was endangering the country. MacDonald, Henderson and Wardle of the Labour Party also urged the unions to call off the strike. Henderson, at least, was impressed by Lloyd George's crisis arguments. He wrote to his son Will that 'the most powerful factor in effecting the settlement . . . is the immediate possibility of war between France and Germany, which meant the withdrawing of all the troops, and the necessity for the Government to get coal for the Navy. This changed the attitude of the Government, and compelled them to bring pressure to bear upon the employers.'[91] This appeal was most probably an on the spot improvisation by Lloyd George. Immediately after the settlement, he burst in upon Haldane saying, 'A bottle of champagne! I've done it! Don't ask me how, but I've done it! The strike is settled!'[92]

Lloyd George succeeded in getting the first direct discussions between representatives of all the railway managements and the four unions. This he had previously 'thought quite impossible'.[93]

The two sides agreed to reinstate strikers without penalties, the immediate recall of the conciliation boards to reconsider the men's grievances, and the appointment of a commission of enquiry, which should report as soon as possible. By Monday 21 August all but the North Eastern Railway were back to normal running.[94]

Lloyd George intervened because of Asquith's failure and because he felt confrontation to be disastrous. He was clearly still concerned about the Moroccan crisis. He also felt that he could repeat his 1907 success in dealing with a railway dispute. As Arthur Murray noted in his diary, 'Lloyd George has gained great kudos from his share in bringing about a settlement.'[95]

The episode ended with Lloyd George denouncing Keir Hardie in the Commons. Before the settlement Lloyd George had succeeded in getting the Labour M.P.s to withdraw a censure motion. But on the 22nd Labour M.P.s protested at the use of troops during a debate on the motion for adjournment. Keir Hardie explained, after being challenged by Lloyd George, that in a speech to railwaymen in Wales he had warned them that troops would be used, and, 'This meant the shooting down, if necessary, of the men.'[96] One observer described the episode:

> . . . Keir Hardie attacked the Prime Minister and the Cabinet in a speech seething with misstatements and inaccuracies, and was severely trounced by Lloyd George, who, pointing his finger at Keir Hardie, declared passionately that 'no word in the category of Parliamentary language' could be applied to him in the circumstances. It may be said with confidence that rarely, if ever, in the history of the House of Commons, has a Member been so hotly denounced for his words or actions as was Keir Hardie by the Chancellor of the Exchequer.[97]

The railway strike and the 1912 coal strike both led to more and more discussion of the role of the State in industrial relations. From the King and the Conservatives there were proposals which amounted to taking an offensive against the unions. In September 1911 the King urged

> most strongly on the Government the importance (and it is also their duty) of their taking advantage of the lull . . . to devise a scheme which, although not entirely preventing strikes (perhaps that is not possible), would to a large extent prevent a threatened strike from coming to a head, and might be the means of preventing 'sympathetic' strikes from taking place. Under any circumstances he hopes that what is now called 'peaceful picketing', which most people condemn, will be put an end to by legislation. Of course the difficulty

of dealing with the men is that they do not feel themselves bound by any agreements, and this in many cases they pay no attention to the orders of their leaders.[98]

Asquith invited his colleague's comments, and replied to the King that these matters had been and were being considered by the Government, but felt there was 'little prospect of any practical scheme of legislation, which would command anything like general acceptance being devised between now and the autumn sitting'.[99] Both he and Grey felt that violent picketing could be dealt with adequately by the existing law. Grey commented to the King on 'the impossibility of putting thousands of men in prison' and said that 'the most serious offence was that of inciting men to break their contracts and leave work without legal notice'.[100] Lloyd George, whilst staying at Balmoral, noted that the 'King [was] disturbed about strikes and labour unrest' and merely observed, 'God help the people if they expect redemption from Kings!'[101]

When the Government came to resolve the 1912 coal strike by legislation, leading Tories showered their leader with proposals for tough industrial legislation. These included stopping picketing and seeing that strike ballots should be run by civil servants not the unions' own officials.[102] Carson and F. E. Smith, like Grey, argued for seeing that contracts should be legally enforceable. Steel Maitland suggested that the 1912 coal strike should be dealt with by compulsory arbitration.[103] Bonar Law himself felt there were two courses of action on this particular strike, 'one to hold aloof but to say and *to prove* that absolute protection by police, special constables, military or whatever was needed, would be given to those who were willing to work; the other compulsory arbitration with effective penalties by imprisonment and by attachment of funds against all who aided, abetted or procured resistance to the award'. Both he and Austen Chamberlain felt the first to be the best course, though the second 'possible and justifiable'.[104]

In fact the Tory leaders took no action either on industrial relations legislation generally or for the coal strike in particular. This was largely because the Tory leaders realised that if they united with the Labour M.P.s to eject the Government, they would afterwards be left to cope with the situation.[105] As Bonar Law put it, 'No Government could deal with such a crisis at the present unless it had a majority in the House of Commons' and 'there could not be an election while the strike was still going on'.[106] They also felt that drastic legislation could only be introduced when public opinion was ready for it.[107] After the strike

Steel Maitland was still urging a confrontation with the unions. He wrote to Bonar Law saying that the Conservative Central Office were repeatedly having to decide whether or not financially to back working men who were bringing actions against their unions, and he urged that a lawyer should be set to work examining trade union law: 'It would involve a close analysis of the various cases which have arisen in connection with Trade Union Law since the passing of the Disputes Act, and a clear statement as to the lines on which cases might be framed for the purpose of breaking down the strength of the trade unions.'[108] But once the coal crisis was past, this contentious area was left alone by the Unionist leaders; perhaps because they did not want to scare away trade unionist votes in the next election. One Tory back-bencher at least urged that their lack of sympathy to Labour's reasonable aims was damaging the party as the trade unionists' distrust of the Tories 'leads them to follow blindly wherever the Lloyd Georgian Will-o'-the-whisp calls'.[109]

The 1912 coal strike was the most serious disruption the Liberal Government had to face. There had been a major disruption in the South Wales coalfields over wage rates for working difficult coal seams in 1910–11.[110] There had been considerable violence in the Tonypandy–Penycraig area after strikebreakers and later police were brought into the area. This caused the Government considerable embarrassment as the police dealt severely with strikers and the military were called in. This was all in spite of the fact that when Macready was called in at the outset, he found 'the Government, especially in view of the approaching General Election, were anxious that untoward incidents should not occur'.[111] However the Cambrian Combine Strike had been limited to one area. The 1912 strike, again centred on the question of the rates to be paid for working 'abnormal places', was national and threatened the whole economy.

The Government decided to intervene just over a week before the 1912 strike was due to begin. The men wanted a minimum wage for miners, whether or not they were working difficult seams, which though varying according to the circumstances of each district, would nowhere be less than 5s for an adult and 2s for a boy.[112] After district negotiations failed, the Miners' Federation balloted its members and in mid-January could declare an overwhelming majority were in favour of strike action. They called a strike for 1 March, and no direct national negotiations took place. After receiving a communication from Askwith and the Industrial Council, the Cabinet decided on 20 February to call separate conferences with both masters and men at the Foreign

Office, with Lloyd George, Sir Edward Grey and Buxton accompanying Asquith.[113]

The negotiations on the 22nd and subsequent days failed to prevent the strike. Cabinet Ministers had been pessimistic from the outset. On 18 February, Lloyd George had predicted, 'the strike would last about a month or industries would be brought to a stop, but that we would be able to get supplies in France and Germany'.[114] Samuel was equally pessimistic, and had laid in extra coal stocks for the Post Office's electric power stations.[115] After several meetings the Ministers were no more optimistic; Grey feeling that 'the only hopeful sign was that both sides appeared anxious to come to a settlement'.[116] Askwith, however, was contemptuous of the Ministers' efforts. He later wrote of these meetings, '. . . there followed the longest series of declamatory speeches and explanations, without any business being done, I have ever heard. The Ministers had no particular plan, and evolved no particular policy. They did not propose that the parties should resume conferences or consider the questions with expert business men, representative of employers and employed . . .'[117] Instead there was 'only a renewed statement of points which everyone except the four Ministers had heard over and over again. Any one of them would probably have got down to the kernel of the case, but the four together never worked it out, Mr Lloyd George keeping conspicuously quiet, and possibly keeping himself in reserve for a crisis.'[118]

When the four Ministers met the 170 representatives of the Miners' Federation on the 27th they submitted proposals for the settlement of the strike. These recognised that there were cases where miners could not earn 'a reasonable minimum wage' and that this should be arranged at rates varying from district to district. But, contrary to the Miners' Federation's position, they felt that to achieve these there should be district conferences and that if any of these failed to reach agreement 'within a reasonable time' the Government representatives at these conferences should resolve outstanding points.[119] The Miners' Federation however would only enter the district conferences on the basis that the minimum rates should be those which their special conference in February had adopted; and like the T.U.C., it was firmly opposed to compulsory arbitration. The majority of coalowners accepted the Government's proposals – though a minority, those from Scotland, South Wales, Northumberland and some of the smaller districts, were against them.

The strike began on 1 March – and soon over a million men were out. Lloyd George was not optimistic of a speedy settlement.

Herbert Lewis noted, 'Lloyd George and Dalziel agreed that it would not be settled soon – the men were determined to have a holiday – if they received all their demands plus 10 per cent they would not go back in many cases. "Smillie", said Lloyd George, "is the evil genius of the men". Whenever the Prime Minister was on the point of persuading the miners to agree, Smillie would intervene.'[120] Few expected the resumed negotiations to succeed.

Asquith and the other Cabinet Ministers saw the miners' leaders on 7 March to see if they would allow their minimum to be negotiable. Joint meetings of both sides chaired by Asquith took place each day from 12 to 15 March. Francis Hopwood was probably right when he informed Bonar Law, 'All these negotiations and conferences are doing no good because the miners' people are certain that the Government, when the pinch comes, will try to coerce the owners in favour of the men.'[121] During the discussions on the 12th Smillie made it clear that the minimums they claimed were only temporary demands, that in August they would want the 5s minimum raised to 7s.[122] By the 13th it was clear the miners were sticking to their position, and were determined not to have anything less than a national settlement and refused to submit the rates to arbitration.[123]

In these early negotiations Lloyd George apparently was particularly conciliatory. Hartshorn told a miners' conference on 15 March, 'I think Mr Lloyd George has shown special anxiety that we should come out of this, at any rate, the miners should come out of this in a favourable light.'[124] Hartshorn's views were no doubt reinforced by the fact that Lloyd George, via Riddell, had made a start the previous night of trying 'to arrange matters with Smillie and Hartshorn', as he felt 'the whole Trinity would not persuade the Scotch and Welsh mine-owners to settle'.[125] On the 14th the Cabinet agreed that in the event of the talks breaking down they would meet to consider 'the whole situation and the question of what is called for in the nature of administration and legislative action'.[126] Asquith told both sides on the 15th that in the circumstances the Government would feel it their duty to go to Parliament and proposed legislation, '(1) to make a reasonable minimum wage, adequately safeguarded, a statutory term of every contract of employment underground on coal mines (2) to provide for the ascertainment of such wage locally, in each district, by a Board on which employers and men would be equally represented with a neutral Chairman.' Asquith felt, 'Neither the owners nor the men expressed surprise at this decision, and both made suggestions as to the form of the proposed legislation.'[127] Askwith similarly felt 'the men were more amenable than they have been, but I think they will do their best to get their people to agree'. He felt the Prime Minister had taken this initiative 'at the first opportunity when it could be done with any chance of success with the men'.[128]

Thus the Government came to legislation to settle industrial unrest. Lloyd George had previously been sceptical of such action. In February Riddell had asked him 'if he thought an attempt would be made to regularise wages by Act of Parliament'. To this Lloyd George had replied that he thought 'this would be the trend of the Labour movement, but did not believe in the practicability of the scheme'.[129] When Lloyd George met Hartshorn at Riddell's house on 18 March, Lloyd George still would not speak in favour of specifying the 5s and 2s minimum in the Bill. He took the type of legalistic view that one would expect of Asquith. He told Hartshorn, 'The Cabinet cannot agree to fix wages by statute. The fixing of the minimum must be left to the Board to be set up under the Act. A vital question of principle is involved,' and, 'It is not Parliament's business to settle rates of wages. Parliament has not the necessary knowledge.' He remained quite firm on this the next day. After Riddell had told him that Hartshorn predicted serious unrest if the 5s and 2s were not included in the Bill, Lloyd George commented, 'If this happens, we shall use every means at our disposal. We shall declare strike pay illegal, and if necessary imprison the leaders.'[130] However within a few days he had changed his mind and felt their inclusion in the Bill to be essential for a settlement.[131] However several of his colleagues disliked legislation of any kind. At the first discussion in the Cabinet Morley and Churchill were foremost in expressing 'doubts as to its expediency' on the Bill even without the 5s and 2s in it.[132]

In fact the Bill was to be vague on rates. Askwith summarised the initial Bill to Bonar Law.

The principle of the Bill will be that the Government, having found as a fact that a grievance does exist, viz. that a reasonable minimum wage is not paid to certain *underground* workers, and having found that no remedy can be got by agreement, propose to establish by law

- making use of and extending the existing system of joint Committees in districts and a neutral chairman, and giving that Chairman power to decide if the parties fail to agree – as he now has power, to try agreement in certain districts, with respect to the rise and fall of standard wages,
- no person to contract out if a man employs underground workmen, or under penalty to pay less than the minimum,

   – elasticity allowed by permission of the joint Committee and conditions of efficiency of work, i.e. safeguards, also to be settled by the joint Committee.

Askwith also commented that the Bill 'will undoubtedly extend a principle, which in the future can probably not be limited to underground men'.[133] However when the Cabinet considered the Bill they removed the penal provision against employers paying less than the minimum 'which was felt to be one sided and not defensible in argument'.[134] Asquith, in his talks with the employers, even hoped that the new wage scale would not be applied for a year in view of the fact that owners had sold their coal output on existing costs a year ahead.'[135]

The main dispute in the Cabinet was over whether or not the 5s and 2s minimum should be stated in the Bill. Lloyd George strongly advocated these schedules of wages should be included.[136] During discussions on the 21st and 22nd they decided that 'while these may be, and probably are, as a rule reasonable figures, they must be subject to local variation in accordance with the circumstances of particular districts'.[137] When Asquith made this clear in the Commons, it came as a surprise to Ramsay MacDonald who 'had been given to understand by two or three members of the Cabinet last night that the "5 and 2" would be conceded on condition that they [the Labour Party and miners' leaders] would advise the men to go back to work'.[138] It is most probable that Lloyd George was one of these, and was trying to reach a settlement on this basis. The '5 and 2' issue was reopened and Hobhouse urged Arthur Murray and other Liberal M.P.s opposed to their inclusion in the Bill to put pressure on the Cabinet.[139]

Asquith told the Cabinet on 26 March that he and his colleagues' attempt to reach an agreement with owners and men on the '5 and 2' had failed. Sir Edward Grey tried to salvage the proposal by suggesting that the Exchequer should indemnify the owners against loss 'up to a maximum amount of (say) £250,000. It was pointed out by the Prime Minister – who was prepared, if *force majeure* compelled, to assent to some such proposal – that it would be difficult to justify to the country a subvention, at the cost of the general taxpayer, to one of the most prosperous industries of the country. Mr Burns, Mr McKinnon Wood and Mr Runciman were very adverse to Sir E. Grey's proposals as was also Lord Morley.'[140] However Grey's proposal was put on one side, and it was agreed to put a suggestion of McKenna's, 'That a National Board should be set up (as distinguished from the

District Boards, which are to deal in districts with the hewers' wages) to determine a national minimum for the day workers and boys', to owners and men that afternoon. This proved to be unacceptable to either party.[141] So the Government allowed the Bill to proceed without inserting the '5 and 2'.

At the third reading Lloyd George defended the Bill against Labour M.P.s' criticism. Arthur Murray noted that, after MacDonald had

> described the Bill as 'mere words' which 'afforded no prospect of settlement whatever', significantly enough the Chancellor in a solemn yet not unkindly rebuke reminded Ramsay MacDonald that none of them could always have their own way but it would be unworthy and inconsiderate action if he were to denounce the Bill simply because all he desired had not been achieved when so much had been gained. The fact that Lloyd George would himself have preferred the inclusion of the '5 and 2' added strength to his argument as this came from one who was, in a sense, in line with Ramsay MacDonald. The power of his retort to the Labour Party immensely impressed the House.[142]

Nevertheless Lloyd George was at odds with his colleagues over this issue – and there were rumours that there was a serious rift.[143]

The Minimum Wages Act did not end the strike immediately.[144] The Miners' Federation balloted their members, a majority of whom were found to be in favour of continuing the strike. This was not by an overwhelming majority, and on 6 April, three days after the result of the ballot had been declared, a special conference agreed to end the strike as there was not a two-thirds majority for its continuance. Thus ended 'the greatest industrial strike of modern history'.[145]

The strike demonstrated the growing power of organised Labour, and further illustrated the outdatedness of the Liberal Party, as Capital and Labour continued to polarise against one another politically. Even some of those Liberals who had been against the '5 and 2' solution of the strike were coming to realise that the State could no longer afford to take a laissez-faire approach to key industries. Arthur Murray noted in his diary, '. . . it will be the duty of the Government to leave no stone unturned to prevent a similar upheaval in the future. Recent events and the railway strike of last summer have made it clear that the two industries, the stoppage of which can dislocate the whole trade and business of the country, must receive differential treatment, and, in some measure at least, be taken under State control.'[146] The coal strike and the other industrial unrest was scaring

many of the upper classes, who became fearful of 'syndicalism'
and 'bread riots'.[147] Many of the miners felt they had been cheated
by the Liberals, who had robbed them of an industrial victory and
given very little in return. Lenin observed that whilst the Government 'pretended to be neutral' and 'secured the recognition in
Parliament of the principle of the minimum', they *'as a matter of
fact*, took the side of capital and did not do anything to secure this
minimum wage'. He felt the workers 'cannot but realise how
important a political organisation, a political party is for them'.[148]
Certainly the miners had cause for dissatisfaction when they found
the joint district boards under the Act gave minimum rates below
5s a day. Similarly, employers in areas which did not accept the
Government's proposals were equally alienated from the Liberal
Party for failing to take a hard line against the miners.[149] After
Asquith had put forward the Government's proposals for a
settlement Lloyd George said, 'Asquith's declaration for a minimum wage sounded the death-knell of the Liberal Party in its old
form.'[150] Asquith's failure, after 'having gone seven-eights of the
way'[151] to satisfy the miners with the legislation was symptomatic of the slowly but steadily growing gulf between organised
Labour and the Liberal Party.

After the coal strike, Lloyd George became chairman of a
Cabinet committee on industrial unrest. Asquith proposed its
setting up at a Cabinet meeting on 16 April 1912. He urged,

> the desirability in view of the existing unrest in the industrial world,
> and of the possibility of serious trouble in the near future in the
> transport and distributive trades, of at once appointing a small
> Cabinet committee, which would see and discuss matters with
> representative men among both employers and employed, with the
> object, if possible, of preventing the stoppage of work, and of
> taking in advance such precautionary measures as the situation,
> actual or prospective, may seem to require. Their work would be a
> useful preliminary to the more general and comprehensive investiga-
> tion of the whole problem which the Cabinet must shortly undertake.

The other members of the committee were Haldane, Beauchamp,
Buxton and McKinnon Wood.[152] Lloyd George discussed the role
of the committee with Riddell the next day. Riddell noted that he
'wants to find some man thoroughly in touch with the Labour
Movement and does not believe that Ramsay MacDonald pos-
sesses the necessary information . . .'[153] On the 25th, Riddell informed Lloyd George, 'I have a "jackal" who knows all the
Labour people and who can always get any information required,'
who was formerly the secretary of a trade union.[154]

Lloyd George was soon involved in the transport strike of the summer of 1912, which was centred on the Port of London.[155] The strike began with a dispute between the Watermen, Lightermen and Bargemen's Union and the employers over the employment of a foreman who was not in the men's union. Dockers began to strike in sympathy, and on 23 May the National Transport Workers' Federation called a strike of transport workers, which was effective in London and on the Medway. Asquith was on holiday in the Mediterranean, and the various moves in settling the strike were referred to Lloyd George.

The investigation of the initial dispute began with Askwith and Mitchell seeing both sides of the dispute, after the Cabinet committee on 9 May asked the Board of Trade to act. Askwith soon found the employers unwilling to reopen the question; they pointed out that many of the agreements had only been recently entered into, and made clear 'that they are averse to discussing the terms and conditions under which officers are employed with officials of a trade union chiefly composed of the men over whom these officials have, in the course of their daily duty, to exercise authority'. Askwith felt that Government intervention 'at the present time' should be broken off.[156] However the Cabinet committee had promised Gosling an enquiry and, contrary to Askwith, Lloyd George felt some enquiry must be held. He informed Buxton, 'I consider an enquiry to be now an obligation of honour which we are bound to discharge. It would be a very serious matter for the influence of the Liberal Cabinet with the workmen of this country if it comes to be thought that their word is not to be relied on.'[157] Haldane also felt there should be an enquiry, though he felt it should be as public 'as that into the loss of the Titanic', as Parliament and the public would expect the Government to 'take a big step'.[158] Lloyd George by this time was in Criccieth, and further discussions were undertaken by other Ministers. After a further conference with those involved in the dispute, at which Haldane, McKenna, Burns and Elibank were also present, Buxton informed Lloyd George that they had decided 'in view of further developments on the Thames to appoint a court to enquire into and report upon the facts and circumstances of the present dispute . . .'[159] Askwith was subsequently scathing of the handling of the strike, in particular the way in which several ministers individually had informal talks with both sides, and he suggested someone other than him would be best to lead an enquiry as 'both sides knew I was aware of every point'.[160]

However the enquiry's report failed to solve the strike. After the report was received, Buxton, McKenna, Burns and Simon composed letters to both sides urging resumption of work.[161] The Sailing Barge Masters made it clear that they would not confer again on wage rates, feeling that Gosling had repudiated previous agreements.[162] The employers also refused to form a federation or recognise the union ticket. One of them also declared they would not listen to 'the cajolery of Mr Lloyd George'.[163] On the 31st a deputation of the Transport Workers' Federation saw Lloyd George who was accompanied by Buxton, McKenna, Burns and Simon. Lloyd George told them that, 'The Government recognised that there were differences of opinion amongst workmen as to compulsory arbitration, but some form of joint conciliation board seemed desirable. He had, therefore, suggested to the employers, and he now suggested to the men, that they should set up machinery that would bring into being a joint board of masters and men.'[164] The men accepted the proposal, but at the same time declared that if the employers did not accept by the next day there would be a national strike. The employers refused to do so, and the National Transport Workers' Federation ended up calling a national strike which proved to be a fiasco.

Asquith was against legislation whilst Lloyd George favoured it. Asquith telegrammed Elibank from Gibraltar on 5 June for information and to tell him that he hoped legislation would be avoided.[165] The strike was discussed at length in the Cabinet on the 12th, after Asquith had returned. At this Lloyd George and Haldane 'were inclined to favour legislation, either to make the rates of wages recognised in representative agreements compulsory in regard to all persons employed in the Port, or to give power to the Port Authority to fix a scale of wages from time to time'.[166] The former course, making contracts legally enforceable, had been urged on Lloyd George by the trade unionists when they saw him on the 31st. Samuel also pressed for such a measure.[167] However the Cabinet as a whole did not agree, 'and at the end of the discussion the Prime Minister stated that he was not convinced of the necessity for any legislation and that in any case it would be premature at the present stage to promise anything of the kind'.[168] The next day the Cabinet agreed that 'there was no case at present for legislation'. Instead they shunted the issue of industrial agreements off to the Industrial Council.[169]

The Government took no further positive steps to intervene, no doubt because the strike was clearly doomed soon to fail.[170] Asquith only took the step of getting Lord Devonport to declare that the employers intended to keep and maintain contracts, a step which Askwith felt would lessen bitterness after the strike. Askwith also gave vent to the Prime Minister to his feelings on the 'absolute failure of ministerial interference by a committee of Ministers in an industrial dispute, and the bad effect upon Government prestige, particularly in the event of a failure'.[171] Askwith records, 'The Prime Minister was so annoyed that he gave strict orders that Ministers, even the President of the Board of Trade, who, if any Minister should intervene, were to leave industrial disputes alone and not mix themselves up with them.'[172] And so political intervention in disputes ended until Lloyd George's initiatives during the war.

In the Port of London dispute, Lloyd George failed, quite uncharacteristically, to take a firm lead in settling the dispute. With Asquith away, and as chairman of the Cabinet committee on industrial unrest he was in a strong position to organise the Government's initiatives on the strike. Instead, during the important early stages of the strike he stayed in Criccieth and left other Ministers to negotiate. Perhaps he was distracted by his plans for the land campaign, or concerned about his relationship with Frances Stevenson, or even worried by early murmurings about the affairs of the Marconi Company.

Thus in the period before the First World War Lloyd George was usually foremost amongst Ministers in coping with industrial unrest. His pre-eminence was due not only to his formidable negotiating abilities but also to his social background and his political outlook. The 1907 railway dispute and the 1912 coal strike in particular threatened to disrupt the national economy. Lloyd George played an important part, as he was to do later in his career, in limiting unrest by taking extraordinary measures – in 1912 with the Coal Mines (Minimum Wage) Act.

This was part of a major trend. Governments increasingly needed to stabilise industrial relations, thereby restraining class conflict within an institutional framework which would act as a safety valve. Asquith's Government made major inroads into the nineteenth-century policy of leaving wages to be determined entirely by free competition. The 1909 Trades Board Act ensured minimum wage rates in certain sweated trades. The fixing of rates was carried out by representatives of these industries plus independent persons organised as a Trade Board, not by Ministers fixing wage rates. The motivation of this measure was humanitarian – concern at the lot of those suffering in sweated trades.[173] Whereas the setting up of the Industrial Council and the passing of the Coal Mines (Minimum Wage) Act were responses to considerable industrial unrest. In the summer of 1911 Buxton observed to his Cabinet colleagues, 'It is generally recognised now that industrial disputes are not merely the concern of the parties who are immediately involved, and the question is not whether the State should interfere more in trade disputes, but what form should their [sic] interference take.'[174] The Board of Trade, viewing with concern the supercession of the old Lib-Lab moderate trade union leaders and the growing militancy of the rank and file, asserted, 'some effort should be made to maintain control'.[175]

The Industrial Council was an attempt to solve industrial disputes by conciliation at national level – a natural response to national strikes in particular industries which affected a wide range of other trades. In essence it brought together all those on both sides who shared Macara's ideal of 'the substitution in the industrial sphere of cooperation for antagonism in the relations between employers and employed'.[176] Buxton felt the setting up of the Council would reassure public opinion that something was being done and might help settle the threatened national coal strike. But for him it was only a tentative move in the field of industrial relations; he informed Asquith that its 'creation . . . would in no way prejudice subsequent legislative action . . .'[177] Lloyd George was s supporter, in general terms, of moves to create more effective conciliation machinery. After the 1912 coal dispute Lloyd George spoke of this in his Mansion House speech, saying of strikes: 'You will always get them until capital and labour arrive at some method acceptable to both for determining the issues which create the unrest.'[178]

The 1911–12 industrial unrest forced upon members of the Government the whole question of what role the State should assume in industrial relations. Lloyd George's interventions, the Trade Boards Act and the Industrial Council all reflected and contributed to the widespread support in the pre-1914 period for conciliation and arbitration machinery in dealing with industrial unrest. After the 1912 coal dispute Riddell asked him whether he felt there was a strong trend towards compulsory wage arbitration. Lloyd George replied, 'I think . . . [so], but at the moment neither employers nor employed are ready to agree to that method. You cannot hope to carry such proposals in the existing state of public opinion, but I agree we are trending that way, and may have State interference within a comparatively short time.'[179] The pre-war experience made Lloyd George's task much easier in setting up a war-time system to control industrial relations.

PART II

The Introduction of the War-Time System of Industrial Relations

IV

Lloyd George organises for victory

With the outbreak of European war, Lloyd George, after many hesitations, decided to remain in the Cabinet and wage war. The violation of Belgium's neutrality was contrary to the basic tenets of Liberal standards in international relations. Lloyd George made this his test as to whether Britain should intervene against Prussian militarism. Lloyd George made clear that for him such intervention was against a military caste, not against the radical and democratic elements of the German nation.[1] For a while he was hesitant in his new role; Samuel wrote to his wife on 3 August that after lunch that day when he 'was warmly cheered by the excited people, waving little Union Jacks', Lloyd George commented, 'This is not my crowd . . . I never want to be cheered by a war crowd.'[2] But once reconciled to the fact of war, he committed himself to taking every necessary action to win, if necessary regardless of Liberal principles held sacred in peace time.

The first obstacles he came up against in his relentless pursuit of victory were organisational ones. His work as Chancellor of the Exchequer and his concern for the efficient conduct of the war led him into taking an active interest in the problems of munitions production. As Lloyd George wrote in his *War Memoirs*, 'At the outbreak of the war my only connection with the problems of munitions supply was the responsibility, as Chancellor of the Exchequer, for finding the money to pay the bills.'[3] He vigorously cut through inter-departmental red tape in order that the War Office might rapidly make sufficient orders to meet the greatly expanding munitions requirements of trench warfare. He was among the first to recognise the need to plan and order huge quantities of munitions well in advance of current needs. This perspective of weighing the need to win the war against the cautiousness of the 'Treasury mind' is reflected in Lord Riddell's diary entry of 13 October,

Von Donop and others who are at the head of Ordnance know all about guns, but have no wide view of a situation. Already L.G. has got orders for guns largely increased. There has been no difficulty. The gun making firms readily took the orders. Von Donop and the others seemed surprised that they could have any money they required. L.G. said to them, 'What are ten, twenty or thirty millions when the British Empire is at stake?'[4]

The War Office's failure to anticipate future needs and later the failure of contractors to meet the orders they had promised brought Lloyd George into greater and greater involvement in the organisation of munitions production. He was the prominent figure, along with Hankey and Churchill,[5] in pressing the Cabinet to set up the Committee on Munitions (which met six times between 12 October and 1 January). He pressed this committee to increase the size of orders.

The activities which stemmed from his desire to wage war with more efficiency soon brought him into conflict with the War Office. He criticised not only the quantity of their orders, but also their policy of restricting contracts to their established contractors. He also attempted to get some priorities into recruitment (which Kitchener for long insisted should be unrestricted) – a major obstacle in organising munitions production, one official complaining in April 1915, 'We are getting into a tremendous muddle between recruiting officers, the Labour Exchanges and the Board of Trade.'[6] The struggle to limit recruiting and to get essential men released from the Forces lasted until well after Lloyd George left the Ministry of Munitions. A second criticism he made of the War Office related to the conduct of war generally – the failure to send sufficient help to Russia, and later at the attrition policy on the Western Front.

Lloyd George's concern with the conduct of the war brought him into conflict not only with the War Office but soon with those with the highest responsibility – Asquith and the Cabinet. In a leter of 31 December 1914, to Asquith, he complained of the infrequent nature of the Cabinet Committee on Munitions: 'Could we not have a series of meetings of the War Committee of the C.I.D. at an early date. Occasional meetings at intervals of a week or a fortnight will end in nothing.'[7] Asquith was slow in transforming Government to meet the crisis of a European war. His belief at first that the war would be short, his reluctance to interfere unduly with what he considered to be the army's prerogative to conduct the war, and his suspicion of introducing businessmen into the Government (apparently a residue from the Marconi

scandal)[8] were constituents of this. By March 1915 Lloyd George
was complaining of Asquith's mode of controlling the British war
effort:

> ... he lacks initiative and takes no steps to control or hold together
> the public departments, each of which goes its own way without
> criticism. This is all very well in time of peace, but during a great
> war the Prime Minister should direct and overlook the whole
> machine. No-one else has the authority. I have raised some questions
> but I have had to do this in the Cabinet. For example, I raised the
> question of guns and ammunitions . . . But I had to fight. I had to
> get a Committee appointed and go there and question the officials.
> All very unpleasant, as it was not my job.[9]

Lloyd George frequently became exasperated with Asquith and
his retention of a large Cabinet to deal with war policy; this led
eventually to Lloyd George's ultimatum of December 1916 and
Asquith's immediate supercession.

It is in this context – Lloyd George's attempts to override all
impediments to what he considered the efficient conduct of the
war – that his response to labour should be set. However, before
examining Lloyd George's handling of labour, it is important to
review his attitude to private enterprise in his organisation of the
nation's resources for war production.

Before the war Lloyd George had a reputation of being a major
enemy of privilege, but as has been shown he was never an opponent of private enterprise, unless it was monopolistic or unduly
profiteering. However, in his rush to get the necessary munitions
he trusted too much that businessmen would all behave un-
selfishly if an appeal was made to them; thus in July 1915 he
proudly spoke of the reduction of Government controls and red
tape: 'That involves a good deal more confidence and trust than
usual. We have no time to go through the same processes of
examination, of bargaining as you usually get in the matter of
Government contracts. Whatever is done must be done with
promptitude. That involves our trusting to the integrity, to the
loyalty, to the patriotism of the businessmen to do the best for us,
and to do it on fair terms.'[10]

However, considerable reliance on the existing production
system was without doubt unavoidable in an unexpected 'war of
munitions'. The scale of munitions production needed was un-
predicted by any of the combatants; as Lloyd George told the
Commons in the debate on munitions organisation in April 1915:
'During the fortnight of fighting in and around Neuve Chapelle
almost as much ammunition was spent by our artillery as during

the whole of the two-and-three-quarter years of the Boer War.'[11] In these circumstances the State needed the willing co-operation of the whole engineering industry. However, Lloyd George's extreme sense of urgency resulted in larger profits being made than might otherwise have been made; in one Minute he urged: 'the first interest of the taxpayer is that supplies should be secured. With this object it may be of public advantage to conclude contracts in the negotiation of which the prime necessity of securing expeditious and satisfactory delivery has been regarded as of more urgent importance than the actual terms of the bargain.'[12] For a short time the orthodox view that better terms might induce greater output may have been reasonable; until it became clear that the Government's need for munitions was virtually unlimited. Also putting contracts out to tender failed to act as a price restraint. Yet better terms could have been negotiated (quite apart from commandeering the necessary industrial capacity). Businessmen in engineering increasingly wished to undertake Government work – for as the war proceeded Government munitions work was the only expanding sector of trade, and firms not participating in it were liable to lose portions of their skilled labour force and, before long, be liable to closure.

The Government's terms to contractors were especially generous in 1914 and 1915. Early in the war engineering contractors were offered generous prices in order to encourage them to take the risk of switching their production to war work (often a costly procedure); this usually meant prices were close to the costs of the least efficient firms, thus leaving high profit levels for the others. In addition, a guarantee of six months' production was made to alleviate the firms' fears that, if the war were short, the investment in new plant would be lost. To facilitate further the rapid expansion of production by engineering firms, direct grants were given to engineering employers during the first year of the war for the installation of this plant and the extension of works. From mid-1915 and after, the inducement took the form of firms being allowed to write down such expenditure out of their excess profits (the resulting plant being evaluated and charged to the firm at the end of the war). As well such forms of grants, firms were given generous advances on contracts, many without interest.[13]

The often grossly inflated prices paid by the Government for munitions in the first year of the war were reduced steadily thereafter. This took place as contractors became experienced in such production and as, from the summer of 1915, the Ministry of Munitions started cost investigations. These cost investigations and the coming-in of National Shell Factory cost returns enabled the Ministry of Munitions from December 1915 to reduce prices substantially. Thus the maximum price for an 18lb shell fell from 22s in July 1915 to a sliding scale price of 14s to 16s at the beginning of 1916.[14] Another effective move was to investigate prices paid to sub-contractors (which was, on the whole, effectively taken in hand from June 1917). This is well illustrated by a contract for gun equipment in July 1916 where a main contractor (Beardmore) quoted £220 for a wagon and £215 for a limber, whilst one of their sub-contractors was willing to quote £116 and £111 respectively.[15]

As well as reducing munitions prices through cost investigations, profit levels were reduced as the war proceeded by the Munitions Levy and the Excess Profits Duty. The former was a result of the needs of the Government to persuade the trade unions to relax trade union restrictions, as will be shown. The latter took 50 per cent of profits over a standard based on pre-war profits; but this, even when raised to 80 per cent after the industrial turbulence of 1917, was never swingeing. The standard in itself was generous in view of the sacrifices called for from all sections of the community; and it has been estimated that instead of 63 per cent of excess profits being collected (the average rate of the Excess Profits Tax during its existence) only 34 per cent was gathered.[16] Even during the period of the 80 per cent incidence of the tax, the Select Committee on National Expenditure noted: 'that excess taxation is only a partial corrective [to big profits] is proved by the fact that contractors have thought it necessary to stand out for as high terms as they can get'.[17]

Even if cost investigations and other steps of the Ministry of Munitions kept down munitions prices, after 1915 the manufacturers had substantial compensations in other directions as the war proceeded. Even with a limited profit margin on each item (especially on goods produced on a cost-plus basis), the quantity required and the constant demand largely removed normal uncertainties for the manufacturer. The Financial Advisory Committee in a report of 30 January 1918 commented on the Ministry of Munitions contracts:

> There is little open competition in the usual sense of the term. In many cases the Government supplies the material at a fixed price and bears the burden of all increases of wages granted by the Government after the date of the contract. The Government in many cases is the sole customer taking the entire output, and in these cases the risk of the contractor is eliminated both on materials and labour, whilst the establishment charges are averaged over a large con-

tinuous output without the necessity of carrying stocks and book
debts, or incurring bad debts. He is thus in the favoured position of
having a fixed demand for his output without the need of incurring
selling commissions and can afford to accept a lower rate of profit on
his turnover.[18]

Lloyd George was apparently surprised at the end of the war,
when investigations into profiteering were made, that fortunes
had been made out of the war. He himself was slow to bring
forward proposals for a general war profit tax. As Chancellor of
the Exchequer, Lloyd George faced a series of questions in the
Commons, from February 1915, as to what steps he would take.
When Chiozza Money asked on 15 February if, 'in view of the
fact that certain trades were reaping extra profits from the war',
Lloyd George would see that firms and individuals 'should pay
a heavily graduated extra income tax', Lloyd George replied, '. . . I
cannot anticipate my next Budget Statement, but my Hon.
Friend may rest assured that this, along with other proposals, will
receive due consideration.'[19] However, when Lloyd George introduced his Budget on 4 May, he made no mention of such a tax.[20]
Perhaps this dilatoriness was due to the Government's voluntary
agreement with munitions employers that if their profits were
limited then the trade unions would relax trade practices in such
establishments; in this instance the unions would clearly get no
quid pro quo out of the Treasury if all profits were limited anyway.
Whatever the reason, general profit limitations were not introduced until McKenna was at the Exchequer,[21] and the contents of
the Treasury Agreement had been made statutory by the Munitions of War Act.

In fact Lloyd George's record in organising war finances as a
whole as Chancellor of the Exchequer appears slow and timid in
contrast to his approach to manpower problems. Lloyd George
and his successors at the Treasury listened far more to the financial
pressure groups than they did to other groups such as the industrialists and the landed interest. Lloyd George did not draft into
the Government a large number of financial experts independent
of the orthodoxies of the Treasury, the Bank of England, the
leading banks or the Stock Exchange. Instead of mobilising funds
in a systematic manner to finance the war, the war-time Governments lurched from crisis to crisis, meeting them with a patch-
work of *ad hoc* measures.

This reliance on orthodox advice and measures is best illustrated
by the famous emergency measures taken by Lloyd George in the
first few days of the war.[22] As the outbreak of war became immi-

nent he became afraid of the effects of its 'violent reaction on the inherently unstable financial equilibrium of the whole world, which is maintained by perhaps the most sensitive organisation devised' – as he reverently put it in his *War Memoirs*. In meeting this threat he initially consulted 'a number of financial and business men', the Governor of the Bank of England and top Treasury officials.[23] Then during the three extra Bank holidays he 'summoned a conference composed of Ministers and other officials and some of the leading bankers and traders, which sat morning and afternoon under my chairmanship'. This included Austen Chamberlain, who even chaired one session; and it was, as Lloyd George commented, 'a foretaste of the coalition'. Professor Pollard has fairly spoken of 'the extraordinary care taken to shelter the money market at a time when the greatest sacrifices were demanded from the rest of the nation'.[24] It is not surprising that this and subsequent policies restored his relationship with businessmen and financiers to the rosy state it was in during his time at the Board of Trade.[25]

Lloyd George was dilatory in raising direct taxation to pay for a larger proportion of the massive war expenditure. His autumn 1914 Budget doubled income tax from 1s 4d to 2s 8d in the pound and doubled the super tax from a range of 5d to 1s 4d to 10d to 2s 8d in the pound on incomes above £3,000. In view of the national emergency and the huge expenditure involved these were low levels – though at this stage Lloyd George could not anticipate the duration of the war. At the same time Lloyd George also increased indirect taxation. The beer duty was raised from 7s 9d per barrel to 25s and tea duty was raised from 5d to 8d per pound. Other rises in indirect taxation also took place. Though most increases in taxation were rightly concentrated on direct taxation these increases contributed to the problems of the poorer sections of the community, who were facing price rises generally, and to a small degree contributed to unrest and the demands for increased wages. Their problems were also increased by the low level of direct taxation in the face of the massive war expenditure which promoted undue inflation.[26]

Lloyd George and his successors depended heavily on raising finance by loans. In his autumn 1914 Budget Lloyd George announced the first War Loan, which was to yield approximately 3·75 per cent. However, McKenna's War Loan of June 1915 gave 4·5 per cent interest. In retrospect Lloyd George blamed McKenna for raising interest levels, but it was under his premiership that the rate was further raised by Bonar Law to 5 per cent, a level which he later described as 'penal'.[27]

D

For a short while in the autumn of 1916 Lloyd George did consider a national levy on all classes to finance the war. At the time McKenna's autumn 1915 Budget was under consideration, Lloyd George urged

> that the financial situation could not be really grappled with unless all classes of the nation were called upon immediately to set aside at least half their income for the prosecution. I suggested that the levy should be partly tax and partly loan, say roughly half and half; that the contribution levied upon the working classes should be in the form of a deduction from their wages; that there should be no exemptions except in favour of workmen whose incomes were only barely adequate to provide them with the necessaries of life.

This, he informed Sir Leo Chiozza Money, 'received a very considerable measure of acceptance from the Cabinet', and he asked Sir Leo to work out the details of the scheme if organised, with exemptions for those earning '(a) £1 a week and less, (b) 25/-d a week and less'.[28] Chiozza Money did this, and very soon pointed out that the figures on the various income groups 'show at once that it is impossible to take by levy as large a proportion as one-half of the total National Income'.[29] Later war taxation measures proved to be much less drastic.

The policy of raising the bulk of the finance by voluntary means was at first in line with the voluntary agreements for greater productivity and with voluntary recruitment. However, as it became increasingly clear that the war was not to be of short duration, and with the introduction of the Munitions and Conscription Acts, the voluntary principle became increasingly untenable. In his *War Memoirs* Lloyd George went a long way in recognising the justice of the Labour Movement's call for the conscription of capital. He observed of McKenna's 4·5 per cent loan:

> Maybe this corresponded to the price that was being offered in the money market for other gilt-edged securities. But in view of the increase in our nominal capital reserves due to war inflation and to the restriction of an overseas market for investment money which was also one of the effects of the War, there can be little doubt that the Government could have continued to obtain as much money as it required by voluntary investment, without raising the interest rate beyond the level of $3\frac{2}{3}\%$ at which my first loan had been negotiated. Investors would have had to take this for lack of an alternative. And if they had been willing to do so, there would have been a clear and popular ground for the conscription of capital for war purposes – a

step which would have been an appropriate corollary to the conscription of manpower which we were soon to introduce.[30]

The considerable dependence on war loans, especially in the early years of the war, allowed the rich to get richer – whilst mortgaging the future. The large profits of the early part of the war, whilst taxation was low and before cost accounting was introduced, were often loaned to the Government, and, as has been remarked, 'the interest which has to be paid upon it is simply transferred within the community from one group of citizens (the taxpayers) to another group (the bond-holders) . . .'[31] The repayment of the capital of such loans was left to post-war Governments. The effects of channelling investment into highly priced Government bonds was not fully felt by Labour during the war – as there was high employment and productivity. However, in the longer term the high rates of interest not only hit the taxpayer directly, but caused interest rates generally to stay high, and so greatly contributed to making money dearer for all public and private enterprise.

Lloyd George's policies in organising the nation for war reflect his considerable reliance on and confidence in the business community to meet the nation's needs. One may instance his desire to introduce businessmen of 'push and go' into Government positions. On the whole this policy proved valuable – with men like the Geddes brothers matching Lloyd George's hope; though now and then it caused friction with the existing civil servants, and a few of those so introduced remained attached to their own business interests.[32] Then, there was little desire to use the strong controls over industry which the Defence of the Realm (D.O.R.) Regulations gave the Government. And Lloyd George and the other Ministers showed little desire to develop the potentialities of the National Factories. Though these factories greatly contributed to the lowering of contract rates, they were barely more favoured by the Government when contracts were given. Another instance was Lloyd George's (and the Government's) preference for using the usual channels for raising capital for new projects (avoiding suggested moves to 'mobilise capital'); this included allowing external capital to be free of national restrictions if these restrictions threatened to frighten such investment away.

It is against the background of his general approach to organising the war effort that Lloyd George's relations with Labour should be seen. On the one hand he had a clear-cut and sincere commitment to win the war; and he was determined to pursue this even though it might mean clashes with the War Office,

Asquith and with Labour. On the other hand, his belief in and reliance on private enterprise often led him to expect very unequal sacrifices from labour. He opposed the extreme compensation to industry that many Tory M.P.s demanded; he told critics when he pushed through the second D.O.R. Amendment:

> ... of course businessmen will be subjected to inconvenience – and some businessmen to a great deal of inconvenience. That is inevitable. But this is a State of War, and we cannot conduct war and allow business to be conducted as usual. Instead of 'business as usual' we want 'victory as usual', and you cannot have that unless everybody in the community is prepared to suffer all kinds of inconvenience and, if necessary, sacrifice.[33]

But the degree of inconvenience often seemed one-sided. The contrast between the generous terms given as incentives to engineering firms and Lloyd George's apparent determination to restrict tightly money for distress resulting from war was not missed by Labour observers; nor was the Government's policy of expecting the working class to assimilate the soaring cost of living.

V

Lloyd George's 'Charter for Labour': the Treasury conference

Within weeks of the declaration of war it became clear that unemployment would not be the main labour problem facing the Government. Lloyd George correctly forecast the war-time situation to a deputation from the War Emergency Workers' National Committee on 7 October:

> I am not at all sure that we are not a little premature in anticipating very considerable unemployment. As the war progresses the demands on the industries of the country will . . . be enormous. There will be industries where not merely will employment be very full, but there will be overtime and shortage of men. You must remember that more than one million men have been withdrawn from ordinary industry for the purpose of war and it looks at the present moment as if that number might be increased by another half million . . . At the same time, you have this abnormal demand upon the manufacturing resources of the country. We are receiving orders from other countries constantly – from belligerent countries which are friendly to us. What does this mean? Far from there being distress and unemployment, I am not sure that you will not have a condition of abnormal employment in a short time.[1]

The war-time 'abnormal employment' and the urgent need for rapid and greatly expanded production of war supplies vastly increased labour's economic bargaining position not only *vis-à-vis* the employers, but also *vis-à-vis* the State. The Government soon realised the need to come to an understanding with the trade union leaders. In March 1915 Lloyd George negotiated at the Treasury a voluntary agreement with most of the unions connected with war supplies.

Manpower was directed to four main priorities as the war proceeded. These were: manpower for the army; adequate skilled and

unskilled labour for a vastly expanded munitions industry; sufficient labour to maintain the export industries, vital at least until
the receipt of large-scale American credit in 1917; and labour to
fulfil the essential domestic needs, of which the production of
food became the most crucial with the German submarine campaign.

The initial widespread belief that the war would be short postponed the full recognition of these priorities. Kitchener's 'Your
Country Needs You' recruiting campaign was phenomenally
successful in its immediate purpose, but its indiscriminate nature
accentuated the Government's problems in meeting its other
priorities. In the case of munitions, Kitchener's adherence to the
Liberal belief in the virtue of voluntary recruiting greatly
acerbated the shortage of skilled engineers, and undoubtedly
brought forward by several months the Government's need to
pressurise the trade unions to suspend many of their hard-won
rights.

After the German advance in France had been held, the
Government's overriding need was to increase munitions production rapidly. Not only did Kitchener's recruits have to be equipped,
but the nature of the warfare on the Western Front called for un-
predictably huge quantities of munitions.

The shortage of skilled labour for munitions production came
to the Government's notice from the autumn of 1914. As early as
October employers pressed this problem as the reason for their
failure to fulfil contracts punctually or to extend production. On
21 December the War Office held a conference with the munitions
manufacturers, at which the latter pressed labour shortage as the
greatest obstacle to greater production. Two days later the
Cabinet Committee on Munitions discussed the report of the conference, and recommended better co-ordination of labour, the
diversion of labour from less urgent industries (using moral persuasion on reluctant employers, and, if necessary, even using such
sanctions as refusal of railway facilities), and the introduction of
Belgian workmen.[2]

The Government was drawn into intervening in industrial
relations in the munitions trade by the failure of the employers
and unions to come to terms to meet the shortage of labour. After
piecemeal local negotiations between employers and the unions,
negotiations at national level between the Engineering Employers'
Federation and the engineering unions began on 10 December
1914, and ended in deadlock in mid-January.[3]

The issues at stake covered the core of trade union practices and
the Government's success in getting the union leaders to suspend

them during the war became a root cause of much of the subsequent industrial unrest. For this reason it is important to examine the employers' proposals. On 10 December they called upon the unions to allow (1) skilled machine operators to control more than one machine; (2) the relaxation of demarcations between trades; (3) the employment of non-union labour (in effect semi-skilled and unskilled men to do skilled men's work) and of female labour; (4) the relaxation of overtime limits. At a later conference the employers agreed that such innovations should only be made where essential (through shortage of labour), that workpeople should receive the rate recognised in the workshop for whatever job they did, and that innovations such as the employment of semi-skilled men in skilled men's jobs would not be permanent but only for the duration of the war.

These were proposals that the union leaders felt unable to accept. The role of the trade union leaders was to safeguard the position of their members: and labour had only its conditions and terms of work to safeguard. When the Under-Secretary of State for War, Tennant, appealed to Labour in the House of Commons for 'some form of relaxation of their rules and regulations, especially in Army work',[4] J. H. Thomas succinctly pointed out: '. . . the simple fact is that the rules and regulations as to the working conditions have been granted after a long struggle and, in many cases, as a result of bitter experience, and the trade unions would not, and rightly so in my opinion, relax easily any of those rules unless they have an absolute guarantee that the Government themselves would see the rules were enforced after the war and that the relaxation would not be taken advantage of'.[5] It was not enough for the trade union leaders that the Engineering Employers' Federation alone should guarantee post-war restoration, for the Federation did not cover all engineering employers, and the remainder would have been free to undercut firms abiding by the agreement. Above all else, the union leaders needed to carry their membership in any agreement. They knew that the skilled men of the union would be deeply hostile to the introduction of semi-skilled and unskilled men who would learn the job and so *de facto* undermine the skilled men's position at the end of the war.[6] And if other hard-won 'rights' were to be sacrificed during the war, they wanted to be certain that they were sacrificed for the national effort and not for the employers' profits. The Government was slow in coming to meet these points.

The union leaders' alternative proposals recognised the fact there was a labour shortage. They recommended that firms not engaged in war work should receive such contracts and that increased labour for war work should be obtained by the transfer of men from firms working short time, by the Government paying subsistence allowances to men working away from their home areas, by the introduction of skilled engineers from the Empire, and by the withdrawal of skilled engineers from the army. These suggestions, to varying extents, were in due course implemented by the Government. But the employers rejected them as inadequate. And this proved to be the case. As more munitions were required, the Government needed far more skilled engineers than had been employed before the war, especially when the building of National Factories extended the country's engineering capacity.

At first the Government faced the problem of increasing production with a reduced skilled manpower very cautiously. When Allan Smith, Secretary of the Engineering Employers' Federation, wrote to the War Office the day after the employer–union talks ended in deadlock, urging compulsory abolition of strikes and lock-outs, the suspension of restrictive practices and the setting up of munitions tribunals, he was informed that such schemes were neither practicable nor necessary.[7] However, the War Office, which at the end of December had already referred the problem of labour supply for munitions to the Board of Trade, now also referred the problems involved in this deadlock. The Board instructed Sir George Askwith, the Chief Industrial Commissioner, to investigate the matter.[8] On 4 February the Government appointed a committee, consisting of Sir George Askwith (as chairman), Sir Francis Hopwood (a Civil Lord of the Admiralty), and Sir George Gibb (a civil member of the Army Council) to investigate means of maximising production; it became well known as the Committee on Production, and after the Government accepted its second Report, it became an arbitration body for disputes.

Government intervention was made more essential by the collapse of the free labour market system, the continuing and increasing urgency for munitions on the Western Front, and the disruptive effect of an outbreak of strikes, most notably on the Clyde, the foremost munitions centre. The collapse of the free labour market became increasingly apparent at the beginning of 1915. In conditions of an absolute shortage of skilled engineers, employer tried to outbid employer for the available men; and Government department (notably the Admiralty) bidded against Government department. The result was disastrous to production; as one commentator has noted 'in the northern centres from a third to a half of the men thus drawn to munitions work proved disastrously mobile'.[9] Eventually such competition for labour was forbidden by a Defence of the Realm Act regulation at the end of April. Anarchy in the labour market could not be tolerated for long when national victory depended on efficient munitions production.

As well as trying to divert the requisite available labour to munitions industries, the Government realised more and more clearly that the relaxation of trade practices and restrictions would be a major element in increasing production to meet the army's requirements.[10] They were all well aware that such a policy was controversial. Llewellyn Smith, in a memorandum of 23 January, stated that the relaxation of trade union restrictions was 'the most difficult and delicate of all the matters which the Board of Trade have undertaken', and added 'I am strongly of the opinion that nothing but disaster would attend any attempt to rush the position by a frontal attack on union policy, or by any Government action which would give the unions the impression that the Government in this matter were acting as the mouthpiece of the employers.'[11]

The outbreak of strikes in February put a more dramatic pressure on the Government to intervene. The widespread unrest, particularly on the Clyde, caused the Government rapidly to extend D.O.R.A., to make the decision to negotiate with the trade unions separately, and to take notice of the widespread calls for profit limitation.

This industrial unrest was rooted in growing working-class resentment at the exploitation of their patriotism. Whilst wages remained fairly static after the outbreak of war for the majority of workers, the retail cost of food soared. In February 1915 it was 22 per cent higher than in July 1914.[12] Part of the rising cost of living was due to war-time dislocation of trade, but a large proportion was due to profiteering. The War Emergency Workers' National Committee's campaign at the beginning of the year failed to get early Government remedies; though allegations of huge domestic coal profiteering were later borne out by a Government committee of enquiry.[13] The inflow of extra labour for munitions made the deplorable housing situation in areas such as Barrow and the Clyde even worse; the scale of rent rises in these areas became a scandal, and the Government eventually limited them.

The Clyde engineers had been pressing for a major wage advance before the outbreak of war. They had upheld a three years' wages agreement which expired in January 1915, and the 2d an hour (8s a week) wage claim that they pressed in December 1914 had been formulated the previous June. The 2d demand was a big one in the pre-war context. It represented an attempt to improve their wages considerably relative to workers in comparable trades. However, in the face of war-time inflation it was by no means unreasonable. The employers stalled for months on this wage claim, and eventually offered only ¾d. The union leaders recommended a ballot in March (that is three months after the old agreement had run out); but the men went on strike.[14] The strike was led by an unofficial socialist shop steward body – the Central Labour Witholding Committee (its title being an attempt to avoid prosecution). Eventually the Clyde workers agreed to allow the dispute to go to arbitration before the Committee on Production who, in due course, awarded an advance of 1d an hour (4s a week) or 10 per cent on piece rates, but only as a war bonus.

Thus the Government followed a stupid policy – which appears even more stupid when it is remembered that Lloyd George and some other Ministers already expected the war to last two or more years[15] – of expecting the working classes to assimilate the steeply rising cost of living. The Clyde engineers received only 4s a week (10 per cent) when the cost of living had already risen 22 per cent.

Soaring prices hurt even more those who were not in strong unions. As W. C. Anderson complained in the Commons, such wage awards were not an answer to rapidly rising prices 'because the advance in wages does not apply to millions of people, many of them the very people who need it most. It is very often the most skilled and best organised work people who are able to force an advance in wages while old age pensioners, charwomen and badly organised women workers who are paid miserably low wages are left to feel the full blast of the rise in prices.'[16]

However, the widespread unrest did prompt the Cabinet into quicker but cautious action. In amending the Defence of the Realm Act in order to gain greater powers of labour regulation, Lloyd George wished to take a tougher line than his colleagues. Even before the Clyde strike Lloyd George had been following up reports that the workmen were idling. At the beginning of the month he enquired of Churchill whether it was true that 'the workmen in the north are refusing to work more than three days a week for Government firms?' MacNamara answered his query, suggesting his reference was to 'broken squads' (a problem subsequently dealt with in the Committee of Production's first Report), and said, though noting wage claims and opposition to dilution, that workmen had generally 'worked with great assiduity'. He did, however, comment that some dockers could not 'be said to be inspired by any very vivid sense of concern. There have been numerous complaints of carelessness, indifference and drunkenness, and in certain cases, large demands for increases in emoluments.'[17] With the rejection of the A.S.E.'s recommendations and the activities of the Central Withdrawal of Labour Committee, Lloyd George felt his worst fears were being realised. In early March Askwith reported to Asquith that Lloyd George mistakenly felt 'that an anti-war set exists in Glasgow and is at the bottom of the Clyde dispute'.[18] When labour regulation was discussed in the Cabinet during the Clyde strike, Lloyd George was amongst those favouring a firm line. Asquith reported to the King:

> A long discussion, exhibiting much diversity of opinion, took place in regard to the best way of dealing with the disputes, whether arising from the greed of employers or the slackness of workmen, which was delaying the execution and narrowing the field of Government contracts for the supply of munitions of war. Various suggestions, some of them of a very drastic character, were put forward; and in the end it was agreed that a Bill should be drafted under the supervision of the Chancellor of the Exchequer and the Attorney General, for the consideration of the Cabinet next week.[19]

The first draft of the Defence of the Realm Amendment Bill directly restricted workmen's choice of employment – giving powers to prohibit them working on non-essential work. On 26 February Lloyd George had much sterner clauses drafted – these were to prohibit strikes and lock-outs or the incitement of them, and to enact compulsory arbitration. However, on 4 March the Government decided on a milder plan than either – to put the onus on the employer to restrict the 'carrying on of work in any factory or workshop' that was inessential, and thus indirectly to restrict labour.[20] Thus the Clyde strike (combined with the labour supply problems) not only speeded Cabinet intervention, but also demonstrated forcefully for the first time labour's potentially very strong position in 'a war of production'. Lloyd George introduced the Cabinet's milder version in the Commons and pushed it through in two days.[21] The measure also enabled the Government to take over factories and workshops essential for the war effort – and the debates mostly revolved around the question of compensation. Lloyd George in his introductory speech carefully avoided the labour aspect, and pleaded the measure as one relieving contractors from their obligations to keep to private contracts and so enable them to concentrate on war work.[22] Even these measures evidently unnerved the rest of the Cabinet at this time. When asked by Riddell why he had introduced it, Lloyd George replied, 'All the others were afraid. They thought that there would

be a terrible row in the House of Commons. It was not my job,
but I agreed to do it.'[23]

The strike also ensured that the Government would seek the
full co-operation of the trade union leaders before taking over the
munitions industry. The suggestion of a Cabinet Minister addressing trade unionists unilaterally (in contrast to Ministers meeting
both sides of industry) had long been in the air. In December
1914 Brownlie and Young of the A.S.E. Executive had twice
pressed that a Cabinet Minister should directly appeal to the
trade unions for co-operation in greatly increasing production.[24]
And from the outset of the Committee on Production, Sir George
Askwith had urged that if the necessary requirements were not
met by the employers and unions coming to agreement then a
Cabinet Minister should make a strong appeal. 'An appeal couched
almost in the language of a demand', he wrote to Runciman, 'is
what the trade union leaders want to strengthen their hands when
they go back to the men.' His ingredients for such a demand – 'a
brief statement of the absolute necessities of the Nation, particularly during the next few months, and the claim of the Nation to
demand temporary sacrifices in her hour of need from all her
people'[25] – were the same as those made by Lloyd George at the
Treasury Conference. On 11 March the Cabinet decided 'to call a
representative meeting of labour people and try to get some sort
of understanding with them before taking over the Armament
works'[26] and the matter was put under Lloyd George's supervision.

The Government's basic position at the Treasury Conference
was prepared by the Committee on Production's four Reports
and by the Shell and Fuses Agreement. The first Report of 17
February dealt with the particular problem of 'broken squads' – to
avoid stoppages by a whole shipyard squad, when a member was
absent, a mobile reserve was formed to fill such gaps. The second
and third Reports (20 February and 4 March) were basically
revisions of the propositions that the employers had put to the
union leaders. The second Report called for no stoppages of work
during the war, but the settlement of disputes by an arbitration
tribunal appointed by the Government (on the 24th the Committee received authorisation to act as such a body); the relaxation
of restrictions on piece rate output, with the Government safeguard that its contractors should not subsequently lower piece
rates; and the introduction of female labour, with reference to
arbitration if differences arose as to the terms. The third Report
called for the suspension of demarcation lines under specific conditions (where there was the lack of the requisite skilled men either

locally or under transfer, with the usual rate for the job paid, and with a record kept of all departures from normal practice); and recommended in such circumstances the introduction of semi-skilled and unskilled workers. All these changes were to be for the duration of the war only, and at the end of the war workers who were in the various positions at its outbreak should receive priority for employment, whether or not they had joined the Forces. A definite agreement was made allowing the introduction of less skilled workers and the relaxation of trade union practices on the manufacture of shell and fuses on 4 March. The Shell and Fuses Agreement was ratified by a ballot of the A.S.E. members, who probably considered incursions on such war emergency items were not too great a threat to their position on ordinary engineering work after the war.[27]

The strikes in February also forcibly impressed on the Government the widespread resentment at large war-time profits. The Labour Party in the House of Commons strongly denounced food profiteering. W. C. Anderson, for example, made it clear that it was unacceptable that the working class should suffer as consumers through lack of State intervention, yet gain nothing as producers because of State control: '. . . if the law of supply and demand in all its nakedness is going to apply to food, then work-people can claim that their labour also shall be subject to the law of supply and demand and can take advantage of the law of supply and demand'.[28] Sir George Askwith in late February warned the Government that the working-class complaints would in some way have to be met: 'unless something were done to correct the view that contractors were entitled to unlimited profits, the work-men would claim corresponding freedom; and they had never been in a stronger position to enforce their demands'.[29]

However, the Government's moves in this sphere, until McKenna's Budget in the summer, were the narrow ones of dealing with profits on direct war work. In a fourth Report (forwarded to the Prime Minister on 8 March), the Committee on Production recommended the limitation of profits in return for the relaxation of trade union restrictions, as well as taking over armaments and shipbuilding firms. The Cabinet accepted this Report; though publication was postponed as it would weaken their hands in negotiating with the trade union leaders at the forthcoming Treasury Conference. Lloyd George postponed it twice more (in April and June) and it was never published.[30] Earlier, in December 1914, Llewellyn Smith apparently mentioned a 10 per cent increase in wages in return for a relaxation of union restrictions in firms doing predominantly Government work.[31]

But as the Government's policy was to avoid wage rises (in order not to increase the cost of the war or the length of time the country could directly pay for it) this kind of offer was not raised again, and hereafter the unions were only offered limitation of profits and guaranteed restoration of pre-war conditions at the end of the war in return for the sacrifice of their trade practices.

The Government therefore did not meet the ills which caused the disruption of production of the Clyde, but for a while longer followed a much more limited policy. Thus, with the adoption of the policy on profit limitation contained in the Committee on Production's fourth Report, the State appeared to be tackling certain excessive profits, motivated, however, by the need to increase munitions output, not because it felt these profits to be unreasonable in the national crisis. Acland (a civil servant at the Admiralty) stated this attitude quite explicitly:

> I believe that nothing would more quickly bring Labour to its better senses than the knowledge that we were not letting the big armament and shipbuilding contractors to have things all their own way. The main argument, I gather, for taking over the armament firms is that nothing else will convince the workers that their work is not simply piling up profits for contracting firms – and thus make them modify their rules which limit output.[32]

So whilst the War Emergency Workers' Committee, the trade unions, and Labour M.P.s pressed profit restrictions in all spheres as a corollary to wage restraint, Lloyd George and the Government were to barter limited profit restrictions for relaxation of trade restrictions in controlled munitions establishments. The failure to meet such a widespread genuine grievance rapidly soured later appeals to patriotism, and failed to remove very combustible material for later strikes.

Even within this narrow area of profit limitation, the Government's terms with the employers were hardly swingeing as a *quid pro quo* for the relaxation of trade union rules and customs. Runciman (keeping in close contact with Lloyd George) began negotiations with employers. It is not surprising he could inform Lloyd George on the 15th that 'we were able to make a good deal of headway on the basis of the proposals which I got them to bring to me themselves'.[33] Runciman accepted the firms' view that there should be no interference with the direction or management of the companies.[34] He would not agree to their suggestions that profits on new orders should be allowed to bear the same ratio to turnover as in normal times (for war-time turnover could be more than treble). But he accepted that net distributable profit might exceed the average of the two previous years by not more than 20 per cent (Runciman had tried to fix it as 15 per cent); and he also conceded that, as well as the usual allowances such as depreciation and expenses of management, capital expenditure specially incurred for Government work (with due regard to its value to the company at the end of the war) might also be charged against profit.

Surplus over this profit limit was to be dealt with either by price reductions or by directly returning it to the Exchequer. Runciman had suggested a bonus to the men as a third alternative. At first the employers did not oppose this, and Kitchener even implied profit sharing in a speech in the Lords,[35] but later the employers did oppose such proposals as 'they felt sure it would lead to trouble'. Similarly the suggestion made by one of Armstrong's representatives that 'the Government should acquire the ordinary shares of the two companies' was received unfavourably by the other employers.

The Government's terms with employers were certainly generous. From at least the beginning of March Lloyd George knew that some leading employers were willing to have their firms and profits controlled[36] and Runciman informed Asquith beforehand that Armstrong for one seemed 'quite to expect taking over'.[37] When these terms were underway it is not surprising that Runciman could report to Lloyd George that the employers were 'not in at all a bad humour'.[38] A fifth extra profit above the average level of unusually profitable years for the engineering trade was obviously far from severe Government control. As a memorandum by Professor Adams and Professor Geldart, drawn up before the passing of the Munitions Act (which incorporated these proposals), noted: '. . . the proposal . . . to allow an excess of one fifth above the standard amount of profit is a large concession where Labour is being required to give up its power to strike'.[39] In urging the fourth Report of the Committee on Production, Askwith had emphasised:

> But I must repeat that the great point is the concurrence of the Government in the recommendation that they object to money being unduly made out of the war, one first practical step to that being the action with the firms and unless that principle as a matter of the gravest policy can be made known it is almost useless to struggle against the trouble there is going to be in the *labour* world without whom we cannot wage war – and the cost which may be more than the country can readily bear.[40]

Runciman's negotiations did not meet this 'great point'; the

Government did not show at all clearly they objected to large war-time profits.

Lloyd George had hopes of considerable advantages stemming from a voluntary agreement with the trade union leaders, including industrial peace for the duration of the war.[41] This attitude can be illustrated by his remarks on receiving the sub-committee of the conference's first draft of an agreement; 'In as much as I hope that we shall be able to work the State direction of factories during the war, every word in it is a matter of very considerable importance, and we do not want to leave any ambiguities at all.' Lloyd George overestimated the power of the union leaders as the Government had overestimated the power of the Labour Party *vis-à-vis* the unions.[42] Lloyd George appears to have been genuinely surprised on the first day of the conference when Brace told him that neither he nor Herbert Smith had the authority to agree or disagree – to which he replied, 'But you can agree to recommend it to your people, surely?' Henderson interposed, 'We are all in the same position, everyone of us.' But this appears to have in no way shaken his belief that such agreement with them was the key to the rapid increase of production and to the prevention of further outbreaks like that on the Clyde.

The Clyde unrest was certainly at the front of his mind whilst negotiating the Treasury Agreement. He complained of the union leaders' first proposals, 'We want machinery to settle every dispute. For instance, on the face of it, this would not enable us to settle the Clyde dispute, or a dispute of the same kind supposing it arose. We want it to appear . . . an agreement for settling every kind of dispute arising out of the war conditions.'

Lloyd George's opening speech put a great emphasis on the need both for no strikes and lock-outs during the war and for the introduction of compulsory arbitration. These were the points Lloyd George had tried to draft into the D.O.R. Amendment Bill at the end of February. Before the Treasury Conference met Llewellyn Smith gave advice on these points.

Llewellyn Smith urged him before the Conference to 'make clear that the object of the conference is confined to work performed directly or indirectly for the Government for war purposes'.[43] Llewellyn Smith made clear that the Labour view that profit should be restricted as a *quid pro quo* for the working-class's acquiescence in rising prices was not to be allowed on the agenda – 'the conference is not concerned with general questions of wages and cost of living which affect all workmen and indeed all citizens alike, but with the particular problems connected with Government supply'. He went on to urge,

Do not connect the appeal to refrain from strikes, etc. *too* closely with the particular operation of controlling the profits of the big armament firms, so as to give an excuse for the representatives of all the other trades (boots, woollen cloth, clothing, saddlery, etc. etc.) *in which it is not practicable to control the thousands of undertakings concerned in the same way*, to say that they are prepared to come under an obligation not to strike *only if they can have the same terms* i.e. nationalization of their industries. The language used will evidently require great care to avoid this danger.

This Lloyd George carefully did. He circumvented discussing the arrangements being negotiated by Runciman with Messrs Armstrong and Vickers and avoided socialist concepts of State control. He made it quite clear that control was to be 'of works which are now exclusively devoted' to munitions; and emphasised that the Government's criteria for taking over firms was not just war need but the adaptability of the business concerned. He linked the restriction of profits to relaxing trade practices not to strike, saying, 'Above all, we propose to impose a limitation of profits because we can quite see that it is very difficult for us to appeal to labour to relax restrictions and to put out the whole of its strength unless some condition of this kind is imposed.' Other than mentioning the need of the Government to come to an agreement with both sides of industry to ensure that they did not combine to the detriment of the Treasury, he avoided further specific mention of profits in his speech.

On stopping strikes and lock-outs Lloyd George took pains to emphasise that the proposal to stop 'important work [being] interrupted by Labour disputes' was 'not a question of who is to blame there', but , 'How is the interruption of work to be prevented whilst you are settling the dispute.' Lloyd George read out a proposition in favour of arbitration and no stoppage, and after suggesting alternative forms of arbitration, he adroitly informed the trade union leaders that he could give them 'good news from the Clyde' – that the result of the ballot on the Clyde (where the trade union leaders' leadership had been humiliatingly rejected) was 'overwhelmingly in favour of accepting the Government's proposals for arbitration in the matter'; news which the assembled trade union leaders greeted with cheers.

The actual form of arbitration was a potentially controversial matter. Earlier in the month Arthur Henderson, on behalf of the parliamentary Labour Party, had written to Asquith (who forwarded the letter to Lloyd George) that if arbitration was to be done by the Committee on Production it should include, to gain greater confidence from 'the workers of the country', at least two of their own direct representatives. The employers later echoed this viewpoint.[44] Llewellyn Smith urged Lloyd George, 'Do not say anything which will weaken' the Committee, for he believed 'it is working very well and smoothly, and it would be disastrous to appear to suggest that its composition is not satisfactory, or that workmen who do not like it can have some alternative'.[45] Lloyd George offered the three choices already existing – 'a single arbitrator agreed on by the parties or appointed by the Board of Trade', the Committee on Production, or 'a Court of Arbitration shall be set up upon which labour is represented equally with the employers'. (The Committee on Production already had the power to set up such a court.) And in the event the Committee on Production was not altered – at least not until 1917.

Arthur Henderson, in his letter to Asquith, had offered an alternative to altering the arbitration body. He suggested

that an Advisory Committee of five, appointed say from the work-men's panel of the Industrial Council or other representative, should be set up with the authority of the Government for the period of the war, such a committee could be open to confer with the parties concerned in all cases where there had been failure to settle locally, and the committee could also, if desired by the workers concerned or their executive officials, assist in presenting the case to Sir George Askwith's Committee in the last resort. It should be clearly under-stood that in all cases this Advisory Committee should be consulted by the workers before any stoppage was attempted.

In the discussions Henderson repeated his suggestion, other speakers also wanted something similar, and so the National Advisory Committee (of Labour) was set up, and the Committee on Production was for the time being left alone.

The second major point of agreement Lloyd George sought was over relaxing trade restrictions, which had been called for by the employers and by the Committee on Production. In his speech Lloyd George seems to have put less emphasis on this than on the stopping of strikes. He emphasised, 'I want to make it perfectly clear that I am only discussing this suspension during the war', and he merely mentioned the questions 'of the number of machines which one man is permitted to attend . . . of the employment of semi-skilled labour, where under normal conditions you would not assent to it . . . and . . . of the employment of female labour'. In the ensuing discussions the trade unionists centred their com-ments on this issue, rather than the suspension of strikes. Brownlie, for instance, once more expressed the skilled men's fears of what would happen at the end of the war to the semi-skilled and un-skilled who would have then been doing skilled work, and bluntly stated '. . . the introduction of unskilled and semi-skilled labour into this industry is a standing menace to the skilled. We have no desire to prevent anyone rising in the social scale, but we do not think we are called upon to allow him to rise in the social scale to the detriment of the skilled workman.' Quite possibly Lloyd George did not fully appreciate at the outset the depth of feeling such proposals aroused amongst skilled workers – for at one point in the discussion on the first day, after Henderson had mentioned the need to safeguard average wages for skilled men put on to harder work, Lloyd George commented, 'We must safeguard the State against giving the same wages for less work, and, thus discouraging output. We would lose by a transaction of that kind instead of gaining.' However, he was astute enough to realise it was the major obstacle in coming to an agreement, and allowed the Treasury Conference to extend to a third day in order to achieve provisions for the safeguard of the skilled men accept-able to the trade unionists present.

Lloyd George achieved agreement with the majority of the unions present on the two main issues of the conference – the substitution of arbitration for stoppages of work and the relaxa-tion of trade union restrictions. The Treasury Conference con-sisted of representatives of the T.U.C., the General Federation of Trade Unions and the chief unions connected with the production of war material; and the Agreement was signed by all except the miners, who withdrew on the second day of the Conference, and the A.S.E. The conditions under which the trade unions should relax restrictions had been well aired before the conference in the proposals the Engineering Employers' Federation were willing to observe and the recommendations of the Committee on Produc-tion. The addition of the condition that, 'due notice shall be given to the workmen concerned, wherever practicable, of any changes of working conditions which it is desired to introduce as a result of this arrangement, and opportunity of local consultation with men or their representatives shall be given if desired', is significant of the trade union leaders' awareness of the need to carry the rank and file in any innovations, an awareness no doubt heightened by the recent events on the Clyde.[46]

However, the refusal of the A.S.E. representatives to sign the Agreement necessitated a further conference – as the A.S.E. was by far the most important skilled union connected with munitions. This conference, again at the Treasury, took place on 25 March.[47] Lloyd George made a strong patriotic appeal at the conference on

the 17th emphasising 'every month that there is delay in the output may mean two or three months added to the duration of the
war, with all its horrors'. But addressing the A.S.E. representatives on the 25th his tone was far more strident and he put greater
moral pressure on them.

> If a powerful body like yourselves, a body which is all powerful so
> far as the . . . [Treasury Agreement] . . . is concerned, cannot see its
> way to extend to the State the necessary relaxation of rules, which in
> themselves and during normal periods are of infinite value to your
> trade, well, we shall be placed, not as a Government, but as a State
> and as a Country, in the worst fix in which this Country has ever
> been placed. I should like you to realise this thoroughly: if Britain
> is beaten in this war it is beaten not by its enemies but by its own
> people.

And trying to put the moral onus even further on them, he concluded:

> We are making no appeal to you which we are not making to every
> other class, and we are making no appeal to you which has not been
> responded to by every other class. I cannot think of any appeal we
> have made to any class of the community for sacrifices which has
> not been responded to. And, if you refuse to make the sacrifice, it
> will be the first refusal we shall have had, acting on behalf of our
> native land.

The A.S.E. representatives remained doubtful of the equality of
sacrifices being made. Button asked that the terms the Government had made with the employers, in particular the percentage
of maximum profits, should be shown to them first. Lloyd George
again emphasised that the crucial point was that there should be
no stoppages, no loss of output and agreed that the unions need
only relax restrictions when they saw profits controlled. The
A.S.E. leaders remained uneasy over the relaxation of trade
practices. Lloyd George showed in the discussion that, though he
had no intention of being dragged into controversy over the rights
and wrongs of trade restrictions and practices, he was obviously
greatly distrustful of them. He replied to their demand of full
restoration of pre-war conditions at the end of the war: 'It does
not mean that any rules and regulations are going to be like the
laws of the Medes and Persians. But that is a matter which you
will have to fight amongst yourselves (employers and unions) at a
future time. Our business is to see, if you press it, that the *status
quo ante bellum* is restored . . .'
In the end the A.S.E. leaders agreed to enter the Treasury

Agreement provided that five assurances of Lloyd George's were put on record. These were that pre-war practices would be restored at the end of the war (recorded without the 'if you press it' of Lloyd George's verbal assurance); that on new inventions the workmen to be employed 'should be determined according to the practice prevailing before the war in the case of the class of work most nearly analogous'; that the Government should certify whether or not work was war work if doubts were raised; a reaffirmation that the Government intended to make arrangements with munitions firms 'with a view to securing that benefit resulting from the relaxation of trade restrictions or practices should accrue to the State;' and that relaxation of trade practices was wanted only for war work.

At the Treasury Conference Lloyd George made a third proposition for increasing output, of different origin from the requests for no stoppages and the relaxation of trade union restrictions. This was a request for support for 'very strong action on the part of the Government' to deal with war work being delayed through excessive drink. Concern about the evils of drink at this time emanated from Admiralty and War Office officials, who complained of it affecting output and transport.[48]

It is difficult to assess the importance of drink as a factor in hindering output. The data compiled in memoranda in the Lloyd George Papers and in the Government White Paper on the subject show that in *some* areas some slackness could be attributed to it.[49] But it is difficult to assess the extent of drunkenness or the amount of production lost through it. Drink was just one cause of bad time keeping – and it was intimately linked with the long hours and the bad housing which many munitions workers suffered.

Lloyd George certainly exaggerated its importance. After listening to a deputation of employers on 29 March he made his famous comment, 'We are fighting Germany, Austria, and drink; and, as far as I can see, the greatest of these three deadly foes is drink.'[50] His temperance past allowed him to pass on uncritically the employers' excuse for slow deliveries of munitions to the King as, 'They attributed the shortage entirely to drink.'[51] He was motivated partly by the belief that the war gave the opportunity for thorough-going temperance reform. This is borne out by a letter he wrote to Samuel, who was helping him draw up a drastic scheme of state purchase; in it he reported a Cabinet discussion and observed, 'The fact that the War Lords take this view helps things because the war emergency is the only ground upon which we can recommend any great change.'[52] His approach to the matter was generally far from dispassionate;[53] and the effect of raising it was to cause great resentment in the Labour Movement, even though he stressed he was accusing only a minority.

However, Lloyd George's choice of occasion in raising the drink issue was shrewd. He raised it first amongst the trade union leaders at this Conference – not in Parliament, let alone in a public speech. And in doing so, he emphasised that he was denouncing a limited number of men:

> I am referring to the effect which excessive drinking amongst a minority in some districts has upon the output. Believe me, I am very loth to mention it; one is so apt to be misconstrued. It may be said, 'You are bringing a charge against the working classes.' I am doing nothing of the kind. I am referring to a minority. But, as you know perfectly well, where the minority do that, they may throw the whole works out of gear, and very often they prevent men who are anxious to go on with their work from continuing that work.

However, the union leaders at the conference were sceptical, doubting if such effects were 'so widespread and so harmful' as Lloyd George suggested. The Tory leaders also had considerable doubts as to the importance of the issue,[54] but were willing to support measures if the Government declared them 'necessary for the successful prosecution of the war'.[55] Despite his disclaimer, Lloyd George was held at Labour meetings and in Parliament as the abuser of the working class.[56] The issue came near even to causing a breach between the Government and the parliamentary Labour Party, Henderson warning, after the publication of a White Paper filled with evidence given by employers and Government officials, '. . . until some method is found whereby the other side of the case can be stated, it will be impossible for the Government to expect from us a continuance of that solid support which we have endeavoured to give during the whole period of the War'.[57] However, amidst widespread scepticism and strong opposition from some quarters Lloyd George's proposed 'very strong measures' became much weakened.

Though his proposition on drink was opposed, Lloyd George did achieve agreement in principle on the two main issues he put to the trade union leaders. The Treasury Agreement was a voluntary agreement – it did not bind the trade unions. The Government was yet to find out whether the trade union leaders could carry their members in relaxing trade restrictions, in foregoing the right to strike and accepting arbitration in return for a promise that profits should be limited to a maximum of one-fifth more than the average of two boom years; and whether the men would acquiesce in the Government's delay in undertaking to control profits in food, shipping and other businesses affecting the cost of living, and so causing their real standard of living to decline in the face of rising prices. Even so, the Treasury Agreement was still important. Not only did it link the trade union leadership to the Government's policy, but it established foundations for legislation a few months later in industrial relations, the most controversial area for State intervention.

VI

The Munitions of War Act

The Government's need of munitions remained extremely urgent in the spring and summer of 1915, despite the Treasury Agreement. The 'shell shortage' became the political issue of 'the shell scandal' and was a major factor in causing the downfall of the purely Liberal Government and in precipitating the creation of the Ministry of Munitions. During the summer complaints continued to come from the Western Front of the dangerous hindrance to the war effort that such shortages caused.

The Treasury Agreement and the D.O.R.A. Amendments failed to cope with the breakdown of the supply of labour to war industries. As Llewellyn Smith commented in June, 'The question is whether some exceptional form of control or motive of not purely economic character can be effectively substituted.'[1] The Munitions of War Act was largely such a substitute, and this innovation in the relationship between the State and industry was confined at this time to one section of British industry—the munitions trade; as Lloyd George frequently commented, whilst Minister of Munitions, the customary free-for-all between employers and employed was not directly affected outside of war work by this measure.

The Treasury Conference had been intended as the remedy – but its results pleased no one. In the face of steadily rising prices, strikes and threats of strikes were on the increase and, as the Government had not controlled profits – an action agreed at the Treasury Conference with the A.S.E. as a prerequisite for dilution and suspending restrictive customs and practices, the trade unions had done little in pressing their members to adopt these policies. The trade unions complained of soaring profits and the rising cost of living. And very soon after the Treasury Conference the employers were complaining of the labour situation;

thus one firm wrote to Booth, '. . . as we have great difficulty in retaining our workmen engaged on War Office and Admiralty work, all of munitions of war, we would like to have further particulars of what steps Lord Kitchener's Committee intend to take, or can take, to provide additional labour, as may be required; where is it to come from?—as so far as our experience goes, all available labour is taken up.'[2] The failure to make the voluntary Treasury Agreement effective and the discontent of the participants at its results left the way open for the Government to take the alternative of legislating an industrial code for the duration of the war, and so control labour by law.

During the spring of 1915 Lloyd George more and more associated himself with the administrative efforts to increase production greatly to meet this need. The War Office had been following a policy (partly for safety reasons, partly through lack of imagination) of giving contracts to the Royal Ordnance Factories and to their pre-war contractors, and so only using other engineering capacity indirectly as sub-contractors. This proved inefficient. Apparently as low a proportion as 16 per cent of shell contracts entered into by businessmen were being delivered on time in the early summer.[3] To meet their labour shortages, the Government needed to move labour and concentrate it on these firms. The policy changed when within the War Office's Armaments Output Committee (created at the end of March) George Booth, Lloyd George's man of 'push and go',[4] pressed for contracts to be spread out, under skilled supervision, to the engineering areas of the country (thus taking work to the men, rather than vice versa).[5] In fact the initiative was taken spontaneously by groups of employers from January 1915; and a group of Leicester manufacturers organised co-operatively received a War Office contract at the end of March.[6]

The War Office's former policy was unpopular with both employers and labour and even became politically embarrassing. Later George Booth, in replying to a complaint at a meeting of employers, observed,

these large armament firms in the rates they pay are taking the last drop of financial blood from these small contractors . . . There will be no more of that, because it will be arranged through the districts entirely . . . We want to have no one feeling that they are piling up profits for a particular firm. That does not suit anyone. It does not suit the political side of the Government, and it is a very important thing to a man like the Chancellor of the Exchequer, who is having that in hand all the time; and it does not suit the Labour Party . . .

There will not be that centralising of huge armament profits for three or four firms that you are thinking of.[7]

At one stage the War Office attempted to revert to its old system. Lloyd George successfully put pressure on Asquith. He informed Balfour, 'the Prime Minister . . . has taken a very strong step. He has appointed our committee not merely to look into the question of organising the resources of this country for war munitions but with full authority to take any action they feel necessary.'[8] 'Our committee' was the Munitions of War Committee ('of which', Balfour observed, 'Lloyd George and I are the two principal members'), which was set up early in April, though its formation had been agreed upon by Asquith, Lloyd George, Balfour and Churchill at about the time of the Treasury Conference.[9]

As chairman of this committee, which had 'full powers to take any steps it thought necessary to increase the output of munitions of war', Lloyd George felt he would be held responsible for any failure to achieve much greater output, and was determined to brush obstacles aside.[10] The shell crisis further strengthened his hand for munitions organisation, and he successfully pressed for the creation of the Ministry of Munitions at the same time as the formation of the Coalition Government.[11]

Legislation of some form or another was needed to cope with the Government's pledge to control profits. This was dealt with in part 2 of the Munitions of War Act. The basis of profit limitation was the same as Runciman had agreed with Vickers and Armstrongs – the profits were to be limited to a fifth above the average of the two pre-war years. At a meeting with Sir Vincent Caillard and Sir Thomas Davison of Vickers on 17 June, Lloyd George reassured them that in introducing the changed policy of spreading contracts 'the Ministry had no desire to interfere with the conduct of their business, but to secure the prevention of overlapping and useless competition and to use the engineering resources of the country in the best possible manner for the production of munitions of work'.[12] In these munitions works, termed 'controlled establishments', strikes and lock-outs (under part 1 of the Act) were forbidden and the relaxation of trade union practices was to be carried out under the safeguard provisions agreed at the Treasury Conferences (these were listed in schedule 2 of the Act). Minor offences against regulations in controlled establishments, such as bad time-keeping,[13] were to be dealt with by local munitions tribunals; and, after pressure from the Labour Party, major offences against the Act (such as strikes) were to be dealt with by the general munitions tribunal rather than by the ordinary courts.[14]

This legislatory enforcement of the Treasury Agreement was the policy recommended by several leading Civil Servants. In early June Sir George Askwith and Isaac Mitchell emphasised the need to prevent strikes;[15] and the Director of Naval Contracts went as far as to urge on 5 June *'compulsion* should be limited to securing arbitration and no strikes'.[16] Llewellyn Smith in addition urged the strengthening of the D.O.R. regulations on labour control by two measures, which were both eventually taken. Firstly 'in the case of workmen engaged on Government work, no new employer should take them on within a certain period of their leaving such employment without either a certificate from the previous employer that he consents or a certificate from some tribunal such as a Court of Referees that this refusal was unreasonably withheld', and secondly, 'the raising by voluntary enrolment of an "Industrial Army of Munition Workers" '.[17] The shortage and lack of discipline of labour had been emphasised very strongly again when the engineering employers of various areas had come to discuss production with the Armaments' Output Committee from 20 to 30 April.[18]

Lloyd George was quite determined to take the action recommended by his advisers and if possible much firmer measures as well. He made his intentions to tackle these problems quite clear in a major speech he gave at Manchester on 3 June: 'With regard to labour, two things are essential to our efficiency . . . The first is that we must increase the mobility of labour; and the second is that we must have greater subordination in labour to the direction and control of the State.'[19]

One measure to achieve this greater control of labour was to include in section 10 of the Act direct restrictions on the employment of labour. These, in effect, were the restrictions the Cabinet had balked at including in the second D.O.R.A. Amendment. However, on 23 April Lloyd George's Munitions of War Committee approved a regulation (8B under D.O.R.A.) which prohibited engineering employers inducing men to leave other such firms to join their firm; but the difficulty of defining inducements limited its effectiveness.[20] The problem of getting sufficient labour from commercial to Government work remained serious; in June it was reported that 43 per cent of persons working in the engineering trade were on private work.[21] The Admiralty raised the question of transferring labour from private work to urgent Government work at the Munitions of War Committee in May, and after consulting the Treasury solicitor as to whether the Government had adequate legal powers to do so, it was decided to strengthen the D.O.R.A. clause.[22] In the event, it was incorporated as section 10 of the Munitions of War Act, which gave power to regulate directly 'the engagement or employment of any workman or all or any classes of workmen' in munitions works.

Much more controversial was the 'leaving certificate' clause (section 7 of the Act) which interfered with the right of men to leave Government work for other work. At first its implications largely escaped notice. The idea was basically an extension of the prohibition which prevented essential employees from joining the army. On 16 April, F. G. Creed of Creed, Bille & Company, wrote to the Director of Naval Contracts (sending a copy to Lloyd George) urging:

> The remedy for this evil seems to us to be easy and simple. Firms engaged on Government contracts are now protected against the enlistment of any of their men in Kitchener's Army. No workman engaged on Government work is allowed to join the Army without a Certificate of Release from his last employer. We suggest that this principle should be extended so as to prevent the migration of workmen from one shop to another in search of higher pay.[23]

Employers interviewed by the Armaments Output Committee also stressed this problem – Dudley Docker, in particular, emphasised that many employers felt the problem would be largely met if they could tell their men 'if they were engaged on War Office Work they would not be allowed to leave without a certificate from the employer'.[24]

As with the clause which became section 10 of the Act, the leaving certificate clause was considered by the Munitions of War Committee and the Treasury solicitor advised that its introduction by regulation was not covered by D.O.R.A.[25] Thus it became another constituent of the Munitions of War Act. Introducing the Bill in the Commons, Lloyd George deviously implied it was as much a measure to stop pilfering of labour by employers as one of disciplining workmen; it was aimed at

> the prevention of the practice which has done more to destroy discipline in the yards than almost anything – that is the practice of employers in pilfering each other's men. It is absolutely impossible to obtain any discipline or control over men, if a man who may be either slack or disobedient to a reasonable order is able to walk out at the moment, to go to the works which are only five or ten minutes off, and be welcomed with open arms without any questions being asked. That must be stopped. It is a practice for which the employers are responsible far more than the men.[26]

Lloyd George succeeded in getting this through Parliament without controversy, but it was intended far more as a restriction on the employee. Indeed Lloyd George, according to Beveridge, was annoyed that the period of compulsory idleness for a man leaving his work without a certificate was six weeks not three months.[27] Though Lloyd George succeeded in passing this through Parliament without trouble, its reception in the country over the next two years was to be anything but acquiescent.

However, Lloyd George's most drastic intentions related to providing sufficient mobile labour for urgent war work. The way for industrial compulsion was paved by Lord Derby's success in March 1915 in getting employers and union representatives to agree to the formation of a Dockers' Battalion of the Liverpool Regiment. This disciplined body of trade union members was to be primarily used for Government work, but could be hired out to members of the Employers' Association of the Port of Liverpool. Even before the scheme was approved in April by the War Office, Derby was envisaging extending the use of soldiers in civilian war work. He wrote to Kitchener of men usually discharged as unfit for foreign service that 'it might be possible in some instances to make them into gangs – still keeping them in the Army – for work in your factories'.[28] A month later he told Kitchener, '. . . I could get as many men as I want. I am sure of the thing, and that is that it is not the extra money which attracts the men – it is the uniform and the medals for home service at the end of the war. Given these two things I would guarantee in this country to get you 10,000 men for your workshops . . . what I would really like to take on now would be the formation of industrial battalions.'[29] The trade unionists who feared the Dockers' Battalion as a strike-breaking body were right to do so. Derby, for one, intended using it as such; writing to Runciman in June of a potential strike which the employers had averted, he commented, 'I had arranged to put the Dock Battalion in to do the work if it had been required.'[30]

For a while Lloyd George appears to have joined Derby in seeing the possibilities of extending this kind of discipline. The first outline of the Bill, drafted at the Board of Trade on 1 June, outlined two proposals – the second being similar to the War Munition Volunteer scheme actually enacted, the first being akin to the Dockers' Battalion. According to this first proposal armament and shipbuilding firms whose profits were to be controlled, should be mobilised, and after seven days' notice, every man in them should be compulsorily enrolled, given uniform, a war bonus and potentially a medal, and then organised under the discipline of a military commandant.[31] On 4 June, Lloyd George chose to visit the Liverpool Dockers' Battalion and made a speech to them approving 'this new experiment in the mobilisation and organisation of labour for the purpose of carrying through this war successfully', and commented, 'I have heard a good deal about your battalion, and everything that I have heard had encouraged me to have a good opinion of the possibilities which you have disclosed.'[32]

Lloyd George publicly aired his intention of taking compulsory powers in his major speech at Manchester on 3 June.[33] In this he argued the fundamental right of the State to command the services of all its citizens, and hinted that the State might soon demand this right:

> It is the elementary duty of every citizen to place the whole of his strength and resources at the disposal of his native land in its hour of need. No State can exist except on the basis of a full recognition of that duty on the part of every man and every woman in the land. To what extent and in what direction the moral duty of each citizen to give his best to the State should be converted into a legal duty, a question not of principle but of necessity, is to be decided from time to time as the emergency arises during a period of war.

Later, after warning that if conscription were necessary for success then none would complain of its introduction, he warned, 'However that is not the real problem, and I say to those who wish us to dismiss conscription for the time being as a means of levying armies for fighting abroad: You ought not thereby to assume that it is unnecessary to enable us to mobilise the industrial strength of this country.' In this speech he also emphasised that labour was organised and disciplined in France, under the direction of the socialist Minister of Munitions.

In early June Lloyd George appeared to be close to calling for the Government to have dictatorial powers to conduct the war.[34] Thus at Manchester he urged,

> These questions spring up with great rapidity and ought to be dealt with with decision and promptitude, and above all, with courage. The primary responsibility must rest with the Government for the time being. They alone possess all the facts. These are facts which are only known and can only be known to the Government. Prolonged public discussion as a preliminary to action is all right in times of peace; you can't afford it in war. The ordinary method of arriving at a great national decision in a democracy – prolonged discussion on the platform, discussion in the Press, discussion in the workshops – these methods are totally unapplicable to a period of

war. The facts, the whole facts necessary in order to enable you to come to a conclusion, can only be known to the Government. There are things you cannot discuss in public; there are facts you cannot make public. It is a question of trusting the Government for the time being with the whole destinies of the Nation, or of dismissing them and setting up another which you can trust.

However, the response to his speech was so strong that Lloyd George found it essential to consult the trade union leaders and moderate his proposals. He acknowledged that he recognised that the good will of the unions was essential in a speech at Bristol on 12 June: 'the word rests with organised labour here whether you are going to turn out double the supply of shells or simply to halve your possibilities'.[35] But for a number of days after his Manchester speech, the outright mobilisation of munitions labour was being considered. On 10 June officials of the Ministry of Munitions interviewed the army representatives on the Clyde and Tyne at the War Office 'with reference to the formation of Regiments of "industrial soldiers" on the lines of the Dockers' Battalion', and both generally 'felt with certain safeguards . . . a solution of many of the present difficulties will be found in the raising of battalions of industrial soldiers'.[36]

On 8 June Lloyd George asked the National Advisory Committee for help to increase the output of munitions. At this meeting it was decided to convene on the 10th a meeting of the unions which had attended the Treasury Conference to discuss the reorganisation of labour.[37] Following their meeting, the N.A.C. prepared a memorandum to give to delegates attending this conference. This made two important points with regard to the unions.[38] Firstly, it did not rule out compulsion, '. . . The application of any form of compulsion to workmen concerned in the manufacture of munitions of war, *except as a last and unavoidable resource*, would be so disturbing as to defeat the object in view.' Secondly, they themselves asserted, 'The responsibility of the trade unions to the country for so increasing, by their assistance, the production of munitions of war as to place the issue of the war beyond all doubt or uncertainty.' Whilst they took this responsibility, they balanced it by pressing, 'The National Advisory Committee rely upon the Government realizing their responsibility . . . for preventing the established position of the workmen from being prejudiced and *for safeguarding their social and economic interests by eliminating the element of excessive profits or exhorbitant prices of the necessaries of life.*'

The N.A.C.'s proposal was for 'a voluntary system of transfer of workmen'; i.e. similar to the second proposed scheme of 1 June – a system which had been used on the Tyne under the name of 'The King's Munition Volunteers'.

Lloyd George, on 10 June, told the meeting of unions represented at the Treasury Conference that the munitions situation was even worse than he thought it was when he was Chancellor of the Exchequer.[39] He urged the need for relaxation of trade union restrictions, especially in allowing less skilled labour to be used, for mobility of labour, for preventing migration of labour from war work, and for stopping bad time keeping. On the issue of transfer of workmen, he told them, 'Now if you tell me that you can get these workmen by merely appealing to them that is all I want, but I want your guarantee.' And he wanted the trade unions to be backed by compulsory powers for transferring such enrolled men,

> . . . the mere fact that you had those compulsory powers would settle it. Believe me it is not a question of universal conscription or of universal compulsory labour . . . The point is that we are quite willing, and not only willing, but we would far rather, as you know your workmen, that it should be worked through your machinery, but we want to know that whatever your requisition is you will also be able to deliver the goods, and that you will be able to say to any recalcitrant employer who tries to stop the workmen . . . 'All right, if he does not go tomorrow he will have to go the following morning, and that on an Order.'

He did not accept the N.A.C. statement outright, he merely commented on it, 'I hope you will go a good deal further.' After Lloyd George retired from the conference, it endorsed the N.A.C. statement and agreed that it should be empowered 'to accept such extension of the proposals contained in these suggestions as may be necessary to provide a fully supply of the necessary munitions required for the speedy termination of the war'.[40]

At the Cabinet meeting that afternoon, Lloyd George expounded a measure in line with the tough statements he had been making earlier in the month. In speaking to the trade union conference Lloyd George did not expand on his willingness to accept voluntary enrolment handled by the trade unions; but in the notes prepared for his speech it is clear that such a policy was intended as a method of involving the trade unions in accepting compulsion – it argued 'a reasonable time' should be given to them, 'this is simply a means of affording them an opportunity of securing an adequate number of voluntary methods before action is taken by the State of a compulsory character'.[41] In explaining his policy to the Cabinet, Lloyd George stated seven days would be given. Austen Chamberlain summarised Lloyd George's proposals thus:

> The new munitions workers so obtained, either voluntarily or by compulsion, and the men already employed in munitions factories will thereafter come under severe restrictions for their ordinary liberties and be subject to penalties for any breach of discipline. Both those who have volunteered knowing the new conditions and those who by the accident of their previous employment are brought under those conditions, will henceforth be as restricted in their ordinary civil rights and as much subject to discipline as men who have joined the colours; and it will be noted that the major portion of the men will in any case be subjected to this discipline, not by their own voluntary act, but by what I have called the accident of their previous employment. This section of the population will, in fact, be under a civil discipline as complete as the military discipline imposed on soldiers.[42]

However, this was presumably too tough a line for the Cabinet to agree to. Some Tory Ministers argued that such action 'is necessarily invidious as well as incomplete, and it is open to the objection . . . that it is directed against a particular section of a particular class of the community'.[43] They felt 'if there is to be power to apply compulsion, must it not be compulsion all round?'[44] This larger discussion was shelved by undertaking Lord Derby's National Registration. Lloyd George altered his first proposals, and had Llewellyn Smith and Beveridge prepare immediately 'a definitely worked out scheme for co-operation with the trade unions more or less on the lines of the Advisory Committee's document'.[45]

When the trade union leaders met Lloyd George at a further conference on 16 June, they were handed a synopsis of the proposed Bill, which was not very different from the proposals Llewellyn Smith had made earlier in the month. This synopsis stated: 'The main object of the Bill is to secure by definite legislative enactment the objects aimed at in the Agreement made at the Treasury', and detailed provisions to prevent stoppages, the working of controlled establishments, a war munitions volunteer scheme in co-operation with the unions. The tighter regulations on labour and the leaving certificate clause were thus summarised at the end: 'The Bill contains also minor provisions amending and extending the Defence of the Realm Act, restricting workmen from leaving Government work without good cause.'[46] This successfully ensured that the discussion centred on the 'main' provisions of the Bill.

E

The provisions of the Bill did not receive much hostility at the meeting. Indeed, a few of the trade unionists (most notably Sexton) wanted stronger measures; several saying that the trade unions wanted more power over their members.[47] Lloyd George made clear that the attempt to transfer sufficient men voluntarily needed to be made to work in order to avoid compulsion:

> This is purely an attempt to avoid compulsion. It is an experiment which, if it fails, will bring us face to face with compulsion. I think it would be a very good thing if the workmen knew that. I think it would help to bring them in as volunteers . . . If we cannot get the workmen . . . then there is only one way of doing it, and that is by laying it down as a principle that every man during the war must render the service the State thinks he can render.[48]

During the discussions Lloyd George also made it quite clear that the Government had no intention of dealing with the working class's deteriorating real standard of living. T. E. Hill reminded Lloyd George of the reciprocal duty of the Government, 'the responsibility to safeguard their social and economic interests by eliminating the element of excessive profits, or exorbitant prices of necessities of life'. Lloyd George replied,

> . . . in a Bill of this kind you cannot have a schedule of prices for food; in fact that is a revolutionary proposal. I think the nation will have to consider it for a very long time before they decide upon it. It has been tried before in other countries not always successfully. I rather think the French Revolutionists tried it, and they did not quite succeed; they only succeeded in depreciating the currency . . . We are taking certain steps with regard to coal and other materials to do our very best to restrict the cost, and the time might come . . . when we shall have to take very strong measures indeed to restrict the prices, even with regard to the cost of other essentials of life. I think it is very possible that we shall have to do it. I rather imagine they are doing it in Germany already, but still they can do things in Germany that we cannot do here.[49]

When the Bill was debated in the Commons, the one-sided nature of it in the face of the spiralling cost of living was one of the most telling points of criticism made. Pringle, a Liberal M.P., commented on the virtual extinguishment of the free market for labour, 'there is no competition for labour, the only commodity which the worker has to sell, whereas there is open competition for every commodity which he has to buy'.[50]

The official *History of the Ministry of Munitions* remarked of the Munitions of War Act, 'Its provisions are, in fact, directed to the control of labour; and such disabilities and limitations as are imposed by it upon the employers are to be understood as a means to that end.'[51] Apart from the low excess profit tax level,[52] these limitations were open to much criticism. Professors Adams and Geldart in their memorandum of mid-June argued on grounds similar to Lloyd George's speech on labour control of 3 June of the State's right to call for sacrifices but applied it to profits: '. . . industries that receive their normal profit are being placed, if there is adequate provision for depreciation and other necessary compensation, in a no less favourable position than they were prior to the war. At such a time, when the safety of the State is involved, and in consequence the security of industries within the State, it should not be too much to ask that when the State is incurring abnormal expense to secure the common safety, all super-normal profits should pass to the State . . .' Like many others they also criticised the selective imposition of the profits tax: 'they will fail to satisfy labour because they leave a large field of what are truly war profits untouched; they will, for the same reason, rouse a sense of injustice in capital because they discriminate between capital and capital . . .'[53]

Criticism of the Bill was not great in Parliament. Though the trade union leaders were made nervous by Lloyd George remarking in the Commons that 'if there was an inadequate supply of labour for the purpose of turning out the munitions which are necessary for the safety of the country compulsion would be inevitable'.[54] On 24 June O'Grady, in a deputation of the General Federation of Trade Unions to the N.A.C., expressed fears that Lloyd George's intention of introducing compulsion if the voluntary system had not succeeded in seven days was incorporated in the Act. The N.A.C. 'could not find anything in the Bill or its Schedules to justify this opinion, but [felt] the speech of Mr Lloyd George when introducing the Bill . . . certainly afforded some justification for that belief'.[55] In consequence, Arthur Henderson agreed to the very unusual step (for another Cabinet Minister) of issuing a press statement to make the matter clear.

Thus the Bill passed Parliament with little fuss, and generally gained the tacit support of the leading trade unionists. But Professors Adams' and Geldart's warning that 'an unsound Bill may pass the House of Commons but before long its application will give rise to serious trouble in the country' went unheeded. Such a one-sided piece of legislation in the field of industrial relations was to prove explosive.

VII

The South Wales miners' strike, July 1915

The Munitions of War Act was put to the test within a fortnight of its enactment when the South Wales miners went on strike. This strike is one of the most significant of the war. First, the Government, faced with a strike on a priority war product of which they had inadequate stockpiles, had to follow a policy of concession, not coercion, to end it. Secondly, the solidarity of the 200,000 miners illustrated the hopelessness of prosecuting strikers – and thus considerably weakened the effect of section 1 of the Munitions Act (the power to proclaim strikes). Thirdly, it demonstrated to the Government how much harder it was to deal with strikers when their union leaders were in line with their members (in contrast to the A.S.E. officials and the February Clyde strike). Fourthly, underlining the Government's attitude to the strike and its solution was the fact that it was virtually a purely industrial dispute (over wages and conditions) not a political or revolutionary one (against the war or a step towards the overthrow of capitalism).

From the outbreak of the war the miners had been as willing to support the war as any other section of labour. At the outbreak of the war the majority of wage disputes had been suspended, but the rapid rise in prices forced the Miners' Federation to put forward a national wage demand of 20 per cent on 17 March. By this time food prices had risen 24 per cent of their pre-war level. After deadlock had been reached with the owners, who refused to concede more than 10 per cent or a national settlement, both parties agreed to refer the dispute to the Prime Minister for arbitration. Asquith decided the matter should be referred to the local districts – and awards were awarded of varying size mostly on the local wage basis.[1]

However, the Welsh miners continued to press for a new agreement. On 3 March, before the Miners' Federation made the national demand, the South Wales miners had given notice of their intention to terminate the 1910 agreement (under which wages had reached their maximum in 1913 before the war-time boom) on 30 June. As the official *History of the Ministry of Munitions* comments, 'Their object was partly to simplify the old system which was exceedingly complicated, but principally to take advantage of their strong position in order to secure a high minimum after the war when they feared a depression and to claim at once an advance in wages should the price of coal rise still higher in the course of the war.'[2]

Time in which to avert the strike was running out during the formulation of the Munitions of War Bill. Because of the crucial need for coal at this time, Lloyd George tried hard on 24, 25 and 28 June to persuade the Miners' Federation to agree to come within part 1 of the Bill – the section prohibiting strikes and lock-outs and introducing compulsory arbitration.[3] During these talks Lloyd George acknowledged that his purpose was to obtain agreement to a means by which to deal with a strike in South Wales: 'I am not discussing the thing in the abstract', he replied to a direct question on this. Though from his ignorance of the details of the South Wales dispute at the first meeting (he thought it was another dispute about union and non-union men), it appears this particular dispute only took precedence in his mind at the last moment.

From the outset, Lloyd George made it clear that he had no intention of coercing them by parliamentary means to accept compulsory arbitration. He stated quite explicitly the reason he particularly wanted their agreement: 'You are the best organised trade union in existence. My difficulty has been very often with other unions that, when I have seen the leaders, there is trouble behind. Your men always follow their leaders: they are a much better organised and drilled army.' Their help was essential to prevent a strike which could be calamitous to the war effort.

Lloyd George put extreme moral pressure on the miners' leaders (just as he did with the A.S.E. leaders at the Treasury Conference).

I need hardly tell you that a strike in the coal mines would be worse for us than a German victory. There is no doubt about that ... The whole basis of the explosive [in shells] is coal, as you know. We are supplying not merely our own country, but the whole of the Allies practically depend entirely upon the coal miners of this country. The engineers are important but only important to the extent that they supply our armies in the field . . . That is why the coal miners of Great Britain are more important in the preparation of munitions of war than even the engineers themselves. Therefore any trouble with the coal miners is a disaster; there is no other name for it.

He also pleaded with them to accept the *status quo* for the duration:

You will agree with me that a strike now would be unthinkable – quite unthinkable . . . It may be that in a few years it will be a country which will be governed perhaps under different conditions and different ideas, perhaps according to the ideas represented by Mr Smillie, or the ideas presented by someone else. But at any rate, it is the same old country, and if it goes under now, it is your country and our country, and we all go under. We must really, therefore, do our best to pull together in order to save this land from a very great disaster . . .

The Cabinet dearly wished to avoid a dispute at this time. Apart from the need for coal for the Allies (most of the French coal mines had been overrun by the Germans), there was urgent need for more coal for the production of the high explosive toluol and for the British navy. Balfour, when recommending solutions to the dispute to Asquith, informed him, 'My expert advisers here cannot tolerate the idea of using anything but Welsh coal for the fleet; and supposing only Welsh coal be used, we should very dangerously deplete our reserves if we went on at our average rate of consumption for more than a fortnight.' He himself was more optimistic, feeling that blending coal would help – and concluded, 'I have sent out orders that in the meantime the fleet is not to go to sea and that every possible economy in Welsh coal is to be used . . . I am convinced that if everything is done that can be done, we would hold out for at least a month without serious danger.'[4] However this was not a matter the Cabinet could view with equanimity in the period before the confrontation with the German fleet at Jutland. The needs of the Allies were as pressing as the need for explosives. Thus, when Smillie suggested, 'We do not require to avoid merely a general strike, because a strike taking away any considerable part of your output would be disastrous', Lloyd George retorted, 'It would mean collapse.'

Whilst Lloyd George on his own initiative discussed the matter with reference to the Munitions of War Bill, Runciman met both sides of the dispute for the first time on 26 June. As G. D. H. Cole has observed, 'the full seriousness of the situation apparently not being realised by the Government until within a few days of the expiration of the three months notice'.[5] The only result of this was that the matter was referred to Sir George Askwith for a report. This he made by 29 June. His report laid down two important principles: (1) 'that during the present grave national emergency no section of the community should take advantage of the needs of the nation to make a profit beyond what is normal in times of peace; (2) that if there is a movement of profits, due to war conditions, such movement cannot equitably take place without a movement of wages, and if the selling price of coal should rise so that coal owners make additional realised profits, the miners should get a share of such profits'.[6] But his specific recommendations for a settlement were unacceptable to the miners' representatives.[7] On the 30th, Brace, a former South Wales miners' leader and now Under-Secretary at the Home Office, after consultation with two of the miners' leaders, suggested concessions which he felt would prove acceptable. These were taken by him and his Labour Ministerial colleagues, Henderson and Roberts, to the Miners' Executive on 1 July, as final terms which were to be accepted or rejected. The Executive agreed to recommend these terms as a basis for negotiation to their delegate meeting. The owners reluctantly agreed to these concessions, though throughout they strongly pressured Runciman against any further concession; their role belying *The Times* statement, 'the colliery owners in South Wales have placed themselves unreservedly in the hands of the Government'.[8]

However, after the Miners' Executive pressed for a wide interpretation of the Government's terms, Runciman on 7 July formally asked Lloyd George if he would be prepared to proclaim the strike under part 1 of the Munitions of War Act. On 13 July, the day after the miners' delegate conference rejected the Government's terms and called for nothing less than their original demands, Lloyd George took this action.[9]

The putting up of copies of the proclamation in the area (which made it quite clear that it would be an offence to stop work) and the setting up of a general munitions tribunal failed to break the strike. The miners successfully called the Government's bluff by a remarkable display of solidarity – on 15 July 200,000 men ceased work and voted down a resolution that they should resume work the next day. Robert Wallace, the chairman of this area's munitions tribunal, wrote to Lloyd George on the 17th pointing out the impracticality of mass prosecutions, 'It is of course impossible to summon and try 200,000 men and only a few at first can be dealt with, and the length of time before there can be any real enforcement of the sentence will I fear only lead the men generally to regard the Act as ineffective.' He emphasised a point which apparently had been overlooked by the framer of the Munitions of War Bill: 'The Act only applies to men employed who have gone on strike. It does not apply to the secretaries and others who have incited the men to strike who may not themselves be actually employed in the collieries', and he argued that prosecution should be used only as a last resort, 'The first prosecution will, I fear, prevent any settlement.'[10] Lloyd George took a similar view and in acknowledging the letter agreed that 'we ought first of all to exhaust every endeavour to bring about a settlement by peaceable means'.[11]

Potentially acceptable terms, drawn up by Vernon Hartshorn, were given to Lloyd George by Riddell on the 18th.[12] Lloyd George also discussed the situation with Mr Nicholas, the miners' solicitor; he urged that 'it would be unwise to make any statement as to the Government's intention to take over the collieries in default of an arrangement, as this would be playing into the hands of the extremist section, who have been advocating that course, and who would therefore oppose a settlement with the object of securing this part of their programme'.[13]

Lloyd George took a much more conciliatory line than his colleagues. This was probably because of this advice, his assessment of the situation when he arrived in South Wales, and the extremely unfavourable response to his own tough proposals in early June. Asquith, writing to the King, of a Cabinet meeting on 18 July, makes it clear that Lloyd George went to South Wales authorised to offer no more than that 'the Government would be willing that they [the miners] should go on from day to day on the Runciman terms on the understanding that the margin between these terms and their demands would be submitted to an arbitral tribunal'. Asquith and the rest of the Cabinet intended him to take a tough line with the miners – indeed a remarkably provocative one which would have been likely to cause national unrest:

> He would, at the same time, make it clear to them that if they did not respond to his appeal the Government would at once proceed to take all necessary measures to paralyse the strike by preventing meetings, speeches and the receipt of strike pay; by taking over as 'controlled businesses' such pits as are needed in the public interest, working them for the profit of the State alone, by securing that they were adequately supplied with labour, and by providing for the proper protection of those who were engaged in working them. Inciters to a continuance of the strike, or to obstruction of the measures taken by the Government, would be prosecuted and punished, and the question would be seriously considered of

strengthening the law by making such offences treasonable as acts 'aiding and abetting the Enemies of the King'.[14]

Lloyd George was willing to pressurise the mine owners into greater concessions. The investigations into profiteering in the price of coal earlier in the year had justified the Labour Party's allegations. Vaughan Nash informed Runciman on this, 'We are dealing with a pretty tough lot of people, merchants and coal owners, and we prescribe accordingly.'[15] And Riddell pressed on Lloyd George on the 19th, 'I wonder whether you could induce the owners to be magnanimous for once . . . the masters are making enormous profits which they are carefully concealing. A hint that the Government intend to have their books examined by independent accountants should occasion arise might have a steadying influence.'[16] Whatever the nature of the pressure Lloyd George put on the owners, the result of negotiations by Lloyd George, Henderson and Runciman on the 20th resulted in the men getting nearly all their demands.[17] Speaking to a mass meeting of the South Wales miners on 21 July all Lloyd George could do was urge the importance of production ('Peace at home is essential to victory abroad') and appeal to them 'to make up for lost time'.[18] Once again the Government made a settlement which undermined the position of Labour leaders – in this instance the Labour Ministers – as the proposition that they had declared to be final had been considerably bettered.

Lloyd George's concession achieved a resumption of work, but the question of interpretation nearly produced another strike a month later. The South Wales Miners' Executive sent by telegram a virtual ultimatum to Lloyd George, Runciman and Henderson to see them to discuss the matter. Llewellyn Smith replied that as a difference it was a matter for the President of the Board.[19] On the first occasion Runciman had been willing to be a little flexible on his 'final terms' – sufficiently, perhaps, to make the Miners' Executive discount them as such, but insufficiently to resolve the crisis. On this second dispute over interpretation in August Runciman stuck firmly to the July award, probably more tenaciously than ever as the South Wales Miners' President told him that he, as he indignantly reported to his wife, 'had violated my honour'.[20] On 28 August Lloyd George joined Runciman in these new negotiations, much to the latter's distrust; Runciman observing, 'but for my influence they would have reopened the award. George as usual would have given them everything and given me away as well. The Cabinet is with me on the award being final.'[21] In the end Runciman had to accept Lloyd George's viewpoint that production in the South Wales mines at this point was of crucial importance and that the issue at stake was not a good one for a confrontation. He wrote to his wife on the 31st that Lloyd George now took 'the whole responsibility for concessions to them' and commented:

> The effect on other trades will be deplorable, but there we are in the men's hands and humiliating as it is, I see no other end to it but Lloyd George surrendering to them. All he says on that is that we shall have to come to grips with them on some occasion but 'the present point is too narrow, and the public won't understand a stoppage when the dispute is reduced to such a small matter'. That is his way of looking at these questions and I cannot gainsay it. Yet the general effect on labour everywhere is calamitous.[22]

However, the need for coal remained crucial throughout the war. In late 1916, after continued unrest, the coal mines were brought under State control. Lloyd George's moment to come 'to grips' with the miners was postponed until after the war.

PART III

Munitions and Manpower, 1915–16

VIII

Lloyd George and the trade union leaders in 1915

Throughout 1915 the crucial need of the Government was to increase munitions production considerably in order to equip the unprecedented volunteer army and to supply the needs of trench warfare. To achieve this increased output the co-operation of organised labour was essential.

From the outset of the war, the bulk of the Labour leaders were pledged to help the national effort and agreed to an industrial truce for the duration. At the time Lloyd George (and Churchill) were advocating compulsion Emmott observed in his diary, 'The worst of it is that neither of them know much about Labour. Fortunately L.G. is teachable and may learn before it is too late.'[1] After the very unfavourable response to his public utterances on industrial compulsion, Lloyd George's policy towards labour was to make maximum use of the trade union leaders – and consequently they became more and more involved in helping the Government get the maximum output out of manpower still in industry.

The impact of the war on British industry gave trade unionism a considerable boost. In 1914 there were over 4 million trade union members; by 1918 there were just over 6½ million members.[2] This increase in membership was particularly noticeable in such unions as the Amalgamated Society of Engineers, which was essential to munitions production; membership increased from 170,000 at the outbreak of the war to 300,000 at the Armistice.[3] The greater power of the unions in circumstances of 'a war of production' resulted in greater gains for their members. As Lloyd George observed to a meeting of trade unionists, 'during the progress of this war more things have been done to further the principles of the Labour Movement than the propaganda of a generation had been able to secure'.[4] By a policy of shrewd concessions during the war, Lloyd George generally succeeded in involving the official trade union leadership in Government industrial policies, and thereby isolated dissidents amongst the rank and file.

From early 1915 onwards the Government were fully aware of the importance of the trade unions in such a war. Allan Smith told employers at the Armament Output Committee meetings in April and May that, 'as a general line of policy, practically on the instructions of the Government, co-operation with the trade unions is essential'.[5] So much so, that at these meetings, which were aimed at utilising the maximum of the nation's engineering output, the Ministry speakers made it quite clear that no contracts could be given to firms which did not recognise the unions and so would be unable to enter local joint committees (of employers and workmen). Allan Smith explained the need to press employers to recognise the unions thus: '. . . unfortunately politics enters into these questions to such an extent that . . . we cannot ignore it, and politics at the moment does not violently favour the position of the employers'.

The Government's policy towards the trade unions was explicitly stated at these lengthy meetings with the employers. One intention of the Government was to strengthen the hands of the central trade union leaders. Thus Allan Smith explained why a system of local joint committees under a central committee was desired:

> We want the co-operation of the Labour Party. The general idea we have is this: we want a committee of the employers appointed to look after the various labour questions that may arise in connection with the production . . . the workmen would be nominated under the control of the Advisory Committee that is set up under Mr Lloyd George's agreement. If they have the opportunity of nominating these members on the local committee, then it is to be assumed that it would be an easier method of bringing discipline to bear on them.[6]

In addition such joint committees would prove to be a buffer between the employers and the men; as he explained: '. . . if we are to . . . rush through this thing at top speed, the rate at which we will have to progress, and the breaking down of trade union restrictions, will be so great that you will require a safety valve, and the only safety valve that we can think of as such is . . . a small joint committee to deal with the question where the two interests bump up against each other'.[7] This desire to centralise led to the abandonment in the summer of 1915 of independent local joint committees. These, particularly on the Clyde and Tyne, had gained considerable local prestige in their dealing with local munitions and other war-time problems.[8]

However, from at least February, the Government had been aware that industrial troubles were taking place in spite of the trade union leaders. In his letter to Lloyd George on workmen on the Clyde, MacNamara noted, '. . . I have received every assistance from the leaders of the trade unions. Throughout these leaders have stoutly deprecated cessation of work at this time of crises, their attitude generally being that there could be no discussion of any problem if the men downed tools.'[9] Opposition to changes of customary working conditions came from the unions' rank and file who, naturally, were quicker to sense a threat to their livelihood than the union leaders. When one member of the Armaments Output Committee commented to a Rotherham employer in April, 'that so far as our experience goes the attitudes of the unions are very reasonable, and they are quite willing for unskilled men to be brought in and put to do simple machine work without raising any opposition to quibbles', the reply was, 'In our case the union do not object, but the men do . . . the men will not work overtime . . . They told me candidly a year ago that they will not work overtime, and they have not worked overtime since.'[10]

Though Lloyd George long felt industrial conscription was the best solution for increasing production, from the summer of 1915 he put all his efforts into achieving the relaxation of trade union restrictions and the introduction of dilution through the cooperation of the trade union leaders. He told the Cabinet Committee on War Policy at the beginning of September that his department believed that by such a policy the workforce could increase its productivity by 25 per cent.[11] Duckham in a later memorandum claimed that this policy was liable to produce better results than even industrial compulsion.[12] Lloyd George's policy was to press the trade unions into aiding this effort. One way he did this was by making frequent threats of industrial conscription if they did not succeed in achieving the required labour mobility by voluntary means. Whilst introducing the Munitions of War Bill Lloyd George threatened that industrial compulsion might be introduced even if the War Munitions Volunteer scheme was a success – 'If we succeed by these means', he told the House of Commons, '. . . then the need for industrial compulsion will to that extent have been taken away.'[13] Lloyd George also regularly pressed the trade union leaders to lead and not to be led. Thus after the discussions with the trade union leaders over the Munitions Bill, when the A.S.E. made a new demand, he forwarded it to Henderson and the National Advisory Committee with the comment: 'This is the same trouble over again. What is the use of coming to terms with leaders when the men behind them also insist on being consulted?'[14]

Unrest over the war-time disregard of trade customs broke out on the Clyde in late July amongst coppersmiths at Fairfields.[15] The strike was occasioned by their anger at the introduction of plumbers into the copper shop without the coppersmiths' agreement. An employer commented to Lloyd George on the distrust between employees and employers, observing that when men were brought by their employers before a tribunal it did considerable harm to future industrial relations in their factories: 'The feeling shown by the workmen puts the firm in a very awkward position as regards the resumption of work the next day. They shout out, "It is *we* who are trying *you*", turning around and looking at one of the firm's representatives speaking to the Tribunal.'[16] On this occasion a nominal 2s 6d fine was imposed on each of the men by the Munitions Tribunal as their Secretary promised to advise the men to return to work and the firm agreed not to use the plumbers in the copper shop until the Board of Trade considered the dispute. Trouble was avoided by the union paying the twenty-eight men's fines.

Lloyd George discussed the working of the Munitions of War Act with the Shipbuilding Employers' Federation on 12 August. At this meeting Lloyd George again emphasised, 'The trade union leaders are fairly reasonable; the difficulty comes from the local leaders and not from the men at the top. I found them very willing to assist . . . but they have not the control over the men in the districts that they would like.' He was willing to agree to setting up rules approved by the unions, employers and Government departments in controlled establishments. Though he was unwilling to agree that the Government, not the employers, should bring all prosecutions before Munitions Tribunals, he did inform them, 'We have been discussing this question of our prosecuting not in every case but in suitable cases – cases where we could make sure we could make a real example.'[17] He developed this further on the following day, when speaking about dilution, at a conference of Ministry officials: 'I think if it is fought out in one good case in each district, then the trade unions will give in in the rest, but, if there is real trouble, you must call the Ministry in, and we must make it a national issue. If the trade unions resent it, if they carry it to the extent of threatening a strike, then we shall have to be called in, and the whole influence of the Government must be brought to bear upon it.'[18]

The Ministry chose as their example another strike at Fairfields, which broke out at the end of August. On this occasion the men had struck over what they considered to be the arbitrary and wrongful dismissal of two men. They did so without consulting either their local or national trade union leaders; and this strike threatened a stoppage throughout the Clyde.

The Ministry prosecuted seventeen ringleaders. The judgment was severe; Sheriff Fyfe threatened the full penalty of £5 a day for further strikes, and awarded a £10 fine or thirty days' imprisonment to each man. This heightened unrest among the men, and on 14 September, the Secretary of the Govan and District United Trades Council wrote to Lloyd George appealing for the fines to be reduced in order to avoid greater trouble.[19] Far from doing this the Ministry was considering preventing trade unions paying fines imposed on their members by munitions tribunals.[20] However, the unrest did not affect Government policy until it reached its head after three of the men were imprisoned on 6 October after refusing to allow their trade union to pay their fines.

Meanwhile Lloyd George was giving a trial to the trade union leaders' proposals of running a voluntary labour mobility scheme and bringing skilled men back from the army, before pushing forward with his dilution programme. The War Munitions Volunteer Scheme was run on clear-cut trade union lines in order to forestall later criticism; Lloyd George saying of the volunteer at the scheme's outset, 'Wherever he goes he will go under trade union regulations, trade union wages and trade union conditions.'[21] However, there was 'an absolute shortage of skilled labour'.[22] Few skilled men could be switched as they found 'nearly everybody in the trades is engaged on work of some degree of importance'.[23] Employers protested over most of those who enrolled (enrolments not contested were mainly of the least efficient workmen). The resulting adjudications were complicated by the need to define what was 'important work' and to fix priorities between munitions, food and export work, and even the small proportion of able men actually available for transfer were not always welcome; many employers being afraid of incurring unrest among their regular men if they took on war munitions volunteers with their subsistence allowance. The result was that, by late September, of 102,000 men who had enrolled, only 8,581 had been successfully placed (and of these only 4,529 had actually started work).[24]

Lloyd George also continued in his efforts to extract skilled men from the army. Even in December 1915, he still complained: 'We are trying to get men from the Colours but it is a rear-guard action. It is like getting through barbed wire entanglements with

heavy guns. There are entanglements behind entrenchments.'[25]
By October 1915 only 5,097 men had been released.[26]

Whilst these policies were being tried but proving insufficient,
Lloyd George publicised the need for greater munitions output
and prepared the public for his dilution campaign. During the
summer the Ministry refrained from enforcing dilution when the
workmen affected strongly objected. This was largely due to the
fact that they could ill afford at this time to lose production and
they hoped for results through negotiations with the trade union
leaders; but it was due also to the fact that the public had not been
adequately advised of the need for such steps.[27]

Lloyd George gave particular publicity to the potential use of
women in industry. On 17 July, Mrs Pankhurst led a huge pro-
cession of women through London. A deputation of these women
informed Lloyd George of the willingness of women to do war
work; Mrs Pankhurst informed him '. . . we feel it is essential, if
we are to . . . release as many men as possible to do their proper
business, fighting, that a system must be set up under which
women may be trained not only to do very valuable work as unskilled workers, but also to do skilled work'.[28] The expenses of
the huge demonstration, 'up to a maximum of £3,500', were met
out of the Ministry's propaganda fund, which was justified to the
Treasury on the ground that 'the proceedings served in a marked
degree the purposes of the Government in obtaining public
attention to the needs of the country in the matter of munitions
supplies'.[29] Also during July Lloyd George took pains to ascertain
the role of women in France; and in a communication to Albert
Thomas he asserted, 'I propose to increase very largely the number
of women employed here in the output of material of war.'[30]

Lloyd George also arranged that all manner of persons – as
various as Mrs Pankhurst, Ben Tillett, and bishops of the Church
– went to the munitions centres to urge the workmen to greater
effort.[31] Lloyd George felt such meetings did good. When a
sceptical employer commented, 'it is only the good men who go
to your meetings', Lloyd George replied,

> The trouble now is the decent fellows are not really exercising
> their influence upon the others. After all the public opinion of a
> community is the opinion of the majority, and if you can get a
> majority of the workmen with some sense of shame and decency,
> having regard to the plight the country is in I rather think they will
> have some restraining influence upon the others. At any rate it will
> make it some much easier for us to punish the others.[32]

Similarly, delegations of workmen (sometimes at the suggestion

of employers and with the support of union leaders) were despatched to the Front in the hope that their reports would increase
output.

But Lloyd George's main policy was to prepare the way with
the trade union leaders for dilution. On several occasions in
August Ministry officials discussed the need for dilution with the
N.A.C. On the 12th, when it was asserted that it was essential to
introduce women workers in the engineering trade, Brownlie said
the A.S.E. had discussed the matter and decided to leave it to the
local committees providing the terms of the Treasury Agreement
were adhered to; if this were done they foresaw no trouble. On
27 August Llewellyn Smith informed them that the War Munition
Volunteer Scheme had failed.[33] After consulting Lloyd George,
Addison informed the National Advisory Committee on the 31st
that 'they estimated that from 70,000 to 80,000 skilled workmen
would eventually be required to man the new factories at present
in the course of construction, of whom some 35,000 would be
required by October'. After mentioning that 'they were not getting
more than 60 per cent of the possible output of their existing
machinery', he asserted, 'he could see no other way out of their
present difficulty than to dilute their present supply of skilled
labour . . . The great necessity at the moment was to impress upon
the workmen to work up the provisions of the Treasury Agreement and to facilitate the employment of women.'[34]

At this meeting of 31 August, the N.A.C. recommended that
Lloyd George should address the forthcoming T.U.C. This was
an alternative to Addison's suggestion that the various local
advisory boards should be assembled in London and be addressed
by Lloyd George. The T.U.C. of September 1915 was the first
large-scale gathering of trade unionists since the outbreak of war –
and the Cabinet was anxious as to the degree of support for the
war expressed at it.

Lloyd George addressed Congress on 9 September.[35] He emphasised the crucial role of labour, stating that 'This is a war of
material' and that 'The war has resolved itself into a conflict
between the mechanics of Germany and Austria on the one hand,
and the mechanics of Great Britain and France on the other.'
Though he told them, 'The Government can lose the war without
you; they cannot win it without you', he still took the attitude
that the trade unions were just one pressure group or sectional
interest in the community; thus he urged them, '. . . I beg you, as
a man brought up in a workman's home, do not set the sympathy
of the country against Labour by holding back its might by regulations and customs when the poor old land is fighting for its life.'

Lloyd George's main purpose was to press the urgent need for dilution. He informed them that sixteen national factories were already completed and eleven more underway, and that to fully staff these and the old factories 80,000 skilled men and 200,000 unskilled men and women were needed. He outlined the terms of the Treasury Agreement, emphasising the importance of dilution, the suspension of restrictive practices, and no stoppage of work, and forthrightly told the T.U.C., 'In many cases I say, Yes, it is adhered to honourably. In far too many cases it has not been carried out.' He then gave illustrations of this. In making such a statement to a trade union gathering and not elsewhere, Lloyd George recognised the vital need to keep the majority of trade unionists committed to the war effort.

After the success of his speech at the T.U.C. – and with, as yet, no comeback on the stern adjudication on the Fairfield shipwrights – Lloyd George proceeded to get the trade union leaders' support for pushing forward with dilution and the suspension of restrictive practices. Lloyd George would probably still have liked to introduce some form of industrial conscription at this time; though, as in June, he probably felt that it was not politically possible.

When Lloyd George confronted a sub-committee of the N.A.C. on 13 September with the failure of the Munitions Volunteer Scheme, he brought with him a scheme described by them as 'a form of industrial compulsion'.[36] Lloyd George did not expect to carry any such scheme, but felt the threat of it would compel the trade union leaders into full involvement in the success of introducing dilution. He had reason to think this approach would work. The N.A.C., in pressing on their local committees the need for the War Munition Volunteer Scheme to be a success, had pessimistically informed them in a circular that it 'was the only alternative to some form of industrial compulsion'.[37] Before the meeting Henderson had apparently pressed dilution as an alternative to compulsion; he argued '. . . if you had compulsion for industry tomorrow I am not satisfied that you could get very many more skilled men placed at your disposal', and that if they introduced this, 'you will be up against the whole of the trade union movement in this country, and we cannot afford it. We cannot afford the next two months fighting them.' Lloyd George certainly took this line four days later in a meeting with the A.S.E. He told them:

When Mr Brownlie stated his views on industrial conscription all I can say is this, the stronger your views about the undesirability of conscription, the more bound are you, if I may say so, to make sacrifices to enable the volunteer system to work. You cannot have it both ways. You cannot say, 'We will not have compulsion, and at the same time we will take the fullest advantage of the voluntary system to make it difficult for you to get the best out of the men.' You must choose one or the other. If you say, 'We will not have industrial conscription' that means the workmen are in honour bound to place every facility in the State's way to getting the best out of the voluntary system. If you don't the only alternative is conscription – no, there is a third, and that is that the State should perish. I should like to know the man who would stand up and say, 'We will like that in this country.'[38]

In this approach Lloyd George was successful. The N.A.C. took it upon themselves to organise dilution. Henderson acknowledged that such encroachments 'will be stoutly opposed by every trade unionist in the country', but he said of Lloyd George's various alternative policies, 'I believe the diluting scheme would be probably the very best thing that could be encouraged', and argued that 'if there was going to be this diluting of skilled with unskilled and with women labour, it would be essential that we should bring together the whole of the executives [of the trade unions involved in making munitions] and throw upon them the responsibility of carrying out this scheme'. Mosses agreed with this, commenting, 'Anyone can take a horse to the water, but they cannot make him drink. The fat will be in the fire if you attempt by means of the ordinary machinery, say the Labour Exchanges, to move men from one place to another compulsorily', and he suggested, 'Let the Government give the numbers and let the local people, who know the circumstances of almost every man in the place, select the men.' When it was pointed out that the unions would have no power to transfer men, Mosses replied that they would have 'a good deal of moral power', and concluded that if someone was intransigent, 'He would have to be dealt with.' Henderson's suggestion was carried out. The executives of such unions (other than the A.S.E.) met on the 16th and 17th and passed resolutions generally in line with the N.A.C. sub-committee's views. And the outcome was the setting up of the Central Munitions Labour Supply Committee, largely consisting of members of the N.A.C. and the Ministry of Munitions, to carry this policy out, attempting to achieve 'complete co-operation between it and the local representatives of the trade unions and others concerned . . .'[39]

The separate meeting between Lloyd George and the A.S.E.

was more realistic as to the consequence of the enforcement of dilution.[40] Various members of the A.S.E. Executive warned that the introduction of women into works on the Clyde and elsewhere would lead to serious trouble; Gorman told Lloyd George, 'immediately female labour is introduced the worst men will stop work', and 'these men are prepared to stop work irrespective of your Act, and irrespective of the law . . .' Despite this likelihood, Lloyd George reiterated the importance of it in securing a greater output, and the potential value of a committee of trade unionists and Ministry officials to investigate the different problems of dilution. However, when pressed with the question of what he would do in the event of resistance to dilution, Lloyd George answered,

> What I wish is to secure that the shell and cannon are turned out at the earliest possible moment. If I thought there was not enough skilled labour to do it, and if by means of the introduction of un-skilled labour to work for which experts are not essential I could do it, I should be a traitor to the men at the Front if I did not insist upon it, and I should have to insist upon it . . . I prefer that an adjudication should be made by a Labour Committee, but I mean the thing to be done, otherwise I think the sooner we make peace the better.

Lloyd George believed throughout the war that, in the last analysis, if the majority of the workmen were faced with the alternatives of special war measures changing their working conditions or national defeat they would choose the former; and he explicitly told the A.S.E. representatives that on this occasion.

In late September and during October, the Central Munitions Labour Supply Committee worked out the details of the conditions under which dilution would be introduced. The committee had Henderson as chairman and included other leading trade unionists.[41] A sub-committee produced detailed regulations on the introduction of women and of semi and unskilled male labour (which were approved and issued by Lloyd George as circulars L2 and L3 respectively).[42] The A.S.E. Executive Committee agreed to co-operate in introducing dilution as long as employers observed the rates and conditions of these circulars; and on 4 November the other engineering unions followed suit.[43] The main defect in these proposals was that they could only be enforced in controlled establishments; the Munitions of War Act did not give the Minister general wage regulating powers. Another important defect in them was that L2, whilst providing that women doing skilled men's work should get the same time rate, did not take account of the possibility of skilled men's work being split into sections and women doing the easier parts; this omission caused considerable discontent during the remainder of the year.

The Central Munitions Labour Supply Committee also advised on the method of diluting. In so doing, trade union leaders associated themselves with the Government's firm policy on enforcing dilution in spite of any local opposition. The committee recommended to Lloyd George a procedure for dilution whereby the employer would explain to a deputation from the shop concerned, plus their local trade union official, the details of the proposed changes; if the men opposed the proposals, then there would be a meeting with trade union representatives present. If deadlock continued, the committee observed in their recommendation, 'It is not intended that the introduction of the change should be delayed until concurrence of the workpeople is obtained. The change should be introduced after a reasonable time, and if the workpeople or their representatives desire to bring forward any question relating thereto they should follow the procedure laid down in Part 1 of the Act.'[44]

But whilst preparations for enforcing dilution were being made, unrest on the Clyde came to a head when three of the shipwrights chose to go to prison rather than pay their fines.[45] They were imprisoned on 6 October. When Isaac Mitchell of the Board of Trade went to Glasgow on 11 October he found the situation critical, and two days later asked for an enquiry into the prevailing unrest; Lloyd George immediately agreed to this. The same evening the Govan Trades Council threatened strike action unless the men were released.

On 15 October Lord Balfour of Burleigh and Lynden Macassey opened an enquiry into the unrest on the Clyde; but their terms of reference instructed them to avoid entering into the shipwrights' case. The local trade unionists insisted that the case of the imprisoned men must be dealt with first and the men released. That same evening Lynden Macassey consulted officials at the Ministry of Munitions and urged that the men should be released on indefinitely prolonged bail to avoid the strike which would otherwise ensue the following day. The Scottish Office officials objected that 'it was quite impossible to release sentenced prisoners on bail'; and all agreed that to bring the three men up in custody would be worse than releasing them. Isaac Mitchell suggested the course that was finally taken – that the men's union should pay their fines without asking for I.O.U.s from the men.[46] However, at this time Mitchell's suggestion was not followed. The Commissioners enquired into the Fairfield dispute by hearing the three men's evidence in prison. Their interim report on the 21st stated that the question before them was not whether the men had genuine grievances but whether they had gone on strike contrary to the law. The trade union representatives had pledged themselves by this time to securing the men's release, and so refused to co-operate further in the enquiry until the men were released. On the 23rd a conference of executive councils or district committees of unions representing 97,500 engineering and shipbuilding workers on the Clyde sent Lloyd George a resolution, virtually an ultimatum, that unless the men were released there would be a complete stoppage on the Clyde. Lloyd George requested that a deputation should see him.

Lloyd George was very reluctant to give way over the imprisonment of these men. He felt that it was a test case as to whether or not the prohibition of strikes could be upheld during the war; he told C. P. Scott before he met the deputation on the 26th that to release the men '. . . would mean . . . that the Munitions Act would become a dead letter. Yet it is my last resort *short of conscription*.'[47] However, a large-scale stoppage at that time would have been disastrous – munitions production would only be adequate in early 1916 with the opening of several more National Factories. Moreover, a dispute over these men and other general grievances would be a highly undesirable prelude to the start of the dilution campaign in the area.

In these circumstances Lloyd George achieved a solution which avoided disruption of munitions production and to a certain extent saved his face. Lloyd George and McKinnon Wood (the Secretary of State for Scotland) met, as well as the deputation, representatives of the N.A.C. and the councils of several of the unions concerned. Frank Smith (of the N.A.C.) said that these latter groups repudiated the resolution sent to Lloyd George on the 23rd, but felt that the three men had been harshly treated. Lloyd George took a firm line. He stated that the Government had conceded an enquiry and the men had refused to give evidence and demanded the release of the shipwrights. He emphasised that the prerogative of mercy could not be exercised under the pressure of threats; and he firmly refused to discuss any grievances until the resolution of the 23rd was withdrawn. At a further meeting the next day it was pointed out by Frank Smith that the resolution could not be repudiated by the deputation, but only by the body that had passed it. Lloyd George then suggested that another course of action would be for others to pay the three fines (which had been reduced to two-and-a-half guineas each). This the trade unions did, and ended this particular dispute.

However, the widespread unrest on the Clyde was due to

deeper causes than the case of the three shipwrights. These included both social issues (such as rent increases and the rising cost of living) and industrial issues (notably disgust at the Munitions of War Act, nicknamed 'The Slavery Act'). The Government needed to meet as many of these as possible if it were to have the co-operation of the munitions workers in increasing production – above all in the introduction of dilution.

Rent grievances were dealt with first; and most dramatically as a consequence of a very successful agitation. Housing in areas such as Glasgow was grossly overcrowded before the war; the influx of munition workers made matters worse, and rents rose spectacularly. The Government recognised only limited liability in the matter in the summer of 1915. Lloyd George observed in June, 'With regard to the housing question it is not a question of increasing the number of houses, because the transfer is purely a temporary one . . . you do not want to provide accommodation for men for six months. We should have to provide billets . . .'[48] In the autumn, unrest on the Clyde was caused by widespread rent increases and attempts to evict soldiers' wives. When a 'rent strike' was successfully organised and evictions successfully opposed, the tenants were sued by the landlords' agents in the small debt court, where the men's wages could be impounded. Sufficient discontent was engendered in both the workshops and in the city at large that, when the first test case was heard, hundreds of people demonstrated outside the court.[49] The case was stopped, and Lloyd George promised a Rent Restriction Act. However, no steps were taken for some time to meet the considerable rise in the cost of living.

As well as the unrest generated by social causes, various provisions of the Munitions of War Act had generated widespread hatred in engineering workshops. The settlement of the dispute arising over the arrest of the three shipwrights cleared the way for the Balfour–Macassey Commission to continue its general enquiry. Though the Balfour–Macassey Report did not reach the Ministry of Munitions until 6 December, the records of the evidence were passed on immediately; by 23 November the trade unions had completed their evidence. Many of the Commission's recommendations were incorporated in the Munitions of War Amending Bill, which Lloyd George brought forward in early December.

As Lloyd George told the Commons, 'The whole of this Bill consists of concessions.'[50] The Amending Bill was aimed at settling labour discontent over the Munitions of War Act before the dilution campaign got underway. The concessions, however, were on the less crucial parts of the Act or, as in the case of leaving certificates, amendments making them a little less objectionable without losing their effect.

An Amendment Bill had been envisaged before the unrest broke out on the Clyde, intended to remedy certain omissions from the Munitions Act. These included provisions for the prosecution of persons inciting strikes and for appeals from munitions tribunals, for extending the definition of Munitions Works and for regulating the administration of leaving certificates.[51] To this kind of point were added certain remedies to the grievances put to the Balfour–Macassey Commission. The trade unions in their evidence named leaving certificates, failure of employers to pay district rates, reduction of piece rates and 'the peremptory discharge of workmen in the name of discipline' amongst the men's main grievances; of these, they said leaving certificates 'have occasioned more irritation than any of the others'.[52] In one respect, the abolition of imprisonment as a penalty for failure to pay fines imposed by munitions tribunals, the Cabinet accepted a recommendation of the Commission which was quite contrary to their recent statements.[53]

During November and December the trade unions and Labour Party successfully pressed for certain amendments to the Government's initial Bill. Lloyd George, speaking on his Christmas visit to the Clyde, told a questioner, 'An examination of the Bill as introduced and as finally leaving the House of Commons will show how generously the Labour Party were met.'[54] However, far more substantial alterations were achieved by the trade union leaders in a series of meetings with Lloyd George, a sure indicator of how much more importance attached to the industrial rather than the political wing of the Labour Movement during the war.

After the N.A.C. had considered the Bill on three occasions, they summoned a more representative gathering of fifty-five trade union representatives to consider it on 30 November.[55] Lloyd George stressed to the representatives the magnitude of concessions Labour had so far already achieved in the war, and asserted once more that the Munitions Act 'cut quite as deeply into the rights of private employers as any provision affecting the workmen'.[56] He was willing to accept many of the less contentious proposals put at the conference. But he firmly opposed the removal of leaving certificates, stating that 'it was not for the men to stand out at such a time for the right to leave one shop to go to another when the whim seized them'. Though he told them he was sympathetic to the argument that if workmen could not leave a job without a certificate the employers should not be able to sack employees without gaining a certificate from a munitions tribunal.

He also felt changing the constitution of munitions tribunals was worth considering.

Lloyd George raised both these last points with representatives of the Engineering and Shipbuilding Federations on 2 December. On the question of employers being required to obtain a certificate before sacking workmen, Lloyd George argued the need for them to find some reciprocal measure for the workmen, given the great effect of leaving certificates on their position; preferably, he said, a measure which would interfere with management as little as possible and without lessening the effect of leaving certificates.[57] Not only did the employers oppose both suggestions, but so did Ministry officials;[58] Lloyd George consequently took them no further.

Amongst proposals for the Amendment Bill drawn up by the A.S.E. in late November were proposals that the conditions recommended in circulars L2 and L3 should be statutory and that local joint committees should be set up to deal with matters arising from the working of the Munitions Act. They argued, 'The war has been the cause of considerable changes in the organisation of industry. Many of these changes profoundly affect the position of the workers, and there can be no guarantee that they will work smoothly unless the workers are allowed a share in administering them.'[59] The proposals were endorsed at the meeting of 30 November. But the proposal for workers' participation never got much further. The employers spoke against the proposals; though Lloyd George himself made clear in Parliament that he favoured some such measure.[60] The lack of enthusiasm (and of agreement) among the unions, and the employers' opposition allowed the Government to put such proposals permanently on one side.[61] These proposals were, of course, only to give the workmen a degree of participation. Lloyd George made clear his opposition, 'especially in war time', to any degree of workers' control in munitions factories when, answering a questioner on the Clyde who wanted the workmen to 'have some direct control of the management of controlled establishments', he replied that, 'Every concession which it is possible to make consistent with the proper management of Controlled Establishments to see that the workers are fairly treated is being made. I am not prepared at a time when successful management is vital to the national interests to make a radical change of the kind suggested.'[62]

The A.S.E. were more determined to press for concessions over wage rates and other problems of dilution than for a measure of workers' participation. An understandable enough order of priorities as Lloyd George was imminently to embark on his dilution campaign. Lloyd George also appears to have been ready to make concessions over wage rates, whilst the civil servants were opposed to it. Thus Llewellyn Smith wrote to Beveridge on 27 December, 'Mr Lloyd George tells me that at Glasgow he was pressed on the point of including semi-skilled and unskilled workers within Clause 5 . . . This seems to be the only point affecting the Bill with which he was impressed.'[63] The same day he also wrote to Lloyd George and urged, 'I am strongly of the opinion that we ought to resist the proposal', arguing part 1 of the Munitions Act provided for dealing with all classes of wages in munitions, and that the special circumstances which justified extra provisions for women did not apply in the case of men.[64]

The A.S.E. Executive Council responding to pressure from their members, called a conference on 30 December to discuss the Munitions Amendment Bill. Before the conference met, the A.S.E. indicated that they would afterwards like an interview with Lloyd George and, if possible, with Asquith. Llewellyn Smith for one opposed seeing them: '. . . if the Minister sees this union he cannot refuse to see other unions, and also the employers' associations. All parties have been already fully and exhaustively consulted – to an extent probably without precedence. We cannot begin this all over again.' However, in view of the crucial importance of the A.S.E. in the war effort generally, and the need for their co-operation in particular, Henderson and Lloyd George felt they must be seen.[65]

In a briefing memorandum, prepared for Asquith before he and Lloyd George met the A.S.E. on the 31st, the officials once again argued against extending the wages provisions and joint committees. Llewellyn Smith in particular emphasised the need to take a firm line with the A.S.E.,

> The serious part of the situation is that we have reached a position in which the nation is being held up by a single union. If we allow the obstruction of the Amalgamated Society of Engineers to prevail there is little or no chance of being able to fill the National and other munition factories. The negotiations with this union appear to be interminable, and no sooner is one agreement arrived at then it is broken, and new black-mailing conditions are proposed. The demand at the last moment for drastic amendments of the Munitions Bill as condition of fulfilling the agreement as to dilution already entered into in the last stage of a series of obstructive tactics, and any yielding will only be the signal for the putting forward of some fresh conditions.[66]

In this statement of the position he made no allowance for the considerable rank and file pressure being put on the A.S.E. leaders.

Lloyd George and Asquith took more notice of the pressure from the members on the Executive Council. Lloyd George commented that dilution had been fought in every works – 'It has not been fought by the executive; it has been a guerilla fight.' Asquith similarly recognised that the Executive had difficulties with men 'who regard . . . the priorities and privileges of skilled labour as almost Gospel; and who feared that it would be impossible to restore their old position at the end of the War.'[67]

Nonetheless, Asquith and Lloyd George echoed Llewellyn Smith that if concession was made over the wages question, then the union must fully co-operate. Lloyd George hinted at industrial conscription once more:

> . . . What I am afraid of is that you will say, 'Yes, we will accept this', and then your men begin again. They do not like dilution, and therefore they are always trying to find some sort of objection to it. They will find another and we shall be no nearer the end. If so, I shall have to put another proposal before the Prime Minister to deal with the situation. That is a ghastly thing to contemplate. It is infinitely better for the Government that it should pay this big price and get the matter settled on these terms. But I want to know that it is settled . . .

When questioned about Orders in Council to arrest men under D.O.R.A., Lloyd George, without dissent from the A.S.E. leaders, explained that he intended to use it on 'men who deliberately foster strikes'.

> We shall be able to deal under the Defence of the Realm Act with those people, and I think it is perfectly right. It is not the trade unionists who are fostering strikes. I met them up in Glasgow. They are men who are trying their level best to overthrow the organisation. They are in revolt against your organisation, a good number of them, and if men of that type go about fostering strikes, I think we ought to deal with them, not under the Munitions Act but under the Defence of the Realm Act.[68]

This firm yet understanding approach by Lloyd George to the A.S.E. Executive was undoubtedly the right tactic. The A.S.E. Executive Council were embarrassed by the way their membership had been coercing them into a more militant posture. The deputation virtually disowned the ultimatum of their conference to the effect that the unions' amendments to the Munitions Bill must be accepted 'as the basis of our continued co-operation' when Asquith took offence at it. And Brownlie explained that he felt the Executive Council 'feels itself in a much stronger position today than it has done at any period during the past nine months . . . You will realise the importance of my words when I say that 80 per cent of the delegates came to London thirsting for the blood of their Executive Council, and the most important resolution [stemming from the E.C.] was carried this morning by 87 votes to 14 . . .'. The A.S.E. Executive Council members went out of their way to plead that the concession wanted was 'a very real difficulty in getting our men to accept the dilution of labour scheme' and repeatedly protested their efforts to carry out dilution. With Asquith and Lloyd George conceding the enactment of the L2 and L3 conditions, the A.S.E. men promised to co-operate fully in enforcing the dilution agreements.[69]

Thus by the very end of 1915 Lloyd George and the Government had prepared the way for the introduction of dilution. The Munitions Amendment Bill was underway as a major antidote to other causes of unrest on the Clyde and elsewhere, lessening these grievances before the predictably explosive dilution programme was really enforced. The trade union leaders by successive agreements from March onwards had gained many concessions from the Government; but at the cost of binding themselves to assist in the enforcement of dilution. Moreover, Lloyd George had made it clear to them beforehand that he intended to take a firm line with militants who encouraged strike action against the introduction of dilution.

IX

Enforcing dilution on the Clyde

The strength of feeling on the Clyde and the amount of support the Clyde Workers' Committee received in the winter of 1915–16 is easily understandable. To a large extent the Government's policy was responsible for the degree of unrest there.

Firstly, considerable hardship was caused there, as elsewhere, by the Government's reluctance to take measures to maintain the working-class standard of living. On the one hand prices had risen during the war with very little restraint; according to the Board of Trade's figures food costs had risen by 42 per cent by early 1916.[1] Yet the Government continued to deny the need for action. Runciman told the Commons on 20 December, 'Steps have been taken to assure adequate supplies, but it is clear that any attempt to fix maximum prices might only have the result of reducing supplies.'[2] Similarly McKenna rejected aiding groups such as old age pensioners who suffered as a consequence, saying '. . . it is feared that if every case of hardship due to special circumstances of the War is met by a grant from the public funds, the heavy expenditure entailed by the War will strain the resources of the country almost to breaking point'.[3] On the other hand the Government followed a definite policy of resisting wage increases, regardless of the soaring cost of living. Under the Munitions Act, differences, including wage disputes, had to go before compulsory arbitration; and trade unionists found the arbitration body, the Committee on Production, far from impartial. By late 1915 it acted under Government instructions to respect the need for economy and that any wage advances granted 'should be strictly confined to the adjustment of local conditions'.[4] This policy on wages derived from the Ministers' growing concern for economising finance as it became clear that there would be no quick victory in the war; Montagu, for example, pressed on Asquith in July 1915 that as 'the war becomes more than ever a war of endurance', 'finance plays a larger and larger part in it'.[5] In the face of rising discontent Asquith appealed at a conference of a thousand trade unionists on 1 December that wage increases should not be pressed whilst war debt was soaring; and McKenna, following him, urged harder work and greater saving as the remedy.[6] By early 1916, engineering workers had only achieved an advance of 10 per cent since the outbreak of war, despite the huge rise in the cost of living.[7]

Secondly the engineering workers had their own specific grievances. The Munitions of War Act particularly affected the conditions of their work, as has already been indicated. Many of the innovations affected the men at workshop level; the dropping of restrictive practices and the introduction of the semi-skilled and unskilled were matters of contention in each workshop. This gave greater importance to the shop stewards who, unlike the remoter trade union officials, were on hand in the workshops as grievances arose and who were able to give them more cogent expression. In particular the introduction of women, a largely untapped source of alternative labour for employers, appeared the thick end of the wedge, devaluing their craft status and threatening their position after the war. As Askwith observed on the engineers' demands for equal rates for women '. . . the Amalgamated Society of Engineers' object is not to get women in, but to ensure getting them easily out, as soon as possible; and probably keeping them out as far as possible'.[8] Not only were outsiders introduced into the workshops, but non-union men were introduced into closed shops. When a questioner on the Clyde spoke of 'unrest caused by the encroachment in controlled shops by non-unionists who use the Munitions Act as a means of flouting the shop stewards', Lloyd George stated, 'the limitation of employment in a particular shop to unionists, though it may be very justifiable in time of peace, was one of the restrictive practices which, in accordance with the Munitions Act, ought to be relaxed for the period of the war'.[9] There was bitter resentment at the verdicts given by the munitions tribunals; they proved to be a major source of unrest in industry throughout the war. Also, despite the modifications in the Amending Act, the leaving certificate clause of the Munitions Act caused widespread discontent because of the greater power it gave employers and the restriction it placed on workmen's movements.

The Clyde had many of the national problems in an acute form. The housing conditions were amongst the worst in the country. Relations between men and management in many of the works were notoriously bad. The arbitrary power assumed by certain of the areas' employers at that time is legend to this day. There was also a stronger background of militant socialism, stretching back to the pre-war period.[10]

Not only was there an abundance of national and particular grievances, but conditions were ripe that winter for direct industrial action. The level of unemployment amongst trade unionists was at the lowest ever recorded (0·06 per cent), an eighth of all industrial firms had machinery lying idle owing to the shortage of labour, and by the autumn of 1915 one in five working-class males were working overtime.[11] Engineers were at a premium – and munitions production was the national priority.

Against this background one is surprised not that there was unrest on the Clyde in early 1915, but that it was not more extensive. The explanation for the degree of restraint is, of course, the war. A large proportion of the working class supported the war, and were willing to acquiesce in the changes in their industrial conditions. Lloyd George was correct in his belief that 'if it were proved to the men that we cannot get the machinery for turning our shell without increasing labour by these means [dilution] the great majority would co-operate'.[12]

By the end of 1915 the Government felt the time had come to press ahead with dilution. The urgent need for this policy to enable the fulfilment of the munitions programme and to economise the nation's financial resources was emphasised by Asquith to the A.S.E. deputation on 31 December:

> Mr Lloyd George cannot carry on his work efficiently and meet the necessities of the war unless dilution is resorted to . . . It is important from . . . the points of view of both military efficiency and financial stability. It is an incalculable gain. I do not think there is anything more important at this moment to the country than that the manufacture of munitions should go on here at home on the largest possible scale and under the best possible conditions.[13]

Lloyd George was quite willing to take firm measures against those he felt to be hindering production and pressed that the Munitions Act should be enforced. In September he asked Llewellyn Smith for information, 'What steps have been taken to initiate prosecutions? The weekly Report supplies no information on this subject';[14] and later still, deploring lack of information, he commented of the Labour Department: 'the whole success of our work depends on the efficiency of this branch of our Department'.[15] Despite the South Wales episode, Ministry officials still believed in the efficacy of prosecuting strikers. Llewellyn Smith,

F

writing on the working of the Munitions Act, noted that the record of strikes in engineering and shipbuilding trades from July to November 1915 was 'a practically negligible quantity' – 'the total is less than 3,800 working-man-days'; 'there is great evidence of the great value of the action of the Ministry, whether by persuasion or prosecution in checking strikes in munitions works. I think it would be well to call attention to this, as the one failure in South Wales is still believed by many to be the only case in which we tried to enforce the Act.'[16]

The activities of the militant Clyde Workers' Committee were soon brought to Lloyd George's attention. The Committee consisted of socialists, the majority of whom were trade unionists, and had evolved from the Labour Withholding Committee which had taken the lead in the February strike.[17] As James Hinton has commented, 'The C.W.C. represented for the revolutionaries a unique break-through from the wilderness of sectarian politics; suddenly they found themselves in the leadership of a genuine mass movement.'[18] The C.W.C. leaders stood for working-class unity; their initial leaflet proclaimed, 'We are out for unity and closer organisation of all trades in the industry, one union being the aim.'[19] Unfortunately for them the greatest grievance of the engineers was the threat of dilution – an issue which tended to divide the skilled from the unskilled worker.

This first leaflet, signed by Messer and Gallacher, was immediately sent to the Ministry of Munitions by Paterson, the local Labour Officer, and by at least one local employer. Paterson advised 'From a general perusal of this leaflet . . . it seems very clear that this body is preparing for a big strike, and it is doing so in such an open manner in this leaflet that I think the two men who have put their names to the paper render themselves liable to action under the Defence of the Realm Act or Regulations.'[20] The Admiralty representative on the Clyde, Captain Bartellot, recommended even stronger action, 'To obtain a reasonably smooth working of the Munitions Act, the Committee should be smashed.'[21] Beveridge recommended Pateron's course of action. Lloyd George referred the leaflet to the Attorney General to ascertain 'the likelihood of a prosecution succeeding'.[22] However, the required legal advice was not forthcoming until the New Year, and Lloyd George agreed with Addison's recommendation: 'In view of the Lord Advocate's very qualified advice, the lapse of time, your visit and the Amending Bill, I cannot advise you to authorise a prosecution on this matter.'[23]

Lloyd George made clear his determination to carry dilution through at the end of his account of the Ministry's work in the

Commons on 20 December. He commented, '. . . the law must be put into operation by some body, and unless the employer begins by putting on unskilled men and women to the lathes we cannot enforce that Act of Parliament [the Munitions Act]. The first step, therefore, is that *the employer must challenge a decision* upon the matter, and he is not doing so because of the trouble which a few firms have had. But let *us* do it. Victory depends on it!'[24]

Before doing so he made his trip to the Tyne and his famous visit to the Clyde. His purpose was primarily to visit the works and speak to the shop stewards and men. This stemmed from the widely held view that once the men had had the munitions position authoritatively explained to them, there would be no further delays in increasing production. Henderson had recommended this course to Lloyd George at the time of the unrest over the imprisoned shipwrights, and it was reiterated by Kaylor after he had had a stormy reception on the Tyne when explaining the Central Munition Labour Supply Committee's dilution proposals in early December.[25] The fulfilment of this was seen as a prelude to dilution; the Government's Tyne representative argued in a brief for Lloyd George's visit, 'It is my unalterable opinion, after the men have this time been addressed by the Minister and the need for dilution pointed out, that dilution should be put into operation with all possible speed and force.'[26] According to Gallacher, Lloyd George pledged himself before arriving on the Clyde not to meet the C.W.C.[27] This would be in line with his policy not to deal with unofficial strike bodies; but it is unlikely he gratuitously tied his hands in advance, and he afterwards spoke in the Commons of hoping to make a bargain with the minority.[28] Anyhow, he intended to speak with the shop stewards; Paterson commenting, 'The Minister's principal object in visiting this district is, I understand, to meet the shop stewards.'[29]

His visit to the Tyne on 22 December passed without incident,[30] but the visit to the Clyde was tumultuous. Lloyd George was prewarned on the extent of disaffection in the area not only by the C.W.C.'s first leaflet and Paterson's Report but also by a memorandum by Lynden Macassey:

> The present state of mind is not the spontaneous product of the workman's own cogitation . . . It was first created by two or three local trade union officials, who deliberately and for their own purposes, circulated only too effectively, untrue statements as to the origins of the Act, and garbled misleading versions of its effects . . . soon the crowd overtook their local leaders. Now these particular local officials to justify their existence are forced to inflate and paint

as crowning tyrannies of the Munitions Act every pettifogging complaint that in peacetime would not have secured report by a shop steward to his union's local branch.

Macassey suggested the removal of these local officials to posts elsewhere, for, 'It would be impossible to obtain sufficient evidence to dispose of them under the Defence of the Realm Act. Even if possible, their prosecutions, in the present state of mind of the workmen, would be attributed unto them for righteousness sake, and would produce an industrial revolution on the Clyde.'[31]

The details of his Clyde visit need only be briefly recounted here.[32] Shop stewards from at least two firms refused to see him. At Parkhead Forge, David Kirkwood told Lloyd George that the men's conditions for improving production by dilution were that they should have a share in management and that the benefits of dilution should go to them. When Lloyd George met a deputation from the Clyde Workers' Committee the next day, 24 December, Johnny Muir informed him that such industrial evolution must be matched by social evolution, and that three conditions needed to be fulfilled before they would acquiesce in the introduction of dilution – that its benefits should be shared, that it should not act detrimentally on any grade of labour, and that organised labour must have a share in controlling it. Lloyd George opposed these two suggested measures of workers' control, replying, 'it would mean a revolution, and you can't carry through a revolution in the midst of a war'.

The degree of tumult in the famous Christmas morning meeting in St Andrews Hall was the result of bad management by Lloyd George. In order that he could first visit the factories his major meeting with the local trade unionists was transferred at a late stage from the night of the 23rd to this time.[33] The C.W.C. capitalised on the local officials' resentment by influencing them to boycott the meeting, whilst their own supporters turned up in force. Lloyd George's plea at the meeting for more munitions to save the nation in its hour of need was severely interrupted. His emphasis that dilution was needed to man 'great national factories . . . State owned, State erected, State controlled, State equipped, with no profits for any capitalists' cut no ice with the militants in the audience.[34] The meeting broke up in disorder.

Lloyd George had expected such a reception when he had learnt that the C.W.C. and not the local union leaders were going to support the meeting. The evening before the Press Bureau had issued to the press a request which included the following, 'Mr Lloyd George will address a meeting at Glasgow tomorrow and it is particularly requested that no report other than the authorised version of his speech should be published. Should any disturbance occur at or in the neighbourhood of the meeting the Press are earnestly requested to refrain from publishing any reference to it.'[35] This request was not sent to the editor of *Forward*, but when a full account and commentary on the meeting appeared in the 31 December issue, Lloyd George (in a meeting which included Addison, Llewellyn Smith, Beveridge and Rey) provisionally decided that it should be seized. This and the seizure of the machinery of the Civic Press were carried out on 2 January, after consultations with the Scottish Law Officer.[36]

It is clear that *Forward* was suppressed by Lloyd George primarily in anger at the publication of what was felt to be a travesty of the meeting.[37] Officials felt very much that there had been undue exaggeration; the secretary of the Civic Press (a socialist) was reported as stating 'that the row was made entirely by from 300 to 500 people out of 3,000 present. On the whole the feeling of the meeting was with Lloyd George.'[38] A memorandum written after the suppression expressed the official wrath,

> . . . Apart from any questions of accuracy . . . and apart from the contents of the alleged report, the whole article is permeated by a spirit of gloating over the hostile reception stated to have been accorded to Mr Lloyd George. All the senseless hostile interruptions are given with the greatest elaboration. The headlines refer to 'Wild Scenes', 'Break-up in Disorder', etc. An earlier part of the article emphasises with obvious glee the opposition of some of the unions to the arrangements for the meeting . . .

Despite Lloyd George's denial that the quotations from earlier issues of *Forward* which he used in the Commons adjournment debate had been gathered after the suppression, it seems highly probable that the Ministry of Munitions at least only accumulated them afterwards.[39] Thus a memorandum of 6 January found: 'As regards previous publications in the *Forward*, it must be said at once that there is practically nothing that can be described as deliberately seditious. The *Forward*, apart from tendencies to describe all war as capitalist conspiracies, does not appear anywhere as an anti-war paper . . .'[40] In his defence of his action in the Commons, Lloyd George linked a few quotations from *Forward* with others from *Vanguard*, which he labelled as an extremer form of seditious paper – and this enabled him to make a somewhat stronger case. But in fact the decision to suppress *Vanguard* came as a consequence of the suppression of *Forward*, and not as part of a unified policy; this is clearly revealed in a memorandum on *Vanguard*:

> It is urged that this paper should be forthwith suppressed as its advanced proofs were found on the premises of the paper already suppressed and indicate a more advanced attack on diluted labour, etc. On the grounds of consistency alone it would be undesirable to leave the *Vanguard* alone as it weakens the justification of the suppression of the *Forward*.[41]

In addition, the Government generally found *Forward*'s journalism very unhelpful for their policies on the Clyde. As the notes of 6 January commented, 'Generally speaking it may be said that the set policy of the paper is (by constant interpretation) to make it as difficult as possible for any *trade union leader* to lend any support to the Government';[42] thus undermining the basis of Lloyd George's industrial policy. Beveridge felt, 'There is no doubt of the thoroughly harmful *effects* of the *Forward*. It is not easy to show the harmful *intention*.'[43] The provisional decision to suppress the paper, made on the very day of its issue, was probably taken in pique at the account of the Christmas Day meeting. That the decision was carried out was due to the fact that firm action would be in line with the dilution policy. As Beveridge was to observe, '. . . the question of the *Forward* is of course bound up with the general unrest on the Clyde'. Reports emphasised that in some militant circles the Government's concessions on rents, the setting up of the Balfour–Macassey Commission, and the action over the three shipwrights were considered a sign that further pressure would get further concessions.[44] Lloyd George's annoyance led him to take a firm line where his case was weak.

Arising also from Lloyd George's visit, was the stay-in strike of 400 men in a department of Messrs Beardmore's works at Dalmuir on the last three days of 1915.[45] This stemmed from the convenor of the shop stewards being dismissed for a false statement over the arrangements for them to attend the Christmas Day meeting; the workmen refused to work, feeling it was a case of victimisation, and twenty-eight of them were prosecuted. Local officials reported the view of the secretary of the Civic Press that the local industrial unrest 'is so divided up that it would require some big thing to make it dangerous, but thinks that the Beardmore prosecutions coupled with the *Forward* raid might cause trouble'. They viewed the trial with foreboding, and observed, 'the police think they will down tools if the verdict goes against them. If the Dalmuir men come out they may be followed by Beardmores at Parkhead.' The Chief Constable wished to know 'how soon he could count upon the military being on the spot if he were to call for them, and if they were sent for at all he begs that a large body be sent so as to overawe the mob at once and completely get them in hand'. The intelligence officers offered the advice, 'there is no doubt that you could clean up the situation a good deal by removing a number of the dangerous agitators under the Defence of the Realm Act as impeding the production of munitions, but this is a matter of policy'.[46] However, the time was not yet deemed ripe for such action.[47] The trial of the strikers took place on 5 January and a £5 fine was imposed on each man. The Ministry tried before and after to get the men to sign a statement recanting their action and promising future good conduct; the men refused and the fines were never collected.

Lloyd George paused for a while in early January before pressing on with dilution in order to see the response to the introduction of the first measure of conscription. He wrote on 6 January to Elibank, who was ill:

> . . . Fortunately for you, nothing much could be done during the next few days owing to the compulsion excitement. Until that is settled one way or other, it would be difficult for you to conduct your operations; and it would be wise not to press for at least ten days the trade union leaders to take any definite action in the direction of diluting labour. The atmosphere is not propitious, and we had better lie low. You have got your organisation ready and you have thought out your plans, so that the moment the temper improves you can start with renewed vigour.[48]

He explained another reason for temporary delay in a letter to Elibank's wife on 18 January: '. . . in nine or ten days' time, when the new factories at Glasgow will be about ready, then will be the moment that we shall need all his tact and skill in handling men and situations . . .'[49]

All in all, the Government was ready to force through dilution by late January. The Ministry had prepared for the dilution campaign from October and November when Elibank and J. B. Adams had been appointed to organise it; at first it had even been intended that there should be a separate Dilution Department alongside the Labour Supply Department in the Ministry.[50] Some of the general grievances of the area had been met by the Increase of Rent Act and by the adoption of many of the Balfour–Macassey Commission's recommendations in the Munitions of War Amendment Act. The A.S.E. Executive had committed themselves to support the enforcement of dilution by the concessions of 31 December. Above all else, the Cabinet felt confident that they had a sufficient stockpile of munitions to withstand a lengthy strike in one, albeit highly important, munitions area; as Lloyd George later commented, in the 'conflict . . . with the Clyde Workers Committee . . . the Government had satisfied themselves that they could stand a strike of six weeks on the Clyde'.[51]

Asquith informed the Commons on 21 January, 'The Government propose to take steps wherever needed, in accordance with the necessities of the situation and on conditions laid down after the agreement with the representatives of the workmen in the Munitions of War Act as amended, without further delay.'[52] He announced the Government's intention to send commissioners to the Clyde and Tyne to carry out dilution.

The scheme the Government had determined on was a tough one. Lloyd George requested Weir to draft it on 17 January; Weir noted it had 'been prepared to meet your express desire to immediately commence labour dilution on the Clyde, and is designed to secure dilution with the minimum risk of an outbreak of feeling which might result in serious trouble. At the same time, on account of the difficulty of accurately assessing the extent of the present Syndicalist movement, the scheme necessarily comprehends the use of drastic measure in certain eventualities.'[53] Weir's draft was somewhat draconian in its details; he suggested when the dilution scheme was explained to the shop stewards 'a shorthand writer should be in attendance and any expression of open resistance or obstruction on the part of any individual should be carefully noted with the name of the man concerned', if a strike broke 'a careful watch by detectives on the actions of the members of the Clyde Workers' Committee and the few others on a private list' and 'at the first attempt of rioting or damage to property martial law should be proclaimed within the district; thereafter any further action must necessarily be opportunist in character.' The approved version omitted this kind of detail – but determined in the event of a strike to prosecute those who incited the strike, prevent trade union funds being used to aid the strikers and to guarantee adequate police and military protection for those willing to work (the original version emphasised that the shops should not be closed, as then 'no opportunity is given of creating the necessary cleavage between the willing and loyal workers desirous of returning to work and of the rebellious element'). The approved plan suggested that, should a widespread strike break, it might have to be left to take its own course – 'without recourse to the union funds it can hardly continue for any length of time, and if, as may be hoped, the strike weakens, the weakening process can then be hastened by prosecuting those who hold out'.[54]

This policy for dealing with strikes was broadly followed in March. The adopted plan suggested that commissioners should go to the Clyde and 'require selected establishments forthwith to submit their definite dilution proposals'. When approved by the commissioners, notice should be given to the men, who may have consultations 'but ... in any case the scheme in its final form will be carried into force' within three days. Firms should consult the commissioners before acting, which would 'enable us in effect to pick and choose our firms for the first experiment ... however, the main point is that whenever at any particular firm the dilution policy is challenged by a definite refusal of the men to agree to it, the challenge should at once be taken up by an instruction to the employers to proceed, and by prosecutions of the men if they carry out their threat of striking.' This part was much moderated by the commissioners in practice.

On the Tyne dilution was introduced with little disturbance, but on the Clyde the commissioners (Lynden Macassey, Sir Thomas Munro and Isaac Mitchell) had a stormy time. But the fact that Lynden Macassey and his colleagues followed a slow and delicate procedure (slower than the Government initially intended)[55] without doubt lessened the resulting unrest. Macassey reported to the Ministry that the commissioners had had the alternatives of following a policy along the lines Weir had suggested or of introducing specific schemes for the needs of a few establishments; Macassey explained, 'In my view [the first alternative] would have been an inexpedient course. It would have meant a more or less general strike on the Clyde against the principle of dilution, as distinct from a local strike against the details only of a particular scheme, the principle being accepted ... The second course is that which we have adopted.' To effect this second method the commissioners took great pains to reassure the men that 'the scheme of dilution is not intended to reduce the employers' cost of output but to increase the amount of output' and to alleviate their other fears, to meet as far as possible the specific problems of each workshop, and to provide instant conciliation whenever necessary.[56] The scheme made progress as separate factories were willing to negotiate on a basis drawn up by John Wheatley and David Kirkwood; thus Kirkwood broke the Clyde Workers' Committee's front of no dealings with the commissioners, and thereafter other works followed Parkhead's lead.[57] It was a much slower process than Weir had planned for. There were great variations in conditions of which the commissioners needed to take account. As Isaac Mitchell explained in a memorandum of 21 February,[58]

Not only do the conditions vary in each district but almost in each shop and even in a shop like Dalmuir [Beardmores] while the men in one Department insist upon piece-work, the men in another Department, members of the same society, strongly oppose piece-work; these variations are multiplied again by each society. The Clyde in fact so far as trade unionism is concerned is in a state bordering upon Chaos; as an example the A.S.E. Local District Committee consisting of 26 members is practically equally divided between supporters of the Committee itself, which follows orthodox trade union lines, and supporters of the Clyde Workers Committee.

However, despite the more cautious approach, the introduction of dilution caused considerable unrest on the Clyde.

The first trouble ostensibly arose out of the ambiguities in circular L2 as to whether women doing an easier part of a skilled man's job should be paid the full district rate. This was referred to the Ministry, and on 29 January Llewellyn Smith replied in the negative.[59] The Paisley Committee of the A.S.E. rejected this interpretation on 1 February, and the same day 400 men at Messrs Lang went on strike.[60] The Clyde commissioners provided police protection for they felt 'it was essential to prevent any efforts being made to induce the three or four hundred men and women who remained at their work to join the others on strike'. The expense was borne by the Treasury, not the local rates, as the matter was felt to be a result of Government policy – 'It will be remembered that the works of Messrs Lang were specially selected as one of three in which the Government Commission on the dilution of labour was to commence by introducing women on a substantial scale. It was not anticipated by the Ministry that the Commissioners should be able to establish dilution without some trouble.'[61] The A.S.E. Executive complained that they had not been informed of the setting up of the Dilution Commission and of the interpretation given to L2. They were promised an interview to discuss the interpretation of L2 – and subsequently called on the men at Messrs Lang to return to work, which they did on 7 February.

When the A.S.E. Executive met Lloyd George on 24 February, Brownlie told Lloyd George, 'your interpretation strikes at the root of our existence as skilled craftsmen'. Lloyd George told them, 'I have been in the Ministry of Munitions long enough to know that no amount of dilution and no amount of introduction of unskilled men will dispense with the services of the highly skilled men', and frankly told them their basic objection was to dilution as such, and not to details. He refused to go back on the interpretation of L2, saying it was based on Kirkwood's arguments that there should be no overall decrease in wages (to the benefit of the employer) but that it should be divided so 'that the more highly skilled the work . . . the higher the pay'.[62]

Isaac Mitchell was probably right when, unlike his fellow commissioners, he felt outright objection to dilution was the cause of the strike at Lang's, and that the overall situation in the area was complex. He wrote of Lang's, 'here again the feeling against the management is very bitter, but it is the "old trade unionism" type of bitterness, narrow and selfish. The recent strike there while ostensibly against the Ministry's interpretation of L2 was really against "dilution" under any conditions.' He commented, 'It will be seen that a general lead from any one of the three forces operating here – the Executive (supported by the narrow old-time trade unionists); the local officials (Bunton and Brodie, who have given us splendid aid in urging the frank acceptance of the Ministry's interpretation of L2 or L3); or the Clyde Workers Committee, would simply lead to the opposition from the other two.'[63]

The Government was determined to have a trial of strength on the Clyde. Their prime object was to break the Clyde Workers' Committee, which was undermining the trade unions. Lynden Macassey warned,

> The outstanding feature of the position is that the official trade unions in the district are in many works now wholly unable to speak for their members. Agreements arrived at between the Commissioners and the local trade union officials or even the shop stewards in the works are promptly repudiated by the members of the Clyde Workers' Committee. The authority of official trade unions in the Clyde District is being steadily undermined . . . I have been convinced for some days that the only effective way of handling the situation is to strike a sharp line of cleavage between the loyal workmen, who undoubtedly comprise the great majority of munition workers, and the disloyal socialist minority who are the pawns of the Clyde Workers' Committee, and those whoever they may be behind the Committee.[64]

Before Macassey wrote this, the Government took action. The Ministry of Munitions had the *Worker* suppressed on 2 February with an article entitled 'Should the Workers Arm?' as the pretext.[65] But Muir, Gallagher and Walter Bell were not arrested until the 7th after the Ministry had learnt that the men had returned to work at Lang's.[66] As Macassey noted in his memorandum these actions were 'a clear and definite act challenging the existence and principles of the Clyde Workers' Committee as inimical to the State'. The day after the arrests there was a strike of more than 2,000 men at Messrs John Brown, G. & J. Weir, Albion Motor Car Company, Coventry Ordinance Works, Beardmore's Dalmuir, and Barr and Stroud; these were the strongholds of the Clyde Workers' Committee's supporters. The arrested men were allowed bail and the C.W.C. called off the strike before it collapsed.

Lloyd George felt that this had sufficiently weakened the Clyde Workers' Committee and settled the dilution question. Thus in a letter of 14 February to Elibank, who was soon to resign his position through continued ill health, he commented,

> The work you were undertaking was far and away the most worrying and unpleasant which the Ministry of Munitions could afford. These squalid labour troubles in the middle of this great struggle are disheartening in the extreme, and it was very gallant of you to have undertaken so thankless a task . . . the work you have already done is bearing fruit. The Clyde opposition has already collapsed.[67]

However, this was premature. Further strikes broke out on the Clyde in March. The strikes began at Parkhead, and were occasioned by Sir William Beardmore forbidding Kirkwood, as convenor of the shop stewards, from going into other departments in the works.[68]

Lloyd George and McKinnon Wood determined to take a firm line. They decided on the 24th to deport the ringleaders, and to follow the policy Weir had outlined in January in the event of a widespread strike. Kirkwood, Messer, Haggerty, Macmanus, Shields and Wainwright were arrested and deported. Consequently strikes spread to Weirs and the Albion Motor Car Company. The Government determined to remain firm, and decided to deport the shop stewards (Bridges, Kennedy and Glass) at Weirs. Addison explained in the Commons, 'The method of deporting these men was resorted to in the first instance because a criminal trial would require an interval of six weeks or two months before it could be held, and it was felt that immediate action was necessary.'[69] He also made clear that the Government intended to maintain this firm line, claiming that the Ministry's action had the support of the trade union leaders (who had repudiated the strikes) and of 'the vast majority of the munitions workers on the Clyde, who are opposed to the dangerous and disloyal action of the Clyde Workers' Committee'.

Lloyd George explained his policy at length in the Cabinet on the 30th. Asquith reported to the King,

It was shown that the principal danger of the situation depends not so much on the proceedings of the small (by comparison) number of workmen holding syndicalist views and revolutionary aims, as on the fear that the vastly larger body of patriotic and loyal trade unionists may be deluded by misrepresentation of the facts into expressing sympathy with the violent minority, believing them to be unjustly treated. Mr Henderson offered to use his best efforts to enlighten his friends as to the true state of affairs . . .[70]

The strike began to break on the 29th, though a demonstration, planned and carried out on the 31st against the Committee on Production's refusal earlier in the month to go above the 10 per cent advance granted the previous year, delayed the return to work. Thirty strikers were prosecuted on the 29th, and as the strike crumbled the last men to return were prosecuted, and Clark, the Treasurer of the Clyde Workers' Committee, was deported.

After this episode, the Dilution Commissioners made rapid progress. Lloyd George's dilution campaign on the Clyde was successful; the new National Factories were fully staffed, and in the first eight months of 1916, 10,000 women were introduced into engineering works, exclusive of shell work.[71] The challenge of the Clyde Workers' Committee had been met. A tough line had been taken with the militants when they struck on relatively poor issues, namely over the suppression of the *Worker* and the rights of Kirkwood at Parkhead, so ensuring that the minimum of public opinion was alienated. Thus by the early summer of 1916 munitions production was adequate to meet the needs of the army in the Somme campaign.

X

Conscription and manpower shortage, 1915–16

Lloyd George moved to the War Office in July 1916. He changed positions at a time when the maintenance of sufficient manpower rather than finding sufficient armaments was the crucial priority for the Western Front. With productivity rising in the munitions industry, the Government's major preoccupation on the Home Front increasingly became the reallocation of manpower between the fighting forces, the munitions industries, domestic essentials and the export trade.

The question of raising manpower for the Western Front by compulsory means was a contentious matter at all levels of the Labour Movement. The majority of trade union leaders were steeped in Liberal principles, of which voluntaryism was a major tenet. They were willing to support the war and to take part in the recruiting campaign, but abhorred the idea of compulsion. As it became apparent that it was not to be a war of movement, this attitude became increasingly inconsistent with their commitment to support the war. Ramsay MacDonald suggested as early as January 1915, 'To cry "no conscription" whilst we are aiding and abetting a foreign policy which imposes obligations upon us which conscription alone will enable us to fulfill is cowardly and dishonest.'[1]

The Liberal Cabinet Ministers, in varying degrees, also found military conscription unpalatable. When the question came to a head, McKenna and others felt that to increase Britain's military contribution would entail jeopardising her financial aid to the Allies and the maintenance of the strength of the navy.[2] Many of them also feared the response from Labour if conscription was introduced. Runciman wrote to his wife, shortly after Lloyd George had pressed him to give way to the South Wales miners,

. . . even if Kitchener and Asquith together declared conscription to be necessary the organised labour of Great Britain would have none of it. These two powerful names might get it through Parliament; no names however powerful could get it through the violent suspicion, hatred and determination of labour . . . those who urged me to give way in face of a stoppage in Welsh coal mines realise that we must bow to the will of the masses in the long run – they should realise that conscription would bring about a stoppage in railways, engineering, iron works and textile mills.[3]

Lloyd George took a pragmatic view of conscription from at least 1910. Conscription was not just a sop to be offered to the Tories; he himself favoured it, at least during periods when international relations were tense. Though before the war he recognised that it was only a political possibility 'in some great national emergency'.[4] Lloyd George first moved towards conscription in industry and then to military conscription in the summer of 1915.[5] This progression was logical enough for a person of Lloyd George's naturally pragmatic outlook. Voluntary methods at first produced enough men; the first problem was to equip men, not to enlist them.

The widespread fear in the Labour Movement that it was intended to follow military conscription with industrial compulsion was well founded, given the views of Lloyd George. When asked by the Cabinet Committee on War Policy what compulsion he considered necessary to increase production,

Mr Lloyd George said he would take the same powers exactly as were taken in France. He would make everybody between certain ages liable to serve in the Army at home or abroad during and only during the course of the war. With this general and basic authority 'you could work the rest all right'. Men who had already volunteered could be ordered to return to the munition factories and work under civil conditions for civil pay just as the 170,000 French soldiers have been ordered to return. The men who had not joined the Army would not be moved directly against their will to a new or different civil employment. But if they did not voluntarily do the work for which they were needed, and do it satisfactorily, they would be enlisted in the Army and used either for home defence or at the front.[6]

Though the Labour Party was firmly opposed to military conscription publicly, leading members showed a readiness to waive this policy. From February to the summer of 1915 Labour figures such as James Sexton, George Roberts, Charles Duncan, James O'Grady and J. H. Thomas all declared publicly that they would be willing to consider conscription if the Government announced it to be essential.[7] When the Cabinet Committee on War Policy interviewed him, Henderson urged that the nation's manpower needs be frankly stated and every effort be made to meet the needs voluntarily, so 'if the effort failed the nation would realise as never before that we were committed to compulsion'. He concluded by telling the Committee, 'From what I have stated it will be seen that I am prepared, as a last extremity, to accept compulsion for a definite and publicly stated object . . .'[8]

In these circumstances both those for and those against military conscription were deeply interested in the verdict of Labour's rank and file which was indicated for the first time at the T.U.C. of September 1915. Smillie and other speakers received warm applause for vigorous speeches against conscription during the debate on this issue. But like many campaigns of the British Labour Movement, it was difficult to judge what the sound and the fury actually signified; the official motion under debate was characteristically innocuous. The result was that both groups in the Cabinet were able to take comfort. Those in favour of conscription saw that it was not labour's greatest fear; as Selborne observed before the T.U.C. met, 'what they really are afraid of is lest factories, mines, etc. should be put under martial law and also that any compulsion applied now should settle the question of compulsion after the war'.[9] H. A. Gwynne, of the *Morning Post*, forwarded to Lloyd George a confidential report on the conference, possibly at Lloyd George's specific request.[10] This gave weight to the view that the earlier comments of individual union leaders were open to question. It commented,

> The fact that a 'no-conscription' resolution was passed unanimously is not to be taken as an indication that in no circumstances will the trade unions accept the principle of compulsion. It represents rather an emphatic declaration against what a leading delegate called 'the attempt to boss or bounce us' into conscription . . . Several of the most influential of the delegates assured me in private conversation that if the Cabinet solemnly declares with united voice that the compulsory principle is essential they will not oppose its introduction.

However, the report did recognise 'that, while the responsible heads of the Labour Party would loyally stand by the Government, the pro-Germans would add to their ranks a considerable number of those who decline to believe that any departure from the voluntary system is required'. Naturally, such an ambivalent attack by the Labour Movement did not sway Lloyd George into giving up the idea of military conscription. But the potential dissent at grass roots level made him cautious at the time of the first Military Service Bill about taking further action on dilution of the Clyde until the response to it had been ascertained.

To Asquith the T.U.C. illustrated that conscription would be vigorously opposed by Labour. In a letter to Balfour in which he made clear his opposition to conscription 'on its merits', he wrote: 'it is now indisputable that any attempt at this moment to establish compulsion, either military or industrial, would encounter the practically united and passionately vehement opposition of organised labour', and cited Shackleton's view that, 'it would mean revolt, if not revolution'.[11]

In the event, when the first Military Service Act was introduced, the Labour leaders' ability to reconcile the irreconcilable to their own satisfaction was quite astounding. On 6 January 1916, at a special conference of bodies affiliated to both the T.U.C. and Labour Party, conscription was clearly opposed, in a card vote of 2 to 1 proportions. At the conference Henderson vigorously spoke up for the Government's policy, even speaking of resigning his seat and fighting for re-election on the issue.[12] A little earlier Runciman wrote, '. . . Henderson has tumbled into Lloyd George's basket, tickled by the flattery of Curzon and Company.'[13] After the conference a joint meeting of the National Executive Committee and the parliamentary Party decided that the Labour Party should withdraw from the Coalition. In spite of all this the parliamentary Party decided that as a body it would oppose the Bill but individual members should be free to vote for it; consequently, by the second reading on 11 January, fourteen Labour M.P.s voted for it and eleven against. Henderson and the other Labour Ministers tendered their resignation to Asquith on the 10th; Henderson assuring Asquith, 'I supported the Military Service Bill in the Cabinet. I shall continue to do so in the House as the representative of my constituents, on the ground of military necessity.'[14] On the 12th Asquith met a deputation of the N.E.C. and parliamentary Party, and after he had assured them, 'I am not in favour of compulsion in regard to any industrial work; I see no reason for it. As far as I am concerned I shall resist it to the last', and had given promises not to extend the measure to married men and to see genuine conscientious objectors received good treatment, the resignations were withdrawn.[15] The Labour Party Conference at Bristol on 26 January absurdly opposed the Bill yet approved the Labour men remaining in office. By the time of the second measure in April the Labour leaders had no qualms at accepting the necessity of it.

However, as 1916 progressed the manpower shortage became acute generally. The Ministry of Munitions, for example, found in June that there was 'a large and continuous unsatisfied demand in the neighbourhood of 32,000', and hoped that more men could be released from the army.[16] Naturally the Ministry was extremely suspicious of attempts by the War Office to 'comb out' munitions workers.[17] Ministry fought with Ministry to retain manpower. This situation led to the creation of the Manpower Board in September 1916 to adjudicate on priorities.

One short-term expedient to meet labour shortage in munitions was to postpone holidays. Lloyd George did this before the Somme with the Whitsun holidays, observing that the three days' holiday at Easter had been 'very disastrous in its effect upon output. It reduced output for two weeks by exactly one half' and urged that holidays should be arranged instead 'for individuals so as not to overstrain their strength'.[18] Holidays were again postponed in mid-July, after the Somme, because, as Addison put it, 'the expenditure of the bigger forms of ammunition above 4·5 inches has been altogether beyond the wildest dreams even of the artillerists'.[19]

Lloyd George and the Government were willing to use soldiers to meet the labour shortage as long as it did not entail a major political row. Soldiers were used for harvesting, for dock work and for certain munitions work.[20] When on 24 August a deputation of Labour M.P.s complained to Lloyd George at the War Office of the employment of soldiers in certain jobs, Lloyd George assured them that military officials loathed this practice and only allowed it in emergencies. He assured them, 'In no instance have we supplied soldiers in the case of labour disputes, and never have they been supplied except in cases of overwhelming military necessity.'[21] However, even if troops were not so in use, the Government were willing to use them if necessary. Thus Derby wrote to Lloyd George shortly afterwards of a potential strike in the South Wales coal field, that, 'We have . . . taken all precautions to provide men if absolutely necessary from the Army to do the work', adding that he would 'only authorise the employment of soldiers if I consider it absolutely necessary'.[22]

The expedient importing of colonial and Irish labour, itself a way of avoiding the difficulties of debadging skilled men for overseas service, soon led to political embarrassments. Esher commented to Haig on the proposed use of African and Chinese labour: 'When you remember Lloyd George and the Radicals on "Chinese Labour" a few years since, you realise the irony of politics!'[23] Later in the year Montagu approached Henderson on the use of 'five to ten thousand African native labourers . . . under their own white overseers for employment on navvy work in the South of England', assuring him that 'they would not compete for the limited amount of work required of the higher degree of skill'. Henderson agreed to recommend this to the building unions if the supply of labour in Britain appeared to be insufficient, and noted that 'prisoners of war were being employed on work in limestone quarries, and that no objections had at present been received from Labour organisations'. In the event, the building unions would not agree to it, and the scheme was dropped.[24]

The trade unions' opposition to such expedients was one reason for the proposal that dilution should be extended to private work, as an alternative way of stretching the labour supply. C. F. Rey, of the Ministry of Munitions, noted in August that the Irish labour supply was 'coming to an end, in as much as it is opposed vigorously by workmen in this country, who refuse to work with the Irishmen'; in consequence he urged, in addition to the measures already being taken, 'that dilution on private work be agreed with the unions'. This opinion was endorsed at a subsequent conference at the Ministry of Munitions at the end of August.[25]

However, if the trade unions disliked the expedients used by the Government to stretch labour as far as possible, they liked even less the incidence of recruiting. It seemed provocative at a time when dilution was being carried out rapidly. As a Ministry journal observed later, 'We are entering upon a period of super-dilution, when no man can be left to do a job that can be done by a man or woman of lesser skill.'[26] In April Brownlie complained that despite their co-operation in dilution and their sending representatives to France to bring skilled men back from the Forces they still found that 'the military people are taking the skilled men out of the workshops and transferring them into the Army notwithstanding the fact that those men are in receipt of War Service Badges and certificates . . .' In this situation the A.S.E. pressed for protection from recruiting. Button succinctly observed, 'Our only claim to special treatment is that our trade is being diluted . . . Our trade is really an essential one whether on war work or commercial work, and that being so, we are entitled to this extra protection for which we are asking.'[27] This question of the recruitment of skilled men was raised again in the Cabinet on 9 May by Henderson, whose 'complaints' were 'strongly supported' by Lloyd George and Balfour. The Cabinet 'resolved that skilled men taken for the Army should be released on giving an undertaking that they will serve on munitions and other necessary work'.[28]

Nevertheless, complaints from the branches on recruiting continued to flood in on skilled unions' executive committees throughout 1916. The A.S.E. sent a further deputation on this matter to the Ministry of Munitions on 27 September. Brownlie warned that, 'discontent will manifest itself in various ways'.[29] Montagu promised to look into their various complaints; but he emphasised that some skilled men would be needed in the army. The A.S.E. representatives suggested that the Government should seek their co-operation in obtaining such men.

On the following day, the Prime Minister addressed a deputation of skilled trade union leaders and heard their grievances. He summed up the Government's policy on skilled workers and recruiting; his statement being the basis of later definitions.

> There are two governing principles . . . The first one . . . is that skilled men (by whom I mean men who from natural ability or training, or a combination of both, have special aptitudes for particular and indispensable kinds of national work, here at home) ought not to be recruited for general service . . . but . . . there are some forms of military work . . . for which skilled men are required. We cannot carry on the operations of a complicated machine like a modern Army . . . without a number of skilled artisans . . . Then the second is this . . . if we are to make the most economic use . . . of our best national resources in the way of personnel for the purpose of the war . . . we must apply, as we have applied and are applying, the principle of dilution . . . Dilution means not that you should get rid of your skilled men and send them to fight in the Army, which many other people can do quite well . . .; it means that you should get rid of your unskilled men, men who are not absolutely essential and indispensable for the technical purposes of their trade, and if, of military age, as far as possible substitutes are found for them . . . It does not mean wasting; it does not mean annihilation or removal; but it means spreading your skilled resources over as wide a surface and in as many channels as they can be effectively employed . . .[30]

From these two meetings, the basis of the Government's later trade card offer can be seen. Asquith in his statement carefully divided the skilled from the unskilled worker in his phraseology of 'get rid of', 'annihilation', 'wasting'; and generally played up the prejudices of the craft unions. As the official history comments, 'At home no maxim is more pernicious than *divide et impera*'[31] – and the Government policy with the skilled unions, especially under the trade card scheme, was precisely this.

Before the Sheffield strike began, the Government had already started to discuss the trade card scheme with the A.S.E. At a meeting on the extension of dilution of private work on 27 October, Henderson revealed, after a barrage of complaints on recruiting, that the trade card scheme was under consideration by the Manpower Board.[32] The A.S.E. Executive saw the Manpower Board on 3 November and warned them that the existing recruiting arrangements were causing very serious unrest in the country; pressed that they should issue an exemption card to their members, which would certify that they were skilled men; and offered to find the required skilled men for the army by voluntary means.[33] Some members of the Executive felt that the card should be issued on condition that the skilled man joined the War Munitions Volunteers, thus making him available wherever needed; but this suggestion was not incorporated in the proposals they drafted after the meeting and presented to the Board on the 7th. At this meeting, on the 7th, greater force was given to the Executive Council's proposals by the growing unrest over indiscriminate recruiting in Glasgow and Sheffield.

The strike which broke out at Sheffield on 16 November 1916, proved to be a major turning point in the attitude of Labour to Government policies. It showed there was widespread distrust of the Government. The immediate cause of the strike was the enlistment of a skilled man, Leonard Hargreaves.[34] But his call-up was merely the straw that broke the camel's back. Complaints about such action by the army authorities had been coming from Sheffield from at least the summer.[35] The day before the strike broke one A.S.E. official, Rose, told Ministers that despite recent promises from the Ministry of Munitions they still found 'that we are getting sheaves of complaints from different districts and works to the effect that absolutely necessary men are being taken into the Army . . .'[36]

On 9 November J. T. Murphy, Secretary of the Sheffield Engineers' Shop Stewards Committee, wrote to Asquith and Montagu warning them that if Hargreaves was not released within a week there would be a strike.[37] On 14 November the Ministry of Munitions consulted Henderson. He advised that the unions should be pacified by recognising all the men who were members of a craft union at the outbreak of war as 'skilled', and to give them exemption from military service. The next day Derby, Montagu and Henderson met representatives of the craft unions, including the A.S.E. Coates, of the United Machine Workers, bluntly told them '. . . you are on the edge of a volcano and the officials of the union cannot prevent an eruption taking place'. The Ministers agreed to release Hargreaves from the army, and offered what was to be the basis of the trade card agreement.

Derby summarised their offer, 'To all your skilled men we allow you yourselves to give a card of exemption but we ask that you in return . . . provide us yourselves with men of the age and skill required for the purposes of the skilled work in the Army.'[38]

Despite the A.S.E. Executive advising the shop stewards to do nothing until a national conference discussed the whole matter on the 16th, they declined to call off the strike unless they were sure Hargreaves had actually been released. They sent a telegram to Lloyd George and received no reply, and learnt from Mrs Hargreaves that her husband had not returned home. The strike began at 5 p.m. on the 16th at Sheffield and Rotherham; and on Saturday, 18th, the engineers at Barrow came out in sympathy. They ignored the pleas for a return to work made by the Ministry and by the A.S.E. The men only agreed to return to work when Hargreaves appeared at a strike meeting in Sheffield on the 18th.

The strike illustrated the disregard the rank and file union members had for both the Government and the official trade union leaders. The men only accepted the proof of their own eyes – the physical return of Hargreaves. The *History of the Ministry of Munitions* comments, '. . . the strike confirmed what events on the Clyde had already shown, that the shop-stewards under capable leadership were a formidable power, which the restrictions imposed on the trade unions by the war were strengthening'. Its verdict '. . . in the annals of the war no strike showed so few signs of indecision or half-heartedness' is unlikely to be disputed.[39]

The details of the trade card scheme were negotiated on 16, 17 and 18 November. The Sheffield strike gave impetus to the introduction of such a scheme, but it most probably would have been introduced anyway. The third Report of the Manpower Board, issued on 9 November, included a recommendation to this effect: 'The Board think that this scheme would provide a simple and effective remedy for the complaint of the trade unions that at present both the provisions of the law and the pledge of the Prime Minister are not infrequently violated, and that they are unable to find any authority to whom they can appeal for redress with any probability of success.'[40] Austen Chamberlain, in recommending the Report to Montagu, commented, 'They are proposals which we have good reason to think will smooth away some of the most acute trouble with the trade unions.'[41]

The A.S.E. conference on the 16th broadened the scope of Derby's proposals, and these were put by a deputation to Ministers on the 17th. The Government quite explicitly went out of its way to cut the ground from under the unofficial leaders of the Sheffield strikes. Montagu frankly told the deputation the next day:

. . . we have decided to agree to the amendment made by your Conference . . . you have conducted your proceedings as we had a right to expect proceedings should be conducted in this war. You have pointed out the things that were, in your opinion, wrong, and you have done your best – and we acknowledge it – to help us. The Sheffield strikers . . . put forward smaller demands than yours, but because you are the representatives of your great union and have negotiated in a helpful spirit, we are prepared to give you what we could never have given to people who have conducted their negotiations by means of a strike, which has prevented the proper equipment of our armies in the field for two long precious days.

Brownlie sincerely commented that he and his colleagues had 'never met in conference people who were more anxious or ready to meet our point of view'.[42] The fact was that the Government was seriously concerned at the extent the unions' control over their members had been undermined. To remedy the situation the Government bolstered up their prestige. As Addison observed of the scheme, 'It is a great feather in the cap of the unions.'[43]

The trade card agreement conceded that only members not working on war work should enrol as War Munition Volunteers. It also met the A.S.E.'s request that all those who were journeymen or apprentices on 15 August 1915, should be exempt from military service. However, whilst the unions pledged themselves to 'do their utmost to provide the Ministry of Munitions with skilled men, who will undertake to serve at the choice of the Ministry either in the Artificers' Corps in the Army or as War Munitions Volunteers in civil life', the Agreement clearly stated, 'If skilled men for the Army are not secured in this way, it is clearly understood that recourse must again be had to the statutory powers.'[44]

Four days later Lloyd George, who had been in France up to this point, chaired a meeting with the other craft unions. Trouble was foreseen. Henderson took Chamberlain's suggestion that he should explain the machinery of the scheme to the meeting: 'if asked about the separate agreement with the Engineers (and craft unions) he will say it is not applicable to the unions generally, but if they are not satisfied with the protection afforded by the machinery let them appoint a committee to confer with the Government and say exactly what they want'.[45] The other union leaders expressed strong feelings at the A.S.E.'s preferential treatment. Montagu's assertion that they had been dealt with first because by chance they had a conference sitting at the time in London which sent a deputation over, did little to appease them.[46]

The majority of the craft unions (to the resentment of such ex-cluded ones as the woodworking trades) were brought within the scheme. In doing this Lloyd George went further than the Ministry of Munitions intended.[47] He was probably right; not to have extended the scheme to them would have created bitterness between them and the Government. As it was the unskilled unions were embittered – but with the skilled unions.

It did little to help the general questions of recruitment to the army or of gaining the most economical use of labour at home. The military members of the Army Council informed Lloyd George on 28 November that unless drastic steps were taken the strength of the armies could not be kept up after April 1917.[48] On 30 November the War Committee decided to accept in principle the adoption of compulsory national service for all men up to the age of fifty-five years. They recognised that they would have to consult Parliament, the unions and other groups to whom pledges to the contrary had been given.[49]

So in the period before Lloyd George acceded to the Premier-ship, critical moves were being made in regard to manpower. There were the moves to get the unions to agree to dilution on private work. There was the trade card agreement. There was the national service decision. The *History of the Ministry of Munitions* summarised the position:

> Thus while the policy of the Government was moving rapidly towards a comprehensive scheme of industrial compulsion, certain craft unions had secured the privilege of exempting their members from military service and recruiting from among them volunteers for the Artificers' Corps of the Army. The privilege was emphasised by the decision to withdraw from all semi-skilled and unskilled munition workers their legal certificates of exemption from military service, although collectively they were essential for the output of munitions, and many thousands of them could not be replaced by any available substitutes. In these circumstances the industrial situation at home was hardly less menacing than the military situation abroad.[50]

PART IV

War-Time Prime Minister

XI

Mounting discontent in the Labour Movement

With his accession to the Premiership, Lloyd George's personal role in dealing with labour changed. Naturally he undertook much less personal negotiation with trade union leaders and employers. His main concern was with the general direction of the war effort, though he did try to keep an eye on all departments. However, in 1917 and 1918 labour matters frequently became central to the war effort.

The overturn of Asquith made the retention of Labour participation in the Coalition even more important than hitherto. The loss of Asquith, himself something of a symbol of national unity was one thing, the additional loss of the Labour Ministers would have been a serious blow to Lloyd George. At the end of the war he frankly told Bonar Law, 'They are not Ministers because they are the most suitable men, but because they represent a large class, who should have a voice in the government of the country.'[1]

Lloyd George made a strong appeal to the M.P.s and the National Executive Committee of the Labour Party of 7 December. As G. D. H. Cole has observed, 'Lloyd George was offering attractive terms – a seat for Henderson in the Inner War Cabinet, the establishment of a Ministry of Labour under a Labour Minister, State control of mines and shipping, an improved policy of food, and various other things for which, in face of Asquith's strong laissez-faire tendency, Labour had hitherto been pressing in vain.'[2] Lloyd George needed to. His position with Labour after his time at the Munitions Ministry and War Office was 'shaky';[3] Henderson stood by Asquith until the end. At the meeting Lloyd George isolated dissidents such as Snowden and Sidney Webb,[4] and gained the necessary support. Beatrice Webb was probably right in feeling that once offered decent terms the majority of Labour would readily support the Government as they clung to 'the illusion that the mere presence of Labour men in the Government, apart from anything they may do or prevent being done, is in itself a sign of democratic progress'.[5]

As has often been emphasised by recent historians, many of the changes in organisation of the war with which Lloyd George is credited began under Asquith. Even so, many were pressed on Asquith by Lloyd George and other preachers of vigorous measures under the pressure of events. To contemporaries a Lloyd George Government meant a considerable change in the style of goverment. Hobhouse, on 2 December, wrote to C. P. Scott that 'we may be sure . . . that a Lloyd George–Northcliffe Ministry will be for a policy of "Thorough" at home and particularly in Ireland'.[6] Beatrice Webb percipiently predicted the contrast with the Asquith Government: 'It was an intensely Whig Government. Asquith and his favourite colleagues hated State intervention either in the regulative or its administrative aspect. The Government will be boldly and even brutally interventionist – it will break all conventions and even control inconvenient vested interests.'[7]

Despite Lloyd George's transformation of Government and creation of the Ministry of Labour, industrial relations were still not dealt with by one department alone. Wages policy might be outlined under the Committee on Production but conflicting wage increases could be given by other departments, notably the Admiralty and the Ministry of Munitions, and the Coal Controller. Strikes were settled by both the Ministry of Labour and the Ministry of Munitions.[8] Similarly there were repeated conflicts between the Ministry of National Service and the Ministry of Labour over the distribution of manpower. Co-ordination in such matters had to be prompted by the May engineers' strike and the $12\frac{1}{2}$ per cent bonus trouble.

Labour, in the persons of Hodge and Roberts, reigned over the Ministry of Labour during the war; and at times Lloyd George delegated supervision over industrial matters to Henderson and Barnes who were successively in the War Cabinet. Beatrice Webb acidly observed that in Lloyd George's Government 'each Department has been handed over to the "interest" with which it is concerned. In this way, our little Welsh attorney thinks, you combine the least of political opposition with the maximum technical knowledge'.[9] This is exaggerating somewhat, though the influx of men such as H. A. L. Fisher and Sir Joseph Maclay gives the statement some substance. But in the case of Labour this was Lloyd George's intention – just as he had been delighted to involve the National Advisory Committee in formulating the regulations for the introduction of dilution.

Labour discontent threatened Lloyd George's conduct of the war in three ways in 1917 and 1918. As in the previous years outbreaks of strikes threatened munitions production, transport and other essential work. Secondly, if there was a substantial decline in the supplies of food and other necessities it could seriously undermine the morale of the cities. Thirdly, war weariness, extensions of conscription and doubts as to the war aims of the Allies threatened to undermine working-class support for a termination of the war by victory.

The production of food in the last eighteen months of the war assumed the importance that the production of munitions had done to Asquith's Government in 1915. With American troops on the way and munitions production under control, the Government needed to maintain the level of manpower in Haig's armies on the Western Front and to maintain the food supplies of the civilian population until the balance of military strength tilted decisively against Germany.

Food supplies had become more of a problem as 1916 progressed – that year's harvest was poor, the German submarine campaign had become increasingly effective, more men were removed from the land, and there were inadequate supplies of machinery and fertilisers. The Asquithian Government appeared incapable of dealing with either food production or prices. Barnes warned the Government in October, 'Nothing has so angered the people of this country during the last years as the enormous profits made out of the people's food, except it has been the shameless excuses put up for them by the Government's spokesmen.'[10] Such concern was not confined to Labour. Churchill, in August, had deplored the way the consumption of food was being restricted, observing, 'you could not do it in a more cruel or more unfair way than by the agency of price, because in regard to food . . . the poorest suffer out of all proportion to any other class'.[11] Labour pressed that food prices should be kept down. Bramley cogently explained their case to Asquith: '. . . if an increase of wages were to be sought in the way of adjustment only those who are well organised . . . will get the advantage; but if action can be taken to keep down the cost of living the community generally will benefit and particularly the very poorest who as a rule represent the unorganised mass of people . . .'[12]

Lloyd George appears to have been too involved in munitions and manpower problems to examine food problems in any detail until late autumn, when Earl Crawford consulted him 'with a view to increasing our agricultural man-power, so as to ensure fair crops next summer'.[13] When Lloyd George did examine it, he complained, 'We have been shuffling and hesitating . . . look at the food question. We have delayed the production of home grown crops until it is nearly too late.'[14] In February 1917 his Government adopted a domestic food production programme substantially similar to the Milner Committee's recommendations of the summer of 1915.[15] He personally ensured that his Ministers were concentrating on increasing agricultural productivity.[16]

However, food prices remained high. In February, at a time when the War Cabinet decided to try to increase the supply of potatoes by giving farmers a guaranteed minimum price (which was deemed to 'yield a bigger profit than was obtained in peace time'), Lloyd George received warnings from the Mayor of Manchester and the Lord Provost of Edinburgh of serious unrest in their cities at the failure to supply sufficient potatoes.[17] In March the War Cabinet had before them a memorandum which pointed out that the working-class cost of living had risen by 65 per cent from the opening of the war, that food had risen by 92 per cent, and that the other mainstay of the working-class diet, bread, had risen 100 per cent (the 4lb loaf going from 5½d to 11d).[18]

The response of the Co-operative Movement at the failure of the State to intervene drastically on food prices was symptomatic of the whole Labour Movement. Its members, like the rest of the Labour world, found themselves confronted with uncontrolled blatant profiteering at a time when wages were falling behind prices and those on fixed incomes or dependent on men in the services were suffering. They responded in May by abandoning their neutral role in politics and launching their own party.[19] Lloyd George unnecessarily gave the co-operators additional ground for complaint by delaying from May to October in agreeing to see them. Though he did ask Barnes 'to make enquiries . . . about a possible [Food] Controller being obtained from the co-operators'; which would have met one of the Co-operative Movement's main war time grievances.[20]

The introduction of conscription and the war weariness at the lack of results after continuous sacrifices, especially after the Somme campaign in the summer and autumn of 1916, began seriously to undermine popular support for the war. Conscription was an issue which united dissidents of all kinds, whereas opposition to dilution and certain other provisions on the Munitions of War Act had often been particularist in nature, dividing the skilled from the unskilled worker. With the abolition of the trade card scheme stark divisions of this kind largely disappeared.

The demand for a 'democratic peace' without annexations increasingly joined together those opposed to the war and the more militant advocates of social change. Middle- and upper-class radicals, such as Clifford Allen, E. D. Morel, C. P. Trevelyan, Arthur Ponsonby, Norman Angell and Bertrand Russell, denounced the war from the beginning – and organised opposition on bodies such as the Union of Democratic Control and the No Conscription Fellowship. To gather maximum support they focussed their efforts on discussing war aims rather than the 'secret diplomacy' which they felt had caused the war.[21] As the war progressed they came to realise the importance of securing working-class support if the Government were to be forced to end the war. Thus Morel wrote to Trevelyan in August 1916 that their best hope lay in converting the Triple Alliance:

> The railwaymen are beginning to feel the pinch of increased food prices and, I suppose, will have to be met with regard to their application for increased pay. We already have a large section of the miners on our side, and probably will have a larger as the result of these South Wales meetings if they are allowed to go through. Of the transport workers I know little. Here then is the greatest centralised Labour force. If the Triple Alliance could be won over, if not in whole at any rate in part, to the definite programme of peace by negotiation, the effect out to be very great, and combined with the steady operating force of economic factors, casualties, rising prices it might be decisive.[22]

Lloyd George had been aware of the activities of pacifists and some revolutionary socialists in the industrial centres from early on in the war. He spoke of such activities on the Clyde and in South Wales to a group of Clyde employers in August 1915: 'You have a section of workmen in the yard who are under evil influences and who are opposed to the war and who are doing their best to create mischief. We have a considerable number of those in South Wales. It is deliberately fermented by a man who is spending his wealth in training people to instruct workmen in doctrines of this kind.'[23] He heard from Mrs Pankhurst that in South Wales 'strikes and rumours of strikes fill the air', and she urged that 'if vigorous action is taken to arouse patriotic and national feeling much can be done to counteract the pernicious influence of the U.D.C.'[24] In the autumn of 1915 he was not unduly worried, observing in reply to Mrs Pankhurst, '. . . the evil effects are for the present confined to a minority of the working population – an active and energetic minority it is true, but every effort ought to be made to counteract their evil influences'.[25]

The introduction of military conscription made the mixture of revolutionary socialism and pressure for a democratic peace a more potent force. This threat was strongly revealed during the Sheffield strike. A local representative informed the Ministry of Munitions that the district secretary of the A.S.E. had told him 'that his men are all joining the "No Conscription Fellowship", as a result of the mass meeting of November 5th ... The A.S.E. have lost all control of their members and have no power whatever. The officials are all against it. The movement is against conscription of any kind.'[26] Earlier in 1916 Lloyd George had described the organisers of the industrial discontent as 'Socialists and Syndicalists whose only endeavour is to set class against class',[27] but as the Military Service Acts took effect the opposition became much more important. By the time he became Prime Minister the situation was described as 'the present crisis' by the writer of one secret memorandum. This observed,

> The outstanding feature of the strike movement we are now considering and the one which differentiates the present situation from all previous troubles is the essential fact that the driving force behind this agitation is not an economic question at all, but has its roots as well as its cohesive force in a widespread antagonism to the Military Service Act and in a common determination to withstand the advent of industrial conscription.
>
> The Military Service Act forces links that bring together factions between whom there is no economic tie. Aggregations of individuals of different grades, of different ideals, and with different material standards are united by a common and personal interest in this new quarrel. As the application of the Military Service Act recognises no territorial boundaries (other than Ireland) so also is the opposition to its provisions unrestricted in respect of locality ... Every turn that is given to the screw of the Military Service Act swells the ranks of the movement and hardens the animosity of the extremists. As food gets dearer the economic factor will come into play and add its quota to what is already a sufficiently formidable combination.[28]

Lloyd George was naturally concerned at the development of a revolutionary movement, but he did not become as alarmist as Milner. The Government kept a close watch on the Left in the Labour Movement,[29] and made attempts to combat it by their own propaganda.[30] His view was probably similar to that of Shackleton (Ministry of Labour) that there would not be a serious likelihood of revolution 'if the workers are convinced that the Government is earnestly and sympathetically seeking a thorough remedy for the evils which undoubtedly exist'.[31]

The collection of causes of discontent which gave greater power to the revolutionary movement also affected the democratic Labour Movement. Labour M.P.s and trade unionists were made aware of growing scepticism about the war among sections of the working class. Dissident groups, including Ramsay MacDonald and the U.D.C., worked to move their peace resolutions and anti-war motions through local trade union branches and Trades Councils upwards through the Labour Movement.[32] The January 1917 Labour Party Conference still had a majority in general support of the war; the Conference in August of that year reversed decisions taken seven months earlier.

The year in which the Government recognised the Labour Movement as a whole as difficult was 1917. Long hours, changing workshop conditions, restricted industrial relations under the Munitions of War Act, high prices, food scarcity, growing war weariness, scepticism as to war aims, the widening incidence of conscription, and popular democratic feelings released by the revolutions in Russia all combined to make Labour uneasy in this year. Lloyd George came to power at the time when these matters and those in other spheres, notably the supreme command of the war and general controls over the nation's resources, came to a head. Most probably he came to power at the time he did because these matters were coming to a head, and because Asquith and his closest associates no longer showed the confidence that they either could or had the will to face and solve the problems.[33] Esher was expressing feelings felt widely in governing circles when on 4 December 1916 he wrote to Haig: 'In view of Lansdowne's Memorandum and of the reluctance of Asquith to give a decision on Man Power, Food, etc. etc. I think L.G. was more than justified in resigning . . . If L.G. does become Prime Minister then his only chance of success is to govern for a time as Cromwell governed. Otherwise Parliamentarianism (what a word) will be the net in which his every effort will become entangled.'[34]

XII

The May engineering strikes

The May engineering strikes made perfectly clear to the Government the large amount of unrest in the country, and gave it warning that the unrest could provide potential support for the Left. As a result of the strikes the Government made considerable changes in their domestic policies.

The main causes of most of the strikes were the Government's proposals to abolish the trade card arrangement made with the engineering unions and to introduce dilution of labour on private work. These changes were motivated by the Government's need to stretch its domestic manpower resources further and to provide more men for the Western Front. The German and French Governments had already been forced to take drastic 'combing out' measures to maintain their military strength.

The proposal to extend dilution to private work was one on which the Government needed to consult the unions carefully. As Brownlie observed, 'The A.S.E. strenuously opposed the principle of dilution in private and commercial work, and was responsible for extracting from the then Chancellor of the Exchequer . . . a promise that he would not apply it.'[1] Rank and file engineers particularly resented breaking down their industrial safeguards for private enterprise.

The consultations with the engineering unions began before Asquith's Government fell. After getting the general approval of the Trade Union Consultative Committee on 16 October, Henderson presented draft proposals of a scheme to a meeting on 27 October. The unions made clear their hostility to the proposals and no decision was taken. On 22 November Addison presented a scheme whereby dilution would be extended under the supervision of local chief dilution officers backed by a committee of which half would be Labour representatives and half Ministry officials. An amended version of this was accepted by the unions other than the A.S.E., which refused to attend.[2] The engineering unions demanded that no better terms should be offered to the A.S.E. The A.S.E. refused to attend because, as Henderson told Lloyd George, 'they said there were certain people who would be represented at the conference with whom they were not going to settle the terms of dilution, or any other question, so far as they were concerned'.[3]

The Ministry of Munitions arranged a meeting with the A.S.E. on 12 December. Addison made a confidential statement on the war situation, explaining why 'the circumstances have become so different now', and informing them that he expected to get an additional 300,000 skilled men by the scheme.[4] The meeting then adjourned for the A.S.E. Executive Council to consider the proposals. Addison felt by the end of the meeting 'we got them . . . into a friendly frame of mind'.[5] However, for the A.S.E. officials the proposal was dynamite. They had lost the confidence of large sections of their members by supporting the introduction of dilution into controlled establishments. In supporting that one of their strongest arguments had been that they had guarantees that it would not be extended to private and commercial work (the work the bulk of engineers would return to after the extraordinary war work in munitions had ended). In these circumstances much as they were impressed by Addison's appeal on the new war conditions, they must have realised they could not carry their members in such an extension of dilution. At the resumed meeting on the 18th Brownlie bluntly stated that they could not accept the Government's proposals; and in the discussion made it clear that even with legal guarantees on the restitution of pre-war conditions and on employers making no extra profits his Executive would not commit themselves. When Addison asked Brownlie 'what suggestions you have to meet the existing emergency if you turn down this proposal?', he avoided committing himself to alternatives by answering that it was not for him to make suggestions.[6]

The Government now took the strong line of proceeding by legislation without further consultations. In making this decision on the 20th Addison was avoiding the danger of the A.S.E. blocking matters by taking a ballot of their members.[7] Addison's diary suggests that this decision was partly stimulated by the A.S.E. Executive's attitude: 'They were very sticky and refused to have anything to do with it, but we got the impression which was confirmed by what some of them said afterwards, that they were afraid to accept responsibility for recommending their members to adopt it, but would offer no opposition if we brought in a Bill to require it . . .'[8] However, the Bill was delayed for several months because of the difficult situation caused by the proposal to withdraw the trade card scheme. Despite Labour opposition, the Bill passed its second reading, and went into committee; but it was dropped at the outbreak of the May strikes.[9]

The second Government decision which sparked off the May strikes was that to end the trade card scheme. Manpower came under increasing scrutiny under Lloyd George's Government. Long, for one, wanted more rigorous classifying of men who could not be taken for the army. He wrote to Austen Chamberlain on 22 January:

> . . . The Minister of Munitions yesterday [in the Cabinet] argued that only he and his officials can tell what labour is essential to their productive power and what is not. This is the argument used by every employer . . . I am convinced that there is only one remedy for this difficulty, namely to give the Director of Man Power absolute power, and to enable him to say whether men shall or shall not be taken in blocks, not of course in individual cases, from the various employments . . .[10]

Derby pressed Addison in mid-February to raise 'whether the Trade Card Scheme should be retained and extended, or should be abolished'.[11]

From early on there were doubts about the scheme within the Ministry of Munitions. Addison at the beginning noted in his diary that whilst the trade card scheme 'looks so attractive' it 'will place us very much in the hands of the unions so far as the issue of cards of exemption is left to them'.[12] Stephenson Kent wrote in November that 'while for political purposes it is no doubt advisable that this scheme should be given a fair trial', he felt it would fail to meet their needs and that legislation would have to be brought in 'as may secure the desired mobility of labour'.[13]

By early 1917 military and shipbuilding needs were such that the Government felt it was essential to gain additional manpower by substituting a rigorous Schedule of Protected Occupations in place of the rather loose trade card scheme. On the Western Front the Germans were re-organising their forces whilst the French armies were diminished and exhausted and the British needed half a million men to maintain the strength of their divisions. On the Eastern Front the Russian armies were on the verge of collapse, and were unlikely to give any major assistance in 1917. At sea the

German submarine campaign made it essential that every skilled man who could be spared and could build ships should help make up the loss of merchant shipping and build more naval craft for protection.

After Robertson and Jellicoe gave a blunt exposition of the military and naval situation on 2 April to representatives of the unions in the scheme, Henderson chaired a discussion on the new proposals.[14] He emphasised that the decision to change the exemption system had not been lightly taken, and justified it by reference to the war priorities and the dissatisfaction of the other unions. Addison explained the new schedule would be based 'upon the man's occupation, upon his skill, and upon his real indispensability' and frankly informed them that 'a certain number of men who are members of your unions . . . will not be exempted'. When a trade unionist asked if they had any option, Henderson bluntly replied, 'Whilst we are prepared to give the fullest consideration to any suggestions or amendments you may have to the scheme the Government has decided that the Trade Card Scheme must be withdrawn and substituted by this . . . much better form of protection.' In spite of this the trade unions resolved that the trade card scheme should be given a fair trial.[15] Nevertheless both Henderson and Addison were optimistic that they would agree to the abolition of the scheme.[16]

In urging the abolition of the scheme the Ministers pointed to the resentment of the unions which were outside it. The N.A.C. heard a complaint that the A.S.E. was using the scheme to poach members from other unions, that there were threats to strike if the scheme was not abolished or broadened, and that there was a general feeling of bitterness.[17] Thus when Addison saw representatives of those unions outside the scheme, Clynes denounced the holding of separate conferences with the skilled unions; 'Why should we be separate in this matter of National Service? Why should we be brought together separately from the aristocracy of labour . . . ? [The Government] . . . should have the courage to tell the skilled unions that they are not to have this privilege against their fellow Christians in the shops.'[18] In replying to the arguments of those outside the scheme Brownlie stated the fear that underlay most of the unrest amongst skilled workers:

> The unskilled unions stand to gain by the system of dilution whereas we . . . in response to the call of the nation, have relaxed our hard won and traditionally cherished trade right . . . The unskilled unions have not relaxed any of their trade practices. As a matter of fact . . . they are now enjoying increased earnings under the scheme . . .

They have also profited by the scheme to the extent they are acquiring a knowledge of our trade which may be used to the detriment of the skilled craftsmen on the termination of the War.[19]

The Ministers were repeatedly warned by representatives of the unions in the scheme that there would be considerable unrest on the shop floors if it was abolished. The officials of the engineering unions (other than the A.S.E.) complained that they would have difficulty in explaining to their members why the trade card scheme, which they had been warmly supporting, was being abolished when, in some cases, the trade cards had not even been distributed to all members. One of them warned,

> . . . I think it is a disaster to withdraw these trade exemption cards. We have had considerable difficulty in more than one district in preventing trouble, and . . . I do know that resolutions have been passed at mass meetings in Sheffield, Liverpool and Barrow to the effect that if the trade exemption cards are withdrawn the men are going to 'drop tools' . . . I am very much afraid that if you cut out the whole lot and initiate a new system it will breed distrust and you will not get a satisfactory result for it.[20]

Similarly when they met representatives of an A.S.E. national delegate conference, one delegate observed,

> . . . the men in the workshops . . . are practically at their wits' end to know when there is going to be any settling down on this question and how they can take the promises of the Government seriously. There have been so many promises and the men become more irritable every time and irritation is such that one hardly knows how to cope with the position and keep the chaps in order.[21]

Henderson and Addison fully recognised the importance of meeting representatives of the A.S.E. delegate conference. Henderson later told other trade unionists, who complained of the meetings, that if they had refused to meet the delegates, 'What would have happened is that instead of having a sectional stoppage affecting guns here and guns there, we should have had a universal stoppage. I do not mind saying that you cannot at this moment risk a universal stoppage without risking a stoppage of the war.'[22] At these meetings on 23 and 26 April Young, the Secretary of the A.S.E., pressed the Government to pledge that before any arrangement was made dilutees 'will be removed from the workshops before the skilled men are taken'. On the 26th Henderson suggested if they would accept the schedule as a basis for negotiation then they could arrange this point. The A.S.E.

representatives asked that the schedule should not come into operation as planned on 1 May but postponed so the delegates could consult their constituents. Henderson offered that the call up of A.S.E. members should be delayed until agreement was reached or negotiations were ended.[23]

The question of postponing the schedule was discussed at the War Cabinet the next day. Derby made it clear that the schedule could not be selectively postponed for men in one union, and Geddes suggested the only way the recruiting machinery could exempt A.S.E. men was to stop recruiting altogether for one week. Henderson and Addison differed in their appraisals of the situation. The former

> stated that the tone of the conference had been very menacing. The delegates had demanded that the Trade Card Scheme should be continued, and threats of an immediate stoppage throughout the country had been used. There was undoubtedly grave unrest in the country, which had been deepened by the Russian Revolution, and as Labour Day [1 May] was approaching, the situation was one which would need careful handling.

The latter 'said he thought that the Executive of the Society and the delegates were not at one on the subject and he believed that the men would yield if the Government took a firm line; but it would be absolutely necessary to stand by the pledge given at the conference, and allow the constituencies to be consulted'. Despite various problems that would be caused by postponing recruiting, the War Cabinet 'agreed that to take any action during the coming week (which includes Labour Day) calculated to increase the resentful temper now prevailing, or to cause a strike which would delay shipbuilding and the output of munitions, would be a still greater evil'.[24] The schedule was postponed until 7 May, but before then the engineering strike was underway.

Lloyd George and the Government were prepared to delay the introduction of the Munitions Amendment Bill and the implementation of the Schedule of Protected Occupations as they were aware that there was considerable discontent in the country which could become serious if it was organised. But the overriding manpower needs ensured that such postponements could only be temporary and tactical. Lloyd George was none the less concerned at the rise of the revolutionary Rank and File Movement. He raised the matter at the War Cabinet on 6 April 1917, saying: 'he had received indications from several sources of a very considerable and highly organised labour movement with seditious tendencies, which was developing in many industrial centres. At bottom there appeared to be genuine and legitimate grievances, but there was a danger of these being exploited by violent anarchists.' In view of Lloyd George's comments the War Cabinet decided that, 'As soon as further evidence was forthcoming the Government should endeavour to remove the grievances without delay in order, as far as possible, to forestall trouble.'[25]

A few days earlier Lloyd George had received a full report on the Strike Movement, which noted amongst other things that at the Second General Conference of the Rank and File Movement at Birmingham on 3 and 4 March, attended by over 120 delegates from the chief British industrial centres, 'their first business was to discover some suitable ground for a General Strike'.[26] The memorandum noted with some alarm that the war had brought together a disparate group of Left organisations:

> Considered as separate entities, none of the factors referred to, with the possible exception of the Rank and File Movement, are sufficiently dangerous to justify alarm; but considered as a whole, the combination may truly be said to be formidable, even perilous to the State . . .[27] It is obvious that such an amalgamation is particularly difficult to handle because specific concessions (short of an absolute surrender of the citadel) made to one group does not mitigate the hostility of the associate groups . . . whilst there are many tributary streams, each draining its own particular valley, the main current of industrial unrest is to be found in the Rank and File Movement. This is the organisation which is increasing in volume, and this is the force which is being directed into the most effective channel for the accomplishment of practical ends. So long as its embankments are kept in repair, and where necessary strengthened, it will remain comparatively harmless, but it is capable of an infinite amount of mischief if once allowed to break its barriers.

The author of the memorandum warned, 'the fact must not be lost sight of that anything like a serious rise in the cost of living would immediately react disastrously on the situation and bring a tremendous access of power and authority to the self appointed leaders of working class unrest'. The measures the author suggested followed the line Lloyd George had taken before on the Clyde and was to follow again:

> (1) The immediate redress of all genuine grievances, (2) Man all the points of public influence and mobilise the patriotic elements, (3) Strengthen the hand of legitimate trade unionism and refuse to bargain with irresponsible and mutinous leaders, (4) Reason with

and attempt to convert those who are still amenable to reason, (5)
Identify the irreconcilable and, wherever they render themselves
liable, proceed against them with the utmost rigour of the Law.

However the outbreak of the May strikes and the rapidity with
which they spread caught both the Government and the Rank and
File Movement by surprise.

The beginning sprang from a sympathy strike stemming from
another major irritant – the slowness of the Government departments to rectify genuine abuses by employers. Again, this was a
matter which the Government recognised before the strikes
broke. Hodge told an inter-departmental meeting on labour unrest on 19 April, '. . . I think we must all be conscious of the fact
that there is a great lack of co-ordination on labour matters between the various Government Departments. I think that it is a
case where the old proverb applies, that too many cooks spoil the
broth.'[28] The Ministry of Munitions took two months from the
time that complaints were lodged with it to prosecute the firm of
Tweedales and Smalleys, which without consultations had tried
to put women on skilled work for which there was no agreement
with the unions. When the firm ordered some of their men to
instruct the women on this new work, the men refused and were
sacked. After this, on 14 March, 400 men gave in their notices.
On 29 March a mass meeting of 2,000 men at Rochdale denounced
the proposals to extend dilution on private work and called for
the prosecution of Tweedales and Smalley within three days. The
following day men at Manchester downed tools, and the strikes
thereafter spread through Lancashire and across the country.[29] By
the finish of the May strikes, 1,500,000 working days were lost,
and 200,000 men had been involved in them.

That the strikes were an expression of accumulated discontent
is clear from the way the different centres cited different things as
their main grievance, though abolition of the trade card scheme
and the extension of dilution were common to nearly all. In the
London area, for example, the abolition of the trade card scheme
was the prime irritation. The Ministry of Labour account commented, 'The strike in the London area, serious as it was, was by
no means inspired by unpatriotic motives and the men came out
very reluctantly and not until a fortnight after their decision was
first taken' and cited as evidence that 'at the Crawford Works it
was resolved that the men engaged on certain work for the de-
feating of submarines should not down tools with the others'.
Whereas at Coventry there was already unrest over food before
the two new proposals became issues. But in Leeds and Barrow

the strike only broke in protest at the arrests the Government made in other centres.

The Rank and File Movement, like the Government, were expecting unrest but were not fully prepared for it when it did break. Their organisation was expanding across the country – but in certain centres they were unable to organise strikes. The Joint Engineering Shop Stewards' Committee first organised a meeting against the extension of dilution and the trade card scheme on 22 April at Manchester and this was translated into action on the 30th. They were successful in the Manchester area, but on Merseyside it was only on the 14th that they got the men out, and then there was little enthusiasm for the strike. Sheffield was another area in which their organisation was strong. The Ministry of Labour account noted, 'The Sheffield leaders were among the most able and extremist in the Shop Steward Movement and remained moreover in close touch with the Strike Committee in Manchester.' Similarly at Coventry: 'At Coventry as at Barrow, local conditions and certain local grievances had produced a truculent frame of mind among the workers and this fomented by unscrupulous extremists eventually brought about the strike.' Elsewhere their organisation was less efficient and successful. The Ministry of Labour account observed, 'the affair at Barrow is an excellent illustration of the want of co-ordination and unity between the various areas and in the strike centre themselves. The Barrow shop stewards are as well organised and compact a body as any in the country yet their conduct was marked by delay, shilly-shallying and want of confidence in themselves and the rank and file.' Shop stewards from Bristol failed to bring out the South Wales engineers. There was no stoppage on the Clyde, despite the area being 'in a very restless condition'. The Ministry account commented,

> The failure of the Clyde to strike is interesting as emphasising the amount of which any given district is swayed by purely local feeling. The most serious moment of the whole period was that at which a protected Clydeman was called up by the military authorities. Only by decisive action on the part of the shop stewards would a strike have been possible, and for them the rush of events was too rapid for realisation of their position. Many of them were men of moderate character and others were swayed by local jealousy and suspicion of English districts which had refused to come out in sympathy when they themselves were out.

During the strikes the Government reached agreement with the A.S.E. on the Schedule of Protected Occupations, but this did not stop the strikes spreading further, let alone end them. On 2, 3, 4 and 5 May Henderson and Addison negotiated with the A.S.E. Executive and delegates conditions under which the schedule could be operated.[30] The agreement reached greatly limited the Government's recruitment field. They agreed not to call up any skilled men or apprentices until all the dilutees fit for military service in a large unit termed 'a munitions area' had been called up; and promised not to call up any man over thirty-two without first consulting the unions and amending the schedule. After reaching this agreement the delegates called on the strikers to return to work, but without success.[31]

The Government then had further discussions with the A.S.E. and the other unions. At a meeting between Addison and Hodge and the A.S.E. Executive on 9 May, Brownlie emphasised that the settlement of the Schedule of Protected Occupation alone was not enough, as Addison seemed to suggest; in Lancashire and certain other areas the major grievance was the extension of dilution.[32] Hodge made quite clear to them that the Government's intention was 'to help you in maintaining Executive authority. The question is in what way can the Executive authority be maintained and how far can we assist you in doing that.' He told them that the previous day a deputation had come to see him, but he refused to see them. 'We got in touch with your Executive to see if the Executive would consent to a deputation to appear along with them, just as a demonstration to them that without the Executive they could not be seen.' The Executive declined to do so, and Shackleton unofficially listened to their comments. 'They said they were out more against their own Executive and their own Society than they were against anybody else or anything else. The Executive had sold the pass. That is the kind of thing which we want, if it be at all possible to kill.' Hodge concluded by calling on the Executive to give a strong lead and issue a manifesto calling on the men to go back to work; and commented, '. . . I think it must be evident to you that this thing, being unconstitutional, it is quite impossible for Dr Addison to give way until the men go back to work. If anything else is done it will, to my mind, weaken your authority very much.' The A.S.E. however felt that a further appeal would do little good, and Brownlie remarked, '. . . there is a feeling abroad that the Executive Councils of the trade unions of this country are more concerned with assisting the Government than they are with promoting the interests of those who have elected them to their present position'. Addison broached with them the question of prosecutions, saying, 'I feel under the present circumstances that if we can show that any particular man is fomenting trouble in defiance of your authority and the authority of everybody else we shall have to take proceedings against him. I can mention the names of one or two . . .' After one of the A.S.E. Executives interjected, 'We can mention half a dozen', Addison continued,

> I know you would repudiate them as strongly as you could . . . We have not decided to do anything at the moment; but I do not want this to prevent our doing it if we think it right on the evidence which is obtainable. I should think in your heart of hearts nobody would rejoice more than you would if we proceeded against two or three people I could mention.[33]

The following day Henderson and Addison had a conference with fifty unions (not the A.S.E.) representing the Engineering and Shipbuilding Federation.[34] Like Hodge on the previous day, Henderson made much of the revolt being against the constitutional leadership. He made the unequivocal offer,

> I have no hesitation in saying that the Government would be prepared to go any length – at any rate, any reasonable length – with you to assist you to stamp this pernicious influence and policy out of the ranks of organised labour, because it is going to be disastrous to the country and disastrous to organised labour . . . I have set my face like flint against anything that is going to undermine the discipline and executive authority of the respective trade unions (hear, hear) . . . let me . . . once more impress upon every representative present . . . that no more serious situation has arisen since August 1914 than the situation which obtains in this country today.

Several of the representatives echoed Henderson in fearing the Rank and File Movement would undermine trade unionism as they saw it; Wilkie, of the Shipwrights, said, '. . . I do ask you to assist us in keeping the trade unions together, for you will have no reason to fear us in the future any more than you have had reason to fear us in the past.' As Addison noted in his diary, '. . . I am glad to say they passed a resolution, after blowing off a little steam, unanimously condemning the strike, and appointed a committee to discuss the Amendment Bill with us in a friendly spirit.'[35]

The next day, 11 May, Henderson, Addison and Hodge conferred with the Public Prosecutor and Scotland Yard. At the meeting they settled on the procedure with respect to prosecutions and decided to issue a proclamation and take action on Monday. However the prosecutions were postponed as the King

was due to make a tour of the northern industrial towns.[36] At a
meeting presided over by Lloyd George on the 17th, it was decided to prosecute eight or ten strike leaders. This was clearly to
be an exemplary measure – the meeting deciding that 'the case for
the Crown should be presented in such detail as to give the public
a full opportunity of forming an opinion as to its merits, and no
restriction should be placed on the publication of the proceedings'.[37] Seven out of ten men selected were arrested the following
morning, and finding no sureties were put in Brixton Prison.

Meanwhile a conference of strike committees summoned a
national conference at Walworth in London. This began on 15
May, and was attended by 100 delegates. The next day a deputation of ten asked to discuss terms for a settlement of the strike
with Dr Addison. He answered according to a War Cabinet decision of that day – 'The Government should adhere to its policy of
recognising only the constituted authorities of the trade unions,
and that no deputation from the shop stewards should be received
except at the request of the executive of the union.'[38] Addison was
criticised in the Commons on the 17th by Anderson and others
for refusing to negotiate with the deputation from the Walworth
Conference. He made it clear that he would deal with only the
official representatives of the unions.[39] The next day the Walworth
Conference and the A.S.E. Executive discussed the situation, and
a committee of the Conference passed the resolution:

> That we hereby request the Executive Council to attend with us at
> the Ministry of Munitions, in order to state our case, and then
> immediately return to our districts, telling them we have carried out
> our mandate, and advise them to return to work, leaving the matter
> with the Executive Council on receiving assurances of no further
> arrests, of no victimisation, and in regard to releases.[40]

The Executive arranged a meeting with the Ministry of Munitions
the following day.

This meeting on the 19th was overshadowed by the arrests.[41]
The deputation at first felt these precluded them from discussing
matters at all – but Brownlie persuaded them to continue with the
meeting. The deputation put their specific complaints. During the
meeting the A.S.E. Executive showed that it was very anxious
about its position. Hutchinson pressed at the meeting,

> ... you could get a general statement made that this trouble has been
> of no value to the workers generally and that it has proved con-
> clusively that they can open no negotiations for any settlement with-
> out them doing it through their organisation. The logical sequence

of all that is that they should take all their grievances to their local and central Society . . .

Addison was conciliatory at the meeting. He pressed three points. Firstly he emphasised that there must be a swift return to work, and hinted that, providing Lloyd George agreed, the arrested men would subsequently be released. After further negotiations with the A.S.E. on the 21st, Addison wrote to Lloyd George that he, Worthington Evans, Kellaway and Shackleton all felt the best policy 'in view of the fact that we have got both the Schedule accepted and the principle of the Bill and the Shop Stewards hopelessly discredited, is to immediately announce the abandonment of the prosecutions as an act of grace'. He pointed out that it was hard to take proceedings against the eight men arrested when they had pledged themselves on the 19th not to arrest anyone else, and also if this were not done quickly it would be interpreted as an act of weakness by the Government, in that their case was not legally sound or that they feared further strikes.[42] The second point Addison pressed on the 19th was 'that if there are any of these grievances or any troubles let us be sure that they are going to be put up by the orthodox channel . . . but do not let us have cyclist despatch riders running from one district to another fetching men out from the shops without the approval of the Executive'. Thirdly, he pressed 'that whilst accepting the general principle of the Bill in the limited application, you shall be parties with us to considering to what extent we can make amendments either in this Bill or in the present Act which will make it more acceptable to your members and remove the causes of irritation which I recognise are very acute in some cases'.

Addison's negotiations with the A.S.E. on the 21st settled the strikes.[43] The settlement followed the line of the motion which the Walworth Conference passed on the 18th, though the question of releases was left to the Government. Lloyd George agreed to the withdrawal of charges against the men when they agreed to sign an undertaking to adhere to the terms settled by the A.S.E. Executive.

The Ministry of Labour officials felt that the Government had backed down considerably by seeing the Walworth Conference delegates. In a memorandum of 18 December 1917, Hope Simpson asserted, 'The interview between the Minister and the unofficial Strike Committee, even though facilitated by the presence of the A.S.E. Executive, in fact amounted to recognition of the right of the former to speak for the men.'[44] However, as has been shown such a joint meeting under the auspices of the A.S.E. Executive Committee was actually desired by Hodge beforehand. The Government stuck by their refusal of the 16th to see deputations from the Walworth Conference on their own, and this led the conference to negotiate the moderate resolution of the 18th with the A.S.E. Executive. Lloyd George and the Government were not pleased to be negotiating with the shop stewards even at a joint meeting, but in the circumstances the Government got the best arrangement it could, and neither Lloyd George nor Addison appear to have seen this meeting as a particular reversal.

The Left tried to keep up the momentum of the May strikes by calling a convention at Leeds for 3 June.[45] This was characterised as a convention 'to hail the Russian Revolution and to organise the British Democracy to follow Russia'. As well as resolutions welcoming the Russian Revolution, there were ones calling on the British Government to follow the Russian Government's lead on foreign policy and war aims, for an end to the wartime system of compulsion inside Britain, and most notably one calling for 'the formation of local workmen's and soldiers councils'. Lloyd George later wrote in his *War Memoirs*, 'Nervousness was expressed in some quarters as to the possible outcome of the Leeds Conference and I was urged to prohibit it, but I thought it would be a mistake to take it too seriously.'[46] At the time Lloyd George raised the matter the War Cabinet 'were informed that the fact that this conference was proposed to be held was well known to the Labour world', and they decided that, 'It would be undesirable to take any steps to suppress further advertisements or to prohibit the meeting itself, though it was of such a revolutionary character. They requested the Secretary of State for War to take the necessary action to ensure that no soldiers in uniform attended the conference.'[47] But as well as being influenced in not banning it by the fact that the arrangements for the conference were widely known, Lloyd George probably did feel that the meeting would not be a major danger. The convention was within a fortnight of the Walworth Conference which had proved reasonable in spirit, those taking part covered a wide political spectrum of the Left (the fairly moderate Will Anderson in fact proposed the Soviet resolution), and, though the Soviets were clearly non-parliamentary, at this time they were less widely understood in Britain and had not acquired quite the ethos they were to gain after the Bolshevik Revolution. After the conference nothing came of the call for British soviets. As Lloyd George observed, '. . . as very many of the "delegates" attending it were individual enthusiasts who came without authority or instructions from any organised bodies, their votes bound no one but themselves.'[48] It is unlikely that the meeting had any great effect on the British Labour Movement. As Ralph Miliband has observed, 'The Leeds Convention had fortuitously brought together revolutionaries and constitutionalists. But the gulf between them remained as profound as it had ever been and the installation of the Bolshevik regime in November 1917 only served to widen that gap.'[49]

In response to the considerable unrest in the country revealed by the May strikes, Lloyd George set up the Commissions on Industrial Unrest. He was determined that the commissioners should 'interpret their terms of reference in a broad spirit', obtain their evidence from 'official *and* unofficial sources' and 'report within a period of four weeks'. Speed was essential as it was felt they were in a brief 'industrial lull', which would not last in view of the steadily rising cost of food.[50]

The eight regional commissions reported on 17 July. The commissioners reported that the soaring cost of living linked with resentment of profiteering was the 'most important of all causes of industrial unrest', and listed as other major causes the operation of the Munitions of War Act (in particular the leaving certificate and the failure of employers to consult the workers when changing working conditions); the operation of the Military Service Acts; lack of co-ordination between Government departments; and lack of confidence in the equality of sacrifices, Government pledges and the trade union leadership. In addition in certain areas inadequate housing, inadequate supplies of reasonable quality beer, and industrial fatigue were major causes of unrest.[51] A secret memorandum of the Ministry of Labour added a further major cause: '. . . the driving force behind the recent strikes is to be found, in large measure, in the activities of the irreconcilables among whom the leaders of the Rank and File Movement are prominent.'[52] Lloyd George saw that the causes of unrest were alleviated as far as possible without gravely hindering the war effort. The Government's actions on food prices, encouraging co-operation in industry, and amending the Munitions Acts are particularly interesting.

Lloyd George responded to the danger of rising food prices before the commissioners' reports came in. The War Cabinet, 'recognising that reasonable prices for essentials are an important factor in maintaining the *morale* of the nation during the stress of war', at Lloyd George's personal instigation set up a committee under Addison on 8 June 'to examine . . . the question of keeping down prices of foodstuffs'.[53] On 27 June the Cabinet decided that Lloyd George should spell out the new policy of subsidies in a major speech in Scotland. He should announce the Government's recognition,

> that, in order to keep up the morale of the nation, it was necessary not only to have sufficient food, but ample food at reasonable prices. The policy of cheapening the essentials of life would be carried out partly by measures to prevent profiteering, and partly, so far as necessary, by an artificial reduction of the price of food at the cost of the Exchequer. This latter course was necessary for the reason that, in the case of imported food, the cost of production was outside Government control . . . It was also decided that the artificial lowering of prices should be confined to absolute essentials, such as bread, meat and sugar.[54]

The reports of the commissioners reinforced their feeling of the urgency of carrying out this policy.[55] The Ministry of Food was expanded in order 'to provide machinery for a considered and comprehensive control rather than a haphazard and piecemeal interference', including a costings department. This enabled the Food Controller 'to fix the prices of those articles of prime necessity over the supply of which he could obtain effective control at all stages from the producer down to the retailer'.[56] In the case of meat speculative middlemen were eliminated and the prices paid for live animals were fixed on a descending scale which reduced prices by 20–23 per cent by January 1918.[57] However the reduction of prices contributed to 34 per cent less meat becoming available in February 1918 than the average for the first five months of 1917; this 'led to the formation of meat queues and accentuated the industrial unrest which was assuming alarming proportions at the time'.[58] In the case of bread there was a direct subsidy, which avoided such side effects. Lloyd George himself suggested 'a scheme of limiting the price of the loaf at the expense of the State' to Addison on 23 May.[59] The Cabinet wanted bread prices reduced by 20–25 per cent by mid-August, but this was delayed, for organisational reasons, until mid-September.[60] In September 1918 Clynes hesitantly (in view of the huge cost of the bread subsidy) suggested that consideration should be given to 'whether any scheme can be framed for securing by an extension of subsidies a greater measure of industrial peace',[61] but the conclusion of the war ended this proposal.

As well as taking firm steps to reduce prices Lloyd George made the increase of domestic production of food a priority. The Cabinet gave the Corn Production Bill a high place in the parliamentary time-table as it was 'of the most immediate urgency . . . its passing being essential to the success of the Agricultural Programme'.[62] They were determined not to make alterations in their measure. When it was reported that there was pressure in Parliament to raise the minimum wage for farm workers from 25s to 30s, the War Cabinet decided to make it clear 'the Government to stand by the policy . . . laid down, and, if unable to carry the Corn Production Bill, to dissolve and appeal to the country'.[63] Earlier in June the War Cabinet had decided that virtually no more men should be withdrawn from agriculture for the army, and that the army should provide some 5,000 men a week for ten weeks for harvesting.[64]

In a similar fashion various other social reforms were carried out. For instance, the Government saw that the giving of pensions (stemming from the war) was done in a much more generous manner. A memorandum of October 1917 noted, 'Prior to April 1917, there had been 65,673 rejections of claims or an average of 2,084 a month. Since then there have only been 484 or an average of 97 a month.'[65] However with housing the Government only met extreme cases of overcrowding, as at Barrow, with a limited number of houses; they were unwilling to spare more manpower.[66] In consequence the War Cabinet only issued a promise of 'substantial financial assistance from public funds to those local authorities who are prepared to carry through, without delay at the conclusion of the war, a programme of housing for the working classes . . .'[67] But an enterprising Minister, such as H. A. L. Fisher, could get reforms through by arguing that they would prevent disaffection. When Fisher pressed for pensions for teachers his colleagues (no doubt with John MacLean in mind) 'were impressed with the importance of raising the quality of the teaching profession and removing from it all reasonable cause of discontent, inasmuch as at present revolutionary movements were to no small extent fomented by dissatisfied school teachers'.[68]

In his summary of the commissioners' reports Barnes noted, 'A proposal which finds general favour is that workshop committees should be set up.' The setting up of local joint committees was a favourite proposal of both the Ministries of Munitions and Labour. Such committees were functioning at G. and J. Weir on the Clyde and Armstrong Whitworth at Barrow. At a conference of the heads of departments dealing with labour problems Hodge, Wolff and Shackleton all spoke up vigorously for them; Shackleton observing that setting them up was 'essential . . . to peace'. Wolff reported that the Ministry of Munitions was 'trying to force Hotchkiss at Coventry to start a shop committee', and the meeting decided they should be pressed on employers and workers.[69] Soon after this meeting representatives of the employers and men at Hotchkiss travelled to London to see Wolff, and an approved constitution for a shop committee was agreed on.[70] A later memorandum observed,

> In these committees we certainly seem to have an organisation which might perfectly well fulfil some of the functions elsewhere fulfilled by the shop stewards. It is likely enough . . . that the men now acting as shop stewards would be elected to membership of the committees but . . . provided they were elected by secret ballot, and that re-election took place at frequent intervals, the employers, at any rate, would . . . know . . . that the men who spoke for the work-people . . . did really represent their desires and sentiments. The result of the ballot for a workers' committee in the Hotchkiss works at Coventry, where not one of the agitators or extremists secured election, proves that this is not invariably the case.[71]

Barnes also warmly supported this policy after the May strikes. In a memorandum of 31 May he urged that the 'establishment in all factories of a workshop committee which will fit into the labour machine without dislocating the existing mechanism' would be a major step in preventing further unrest.[72]

The proposal for joint local committees was also the third tier of the Whitley Committee's proposals for joint industrial councils.[73] The Committee's first interim Report wanted the Government to propose to 'the various associations of employers and employed' that joint councils should be set up in well organised industries at the national and district level and in the workshops.

The War Cabinet was slow in taking up the Whitley proposals. They received the Report on 2 May, but it was not until 7 June that they considered it. At this meeting they decided not to publish it, as Montagu proposed, but to circulate it to employers' associations, trade unions and the Commissioners on Industrial Unrest for their response.[74] Somewhat reluctantly they agreed to its publication on the 19th, and after being assured that it 'had been very favourably received by the trade unions', on 9 October they endorsed its principle and authorised the Ministry of Labour to take 'the steps proposed . . . for setting up' councils.[75] There-after the Cabinet showed little enthusiasm in pushing the policy, even amongst civil servants.

Their response is not as strange as it seems to enthusiasts for the Whitley proposals. The Whitley Committee formulated their Report between November 1916 and early March 1917, and their aim was to utilise the mood for co-operation in industry which stemmed from the war. But the May strikes showed that whilst the trade union leaders might be in such a mood there was a real

danger of the men in the workshops being led away from 'con-
stitutionalism' by militant shop stewards. In this situation there
was much less appeal in national and district councils; as the
commissioners for the north-west and David Shackleton argued,
in the crucial engineering industry much more would be achieved
by beginning with the shop committees and working up.[76] It soon
became clear that there was an inability to reconcile effective
works committees with the Government's policy of dealing with
the central trade union organisations.[77]

An equally fundamental weakness in such proposals was their
explicitly voluntary nature. All the proposals stressed 'that the
innovations recommended should not, if it can be helped, be
imposed from above'.[78] The memorandum, which the Cabinet
endorsed, outlining 'the steps proposed' for setting up the
Whitley Councils, quite explicitly stated, 'If the associations do
not respond, the recommendations fall to the ground . . .'[79] The
Government soon found neither employers nor trade unions in
the engineering industry were interested; and the same proved to
be true in other key industries which suffered from poor industrial
relations. Despite their fervour the Ministry officials recognised
that many employers distrusted joint committees ('they dislike
interference in general, and they scent syndicalism in particular')
and that the union officials would be far from keen.[80]

Lloyd George had a more realistic appraisal of the chances of
the scheme being successful. In May Addison, when asked by
Lloyd George for his observations on joint committees, observed
that in the past they had never proved 'really effective', that employers and local trade unionists did not desire them and had
'never rendered much assistance in obtaining them'.[81] When there
were doubts in the War Cabinet about publishing the Whitley
Report it was urged against doing so that 'there were difficult and
unsolved questions connected with the future position of unskilled and semi-skilled persons',[82] and union fears about the
restoration of pre-war practices were a major cause of the non-
adoption of the scheme in the engineering industry. But naturally
Lloyd George was willing to praise the scheme in general, to
allow such attempts to be made to set up an improved voluntary
conciliation scheme, and to lavishly praise examples of co-operation in industry.[83] But his immediate concern was in preventing
further strikes like the May ones, the causes of which were only
in part in the area of industrial relations.

The Ministry of Munitions started lengthy negotiations with
both sides of industry about amending the Munitions Acts before
the Commissioners on Industrial Unrest reported. Enacting

amendments to reduce unrest was seen as a matter of great urgency; Addison informed Carson that he would take their 'recommendations into consideration' if they reported by the time the A.S.E. had formulated their views, 'but otherwise we should not propose to take the risk of further delay'.[84] The Government also made rapid changes in the administration of labour, including replacing the N.A.C. by the broader based Trade Union Advisory Committee; and the War Cabinet ensured it was better informed on labour matters.[85]

The series of negotiations resulted in the Government reluctantly giving up its proposal to extend dilution to private work and abolishing the leaving certificate.[86] Addison at a meeting with the A.S.E. on 15 June urged that extending dilution to private work was the only way they could find the necessary labour to make and repair big guns, to increase the production of merchant shipping in order to meet the losses by submarine action, to make aeroplanes and tanks, to replace broken domestic transport equipment, and to provide the necessary tractors for agriculture.[87] However an A.S.E. ballot revealed that 84 per cent of those voting were against such a proposal. On 13 August Churchill (who took over from Addison) again raised the matter, but from the outset declared that 'ill-considered action' on the matter could easily lead to 'a greater loss of output through disturbance than we should gain'.[88] However this meeting of all the unions concerned (including the A.S.E.) made clear their hostility to the proposal and it was dropped.

Addison hoped to remove most of the grievances stemming from leaving certificates without abolishing them. However Allan Smith, going beyond the view of the Employers' Advisory Committee, urged that it would be better to abolish them altogether than drastically modify the scheme.[89] Addison unsuccessfully tried to offer its abolition as an inducement to the unions to agree to dilution on private work.[90] Later Churchill, impressed with fears that if legislation was not enacted before Parliament's summer recess 'revolutionaries of the engineering trade' would get up an agitation on leaving certificates, rushed the new Munitions of War Amendment Bill through the Commons.[91] The Government was very wary of abolishing the leaving certificate outright as they feared migration of labour on a large scale would follow and so 'abruptly interfere with the munitions programme'.[92] The Government took precautions in the Act against large-scale migration, one of which empowered the Minister to increase the skilled workers' hourly rates of pay in order to remove financial inducements for skilled men to transfer to less skilled work.

Churchill's use of this power caused grave unrest in the autumn.

The Commissioners on Industrial Unrest recommended that publicity should be given on the Government's actions to remove grievances. Accordingly press statements were made on 23 August and on 15 and 25 October. However on one issue, recruiting, the basic problem could not be removed. Whilst steps could be taken to try to prevent anomalies in administration, the basic need for enlarging the scope of conscription could not be avoided if Lloyd George's 'knock-out blow' war policy was to be carried out.

XIII

The Stockholm Conference

The basic difficulties involved in Labour's participation in a War Coalition Government which controlled much of industry came to a head not on an industrial issue but over Labour's wish to participate in a proposed Second International gathering at Stockholm. Henderson's refusal to put the War Cabinet before his position as Secretary of the Labour Party led to his resignation and a personal rupture with Lloyd George.

As the leading Labour figure in the Government Arthur Henderson embodied the conflicting loyalties involved. As a member of Asquith's Government he was a key figure in negotiating the introduction of dilution and the other industrial innovations of the Munitions Acts; yet as a trade unionist his task was to protect the industrial interests of fellow trade unionists. As a member of the Government (after first offering his resignation) he supported the conscription measures of 1916; yet the Labour Party repeatedly opposed such measures, opposing general compulsion as well as fearing them as a prelude to industrial conscription. In mid-1916 the additional odium of being a dummy head of the Education Department, because of Asquith's refusal to have a Minister Without Portfolio,[1] proved too much of a strain on top of these other matters. He wrote to Asquith:

> I have never hesitated, as you know, to share with my colleagues full responsibility for the policy of the Government but it must not be overlooked that I am in the Cabinet as the leader of a party, and perhaps you will not be surprised to hear that my position in the party has already been seriously prejudiced. Through my association with the Military Service Acts and the Labour policy of the Munitions Department I believe I have permanently forfeited the confidence of certain sections of the organised workers.

He asked to be relieved of the post.[2] Asquith took no action, until Henderson firmly pressed his resignation on 8 August.[3] Subsequently Henderson remained in office as Paymaster General and continued to handle labour problems for Asquith's Government.

In Lloyd George's Government Henderson had a more prestigious position as a War Cabinet member; but he still had a problem of divided loyalties.[4] His justification was the need for victory; and he could point to the guarantees of a return to 1914 conditions he had obtained from the Government as the price of the drastic innovations introduced into industrial conditions. Nevertheless, his position as Secretary of the Labour Party and as a trade unionist continued to be strained as a War Cabinet member. Under Asquith, as a leading figure on the National Advisory Committee, he had drafted the terms for the introduction of dilution. Under Lloyd George, it was he who told the A.S.E. delegation that the trade card scheme must be considered dead. At the Labour Party Conference at Manchester in January 1917 he was fiercely attacked for the various unpopular actions of the Government. He broke with the Government, at last, when he had a major policy difference with Lloyd George over whether British Labour should attend the Stockholm Conference. On this issue his loyalties as Secretary of the Labour Party and member of the War Cabinet clearly and completely conflicted.

The calling of a conference of all socialists (allied, neutral and enemy) stemmed from enthusiasms aroused by the March Revolution in Russia and the emergence of the Petrograd Soviet.[5] The Second International's prestige had collapsed with the failure of the various national Labour Movements to prevent the outbreak of war. In April 1917 a joint Dutch–Scandinavian committee issued an invitation to all socialists to attend a conference at Stockholm to agree on war aims and then to enforce them on the various belligerent governments.

Both British and French majority socialist groups still remained committed to winning the war, and viewed such an invitation with suspicion. The Labour Party's Conference in January 1917 voted by 1,036,000 votes to 464,000 to fight German militarism to the finish. The Executive of the French Socialist Party decided in late April to reject the invitation to Stockholm, and sent instead a delegation to the Petrograd Soviet; 'their object', Henderson told the War Cabinet, 'being to persuade that Party to do all in its power to bring the war to a satisfactory conclusion'. On the basis of this information, the War Cabinet decided that, 'Mr Henderson should use his influence to secure that a suitable composed British Labour Deputation should accompany the French Party with the same object.'[6] This he did. Thorne and O'Grady joined the French group.

The British and French Governments naturally had no desire to have peace terms dictated to them by an international socialist conference. Nor had they any desire to see a revival in the prestige of the Second International. They also genuinely feared that if such a conference materialised it would be exploited by the German Government. As early as the beginning of April, Horace Rumbold informed Balfour from Berne that '. . . there is reason to believe that the German Government has tried, or are trying, to use German Socialists with a view to bringing about the withdrawal of Russia from the war'.[7]

In May 1917 Lloyd George and several Ministers felt there would be advantages in allowing a pre-war British Labour group attend the conference if it took place. The matter was first discussed in detail at the War Cabinet on 9 May.[8] Robert Cecil informed them that the French Government wanted to prevent the French minority socialists from attending and asked the War Cabinet to co-operate with them in this. The major argument for allowing a Labour Party delegation to go concerned the Russian internal political situation.

> It was pointed out that all the leading German Socialists, including some very prominent men, would be present at the conference, where they would meet representative Russian Socialists. If the Allies abstained altogether from the conference the German representatives would impress on the Russians that the British Empire and France were alone standing in the way of peace, and would have a chance of making misrepresentations on the subject.

This sounds like the kind of argument Lloyd George would urge. However it was felt the delegates must be suitable persons 'who would represent our national aims in the War in their true light'. The Cabinet suspended judgment until after the Executive of the Labour Party met and Henderson had ascertained

> (1) An indication of how the Pacifist Members of the Labour Party interpreted the policy of peace without annexations or indemnities in relation to peoples such as those of Poland, Armenia, and to the native populations of German South-West Africa and German East Africa who have no desire to live under governments which had previously oppressed them. (2) Who would be the representatives of the Labour Party in the event of a decision to attend the Conference.

However at this stage the Labour Party was against accepting the invitation to Stockholm. After a meeting of the Labour Party Executive on 9 May, Henderson told his Cabinet colleagues that 'in accordance with the view of the War Cabinet he had used his influence with the Executive Committee of the Labour Party not to take part in the Stockholm Conference'.[9] Instead he had successfully moved a motion calling for an Allied Socialist Conference in London in June. He also reported to them that Purdy, Roberts and himself had been selected by the Executive to go on a special mission to Russia. The War Cabinet approved, but decided 'in view of the industrial situation at home, it was not desirable that Mr Henderson should leave the country', but were quite willing to allow Roberts, another Minister, to go.[10]

When the Petrograd Soviet called on the Allied governments to allow representatives of minority as well as majority socialist groups to visit them, Lloyd George and his colleagues consulted the other governments as to their reply – suggesting that an indefinite reply should be sent, which observed 'owing to submarine warfare, the means of communication between Western Europe and Russia are very much restricted, and only those persons can be allowed to travel in that direction who wish to do so for business of national importance'. The Cabinet again felt it was impossible 'to give a definite reply on the subject until they know what persons wish to go to Russia and what is the object of the proposed journey'. In refraining from bluntly vetoing the Petrograd Soviet's request the Government was again influenced by the internal situation there. They suggested to the other Allied governments, 'to reply by a direct refusal would irritate the Russian extremists and perhaps discourage their moderate colleagues'.[11] On the 16th Henderson informed the War Cabinet that the Labour Party had decided 'to take no action . . . until further information has been received from the Russian Socialist Party as to the nature of their proposals'.[12] At a Cabinet meeting on the 21st Lloyd George and his colleagues even considered allowing Ramsay MacDonald to go.[13] The discussion was notable for the lack of animosity shown towards him; this was in marked contrast to their comments on him in public.

At the same meeting the Cabinet reconsidered the question of allowing delegates to Stockholm. This time Robert Cecil emphasised the danger of not counteracting German influences at such a conference if it took place. Henderson was sceptical. However the feeling generally at this meeting was in favour of British representatives going if the conference took place. The War Cabinet decided to inform Albert Thomas, who was at Petrograd on behalf of the French Government, of their opinion and ask him for his. The text of the telegram followed closely their discussion.[14]

However the Cabinet's attitude on the 21st was tempered by the condition 'if a conference should take place', and this part of their decision was emphasised more and more by Lloyd George later. At the Cabinet meeting on 1 August it was probably him who 'pointed out that in May 1917 the War Cabinet had no more favoured the holding of a Stockholm Conference than they do now, and it was only in the event of such a conference being inevitable that the attendance of British representatives had been contemplated'.[15]

None the less, there was a considerable change in Lloyd George's and the Cabinet's attitude to Stockholm. In May Lloyd George still hoped Russia could at least prevent the Germans transferring their troops on the Eastern Front to the Western Front and, until Kerensky's disastrous offensive, Lloyd George still had some hopes that the Russian Revolution, like the French Revolution, would revitalise the country for greater military efforts. Lloyd George may well genuinely have feared that German representatives on their own at such a conference would be a serious danger in view of the Russian internal situation. Cecil cited a report of the British Minister at Stockholm, in support of this fear, at the Cabinet on 21 May. It could be that a subsidiary consideration in Lloyd George's attitude at this time was his awareness of the growing popular concern over the war aims, which he would be willing to accommodate providing it did not run counter to his policy of strengthening the Russian Government *vis-à-vis* the Petrograd Soviet.

At the War Cabinet on 23 May it was decided that Henderson should go to Petrograd and consult with the Russian Government and, if he felt it best, take over as ambassador. At the same meeting they agreed to issue passports to British minority socialists (MacDonald, Jowett and Inkpin) to travel to Russia, but arranged that they would be prevented from arriving there before Henderson.[16]

However in late May it is clear that on balance Lloyd George and the Cabinet were in favour of allowing British socialists to go to Stockholm. This was primarily in response to the internal Russian situation threatening their hopes that Russia would keep the Germans busy on the Eastern Front. In June Lloyd George went as far as to say, 'If Russia made a separate peace he would be almost inclined to agree . . . that the War could not be continued next year. At any rate, you could not in those conditions achieve complete victory.'[17] It is equally clear that before his visit to

Russia Henderson had little enthusiasm for the Stockholm project; on his return, however, he was a strong advocate for it, and Lloyd George was adamantly against it. Both of them claimed that the key reason for the change in their views was the new developments in Russian internal conditions.

In Russia Henderson became convinced that a revision and declaration of democratic war aims would stabilise the Provisional Government, and help them to maintain the war effort. He had no sympathy with the Left there, any more than he had for it in Britain. 'The comrades in the soviets bewildered him. He did not understand their language. He did not like their manners.'[18] He found Russian industry in a poor condition, and observed, 'Difficulty accentuated by absence of proper labour organisation.'[19] He was glad to find that both employers and labour were coming to respect the authority of the State over both.[20] Therefore he advised Lloyd George, '. . . I am convinced that our best course is to go steadily forward, losing no opportunity to strengthen the hands of the Government and being most careful to avoid any act or word which might give the extremists a handle against them.'[21] He bluntly told the Labour Party Conference on 10 August,

> I have not wavered in the slightest degree in my attitude to this war, nor have I changed my mind as to the need for a final and complete settlement, but I want to say that in a war in which losses of such terrible magnitude are being imposed on all the nations it appears to me not only wise but imperative that every country should use its political weapon to supplement all its military organisation, if by so doing it can defeat the enemy. That is why I'm in favour of a consultative conference with proper safeguards and conditions.[22]

On his own initiative he consistently pressed for a consultative conference. He was quite explicit at the War Cabinet on 1 August that this was 'the line which he had decided on on his return from Russia to be best calculated to promote the national interests'.[23] Yet despite his consistency a grave misunderstanding as to his intentions grew up between him and his colleagues.

Lloyd George exaggerates in his memoirs when he writes that he returned with 'more than a touch of the revolutionary malaria'.[24] But Henderson does seem to have regained his faith in socialist war aims. Quite probably the success of the Petrograd Soviet reminded him of the growing strength of the shop stewards movement in Britain, and news of the Leeds Conference of 6 June may well have impressed him that the popular mood at home also required a considerable revision of war aims. He also knew that pacifist sentiment had long been spreading in France.[25]

Arthur Henderson returned to England on 24 July. He attended the Labour Party Executive the next day, without prior consultation with his colleagues in the Cabinet (Lloyd George was in Paris at an Inter-Allied Conference). Henderson pressed the Executive to support Stockholm. They decided that MacDonald, Wardle and he should go to Paris to discuss the matter with the French socialists before making a decision on Stockholm. Henderson agreed to go. Lloyd George in his *War Memoirs* fairly comments that his acceptance 'was a profound blunder. As a member of the British War Cabinet he had no right to go off to Paris without even consulting his colleagues in the Cabinet . . .'[26] Lloyd George's indignation over Henderson going 'arm in arm with Ramsay MacDonald, who was openly opposed to the war, and to all measures for its effective prosecution, and had been organising pacifist propaganda' was, despite the catalogue of MacDonald's iniquities, directed at the trip's purpose. This is illustrated in the next paragraph of his memoirs where Lloyd George himself observes that Henderson had cabled him in Paris 'stating that he was coming to Paris with four Russian delegates and Messrs Wardle and MacDonald – not, however, stating their business'. When Henderson saw the War Cabinet members on 26 July and revealed the plans he had made to visit Paris they made clear their disapproval. Henderson offered to resign – but with Lloyd George away, this was not a matter for them.[27]

At this meeting on the 26th, the other War Cabinet members were influenced by a copy of a telegram from Lloyd George to Henderson of the 25th, which stated Lloyd George 'approves *allied* Socialist conference and hope that you will make such arrangements as will ensure you have a leading voice in deliberations' but 'suspends judgment as to later steps until he has seen you and Russian situation in light of conclusions of the conference now sitting'.[28] They were even more annoyed when they learnt that Lloyd George's telegram had been sent when 'he had no idea that this would involve negotiations in Paris, and much less that Mr Ramsay MacDonald would be one of the parties to such negotiations'; Lloyd George's other colleagues observed on the 30th that when they had previously seen Henderson they 'had been under the impression that the Prime Minister had consented to the visit to Paris'.[29]

The prime reason for Lloyd George and the Cabinet's change in attitude on the Stockholm Conference was the change they felt had taken place in Russia.[30] At the Allied war conference in Paris on 25 and 26 July Lloyd George learnt that the Russian summer offensive had failed, and so now knew that the Russian alliance was unlikely to be of much military value. Also the War Cabinet felt that the Russian Government was at last 'taking measures to re-establish discipline in their forces by means that were absolutely contrary to the principles of the Soviet'. They felt:

> To permit the attendance of British representatives at the Stock-holm Conference, which was tantamount to countenancing frater-nisation between one section of the Allied British public and one section of the enemy public, would be very prejudicial to the policy which the Russian Government was engaged on and was pressing forward, the very first item of which was the prohibition of frater-nisation between Russian troops and those of the enemy.[31]

This desire to help the Russian Government restore discipline was very great with Lloyd George.[32] He was naturally deeply distressed at these events on the Eastern Front, and the mutinies in the French army and the strikes and demonstrations in France. He wanted a return to discipline in all the Allied countries.

Lloyd George and the Government were also very concerned not to take a different line from the other Allied governments. Ramsay MacDonald felt that 'in opposing Stockholm the Govern-ment were under the thumb of the French Government'.[33] The French, Italian and American Governments indicated by early August that they disapproved of the conference. This situation contained considerable political danger for Lloyd George. The Coalition supporters took considerable exception to Ramsay MacDonald being granted a passport for Russia[34] and Henderson and MacDonald going to Paris together,[35] and might have re-volted at Lloyd George allowing delegates to go to Stockholm if the other Allies had banned their's from going.[36]

Moreover Lloyd George was not willing to encourage the British socialist Left. The May strikes had revealed the wide-ranging discontent in the country which the Left could mobilise. The Government immediately set about meeting popular grie-vances by industrial and social reforms, to remove this potential. The War Cabinet clearly felt Stockholm was another major threat to the existing order:

> At an extra secret session of the Cabinet in the Chancellor of the Exchequer's room on 30th July, the discussion centred on the danger of the Left exploiting the situation against the Government. 'It was pointed out that the influence of the Independent Labour Party and of the pacifist organisations would probably be exerted to manoeuvre the Labour Party and the British Government into a

difficult position. The series of conferences now contemplated would give an opportunity for this. One step would lead to another . . . If the Paris Conference was followed by an Inter-Allied Conference which decided, as it might do, in favour of representation at Stockholm, it was possible that the British Labour Party, in its subsequent meeting, would not feel justified in disassociating itself from such representation. If once the Stockholm Conference took place, it was possible that the hands of the Government might be forced; that one or other of the Allied Governments might find itself practically committed to terms of peace which did not meet the views of the Allies as a whole; and that the situation in regard to the making of peace might be taken, to a great extent, out of the control of the Governments.'[37]

Nor was Lloyd George willing to abdicate the expression of popular opinions to Labour. He was always willing to bend his policy to the Left if the occasion required it – as he did in early January 1918 in his statement of war aims to the trade union meeting. But he was not willing to allow Labour the role of democratic voice of the nation. In the Commons debate of 13 August he said, 'I am the last man to disparage the power of Labour. I am the last man to say anything derogatory to their influence and to their weight and their power in the community, but they are not the whole community. When peace comes to be made, it must be made by the nation as a whole.'[38]

The events from the time of Henderson's Paris visit to his resignation are well known. In Paris he became a member of a sub-committee composed equally of right- and left-wing socialists to revise the arrangements for Stockholm.[39] He returned to London on 1 August, and informed Lloyd George he intended to continue to work for a consultative conference in Stockholm. The rest of his colleagues had met in, what Milner described as, a 'very agitated Cabinet', in the morning.[40] Lloyd George invited him to discuss the matter with the Cabinet that afternoon, when Henderson was kept waiting an hour whilst the others discussed his position. Barnes was then despatched to him to summarise the discussion. Henderson demanded entry to the meeting, and made clear he deeply resented this, the 'doormat', incident. Henderson explained his conduct to the Commons that night, and in the debate Lloyd George praised his past services.[41] On the 8th Lloyd George and the other Cabinet members came out of a Cabinet meeting with Henderson believing that he would advise a special Labour Conference called on the 10th not to support the Stockholm Conference. Henderson, on the other hand, came away believing he was free to follow his own course. The Cabinet was amazed when they learnt of Henderson's speech, and of the huge majority of more than three to one which voted for the Stockholm Conference. On the following day Henderson resigned, and his resignation was debated on the 13th in the Commons.

The important question is why was it so long after the Paris visit that Lloyd George dispensed with Henderson. In retrospect Lloyd George explained that Henderson had rendered invaluable past services in dealing with organised labour and that he 'had a warm personal esteem for him'.[42] However Lloyd George's career shows, if nothing else, that past services and personal esteem never saved any colleague if his retention was politically embarrassing. A strong case for Henderson's early removal was made at a special Cabinet meeting on the morning of 1 August before his interview with Lloyd George.[43] They felt after Henderson's Paris visit he owed the Cabinet an explanation 'as to why he had . . . acquiesced in, if not advocated, that the Western Allies should be represented' when 'it had been made clear, in Mr Henderson's presence, that the War Cabinet were not committed to the Stockholm project, and to the additional fact that the Prime Minister had left Mr G. M. Young at Paris with a personal message to Mr Henderson asking him not to take any action which would commit the Government to the Stockholm Conference'. They felt his action 'gravely compromised' the Government's position on the conference. And that his support was being misunderstood by the Labour Party and certain trade unions as indicating that the Government were in favour of the Stockholm meeting.

But there were substantial reasons for not breaking with Henderson at this time. Firstly the loss of Henderson would be a matter of international significance. At the 1 August Cabinet meeting they were impressed by the fact that '. . . Henderson's resignation on this question would be equivalent to a repudiation of the plan of a Stockholm Conference in the most dramatic manner, and that the effect of this in Russia might have the most serious reaction on the whole prospects of the Allies in the War'. Further, as Henderson said in the Commons on 13 August, if he had resigned before the Labour Party Conference on 10 August, the vote on Stockholm would centre on his resignation and not the question of British participation. Lloyd George and his colleagues had hopes until the last that the conference would itself reject British participation. Bonar Law observed that Henderson's departure 'would have a very bad effect on Labour and might just have made the difference in turning the scale in favour of the pacifist movement'.[44] Lloyd George informed Carson that the Government refrained from announcing they would prevent delegates going to Stockholm 'on the advice of the anti-Stockholm Labour men . . . They want to capture the Labour Conference and think they can do so provided the Government does not put up the backs of the trade unionists by telling them in advance that we take no heed of their opinions.'[45] Finally, Lloyd George's political position in the summer of 1917 was none too strong. He could not afford gratuitously to alienate the Labour Party – and for this reason would not wish to lose Henderson, the leading pro-war Labour figure.

The misunderstanding at the 8 August Cabinet meeting as to what Henderson would say at the Labour Conference ensured the break between Henderson and Lloyd George was not an amicable one. Lloyd George was convinced that Henderson had deliberately misled him,[46] and he stated in the Commons that the Cabinet had understood that he had been induced to change his mind and oppose the Stockholm meeting because of 'the opinion of the Attorney-General that it would be illegal for British subjects during wartime to meet the enemy' and because of 'the change that had taken place in Russia itself'.[47] He was also annoyed that Henderson had not laid before the Labour Conference the contents of a telegram from Russia (arranged by Nabokoff of the Russian Embassy in London), which was to the effect that the Russian Government considered Stockholm 'a party concern, and its decisions in no way binding upon the liberty of action of the Government'. Lloyd George claimed that the Labour Conference might have reached a different decision if it had had this information.[48] In fact Lloyd George misjudged the situation when he left it to the Labour Conference to vote down the Stockholm proposal. Henderson acted contrary to his expectations, in presenting Stockholm in the highly reasonable terms of a consultative conference which would have the dual purpose of resurrecting international socialism as well as helping to maintain in Russia a Socialist Government committed to winning the war. Lloyd George therefore saw Henderson as the cause of the Government's embarrassment in having to stop attendance at Stockholm immediately after the Labour Conference had voted in favour of sending delegates.

Henderson was even more bitter. He had been humiliated by his War Cabinet colleagues. He had been hounded unmercifully by press and Parliament. In the debate in Parliament he had felt restrained in what secret material he revealed.[49] In contrast Lloyd

H

George had not hesitated to use any material to his advantage, and to suppress as secret anything else. On the other hand, Henderson was glad to be out of his double role, which had been embarrassing him in the Labour Movement. After the Commons debate, he frankly told Arthur Murray, 'The dual position of a Member of the War Cabinet and Secretary of the Labour Party was of course becoming quite impossible.'[50]

The most important effects of the Stockholm incident were on long-term Labour Party policy and on relations between Lloyd George and the centre of the Labour Party. As is well known, Henderson's freedom from office led to his co-operation with Sidney Webb and others in reformulation of the Labour Party's organisation and constitution.[51] It also led to a fruitful reunion of both wings of the Party, and the formulation of a democratic Labour foreign policy. Ponsonby wrote after the debate, 'I believe Labour will rally to Henderson and new recruits will come in, and H. himself will be forced more and more in our direction . . . International Socialism will see by the refusal of passports that the Government are determined that Labour shall have no say in the settlement, and I think we can expect a pretty hot agitation.'[52] Henderson's resentment at his treatment by Lloyd George caused a deep breach between them, but mainly on a personal level. For Henderson was still willing to co-operate with Lloyd George in his National Industrial Conference after the war, whilst the Left outrightly refused to have anything to do with it. But Lloyd George's political chances of ever linking up with Labour were diminishing. As Samuel commented to his wife on 14 August, 'The net result so far is that another section of the House and the country – the centre of the Labour Movement – is now alienated from the Government.'[53]

Stockholm did not however lead to an immediate break with the Labour Party or seriously undermine the Government's political position. Although at the time it seemed extremely serious – Lloyd George thought his days were numbered as Prime Minister,[54] and the Cabinet considered whether or not to hold a general election to gain new authority for their conduct of the war[55] – it did not lead to major political change. The bulk of the Labour Movement still supported the war, and Henderson was merely replaced. The incident between Lloyd George and Henderson had been a personal one; Henderson had not explained or confided in his fellow Labour Ministers, who apparently resented this.[56] Lloyd George had been correct in supposing that though the pacifist feeling had been growing, it by no means dominated the upper reaches of the large trade unions.[57] At the special Labour Conference on 10 August, Adamson of the miners, seconded by Ernest Bevin, succeeded in limiting the delegation to nominees of the Labour Party and T.U.C., excluding delegates from the socialist societies. This was endorsed at an adjourned meeting of the Conference on 21 August, and by a bare majority only (the miners reversing their block vote) they re-affirmed the decision to send delegates to Stockholm. However the refusal of passports and similar equivocation by the French socialists finished the Stockholm project. When an international conference was held at Berne later in the year British Labour did not even apply for passports, whilst the French socialists did, but had their request refused. The account of the Berne Conference sent to Balfour is a fitting conclusion on the attitude of the majority of British trade union leaders: 'A letter was read from the British trades unions refusing to sit at the same table as Germans, on the grounds that these had begun a war of aggression and trampled the Hague Convention under foot. One of the German delegates replied at length denouncing the English letter as Chauvinistic.'[58]

All in all the Stockholm incident was unfortunate for Lloyd George. The likelihood was that Henderson would resign sooner or later, as his positions as a leading Labour official and as a Cabinet Minister were incompatible (industrial unrest repeatedly made this clear), but the occasion for their parting was unfortunate. It is hard not to come to the conclusion that Lloyd George, influenced by the chaos in Russia, the army mutinies and strikes in France, and the widespread unrest in Britain revealed in the May engineering strike, either over-reacted to the Stockholm project, or gave way unduly to the horror of the Right to such a project. The meeting of Allied Socialists in London on 28 August showed they were unable to agree on war aims. The Stockholm Conference, if it had taken place, would surely have been more chaotic, and cast the Second International into further disrepute. Lloyd George's fears of cunning pacifist, extreme Left or German manipulation at such a conference seem – with hindsight – to have been unrealistic.

XIV

The manpower crisis, 1917–18

The last twelve months of the war were marked by an acute shortage of manpower. The British army fought on the Western Front from March to the beginning of December 1917. The disastrous Passchendaele campaign killed three British soldiers for every two German.[1] Lloyd George and the War Cabinet had been extremely dubious of its likelihood of success, and consequently Lloyd George tried to remove Haig and Robertson.[2] But with Russia out of the war and American troops unlikely appreciably to affect the Allied strength on the Western Front until late in the 1918 campaign, the Government felt the strength of British forces had to be maintained on the Western Front in order at least to be able to resist German offensives.

From mid-1917 Lloyd George increasingly recognised that outright victory depended not only on finding manpower for the Western Front but on maintaining support for a policy of victory at home. He observed in the autumn, '. . . the question is . . . whether the people of these islands are prepared to undergo hardships and privations in order to see this thing through. If they are, we can manage all right.'[3] In the War Cabinet in January 1918 he observed that, '. . . the great factor of the War this year would be either military or morale, and . . . he was inclined to think it would be the latter. Food was our first line of defence. Labour was already inclined to demand the cessation of hostilities, and the food position, unless improved, would aggrevate this demand.'[4] The last year of the war was marked by the need to keep a balance between supplying manpower for the army and maintaining sufficient manpower at home to provide essential munitions and consumer requirements.

The Government became increasingly concerned in the autumn of 1917 at the continued failure to recruit enough men. In October Lloyd George complained, 'During the present month we had hoped for recruits at the rate of 18,000 a week . . . [but]

only some 9,000 men a week were coming forward.'[5] In the following month the War Cabinet felt Auckland Geddes' manpower proposals were 'in the main not practicable at the present moment'. They doubted if Parliament would agree to lowering the age for conscription or raising it to fifty, or that 'the country would accept a general "comb out" of workers in munitions works and other essential trades', or that applying conscription to Ireland would be wise or expedient whilst there was 'any hope of a satisfactory result to the Convention'. They felt 'shipbuilding should have precedence in man-power even over fighting forces'.[6] At a further discussion of these proposals Geddes warned that 'this country was straining all its resources to the utmost, and was nearing the breaking point'.[7] However shortly afterwards Derby warned them that at the current rate of recruitment Haig estimated that 'the British infantry divisions would be 40 per cent below their present establishment by 31st March, 1918' and that 'so far from there being any question of our breaking through the Germans it was a question whether we could prevent the Germans breaking through us'.[8] There was considerable scepticism at army estimates of the numbers needed and the comparative strengths of the opposing forces on the Western Front.[9] A Cabinet committee, chaired by Lloyd George, was set up to review manpower priorities. This was unimpressed by the army's approach to manpower, but nevertheless felt that an additional 150,000 top quality and 100,000 other men should be recruited. In consequence on 20 December Lloyd George explained in the Commons the need for new recruiting measures and said that the promise to the unions not to change the Schedule of Protected Occupations without consulting them would be honoured. [10]

The importance of achieving this increased level of recruiting was not far from the minds of Ministers dealing with the unrest stemming from a 12½ per cent wage bonus to skilled workers on hourly rates, or from Lloyd George's mind when he declared his war aims to a meeting of trade unionists. The 12½ per cent bonus had been intended to end a grievance long known to the Ministry of Munitions, which had been referred to the Commissioners on Industrial Unrest by Barnes and on which nearly all of them commented. This grievance was that skilled men on time rates often earned less than the semi-skilled men on piece rates whom they supervised; and the August 1917 Munitions Amendment Act gave the Ministry power to deal with men's wages, in order both to allay unrest and to prevent skilled men moving into less skilled work.[11]

The bonus was granted from 14 October, after much hesitation on the part of the War Cabinet in view of the grave doubts expressed by Ministry of Labour officials and Sir Lyndon MacCassey, the Director of Shipyard Labour.[12] Shackleton and Askwith warned that such a bonus would upset the differentials between piece-workers and time-workers, would set off an almost unlimited chain of claims, and would cost the country millions of pounds. They were particularly concerned at the failure of the Government to co-ordinate and centralise wages policy. The expensive and disruptive results of this had been well illustrated by an isolated advance given to the miners by the Coal Controller in early September.[13] MacCassey protested against it as it cut across the controversial policy the Cabinet had adopted in January of extending the system of payment by results in the engineering and shipbuilding yards.[14] The War Cabinet felt the 12½ per cent had to be granted in view of promises given to remedy the grievance and 'the constant demands for increased wages'. However at the same time as deciding the bonus would have to be made, Milner and Barnes insisted that there must be co-ordination in 'the settlement of labour disputes involving increases of wages'.[15]

From November until the following spring there was a series of strikes aimed at extending the award to other groups of workers. Milner warned Lloyd George on the 17th that 'a very serious and very immediate labour situation has arisen' because of the bonus.[16] A week later an Admiralty official warned him that the unrest would continue 'until the 12½% difficulty is finally adjusted and until piece workers either accept their exclusion from this increase or receive some compensation'.[17] On 21 November the Government promised that the bonus would be extended to all time-workers (semi-skilled and unskilled as well as skilled) in engineering and shipbuilding works and foundries; this was given effect from 11 December.[18] Further extensions were granted to time-workers in allied trades, but by the time the Government decided on a new Schedule of Protected Occupations there was considerable unrest amongst piece-workers.

The War Cabinet dealt with the dilemma of where to restrict the bonus in December and January. There were two schools of thought. Churchill urged Lloyd George that the bonus should not be extended at a flat 7s rate to all piece-workers but that special guarantees should be given to bring up the wages of those on low piece rates. He also felt that as, 'whatever is done now is the prelude of Auckland Geddes' National Service Man-Power negotiations', the Government should link the limitation of the extension of the bonus to a wide policy, including enforcing 'the standardisation of food prices' and taking all excess profits.[19] In a Cabinet memorandum Auckland Geddes supported the proposal to take all excess profits, and in the War Cabinet urged that the workers' resentment of them 'vitally affected the reception that would be given to the Government's proposals regarding manpower and recruiting'.[20] Lloyd George, however, aired the objections of the employers and of Austen Chamberlain to this; and after further consultations with these this proposal disappeared. In contrast to Churchill, Lloyd George and others felt it would be impossible to prevent the demand spreading. At the War Cabinet meeting on 1 January he observed that '. . . it was now impossible to stop. We were not in a position to face a serious strike, as there was no logical ground upon which to take the strike.' Alongside this was continued concern that to deny the piece-workers would undermine the moves to extend piece work. Shackleton commented that 'the $12\frac{1}{2}\%$ increase had done more to kill the premium bonus principle than anything else in the last ten years . . . [The men] considered the refusal to extend the $12\frac{1}{2}\%$ to piece workers and premium bonus workers a penalty on higher wages due to increased effort.'

The case of those believing it necessary to extend the bonus grew stronger as labour unrest on the issue became more menacing. In a resumed discussion on 5 January Geddes observed that 'he was anxious to check the rank and file movement, and by means of a proclamation make it clear that the extension of the $12\frac{1}{2}\%$ to an industry was not due to the power of the local leaders'. He also warned that 'piece workers were going back on to time rates and doing less work per man than they were doing a month ago'. The War Cabinet decided to adopt Barnes' policy of issuing a proclamation clearly stating that the Government would go 'so far and no further' in these wage concessions.[21] On the 7th the Cabinet decided that the recently formed co-ordinating Committee on Labour Disputes would be replaced by the Ministry of Labour which should supervise the making of awards to premium bonus and piece-workers within a maximum 7s per week. In the discussion the 7s had been deemed to be 'less than the full equivalent of the $12\frac{1}{2}\%$' and 'a gain of nearly 2/6 to the Government'.[22] Subsequently, on the advice of the Committee on Production, it was decided to give a $7\frac{1}{2}$ per cent increase to these categories, which was deemed to be rather less than 7s per week in the majority of cases.[23] It was felt that it would be impossible to revise the lower piece rates as that involved complicated and lengthy negotiations.[24] The award was announced publicly on the 24th – and right up to the last minute Churchill and his officials opposed a flat 7½ per cent increase rather than a revision of the lower rates.[25]

When Lloyd George made his statement of war aims to the conference of trade unionists on 5 January 1918 he was aiming his appeal not just at the leaders but at Labour in general – to counter a statement of democratic war aims issued by the Central Powers on 25 December and to smooth the way for the new manpower proposals. Lloyd George had been considering possible peace formulae since his accession to the Premiership; during 1917 he repeatedly hoped to detach Austria–Hungary from Germany by offering them acceptable peace terms.[26] In late September, depressed at the imminent Russian collapse and the lack of progress of the offensive on the Western Front, he had considered peace proposals which would have ended the war at the expense of Russia. But during 1917 the War Cabinet avoided public discussion of war aims as it was deemed likely to encourage pacifists and encourage the enemy.

However in the autumn of 1917 pressure grew for the War Cabinet to make a public statement. They were well aware of the growing war weariness. Barnes, for example, observed that the majority of the working class 'are as yet quite sound, but . . . the pacifist element is amongst them and there is a good deal of war weariness which might easily be turned to disaffection by any great reverse or untoward circumstances here at home'.[27] Lansdowne's letter to the *Daily Telegraph* (29 November), President Wilson's message to Congress (4 December), the publication of the 'secret peace treaties' released by the Bolshevik Government in the *Manchester Guardian* (from 12 December), all contributed to the Government's need for making a statement. The Central Powers' statement of democratic war aims, issued by Czernin on 25 December, ensured that Britain and France would have to respond.

Alongside these matters there was growing pressure from the Labour Movement. Concern over war aims was repeatedly expressed with other demands by Labour. Events in Russia served to heighten this concern. On 13 December Bowerman sent Lloyd George a resolution calling on the Government to 'make a public and authoritative declaration in very definite terms as to the aims and objects' of the Allies, which resolution the parliamentary Committee of the T.U.C. and National Executive Committee of the Labour Party were going to submit to a joint conference of their bodies on 28 December, and asked him for his decision on it.[28] After a further letter in which Bowerman reported doubts at the Allies' intentions Lloyd George declined to make a public statement without consulting other governments and reiterated in general terms the 'ideals . . . for which the British Empire entered the War'.[29] However, after the conference, at which a statement of war aims was adopted, a deputation saw Lloyd George. Lloyd George appears to have been well pleased with the meeting. He told his War Cabinet colleagues that it had been 'an interesting and successful interview' and that their

> view . . . seemed to coincide with that of the Government. They evinced no desire to throw over the demand of the French democracy with regard to Alsace–Lorraine, or to raise a quarrel with the Dominion Governments regarding the non-tropical colonies. With regard to German colonies north of the Zambesi, they agreed that they should not be handed back to the Germans, and advocated some super-national authority being established to administer them.[30]

This statement suggests that he had feared that Labour might have been willing to allow Germany to retain all these areas.

The Czernin statement forced Lloyd George quickly to make a public statement of war aims.[31] Though there are several indications in the days before it was issued that he was coming to feel this necessary.[32] The aim of Lloyd George's statement was 'to maintain our own public opinion and if possible lower that of the enemy', not to make serious peace overtures. In the War Cabinet Lloyd George was quite explicit that 'personally he did not believe that the enemy's statement was a *bona fide* peace offer. Its object was to sow dissension among the Allies and to rally the German people', and that his declaration would 'provide a counter-offensive' after 'the Germans had got their blow in first in this peace offensive'.[33] His counter-offensive carefully related the principle of self-determination to Europe not to the British Empire.[34] His failure to say much about Russia may well indicate that he was leaving open the possibility of negotiating a peace at Russia's expense if circumstances made it expedient as well as expressing his annoyance at Russia leaving the war. He spoke on these lines to the Webbs at the end of February, and in June was willing to no more than observe, 'Russia . . . must be left to take care of herself.'[35]

The Czernin statement may have forced him into rapid action, but the need to negotiate new manpower proposals with the unions was another major consideration for an early statement. Quite independent of all this Geddes had been urging that Lloyd George should 'read a carefully weighed statement' on war aims to the trade union leaders 'since it was understood that the trade unionists would raise the question of war aims' in the discussions on altering the Schedule of Protected Occupations.[36] The fact, that Lloyd George made his statement to a trade union meeting not Parliament was due to the latter not being in session; 'no other convenient opportunity' was available, and 'a statement to the trade unionists was desirable'.[37]

Auckland Geddes had a general conference on the new man-power proposals with all the trade unions on 3 January, and thereafter negotiated with the various trade groups.[38] The A.S E. refused to attend any further general conferences on the basis that the agreements that were now to be broken had been negotiated with them and that they felt there was no justification in taking skilled men before dilutees fit for general service. On 16 January Geddes urged Lloyd George to speak at a further general conference on the 18th, arguing that if he did not '. . . it will be said that the Government are wavering on the man-power proposals.'[39] Lloyd George attended it and reviewed the need for the new proposals and spoke again on war aims.[40] Whilst these negotiations were underway Geddes brought into the Commons the first Military Service Bill of 1918, which empowered the Minister of National Service to cancel exemptions on the basis of occupation and abolish a two months' period of grace which had been hitherto granted on the withdrawal of certificates of exemption. The Bill was rapidly pressed through Parliament before opposition to it could grow, despite requests by the Labour Party that it should not be hastily passed.[41] At the same time the Schedule of Protected Occupations was revised, which enabled almost a 'clean cut' to be made of men under twenty-three, and dilution officers were instructed that men were now to be taken before substitutes were provided.[42] These measures indicate that the Government increasingly made the supply of manpower for the army a higher priority than maintaining the planned output of key war industries.[43]

The Government's new policy received a hostile reception in many engineering and mining centres. There were many threats of strikes and several local strikes in late January, and every indication that the Rank and File Movement would rally discontent. The Cabinet had been very disinclined to see the A.S.E. separately,[44] but on 1 February the Cabinet were informed, 'It seemed certain that a strike would take place unless some means were devised to reopen negotiations . . . It appeared the whole of the press took a view opposed to the Government, and in such circumstances it would be difficult for the Government to refuse to meet the Engineers.' Geddes, who had offered to resign, was instructed not to 'close the door against negotiations with the Engineers'.[45]

However the Government soon felt its position strengthened by the conflict between the A.S.E. and the other unions. Geddes felt the difficulties would be overcome if the two groups could agree

> on the meaning of 'dilutee' . . . These unskilled unions wished to confine the meaning of 'dilutee' to those who were not working in or about engineering works before the War. It would not be possible to agree to the claim of the Engineers that all 'dilutees' should be taken first. The effect of doing so would be most seriously to hamper production. It would also be unjust, because it would discriminate unfavourably against older members of the unskilled unions.

Geddes reported that the other unions were urging their members 'on no account to strike' and observed that he 'was certain that the present conflict had had the effect of increasing the support obtained by the Government from these other unions'. The Cabinet decided to hold a conference of the other unions, and to be prepared if there should be 'a trial of strength with the Engineers' (as Churchill put it). They appointed a committee 'to consider the steps to be taken in the event of serious industrial trouble'.[46]

However though the A.S.E. continued to refuse to take part in a general conference there was no widespread outbreak of strikes. The A.S.E. held a ballot on their policy of opposing the Government manpower proposals until an agreement was reached by separate negotiations; and 81 per cent of those voting endorsed their line.[47] Nevertheless Geddes felt 'fairly safe just now in sitting tight' as the other unions were 'much incensed' by the A.S.E., it was 'from among their members that by far the greater number of recruits would be taken', A.S.E. apprentices were volunteering in large numbers anyway, and the $7\frac{1}{2}$ per cent award to piece-workers had contributed to the industrial situation being 'pretty good'.[48] When the A.S.E. telegrammed Lloyd George asking him to receive a deputation of delegates 'to consider the position of their organisation' Geddes saw no objection to him seeing them 'within the limits laid down in the telegram'.[49] When Lloyd George saw them on 28 February they gained no advantage from such a separate meeting. On 8 March Lloyd George saw them again and made it clear that he would give no guarantee that dilutees would be taken first.[50] In consequence of these meetings the A.S.E. took a ballot on whether the Government's proposals should be accepted, which, when it was announced, showed a small majority in favour. Meanwhile the Government, no doubt influenced by the failure of shop stewards on the Clyde to bring about a strike and the relative industrial calm, decided to prosecute John MacLean again for making speeches contravening the Defence of the Realm Act.[51]

The situation was transformed by the German offensive which began on 21 March. On the 23rd the War Cabinet instructed Geddes to prepare new manpower proposals and in so doing 'to bear in mind that the present military situation might afford an exceptional opportunity for overcoming difficulties that had hitherto proved insurmountable'.[52] Lloyd George later observed that the crisis measures taken that spring 'were measures which only that crisis rendered psychologically possible. Had any attempt been made to enforce them previously, it would have provoked civil disturbance and domestic collapse.'[53]

The second Military Service Act of 1918 (introduced on 9 April and taken through the Commons in a week) gave the Government power to do all the things they had hesitated in doing before.[54] It fixed the recruiting age limits at eighteen and fifty, gave the Government power to extend the operation of the Act to Ireland, and to extend the 'clean cut' on all but crucial work. The Government took the 'clean cut' up to twenty-three, though on Munitions and Admiralty work it was decided to operate it only to twenty-one.

This withdrawal of further labour from key industries had a serious effect on output. The greatest number were withdrawn from agriculture, and the Government was reconciled to no increase in food production.[55] Munitions production fell off as 1918 progressed, and by the autumn there were reports of plant and machinery standing idle and unskilled labour unemployed through lack of skilled supervisors.[56]

Perhaps the most dangerous drop in output was in coal mining where the Government pressed ahead with enlistment despite considerable opposition. There had been unrest in 1917 (notably in South Wales) when enlistment amongst miners had been extended; and the Coal Controller reminded the War Cabinet in July 'that the miners can be led but not driven' and warned, '. . . although it is not entirely absent, there is less unrest among the miners than among any other class of workmen and I believe this to be due to the fact that we have never broken a bargain with them and have always taken them into our confidence'.[57] The new Schedule of Protected Occupations of February 1918 aroused the opposition of the Miners' Federation, and they insisted on taking a ballot of their members. The War Cabinet authorised Geddes to continue recruiting regardless of this.[58] When the ballot showed 53 per cent were against the Government's proposals,

Lloyd George told them on 21 March that recruitment would continue in spite of it. On the 22nd Lloyd George addressed a delegate
meeting again. He spoke of the German offensive on a 57-mile
front, and said the miners and engineers could not be given a
privileged position.[59] The failure to obtain a two-thirds majority
against the proposals and the German offensive ensured that a
large withdrawal of miners for the army took place. In ensuing
months the Coal and Shipping Controllers repeatedly expressed
concern at the great loss of coal output, which seriously affected
fuel for domestic and war purposes. The situation was made worse
by strikes in South Wales and by a serious outbreak of influenza,
which in July alone cut output by nearly 3 million tons.[60] Lloyd
George launched a campaign to increase production on 10
August when he urged Welsh miners to 'hurl coal' at the enemy.[61]
Steps were taken to reduce consumption of coal, and eventually
miners were brought back from the army.[62]

The new situation during the German offensive led to an extension of the War Munitions Volunteer scheme, which brought
outright industrial compulsion much nearer. As Lloyd George
later observed, '. . . as the War progressed, social pressure and
economic measures taken by the Government combined to bring
about a state of affairs more and more nearly approximating' to
it.[63] It was deemed necessary to extend War Munitions Volunteer
in order to increase the mobility of the scarce skilled labour. New
proposals were put to the Trade Union Advisory Committee on
16 April.[64] Stephenson Kent informed them that 'the fitting of the
right men into the gaps which will be created by the withdrawal
of men for the Army' was becoming increasingly difficult,
especially since the abolition of leaving certificates, and that
'while industrial compulsion is not under contemplation, the
complete freedom of movement which skilled labour at present
enjoys must come under review'. The intention was that skilled
labour surplus to requirements in a particular factory would be
required to enrol as War Munition Volunteers or be enlisted in
the army. Dawtrey and Gorman said, in response, that the
Government should go ahead with their proposals and then offer
them to the Committee for simple acceptance or rejection; the
latter going as far as to say, 'What I am annoyed about it that a
Government Department should come to us and ask us for our
opinion when they ought to do something and the trade union
officials will back them up.' However, A. E. Smith brought them
back to a more cautious frame of mind, warning, 'If we . . . agree
to some form of industrial compulsion it is going to lead to a very
grave outburst of feeling . . . I know the vast majority of these

men are not going to have any extra restrictions put upon their freedom if they can possibly avoid it.' In consequence the Committee recognised the need for increased mobility without committing themselves to any details.

Churchill reported the views of the meeting in the most favourable light to the War Cabinet on the 24th.[65] Roberts said that 'he was in favour of the proposals, provided only moral pressure was used to secure enrolment. If there was any open threat of compulsion there was sure to be trouble.' Chamberlain echoed his fears, and the War Cabinet agreed that the proposals should be modified to remove the threat of compulsion.[66] On 5 June the Trade Union Advisory Committee agreed to urge trade unionists to enrol voluntarily – and sufficient men enrolled to avoid the need to force the Government to resort to compulsion.[67]

At the same time as the extension of the War Munition Volunteer scheme was made public (8 June), the Government announced another proposal to economise skilled labour. This was to use the D.O.R.A. regulations to restrict the employment of workmen in order that certain firms might not gain a disproportional quantity of skilled workmen. This policy was adopted as there were continued reports of 'the increase in demand for higher wages, the "auctioning" of labour amongst employers, and the continual migration of labour seeking the most favourable conditions' as skilled labour became even more scarce.[68] Geddes wrote to Lloyd George at the end of April urging the creation of a Manpower Ministry with sole control of labour supply, observing, '. . . the Admiralty, Ministry of Munitions, War Office contracts, Board of Agriculture, Ministry of Labour, National Service are all fishing in the same pool and the employers and the men are playing us off, one against the other'.[69] The Admiralty appears still to have been the worst offender, operating 'less stringent principles and standards' for dilution than the Ministry of Munitions.[70] As a consequence its factories attracted labour from elsewhere; in one instance one firm 'engaged on most urgent manufactures of range finders . . . lost 200 men to an Admiralty establishment next door where better protection from military service was expected'.[71] In the event the two proposals for regulating the supply of skilled labour were applied to the Admiralty's marine engine shops but not to its shipyards.

The embargo policy, on top of the workers' distrust of the Government's intentions and annoyance at a wide range of grievances, was the one addition necessary to spark off a serious strike. The strike took place at Coventry, where the Hotchkiss firm put out a notice which gave the misleading impression that preferential treatment would be given to all but 'skilled men of any type'.[72] It is not surprising that the scene of the strike should have been Coventry. Earlier, at a meeting of aircraft dilution officers, Coventry was cited as the prime example of a place with 'a great deal of excess labour' and hopes were expressed that the new Schedule of Protected Occupations 'will clear Coventry very much. There are roughly 43% of Class A recruitable men . . .'[73] A committee of the local officials of all the engineering unions demanded the withdrawal of the embargo on 12 July; when this was not done, the men handed in a week's notice on the 16th.

Churchill brought the matter before Lloyd George and the War Cabinet on the 16th.[74] He told them that he 'thought the present a good occasion on which to enforce the principle that if a man refused to do the special skilled work for which he was protected he should be conscripted, if fit, to fight', and observed that 'it would be an illegitimate use of the Military Service Acts to compel workmen to put up with industrial conditions against which they were striking in the ordinary way, but this was not an ordinary dispute between capital and labour'. Geddes also felt that 'as the threatened strike was one against recruiting it should not be tolerated' but warned that 'if, as seemed probable in the present temper of labour there was a widespread strike it would be physically impossible to conscript the thousands of men affected, while if it were possible it would have the effect of stopping output'. The War Cabinet endorsed Churchill's policy and authorised him to issue a warning statement to the strikers.

The Government made it clear that they would not negotiate with a local body or withdraw the embargo policy but would discuss the general problem of the most efficient use of skilled labour with the trade unions at a national level. The Coventry Joint Committee consequently called on the men to suspend their notices whilst a national conference was held to consider a general strike. Churchill told the War Cabinet on the 22nd that strikes were possible also in Manchester and Birmingham, and that so far he had refrained from making any public pronouncement.[75] The War Cabinet decided to take no action 'in order to see what developments took place in Coventry at the termination of the notices'. On the 23rd 10,000 engineers struck there, and the following day 12,000 men in Birmingham also came out.

In the face of what appeared to be the beginning of widespread strikes the War Cabinet determined on the 24th to take firm action.[76] Churchill urged that a statement of the Government's intention to withdraw protection from enlistment from strikers should be made at once as 'the general impression conveyed by the reports was one of hesitation, as if the men were not quite certain of their powers'. He felt that this should be issued before he saw the Trade Union Advisory Committee as 'it was useless to hope it would take a strong line'. Lloyd George pressed that 'there was no question of the Government going back on its announced policy, but only of deciding the precise moment at which to make a counter-offensive'. He emphasised 'the importance of the State winning the struggle with the strikers. If to put men into the Army would help the State to win, then they should not hesitate to use the Military Service Acts, but it was a mistake to extend unnecessarily the difficulties of the State'. Roberts urged 'that nothing should be done which would throw the trade unions into opposition' and so felt the Trade Union Advisory Committee should be consulted. After Shackleton also said he felt it should be consulted, Churchill made the suggestion that he would see them and 'invite them to endeavour to settle the dispute, which was a strike against them as much as against the State. They could assume the role of standing between the Government and labour, and could point out to the men that, unless the embargo scheme were allowed to operate the Government would have no alternative but to withdraw the exemptions from military service of the men on strike'. This policy was adopted.

Churchill put this to the Trade Union Advisory Committee the next day.[77] He emphasised that soon the prime need would be for munitions to equip the American troops, and so output must be maintained. He repeatedly urged, '. . . it would be a great advantage if the trade unions could thoroughly re-establish their control at this juncture' and that the Shop Stewards' Movement was 'subversive . . . not merely to Law and Order and the prosecution of the War, but to Labour progress'. Barnes and Roberts reiterated this theme, the former observing, 'It will be absolutely impossible for us to maintain trade unionism in this country if this sort of thing is to go on.' Several members of the Advisory Committee were equally impressed with the threat to their position by militants, and the Committee called the men to return to work and the Government to institute an inquiry into the causes of the strike. Lloyd George prepared a statement calling on the men to follow the Committee's advice by Monday, 29 July or they would be enlisted.[78] That he considered the situation to be critical is revealed by the almost hourly reports on the 26th from the engineering centres which are in his Papers.[79] The Government's firm policy settled the strikes.

The German offensive of March 1918 resulted in the enlistment of all possible men for the army, even at the cost of reducing essential production. On 30 August Lloyd George carefully analysed Britain's manpower position in a memorandum to Clemenceau, showing that she had exceeded her limit and had been compelled to return men to industry.[80] He concluded, 'The only way in which we can liberate more workers is if you and your Allies can dispense with the shipping, the coal, the steel and other supplies which are sent you at the present time.' Britain reached victory with her resources fully stretched, and with unrest growing amongst her industrial workers.

Conclusion

Lloyd George's relationship with the Labour Movement often hinged on his role in industrial relations. This was particularly true of the First World War when he was deeply involved in the widespread extension of state intervention in British industry. It is largely true of his long tenure of Cabinet positions (1905–22) as a whole.

Lloyd George's period as a Minister coincided with the rapid growth of state intervention in industrial relations. He was a major figure in this, as many of the posts he held dealt with labour matters. In view of the potentially disruptive effect of many of the strikes on the economy and on society any holder of such offices would have had to become involved. But Lloyd George's role was distinctive. At the Board of Trade he was much more disposed to intervene in disputes than his predecessors had been – and made considerable political capital out of these activities. Though Chancellor of the Exchequer, his widely recognised prowess as a negotiator brought him into several of the major pre-1914 strikes and greatly facilitated his taking the initiative in labour matters in the first winter of the First World War. His overriding commitment to victory and his early recognition of the economic implications of a major war between industrial powers led him to take a much tougher line on the organisation of labour both for industry and for the armed forces than his Liberal colleagues in the first war-time Coalition Government. His activities with regard to labour led him from the Exchequer to Munitions, then to the War Office, and were a major factor in his rise to the Premiership.

The First World War transformed the role of the State in industrial relations. Labour scarcity forced the Government to regulate its supply. This and other scarcities led to State control of large sections of the economy. As a result the State became a very large employer and had an even greater interest in collective bar-

gaining. The Government became increasingly involved in regulating wages and workshop conditions, as well as dealing with
industrial disputes to an unprecedented extent.

During the war there were also major changes in the relationship between the Government and the trade unions. The need to
organise Britain's industrial resources for modern warfare forced
the Government to consult the T.U.C. and the executives of the
key trade unions much more frequently—and to treat them with
much greater respect. Pro-War leaders of the Parliamentary
Labour Party entered the Government and eminent trade unionists
entered Government committees organising labour supply for
several key industries. In the case of the trade card scheme, certain
skilled unions were even briefly involved in administering an
aspect of conscription. There were pre-war precedents for unions
being consulted and involved in administration, notably with
insurance, but the change in the extent and importance of the
involvement of some major trade unions was dramatic. The
identification of these trade unions' leaders with Government
policy throughout the war encouraged the rise of 'unofficial' rank
and file movements in the unions. In sharp contrast there was no
such major split between the miners and their leaders, who
refused to become actually involved in the formulation or application of Government policy.

Lloyd George was a key figure in evolving a Government
policy towards strikers during the war. From the summer of 1915
he took pains to identify the trade union leaders with Government policies (notably on dilution), involving them in committees
and putting the onus on them to present alternatives to the threat
of industrial conscription, which faced them throughout the war.
When dealing with unofficial strikes after 1915, he generally supported the official trade union leadership at the national level and
avoided negotiating with unofficial bodies. He frequently followed
the principle of divide and rule: isolating militants and dividing
them from the trade union leadership and from moderates, playing
the unskilled workers off against the skilled, and splitting those in
favour of Britain's war effort from those opposing it. He increasingly recognised the need to maintain the support of public
opinion when dealing with strikes and took pains to remove grievances the public would deem to be intolerable. The widespread
working-class support for the war made it easier for him to take a
tough line on strikes in these years, but the question of war
priorities often limited such action. Thus, in the case of the Clyde
in early 1916, when the Government had a reserve of munitions
and could face a local dispute, the strike was smashed; but in May

1917, when faced with a national engineering strike before the summer campaign on the Western Front, major concessions were made.

After the War Lloyd George and the Government extended and developed these policies.[1] In the critical first half of 1919 Lloyd George induced many trade union leaders to participate in the National Industrial Council and the miners to accept the Sankey Commission; and later the Transport Workers agreed to the Shaw Inquiry. In the post-war period even greater care was taken to keep public opinion favourable to the Government. The Government spent considerable sums on propaganda against the Triple Alliance unions' strikes. Lloyd George himself was a master at publicising the Government's case in its best possible light – especially in his public letters to the miners in 1920 and 1921. After February 1919 the big strikes were official ones, and though he could not so easily play the rank and file off against the leadership, he successfully played the Triple Alliance unions off against one another. The main innovation after the end of the war was the evolution from February 1919 of the Government's strike-breaking organisation, based to a large degree on civilian volunteers rather than on the Forces. In a resurrected form this was to be used by the Government in 1926 during the General Strike.

Lloyd George was, however, politically harmed by his successes in the field of industrial relations. Many of his successes, especially earlier on, owed something to his reputation as a radical and social reformer, which made trade unionists better disposed to him than they would have been to a Tory Minister. But in time his industrial interventions earned him the distrust of important sections of the working class and soured his relationship with the Labour Movement as a whole. The extraordinary war-time measures (in particular the Munitions of War Act and conscription) which alienated large numbers of trade unionists were closely identified with his name. After the war the Sankey Commission, the treatment of the National Industrial Council, his branding of Labour Party leaders as 'Bolshevists' and the railway leaders as 'anarchists' did much to reinforce distrust of him in the Labour Movement. The State (and Lloyd George) increasingly appeared to be on the side of the employers – this was so in the 1912 coal strike and was most notably so in the 1921 strike. His record in industrial relations made it increasingly improbable that he could move over to the Left in British politics after the collapse of his Coalition Government.

But equally important in determining his ultimate political isolation was the dramatic change in the Labour Party. This was due not just to its growth in political power, as the Liberal Party disintegrated and failed to appear an alternative to the Tories, but also to the fundamental rethinking of policies. During the war the extension of state intervention in industry and industrial relations and the growth of Government control over the necessaries of life forced the whole Labour Movement, in bodies such as the War Emergency Workers' National Committee, to define its attitude to these matters. As Royden Harrison has observed, this led it to demand that the State '*should* manage the economy, and that it should manage it upon equalitarian lines'.[2] Linked to this, the need for the Labour Party to have its own reconstruction policy ensured that a wide range of policies were formulated in a collectivist spirit. These pressures were reinforced by the impact of the Russian Revolutions, which demonstrated the potential power of the working class. In the post-war period unemployment played a major part in rousing class consciousness amongst the working class, as it had done before the war. Fears of unemployment after the Armistice led to the successful reduction of working hours across many industries in 1919, the struggles against reductions in wages in 1920–2, and growing support for the Labour Party in national and local elections.

Whilst Lloyd George had appeared advanced in his views at the time of his Limehurst speech, after the war he increasingly appeared timid in contrast to the Labour Movement. To a large extent this was because his hopes for reconstruction were thwarted by the Tory strength in the massive Coalition parliamentary majority and by the international economic difficulties. But in part it was due to his limited views on social reform. Before taking office his career had been based largely on old-fashioned radical issues – temperance reform, disestablishment, devolution, and moderate land reform. The Liberal social reforms associated with his name, great as they were at the time, only alleviated poverty and did nothing to reshape the economic system which produced such inequality. Positive action was not taken to improve the overall standard of living of the working class. During most years of the Campbell-Bannerman and Asquith Governments the real standard of living of the working class fell. During the war Lloyd George failed to ensure that there was an equality of sacrifices between labour and capital. Government control of large sections of industry ensured that the companies concerned received guaranteed profits at a generous level; and control did not rule out what the Government itself deemed to be 'excess profits'. In contrast, for the working class the Government allowed a free market in prices but not in wages to exist until serious unrest modified this. The Government's policy of opposing wage increases (a policy which could be, and was, enforced by compulsory arbitration under the Munitions Act), despite rapidly rising prices, acerbated working-class discontent arising from other war-time measures.

It was not just a matter of who was most advanced in promoting social reform. Lloyd George was simply not in sympathy with the aspirations of the strongest elements in the Labour Movement. Whilst he maintained a strong sympathy for the underdog he never understood or sympathised with the aspirations of the skilled workers.[3] His appeal was never to the men in a strong trade union but to 'the average man who would suffer' from class war, and he urged that 'the interest of the vast majority of the people of this country rests in establishing a reign of strict fair play between all classes'.[4] Though he had no time for the landed interest or the more blatant capitalist, he became increasingly impressed with the self-made entrepreneur. Thus in September 1919 he observed, 'You cannot have adequate production unless you invoke the aid of the clever manufacturers and business men working for their own profit. But you must see that they do not get too much and . . . grind the other classes under their heel.'[5]

Indeed Lloyd George never fully understood the Labour Movement. He was more used to bargaining with leaders of interest groups, who were powers in their own right. Of course many of the Labour leaders carried great prestige, but Lloyd George made a mistake at the end of the war in feeling he could buy with office significant Labour support just as he could buy off a press baron or a difficult unionist like Carson. Once Barnes and the other Coalition Labour Ministers severed themselves from the Labour Movement they added little strength to his Ministry.

Lloyd George's relationship with the Labour Movement during the war and in his post-war Coalition Government ensured that, as the Liberal Party crumbled, he was isolated from the Left after 1922. His background, career and temperament equally alienated him from Stanley Baldwin's Toryism. He looked fruitlessly for developments in line with his past career. For a while he watched approvingly those elements of Mussolini's and Hitler's policies which seemed close to his old themes of efficiency and national purpose He harked back to the days of nonconformist leadership in politics with his Council of Action in 1934–5. But, isolated from Labour, even those constructive reassessments of social problems that he sponsored in the 1920s, were destined to fall on stony ground in Britain.

Appendix

APPENDIX

The South Wales Coal Strike, July 1915[1]

	Men's Original Demands	Government Determination	Final Settlement
1. Revision of Standard	The standard to be called that of 1915 and to equal 50% on the 1879 rate (and 35% on the 1897 standard).	Conceded in its general terms, i.e. 50% on the rates of 1879, other standards to be altered accordingly.	Conceded, except as regards anthracite areas which were to be subject to enquiry.
2. Minimum percentage above Standard	Wages not to fall below 10% above the standard: this minimum to be paid whenever the selling price of coal was at or below 15/6 a ton. No maximum to be fixed.	With reference to this demand Mr Runciman abolished both the minimum and the maximum. Further he declined to embody in the agreement any immediate percentage rise in wages, this he thought being best left to agreement between the parties.	Minimum of 10% above new standard rate but no equivalent selling price. No maximum.
3. Interpretation of Standard as regards underground day workers	In effect the demand was that in the case of such men the standard should be raised in all cases to at least 3s 4d + 50%, i.e. 5/- a day or higher where the establishment of the new standard would otherwise	According to his interpretation it was not intended that 'the alteration of the standard shall in itself effect an immediate rise in wages'. It was therefore left to the parties by agreement or failing that to an independent	Conceded except that doubtful cases where the rates were fixed under the Minimum Wage Act should be subject to the decision of an Arbitrator appointed by the Board of Trade.

4. *New Standard for Surface Workers*	The standard for these to be at least 3s 4d a day plus 50%.	Conceded for 'able bodied men as understood at the various collieries'.
5. *Men on Afternoon or Night Shifts*	To receive the equivalent of six 'turns' for each five worked.	Conceded.
6. *Hauliers employed on Afternoon or Night Shifts*	To receive the same as those on day shifts.	Conceded.
7. *Classes to be covered by Agreement*	All men employed in or about collieries.	Too technical for immediate decision. To be discussed at the meeting of the parties and if necessary settled by the Chairman mentioned above.	Agreement to apply to all workers now employed or who might hereafter be employed at the Collieries of the Owners *and who may be Members of the South Wales Miners' Federation*, i.e. to unionists only.
8. *Duration of Agreement*	Three years.	Left to the Board of Trade to decide, on application from either party, what date should be regarded as terminating war conditions and to settle what length of notice after that date should be given before the agreement expires.	The agreement to last until six months after the termination of the war and thereafter subject to three months' notice by one of the parties.

---

[1] Steel-Maitland Papers, GD 193/73/16. There is a similar analysis in the Ministry of Munitions Papers, MUN 5-79-341/11. Asquith informed the King that Runciman's proposals 'would have decided 5½ points out of 7 points in the men's favour; 19 July 1915; Asquith Papers, vol. 8, fo. 69.

Notes to the Text

Introduction

1. A point made as long ago as 1953 by W. S. Adams in 'Lloyd George and the Labour Movement', *Past and Present*, no. 3.
2. For Asa Briggs's recent defence of this concept see his introduction to A. Briggs and J. Saville (eds.), *Essays in Labour History 1886–1923* (1971), pp. 3–7.

I *The Welsh Radical*

1. *Welsh News*, 1 March 1917.
2. Lloyd George's contribution to a magazine series, 'In the Days of My Youth', September 1898; copy in Herbert Lewis Papers, 10/13. For more realistic appraisals see William George, *My Brother and I* (1958), p. 11, and *South Wales Daily News*, 1 March 1917.
3. A. J. P. Taylor (ed.), *Lloyd George: A Diary by Frances Stevenson* (1971), p. 31.
4. At the Welsh Baptist Union, 30 September 1895; *Carnarvon Herald*, 4 November 1895.
5. As early as 1895 (at Aberystwyth, 17 April) he was declaring himself in favour of women securing equal rights; *Carnarvon Herald*, 19 April 1895.
6. Speech at Cardiff, 11 October 1894; *Carnarvon Herald*, 12 October 1894.
7. At Carnarvon, 11 November 1890; *North Wales Observer*, 14 November 1890.
8. At Bangor, 12 November 1890; *Carnarvon Herald*, 14 November 1890. In 1886 he had been Secretary of the South Carnarvon branch of Gee and Parry's Anti-Tithe League. For this and the whole background of the Welsh nationalist revival, see K. O. Morgan's excellent *Wales in British Politics 1868–1922* (1963) and his valuable brief monograph, *David Lloyd George: Welsh Radical as World Statesman* (1964).
9. At Carnarvon, 5 July 1895; *North Wales Observer*, 12 July 1895.
10. At Chester, 16 June 1894; *Chester Guardian*, 23 June, 1894.
11. 9 January 1897; *South Wales Daily News*, 11 January 1897.

12. *House of Commons Debates* (hereafter *H.C.D.*), 4th series, vol. 40, cols. 237–40; 30 April 1896.

13. Ibid. col. 1638; 18 May 1896.

14. Thus at Conway on 25 November 1891 (*Carnarvon Herald*, 27 November 1891): 'The Conservatives have boasted of an increase in trade since Lord Salisbury has entered into power, but how about the wages of the working man? They are still degradingly low.'

15. At Bangor, 21 May 1891; *Carnarvon Herald*, 22 May 1891.

16. At Llandrindod, 21 August 1894; *North Wales Observer*, 23 August 1894.

17. Cited in H. Pelling, *Origins of the Labour Party* (1954), pp. 119–20.

18. At Newcastle, 4 April 1903; printed in his *Better Times* (1910), p. 2.

19. 'In Wales we want Disestablishment, land, temperance, educational and other reforms, but the most urgent question of the hour . . .' was devolution. At Llandrindod, 5 August 1898; *South Wales Daily News*, 6 August 1898.

20. On 20 September 1894; *Merthyr Express*, 22 September 1894.

21. 'The Liberal policy is no more subsidies, no more grants, but the power to the people to work out their own salvation.' 17 January 1895; *South Wales Daily News*, 18 January 1895.

22. At Maestag, 15 October 1891; *North Wales Observer*, 16 October 1891.

23. Lloyd George to Tom Ellis, 27 November 1890; Ellis Papers, fo. 682. He urged it as the foremost issue in his speeches at this time.

24. At Merthyr, 20 September 1894; *Merthyr Express*, 22 September 1894. This speech is a striking contrast to his earlier position: 'The temperance question must not be deferred; temperance reform must precede all other social reforms. What is the use of reducing the working hours of the people, for example, unless the reform is accompanied by prohibition. Increased leisure will simply mean increased opportunities that will lead to intemperance.' *Carnarvon Herald*, 24 November 1890.

25. See, for example, Keir Hardie in the *Labour Leader*, 14 January 1899.

26. At Bangor, 15 December 1896; *North Wales Observer*, 18 December 1896.

27. See V. L. Allen, *Trade Unions and the Government* (1960), pp. 46–7, for a discussion of these.

28. The threat of strikes to the economy increasingly emerged as an argument for Government intervention in industrial relations by the 1890s. Thus a motion in the Commons in 1890 calling for compulsory arbitration spoke of strikes being 'prejudicial . . . to the producing power of the country'. Cited in E. Phelps Brown, *The Growth of British Industrial Relations* (1959), p. 188. Nevertheless, by later standards the numbers of days lost remained small.

29. J. H. Porter, 'Wage Bargaining under Conciliation Agreements, 1860–1914', *Economic History Review* (1970), pp. 460–75.

30. For details, see H. Clegg, A. Fox and A. H. Thompson, *A History of Trade Unionism*, vol. 1, *1889–1910* (1964), p. 108.

31. *H.C.D.*, 4th series, vol. 33, col. 962; 10 May 1895. He had made earlier attempts to get the matter discussed on 25 April, ibid. vol. 32, cols. 1605–9, and 9 May, ibid. vol. 33, cols. 782–3.

32. 10 May, ibid. cols. 963–4.

33. Ibid. col. 991.

34. Ibid. col. 971. Sentiments endorsed by G. J. Goschen, Chancellor of the Exchequer in the recent Tory Government, ibid. col. 985.

35. Ibid. cols. 994–5.

36. At Carnarvon, 5 July 1895; *North Wales Observer*, 12 July 1895.

37. Cited in H. Du Parq, *Life of David Lloyd George*, vol. 1 (1912), p. 174.

38. At Holywell, 19 November 1894; *Carnarvon Herald*, 23 November 1894. See his letter to his wife, at the time of the earlier incident 8 April 1892, in K. O. Morgan (ed.), *Lloyd George: Family Letters 1885–1936* (1973), pp. 47–8 (hereafter cited as *Family Letters*).

39. At Llandrindod, 24 October 1894; *Carnarvon Herald*, 26 October 1894.

40. 16 November 1894; *Carnarvon Herald*, 23 November 1894.

41. Entry of 5 February 1895, Welsh Parliamentary Party Minute Book 1890–95; J. H. Lewis Papers, part 2, fo. 15.

42. See J. Roose Williams, 'Quarrymen's Champion', *Carnarvonshire Historical Society Transactions*, vols. 23–6 (1962–5), and J. Lindsay, *A History of the North Wales Slate Industry* (1974), chs. 10 and 13.

43. Lord Askwith, *Industrial Problems and Disputes* (1920), pp. 80–1.

44. At Carnarvon, 12 August 1893; *North Wales Observer*, 18 August 1893. Lloyd George was but one of the local M.P.s to whom the quarrymen turned. See their Secretary's letters to Tom Ellis, 22 July and 5 August 1893; Ellis Papers, fos. 2132 and 2133.

45. At Rhyl, 6 January 1897; *Rhyl Recorder and Advertiser*, 9 January 1897.

46. On 2 January 1897; *Merioneth News*, 7 January 1897.

47. Ibid.

48. *Trade Union Congress Report for 1902*, p. 64.

49. Roose Williams, 'Quarrymen's Champion'.

50. 28 April 1903; *Daily Chronicle*, 29 April 1903. He particularly heavily marked the passage, 'It is as if a big English landlord, owning some big town like Devonport, were to give notice to quit to the whole population' in his copy of the pamphlet 'Penrhyn Quarry Dispute – Sir Edward Clarke's Negotiations, March 1903', Lloyd George Papers, A/5/10.

51. At Carnarvon, 12 August 1893; *North Wales Observer*, 18 August 1893.

52. 22 January 1892; *North Wales Observer*, 29 January 1892.

53. 3 May 1897; *North Wales Observer*, 7 May 1897.

54. 9 January 1897; *Carnarvon Herald*, 15 January 1897. I have italicised the radical-nationalist emotive words and phrases to illustrate Lloyd George's rhetoric.
55. Cited in Phelps Brown, *Growth of British Industrial Relations*, p. 202.
56. 4 August 1892; *North Wales Observer*, 12 August 1892.
57. 31 January 1894; *North Wales Observer*, 2 February 1894.
58. *H.C.D.*, 4th series, vol. 42, col. 1642; 16 July 1896.
59. At Huddersfield, 6 May 1905; *Huddersfield Daily Examiner*, 8 May 1905.

II *Lloyd George, Labour and social reform*

1. At Liverpool, 30 November 1900; *Liverpool Mercury*, 1 December 1900.
2. See for example, the 'Brutus' articles he wrote in his youth; Du Parq, *Life of David Lloyd George*, vol. 1, pp. 34–9.
3. Editorial in the *Labour Leader*, 6 January 1900.
4. For examples see his speech at Nottingham, *Nottingham Daily Press*, 28 March 1900; in Kings Road, Chelsea, *Daily News*, 17 February 1902; and on the text 'Thou shalt not steal' at Swansea, *Cambria Daily Leader*, 26 April 1902.
5. Cited in Du Parq, *Life*, p. 218.
6. On 18 May 1901; *Oswestry and Border Counties Advertiser*, 23 May 1901.
7. Cited in P. Poirier, *The Advent of the Labour Party* (1958), p. 165.
8. *The Young Man*, March 1903.
9. One of the best examples is his address to the Leicester Federation of Free Churches on 26 March 1900; *Leicester Daily Post*, 27 March 1900. No doubt part of his purpose in making these speeches was to keep as much Nonconformist support as possible whilst he carried on his campaign against the Boer War.
10. Thus at the end of 1903 Campbell-Bannerman spoke at Tredegar of sectarianism as 'the taunt constantly hurled at Mr. Lloyd George and his friends – Mr. Lloyd George your foremost champion, yes, and the champion of us all – against clerical pretensions and political injustice'. Du Parq, *Life*, p. 369.
11. A frequent statement in the country and in Parliament. Examples: at Pwllheli, 3 April 1902, *North Wales Observer*, 4 April 1902; and during the second reading of the Education Bill, 8 May 1902, *H.C.D.* 4th series, vol. 107, cols. 1098–1116.
12. For example at Criccieth, 12 May 1902, he warned of a return of Roman Catholicism; *Carnarvon Herald*, 16 May 1902.
13. Ripon to Campbell-Bannerman, 30 May 1903; Ripon Papers, 43, 518, fo. 13.
14. On 9 January 1892; *Pontypridd Chronicle*, 15 January 1892. His 1903–6 anti tariff speeches were similar.
15. On 10 October 1903; *Oldham Chronicle*, 17 October 1903.

16. But Snowden did recognise that Free Trade was no panacea for social and economic problems. He felt merely 'to exchange Free Trade for Protection would aggrevate every social evil and inequality'; L.R.C., *Annual Conference Report 1904*, p. 41.

17. Ibid p. 21.

18. In the space for the editorial, *Labour Leader*, 7 March 1903. The appeal to Morley was captioned, 'On the Banks of the Rubicon'; ibid. 16 June 1900. The appeal to Burns was in the issue of 28 March 1903.

19. *The I.L.P. Programme*, published January 1899; cited in Poirier, *Advent of the Labour Party*, p. 114. Shackleton also made use of the 'Independence not isolation' phrase at the 1905 L.R.C. Conference.

20. *Labour Leader*, 4 March 1899.

21. Ibid. 20 May 1899. With the deep split in the Liberal Party and much talk going on of a coalition for 'National Efficiency' a Rosebery–Chamberlain alliance was a stronger possibility than usual.

22. Ibid. 4 August 1900. Glasier had first raised the question of a 'White List' in the *Clarion* in May; Poirier, *Advent of the Labour Party*, pp. 124–5. Dr Clarke, a champion of many Left-wing causes, helped to found the Scottish Labour Party.

23. *Labour Leader*, 1 September 1900.

24. Hardie and MacDonald's relations with the Lib-Labs and with erring independents such as Bell are described in F. Bealey and H. Pelling, *Labour and Politics 1900–06* (1958), and Poirier, *Advent of the Labour Party*.

25. On 26 July 1904 at the time of the Welsh rate revolt; Samuel Papers, A/157/213.

26. See the letters in the Campbell-Bannerman and Herbert Gladstone Papers of this period. For Grey's approach to him with regard to the Relugas Pact, see *Family Letters*, p. 140.

27. Diary entry for 10 October 1914; Lord Riddell, *War Diary* (1933), p. 35.

28. On the occasion of Davitt's visit; *Cambrian News*, 12 February 1886.

29. Thus at Carnarvon on 23 November 1891: 'Let the working men of the Boroughs be thoroughly imbued with Liberal principles, and I will defy any influence, be it of the Castle or Mansion, to bend them or lead them astray'; *North Wales Observer*, 30 October 1891.

30. At Bangor, 21 May 1891; *Carnarvon Herald*, 22 May 1891.

31. At Bethesda, 22 October 1892; *North Wales Observer*, 28 October 1892. The italics are mine.

32. L.R.C., *Annual Conference Report* (1902), p. 11.

33. On 4 April 1903; *Newcastle Daily Reader*, 6 April 1903.

34. 18 October 1904; *Carnarvon Herald*, 21 October 1904.

35. Grey to Herbert Gladstone, 18 September 1903; Herbert Gladstone Papers, 45, 992. fo. 100.

36. 19 November 1903; *Falkirk Herald*, 21 November 1903.
37. At a National Reform Union meeting at Bacup on 5 November 1904; *Manchester Guardian*, 7 November 1904.
38. At the Eastern Counties Liberal Federation meeting; *Lincoln Leader*, 13 December 1902.
39. In a Southport Baptist Chapel on 5 March 1908; *Southport Guardian*, 7 March 1908.
40. See his speech of 8 January 1906 at Darlington, *Northern Echo*, 10 January 1906; and at Middlesborough in support of Havelock Wilson on 9 January; *North Eastern Daily Gazette*, 10 January 1906.
41. At Cardiff on 11 October 1906; reprinted in *Better Times*, pp. 30–6.
42. At Madeley, 1 November 1907; *Wellington Journal and Shrewsbury News*, 2 November 1907.
43. Gladstone to Campbell-Bannerman, 9 November 1904; Campbell-Bannerman Papers, 41, 217, fos. 139–40.
44. Campbell-Bannerman to Gladstone, 23 November 1904; Herbert Gladstone Papers, 45, 988, fo. 129.
45. Campbell-Bannerman to Gladstone, 29 November 1904; Campbell-Bannerman Papers, 41, 217, fos. 141–2.
46. At Bangor, 22nd December 1905; *Carnarvon Herald*, 29 December 1905.
47. Campbell-Bannerman to the King on the day's Cabinet meeting, 14 December 1905; Campbell-Bannerman Papers, 52, 512.
48. Knollys to John Burns, 6 February 1906; Burns Papers, 46, 281, fo. 6.
49. Campbell-Bannerman to the King, 18 July 1906; Campbell-Bannerman Papers, 52, 512.
50. Asquith's Cabinet Report to the King, 11 March 1908; Asquith Papers, vol. 5, fo. 14. The history of this almost perennial Bill and Labour agitation generally on the issue are examined in K. D. Brown, *Labour and Unemployment 1900–14* (1971).
51. Burns diary, 11 March 1908; Burns Papers, 46, 326. See Brown, *Labour and Unemployment*, pp. 90–1.
52. Speaking on behalf of Churchill at a by-election on 21 April 1908; *Manchester Guardian*, 22 April 1908.
53. Ibid.
54. Herbert Lewis diary, 8 September 1908; J. H. Lewis Papers, 10/131/79. Though, as Jose Harris observes in her excellent study *Unemployment and Politics* (1972), p. 276, the idea had been discussed in the Royal Commission on the Poor Laws well before the German visit.
55. Lord Riddell, *More Pages from My Diary 1908–14* (1934), p. 3.
56. Arthur Murray, *Master and Brother* (1945), p. 88. For the development of unemployment insurance see B. B. Gilbert, *The Evolution of National Insurance in Great Britain*, ch. 5.
57. Lloyd George to Elibank, 17 April 1911; Elibank Papers 8802,

fos. 209–14. The memorandum printed in *Master and Brother*, pp. 88–9, appears to be a summary of this letter.

58. Lloyd George to McKenna, 11 September 1908; McKenna Papers MCKN 3/20/1.

59. McKenna to Lloyd George, 12 September 1908; ibid MCKN 3/20/4.

60. Churchill to McKenna, 19 September 1908 and McKenna to Churchill, 24 September 1908; ibid. MCKN 3/20/8 and 3/20/11.

61. Asquith's Cabinet Report to the King, 20 October 1908; Asquith Papers, vol. 5, fos. 55–6.

62. Herbert Lewis diary, 8 September 1908; J. H. Lewis Papers, 10/131/79.

63. Burns to Asquith, 2 November 1908; Burns Papers, 46, 282, fo. 67.

64. Lucy Masterman, *C. F. G. Masterman* (1939), p. 111.

65. See the Cabinet paper, 'The Unemployed', 17 October 1908; CAB 37/95.

66. Masterman, *C. F. G. Masterman*; Brown, *Labour and Unemployment*, p. 104; J. Harris, *Unemployment and Politics* (1972), p. 275.

67. Asquith to the King, 20 October 1908; Asquith Papers, vol. 5, fos. 55–6.

68. Asquith's Cabinet Report to the King, 28 October 1908; Asquith Papers, vol. 5, fo. 57.

69. *North Wales Observer*, 28 September 1906.

70. As at Carnarvon on 10 July 1901; *North Wales Observer*, 12 July 1901.

71. At Glasgow, whilst supporting Asquith's candidature for the Rectorship of the University, 1 November 1905; *Glasgow Herald*, 2 November 1905.

72. At Criccieth, 28 June 1892; see complementary reports in the *Carnarvon Herald*, 1 July and *North Wales Observer*, 8 July 1892.

73. At Carnarvon on 5 July and at Holywell on 10 July 1895; *North Wales Observer* and *Flintshire County Herald*, both 12 July 1895.

74. See his letters to his wife of 21 and 26 July 1899, in *Family Letters*, pp. 117–18.

75. At Carnarvon, 18 January 1906; *North Wales Observer*, 26 January 1906.

76. G. J. Shaw-Lefevre to Campbell-Bannerman, 11 April 1907; Campbell-Bannerman Papers, 41, 227, fos. 261–2.

77. Alfred Emmott's diary 1907–11, fo. 24; Emmott Papers, vol. 1.

78. William George, *My Brother and I*, p. 220; cited Gilbert, *Evolution of National Insurance*, p. 219.

79. During the second reading, 15 June 1908; *H.C.D.*, vol. 190, col. 565.

80. *H.C.D.*, vol. 189, col. 871; 25 May 1908.

81. See Gilbert, *Evolution of National Insurance*, pp. 223–4.

82. Dated 19 May 1908; CAB 37/93/62.

83. Asquith Papers, vol. 5, fos. 25–6.

84. William George, *My Brother and I*, p. 221. For the 1908 controversy in the Cabinet over the dreadnought programme see A. J. Marder, *From the Dreadnought to Scapa Flow: Volume I, The Road to War 1904–14* (1961), pp. 138–43.
85. *H.C.D.*, 4th series, vol. 189, col. 1662; 1 June 1908.
86. Ibid. col. 869; 25 May 1908.
87. For a recent discussion of the budget see B. K. Murray, 'The Politics of "The People's Budget"', *The Historical Journal*, vol. 16 (1973), pp. 571–96.
88. Asquith's Cabinet Report to the King; Asquith Papers, vol. 5, fo. 94.
89. Diary entry for 27 May 1912; *More Pages*, p. 65.
90. Herbert Lewis's diary, 8 September 1908; J. H. Lewis Papers, 10/131/81.
91. Lloyd George to Spender, 16 July 1909; Spender Papers, 46, fos. 388 ff. For the Cardiff speech, *South Wales Daily News*, 22 December 1909.
92. Herbert Samuel to Herbert Gladstone, 29 April 1909; Herbert Gladstone Papers, 45, 992, fo. 219.
93. Herbert Samuel to Herbert Gladstone, 12 May 1909; ibid. fo. 222.
94. See for example Elibank to Knollys, 7 November 1906, on Dundee; Elibank Papers, 8801, fos. 99–102. Also F. C. Gardiner to Bonar Law, 22 November 1907, on the Clyde area; Bonar Law Papers, 18/3/47. There is an important memorandum on the overall position in Scotland, prepared for Asquith in February 1908; copy in the Elibank Papers, 8801, fos. 145–51. There is an equally important one (apparently by Vernon Hartshorn) on Wales in Lloyd George Papers (hereafter L.G.) C/17/4/1.
95. This is Philip Snowden's description; *An Autobiography* (2 vols., 1934), p. 199.
96. Herbert Samuel to Herbert Gladstone, 22 January 1910; Herbert Gladstone Papers, 45, 992, fo. 235. Samuel's views on these voting patterns are confirmed in the analysis by N. Blewett, *The Peers, the Parties and the People* (1972), pp. 110–11 and 404–6.
97. The earlier remark was on 25 May 1908; *H.C.D.*, 4th series, vol. 189, col. 872. The later on 15 June 1908; ibid. vol. 190, col. 585.
98. *Manchester Guardian*, 22 April 1908.
99. See the excellent account in Gilbert, *Evolution of National Insurance*, pp. 289–399.
100. This example, 18 January 1910; *Montgomeryshire Express*, 25 January 1910. He was equally fervent in the Commons when introducing the 1909 budget on 29 April; *H.C.D.*, 5th series, vol. 4, cols. 483–5. The Board of Trade letter is dated 22 December 1905; BT–20–1440.
101. Reprinted in *Better Times*, pp. 48–59.
102. Riddell's diary entry for 31 October 1908; Riddell, *More Pages*, p. 6. For an example of the latter, see the letter to Dawson, 23 December 1908; W. H. Dawson Papers, 173.

I

103. Lloyd George's coalition proposals have been admirably analysed in G. R. Searle, *The Quest for National Efficiency* (1971), pp. 177–204. See also Gilbert, *Evolution of National Insurance*, pp. 326–32.

104. Crewe and Grey to Asquith, 22 and 26 October 1910; Asquith Papers, vol. 12, fos. 197 and 214 respectively.

105. *The Times*, 18 October 1910.

106. Herbert Lewis's diary, 10 April 1911; J. H. Lewis Papers, 10/131/100.

107. For details of the drawing up of the Bill see Sir H. N. Bunbury (ed.), *Lloyd George's Ambulance Wagon: the Memoirs of William J. Braithwaite, 1911–12* (1957), R. W. Harris, *Not So Humdrum* (1939), pp. 113–89, and Lloyd George's letters to Elibank (undated); Elibank Papers, 8802, fo. 368 and fos. 369–72.

108. Herbert Lewis's report of Lloyd George's conversation, his diary entry, 7 April 1911. However on the 10th Asquith was reported as being 'now very strongly in favour of the scheme'; J. H. Lewis Papers, 10/131/99 and 100.

109. See C. P. Scott's diary entries for 15 and 21 June 1911; C. P. Scott Papers, 50, 901, fo. 13 and fos. 17–18.

110. P. Rowland, *The Last Liberal Governments*, vol. 2: *Unfinished Business 1911–14* (1971), p. 56.

111. Elibank to Lloyd George, 5 October 1911; L.G. C/6/5/5. Cited in Owen, *Tempestuous Journey*, pp. 207–8 and Rowland, *The Last Liberal Governments*, vol. 2, p. 76.

112. MacDonald to Elibank, 9 October 1911; Elibank Papers, 8802, fos. 336–7.

113. Diary, 6 January 1912; Elibank Papers, 8814, fos. 55–6.

114. Clifford Sharp to Beatrice Webb, 6 March 1912; Passfield Papers, 2 f, fo. 59.

115. At Bath, 24 November 1912; *Manchester Guardian*, 25 November 1912. The Liberals' land proposals are discussed in H. V. Emy, 'The Land Campaign: Lloyd George as a Social Reformer 1909–14', in A. J. P. Taylor (ed.), *Lloyd George: Twelve Essays* (1971), pp. 35–68, and his book, *Liberals, Radicals and Social Politics 1892–1914* (1973), ch. 6.

116. Arthur Murray's diary, 19 July 1912; Elibank Papers, 8814, fo. 84. See also Robert Cecil to Bonar Law, 20 July 1912; Bonar Law Papers, 26/5/32.

117. See, for example, Arthur Murray's diary, 25 July 1912; Elibank Papers, 8814, fo. 85.

118. Riddell, *More Pages*, p. 64. For the Cabinet see Runciman's letter to his wife 24 July 1912; Runciman Papers, WR 303.

119. Speech to a deputation of the slate trade, 30 May 1914; *Manchester Guardian*, 1 June 1914.

120. D. A. Reader, 'The Politics of Urban Leaseholds in Late Victorian England', *International Review of Social History*, vol. 6 (1961), pp. 429–30.

121. On 8 November 1913; *Manchester Guardian*, 10 November 1913.

122. C. P. Scott's diary, 16 January 1913; published in T. Wilson (ed.), *The Political Diaries of C. P. Scott 1911–28* (1970), p. 69.
123. Ibid.
124. See Riddell's diary entry, 19 June 1912; *More Pages*, p. 70.
125. C. P. Scott's diary, 3 February 1913; C. P. Scott Papers, 50, 901, fo. 89.
126. Herbert Lewis's diary, 22 September 1912; J. H. Lewis Papers, 10/131/105.
127. At Middlesbrough, 8 November 1913; *Manchester Guardian*, 10 November 1913.
128. See, for example, Riddell's diary, 9 July 1913; *More Pages*, p. 168.
129. Speech of 29 November 1913; *Manchester Guardian*, 1 December 1913.
130. Donald Read suggests that Liberal performances in rural areas in 1913 by-elections were improved a little by it; *Edwardian England* (1972), p. 192.
131. Llewellyn Davies to Lloyd George, 4 August 1912; L.G. C/9/3/10.
132. See for example the letter from Talbot and Steel-Maitland to Morrison-Bell, 30 October 1913; Carson Papers, D 1507/1/1913/7.
133. Riddell's diary, 1 July 1912; *More Pages*, p. 77. Churchill remained favourable to such ideas after the secret coalition proposals. See his letter to Asquith, 3 January 1911; Asquith Papers, vol. 13, fo. 3; and *More Pages*, p. 130 (21 March 1913).
134. For very explicit utterances to F. E. Smith see his letter of 6 October 1913; L.G. C/3/7/2. This speech was given at the National Liberal Club, 17 January 1913; *Manchester Guardian*, 18 January 1913. He also extolled a Party truce at Oxford on 21 November 1913; *Oxford Chronicle*, 28 November 1913.
135. On Wales see K. O. Morgan, 'The New Liberalism and the Challenge of Labour: the Welsh Experience 1885–1929', in K. D. Brown (ed.), *Essays in Anti-Labour History* (1974), pp. 159–82. On Lancashire see P. Clarke, *Lancashire and the New Liberalism* (1971).
136. Blewett, *The Peers, the Parties and the People*, pp. 234–65 and 389–95.
137. For London as a whole see P. Thompson, *Socialists, Liberals and Labour. The Struggle for London 1885–1914* (1966), and for one working-class area see C. J. Wrigley, 'Liberals and the Desire for Working Class Representatives in Battersea 1886–1922', in Brown (ed.), *Essays in Anti-Labour History*, pp. 126–58 (which emphasises the importance of unemployment in the growth of support for Labour). Labour's strength was also growing very markedly in industrial areas such as South Wales and the Clyde.
138. C. F. G. Masterman, 'Liberalism and Labour', *The Nineteenth Century* (November 1906).
139. On 29 November 1912; *Aberdeen Free Press*, 30 November 1912.
140. See Esher's journal of 4 October 1911; Viscount Esher (ed.), *The*

Journals and Letters of Reginald, Viscount Esher, vol. 3: *1910–15* (1938), p. 61.

141. Beatrice Webb's diary, 30 November 1910, printed in her *Ovr Partnership* (1948), p. 465.

142. 6 July 1912; Riddell, *More Pages*, p. 79.

143. Riddell's diary, 2 July 1912; ibid. p. 76.

144. Thus W. S. Sanders, writing to Sidney Webb on 19 April 1912, observed; 'MacDonald appears to be taken in by George every time he sees him on business.' Passfield Papers, vol. 2, f, fos. 102–3.

145. In the *Christian Commonwealth*, 2 February 1910; cited in S. E. Hassam, 'The Parliamentary Labour Party and its Relations with the Liberals 1910–14' (Aberdeen M. Litt. Thesis, 1967), p. 26.

146. Beatrice Webb to Betty Balfour, 22 August 1913; Passfield Papers, vol. 2, f, fos. 153–4.

147. K. O. Morgan article, in Brown (ed.), *Essays in Anti-Labour History*, p. 170. Henderson thought such a move had occurred at the time of the 1910 secret coalition talks, but this was doubted by Lord Elton (who discussed this with Lloyd George, Churchill and Crewe). Most likely Henderson was thinking of 1913. See Mary Agnes Hamilton, *Arthur Henderson* (1938), p. 74 and Lord Elton, *The Life of James Ramsay MacDonald* (1939), p. 184.

148. Cited by Roy Douglas, 'Labour in Decline 1910–14', p. 122, in K. D. Brown (ed.), *Essays in Anti-Labour History*, pp. 105–25.

149. *Observer*, 16 June 1912. Over the 1914 naval estimates Haldane for one felt that Lloyd George felt 'some personal desire to break away from the Government and to take the lead of the Radical and Labour Party'. Esher to the King, 6 January 1914; Esher, *Journals and Letters*, vol. 3, p. 151. See also A. J. P. Taylor, *The Struggle for Mastery in Europe 1848–1918* (1954), p. 513.

150. As F. W. Wiemann has suggested in his, 'Lloyd George and the Struggle for the Navy Estimates of 1914', in A. J. P. Taylor (ed.), *Lloyd George: Twelve Essays* (1971), pp. 81–2 and 84.

151. Masterman, *C. F. G. Masterman*, p. 235.

152. Lloyd George to Addison, 10 November 1913; L.G. C/10/2/24. See also his role in the Cabinet, Asquith to the King, 12 November 1913; Asquith Papers, vol. 7, fo. 69. He took a similar line on the subject of the Triple Alliance in July 1914; Herbert Lewis's diary, 21 July 1914; J. H. Lewis Papers, 10/131/109.

III *Trade and Industrial relations*

1. Though joking, it was with pride, he told an audience at Carnarvon on 21 December 1905, 'It has been said that I am the first Welshman to be a member of the Cabinet since the days of Archbishop Williams'; *Carnarvon Herald*, 22 December 1905. See also his speech the same day at Rhyl; *North Wales Observer*, 29 December 1905.

2. Herbert Lewis's diary, 18 May 1907; J. H. Lewis Papers, 10/131/56. For Lloyd George's Cabinet paper on the subject, see CAB 37/83/56.

3. 28 June 1907.

4. At a dinner at the Trocadero on 20 November; *Shipping Gazette and Lloyd's List*, 21 November 1906. He repeated these sentiments at a banquet of the Walsall Chamber of Commerce on 28 January 1907; *Walsall Observer*, 2 February 1907.

5. At the December Eastern Counties Liberal Federation Meeting; *Lincoln Leader*, 13 December 1902.

6. 29 August 1907.

7. Llewellyn Smith to Lloyd George, 24 December 1907; L.G. B/1/1/10. Lloyd George apparently did not anticipate the administrative difficulties involved; Llewellyn Smith commented, '. . . you were rather startled when I hinted that the existing staff without further expert statistical aid are not . . . capable of taking a Census which will be creditable to the Board of Trade'.

8. Report of a meeting with M.P.s, 25 October 1906; B.T. 11–2–6378.

9. Lloyd George's Cabinet paper, 5 December 1907; CAB 37/90/ 107.

10. Speech at a dinner at the Trocadero on 20 November 1906; *Shipping Gazette and Lloyd's List*, 21 November 1906.

11. Owners' pamphlet by Norman Hill in a file with the Draft Bill and other outside comments on the Bill: B.T. 13–40–E18003.

12. However the case against Lloyd George was exaggerated by Hyndman in a speech to the British Socialist Party on 14 April 1913, reprinted as a pamphlet, *The Official Murdering of British Seamen by Lloyd George, the Liberal Government and the Board of Trade*. See also his *Further Reminiscences* (1912), pp. 495–8. The proceedings of the British Socialist Party meeting have been rather uncritically used in a sensational account in D. McCormick's, *The Mask of Merlin* (1963), pp. 58–9.

13. For Lloyd George's justification of raising the load line see *H.C.D.*, 4th series, vol. 165, col. 237; 16 November 1906. For the benefits to sailors see his comments in the Commons, 23 October 1906; *H.C.D.*, 4th series, vol. 163, cols. 162–3; and his jubilant letter home 'Shipowners and Sailors blessed the Bill'; 21 March 1906, George, *My Brother and I*, p. 208.

14. Owners' pamphlet by Norman Hill in a file with the draft Bill and other outside comments on the Bill; B.T. 13–40–E18003.

15. This Act also stemmed from the report of a commission set up by the Balfour Government. Lloyd George certainly took a nationalist approach to these matters, though the inspiration may well have come from within the Board of Trade. See Halevy, *The Rule of Democracy 1905–14* (1932, paperback 1961), p. 104.

16. *An Economic History of Modern Britain*, vol. 3 (1938), p. 435.

17. Askwith, *Industrial Problems and Disputes*, pp. 103–8; Halevy, *Rule of Democracy*, pp. 106–7.

18. The best accounts are Phelps Brown, *Growth of British Industrial Relations*, pp. 298–302; Clegg, Fox and Thompson, *History of Trade Unionism*, pp. 423–7; Halevy, *Rule of Democracy*, pp. 107–14; P. Bagwell, *The Railwaymen* (1963), pp. 262–73; P. S. Gupta, 'The History of the Amalgamated Society of Railway Servants 1871–1913' (Oxford D. Phil., 1960), ch. 11.

19. 19 October 1907, pp. 1754–5.

20. Bagwell, *The Railwaymen*, p. 262.

21. Halevy, *Rule of Democracy*, p. 109; Phelps Brown, *Growth of British Industrial Relations*, p. 299.

22. Gupta, 'History of the A.S.R.S.', fos. 367–85.

23. The Secretary of A.S.L.E.F., on the contrary, felt this to be comparatively unimportant; Clegg, Fox and Thompson, *History of Trade Unionism*, p. 423. For the programme see *Report on the Strikes and Lockouts of 1907*, Cd. 4254 (1908), p. 49.

24. 19 October 1907, p. 1754.

25. Herbert Lewis's diary, 30 December 1906; J. H. Lewis Papers, 10/131/49.

26. *H.C.D.*, 4th series, vol. 183, cols. 1639 and 1642; 11 February 1908.

27. *H.C.D.*, 3rd series, vol. 33, cols. 963–4; 10 May 1896.

28. CAB 37–90–116.

29. *H.C.D.*, vol. 183, col. 1645; 11 February 1908.

30. Ibid. col. 1644.

31. At the Board of Trade, 16 February 1906; *The Times*, 17 February 1906.

32. At the Board of Trade, 31 January 1908; *Daily News*, 1 February 1908.

33. Askwith, *Industrial Problems and Disputes*, p. 121.

34. George, *My Brother and I*, p. 212.

35. Owen, *Tempestuous Journey*, p. 155; a widely quoted passage.

36. Letter home of 29 October 1907; George, *My Brother and I*, p. 212.

37. The notes for this speech are in L.G. B/3/2/6. He repeated the warnings about a trade depression in his letter to Campbell-Bannerman; Owen, *Tempestuous Journey*, p. 155.

38. Letter of 25 October 1907; George, *My Brother and I*, p. 212.

39. Herbert Maxwell to Lloyd George, 25 October 1907; L.G. B/1/1/6 (c); cited in M. Thomson, *David Lloyd George: The Official Biography* (1948), p. 169. Maxwell represented the Glasgow and South-Western Railway. Another director, Mark Lockwood, wrote in similar tone on the 26th; L.G. B/1/1/7.

40. Sir Herbert Maxwell, *Evening Memories* (1932), pp. 305–6.

41. Letter of 31 October 1907; George, *My Brother and I*, p. 212; cited in P. Rowland, *The Last Liberal Governments*, vol. 2: *The Promised Land 1905–10* (1968), p. 128.

42. *Royal Commission of the Working of the Railway Conciliation and Arbitration Scheme of 1907*, *Minutes of Evidence*, Cd. 6041; sum-

marised Clegg, Fox and Thompson, *History of Trade Unionism*, p. 425.

43. Recorded in his diary, 9 November 1907; J. H. Lewis Papers, 10/131/59.

44. Askwith, *Industrial Problems and Disputes*, p. 121; cited Clegg, Fox and Thompson, *History of Trade Unionism*, p. 425; Bagwell, *The Railwaymen*, p. 268.

45. For J. H. Thomas's complaint that the union only had a short time to discuss it, see Cd. 6014; cited, Clegg, Fox and Thompson, *History of Trade Unionism*, p. 425. One account claimed they were only given twenty minutes to decide on the scheme; *Manchester Guardian*, 18 August 1911; cited Bagwell, *The Railwaymen*. p. 269.

46. Lancashire and Yorkshire Railway Proceedings of Directors' Board, vol. 16, fos. 597f; cited Gupta, 'History of the A.S.R.S.', fo. 395.

47. The nature and working of the scheme are described in Clegg, Fox and Thompson, *History of Trade Unionism*, pp. 426–8; Bagwell, *The Railwaymen*, pp. 270–3. Also letters of W. H. Clark (Board of Trade) and G. R. Askwith to Lloyd George on 7 and 8 January 1908 comment on union unrest over the scheme: L.G. B/1/1/22 and 23.

48. A point Lloyd George proudly emphasised in a speech at Cardiff on 24 January 1908; *South Wales Daily News*, 25 January 1908.

49. Vol. 65, p. 1904; 9 November 1907.

50. Cardiff speech, 24 January 1908; *South Wales Daily News*, 25 January 1908.

51. W. H. Clark (on behalf of Lloyd George) to J. A. Spender, 14 December 1907; J. A. Spender Papers, 46388 fo. 194. For Lloyd George's earlier letters to Spender, see ibid. fo. 192. It is doubtful if this achieved anything; Herbert Llewellyn Smith doubted if the companies would co-operate; Llewellyn Smith to Lloyd George, 29 December 1907; L.G. B/1/1/11.

52. A point made much of in Bagwell, *The Railwaymen*, pp. 269–70. See also Gupta, 'History of the A.S.R.S.', fo. 393 and G. Alderman, *The Railway Interest* (1973), pp. 199–200.

53. George, *My Brother and I*, p. 213.

54. At Madeley on 1 November 1907; *Wellington Journal*, 2 November 1907, and at Glasgow on 22 November 1907; *Glasgow Herald*, 23 November 1907.

55. Accounts in Halevy, *Rule of Democracy*, pp. 114–15; Clegg, Fox and Thompson, *History of Trade Unionism*, p. 459.

56. *The Economist*, 4 December 1907.

57. 13 December 1907; cited Clegg, Fox and Thompson, *History of Trade Unionism*, p. 459.

58. Llewellyn Smith to Lloyd George, 23 December 1907; L.G. B/1/1/10.

59. Either Llewellyn Smith intervened on his own initiative, as Lloyd George observed in a letter home (*Family Letters*, pp. 150–1), or

the officials muddled their instructions; see Llewellyn Smith to Lloyd George, 29 December 1907; L.G. B/1/1/11.

60. Llewellyn Smith to Lloyd George, 2 January 1908; L.G. B/1/1/17.

61. Llewellyn Smith to Lloyd George, 11 January 1908; L.G. B/1/1/25.

62. Halevy, *Rule of Democracy*, pp. 115–16; Clegg, Fox and Thompson, *History of Trade Unionism*, pp. 433–4; Phelps Brown, *Growth of British Industrial Relations*, p. 312; James B. Jeffrys, *The Story of the Engineers* (1945), p. 153.

63. Speech at Carnarvon on 13 March 1908, when receiving the Freedom of the Town; *North Wales Observer*, 20 March 1908.

64. Of recent literature on this see the sensible survey in R. Charles, *The Development of Industrial Relations in Britain 1911–39* (1973), pp. 42–7; R. V. Sires, 'Labour unrest in England 1910–14', *Journal of Economic History*, vol. 15 (1955), which surveys the main strikes without examining the causes; and Henry Pelling, 'The Labour unrest 1911–14', in his *Popular Politics and Society in Late Victorian Britain* (1968). The main accounts are Halevy, *Rule of Democracy*, pp. 441–86; Askwith, *Industrial Problems and Disputes*, pp. 148–355, and the controversial G. Dangerfield, *The Strange Death of Liberal England 1910–14* (1935).

65. Taking 1900 as the base year (100) for retail prices and wages, the former had risen to 106·6 while the latter had risen to only 100·23; 'The Present Unrest in the Labour World', June 1911, fo. 8; CAB 37/107.

66. Herbert Lewis's diary, 18 February 1912; J. H. Lewis Papers, 10/130/102.

67. Cited in Askwith, *Industrial Problems and Disputes*, p. 183.

68. Herbert Lewis's diary, 8 September 1908; J. H. Lewis Papers, 10/131/79.

69. In his penetrating Leslie Stephen Lecture (1961), 'Lloyd George: Rise and Fall', reprinted in his *Politics in Wartime* (1964), p. 136.

70. Herbert Lewis's diary, mid-September 1912; J. H. Lewis Papers, 10/231.

71. Speech at the Coal Exchange, Carnarvon, 22 September 1908; *Carnarvon Herald*, 23 September 1908.

72. Asquith's Cabinet Reports to the King, 21 July and 11 August 1911; Asquith Papers, vol. 6, fos. 58 and 66.

73. For details of the railway strike see Bagwell, *The Railwaymen*, pp. 289–307; Phelps Brown, *Growth of British Industrial Relations*, pp. 321–4 as well as general references to the 1910–14 labour unrest, above.

74. Askwith, *Industrial Problems and Disputes*, p. 160.

75. Bagwell, *The Railwaymen*, p. 282.

76. H.C.D., vol. 29, col. 2045; cited in Halevy, *Rule of Democracy*, p. 460; see his letter to his wife, written later that evening; *Family Letters*, p. 158.

77. Asquith's Cabinet Report to the King, 17 August 1911; Asquith Papers, vol. 6, fo. 70.
78. Askwith, *Industrial Problems and Disputes*, p. 164; Ramsay MacDonald described Asquith's manner in similar terms, A. Chamberlain, *Politics from the Inside* (1936), p. 346.
79. Askwith, *Industrial Problems and Disputes*.
80. Samuel to his wife, 17 August 1911; Samuel Papers, A157, fo. 615.
81. Asquith's Cabinet Report to the King, 16 August 1911; Asquith Papers, vol. 6, fo. 69.
82. Crewe to Hardinge, 16 August 1911; Crewe Papers, C/23.
83. Samuel to his wife, 16 August 1911; Samuel Papers, A157, fo. 606. On the 17th he still reported to her that the companies felt they could keep the main lines working but commented, 'The railwaymen will probably be beaten, but it will be a disastrous struggle'; ibid. fo. 615.
84. Churchill's role is described in R. S. Churchill, *Winston S. Churchill: Young Statesman 1901–14* (1967), pp. 383–6. For a more critical account see Bagwell, *The Railwaymen*, pp. 295–6, and Harcourt's letter to Gladstone, 12 September 1911, in which he observed, '. . . Winston glorified a little too much in his position as temporary Commander-in-Chief and has thereby brought some retribution upon his own head'; Harcourt Papers, Colonial Office, 2/61.
85. Masterman, *C. F. G. Masterman*, p. 204.
86. For Lloyd George's note to Elibank; Elibank Papers, 8802, fo. 307.
87. Samuel to his wife, 18 August 1911; Samuel Papers, A157, fo. 620.
88. *H.C.D.*, vol. 29, cols. 2196–8; also Askwith, *Industrial Problems and Disputes*, p. 164.
89. See Buxton's account of the negotiations, Asquith Papers, vol. 92, fos. 184–7.
90. Masterman, *C. F. G. Masterman*, p. 207.
91. Mary A. Hamilton, *Arthur Henderson* (1938), pp. 87–8. The letter is incorrectly attributed to 11 August; it was most probably written on the 21st.
92. See A. Chamberlain, *Politics from the Inside*, p. 437, and the slightly different version, p. 320. A. J. P. Taylor was wrong to suggest of the Mansion House speech of 21 July (some days before the first local strikes): 'Perhaps it was with this [settling the railway strike] in view that he made the Mansion House speech in the first place'; *Politics in Wartime* (1964), p. 59. He is more accurate in his *The Struggle for Mastery in Europe 1848–1918* (1954), p. 473.
93. His letter home of 19 August; *Family Letters*, p. 158. Samuel apparently suggested a direct talks about direct talks solution to Lloyd George; Samuel to his wife, 20 August 1911; Samuel Papers, A157, fo. 637.

94. See the excellent analysis of why the companies so soon came to see the unions and of the effects of the strike in Bagwell, *The Railwaymen*, pp. 297–307. Askwith told Emmott, 'Both railway directors and the union leaders were a little frightened and this helped to bring about a settlement.' Diary entry for 21 August 1911; Emmott Papers, vol. 2, fo. 31.

95. Diary, 19 August 1911; Elibank Papers, 8814, fo. 35.

96. *H.C.D.*, 5th series, vol. 29, col. 2347; 22 August 1911. See also Du Parq, *Life*, vol. 3, pp. 591–2.

97. Arthur Murray's diary, 22 August 1911, Elibank Papers, 8814, fos. 35–6.

98. Asquith had this reproduced for the Cabinet; CAB 37–107–107. All but the last sentence is cited in R. Jenkins, *Asquith* (1964), p. 261.

99. Ibid.

100. Grey to Asquith, 13 September 1911; Asquith Papers, vol. 13, fo. 42.

101. Lloyd George to Elibank; Elibank Papers, 8802, fo. 320.

102. Charles Bathurst and Lord Selborne to Bonar Law, 16 and 14 March 1912, respectively; Bonar Law Papers, 25–3–40 and 31.

103. F. E. Smith, Carson and Steel-Maitland to Bonar Law, 1, 18 and 24 March respectively; ibid. 18–7–161, 25–3–44 and 25–3–30.

104. Chamberlain, *Politics from the Inside*, p. 441.

105. For the Tory Whip's reports on the Labour M.P.s probable actions, Balcarres to Bonar Law, 20 and 25 March 1912; Bonar Law Papers, 25–3–49 and 26–1–57.

106. Bonar Law to the Duke of Somerset, 23 March 1912; in a letter to Carson he said if they divided on the second reading and the Government kept their majority, 'we shall take no further steps to interfere with them in carrying out their policy', 20 March 1912; ibid. 33/4/26 and 24.

107. Chamberlain, *Politics from the Inside*, p. 441.

108. Steel-Maitland to Bonar Law, 30 May 1912; Bonar Law Papers, 26/3/43.

109. Fitzherbert Wright to Bonar Law, 1 February 1913; ibid. 29/1/3.

110. As well as works cited above, see R. P. Arnot, *The Miners: Years of Struggle* (1953), pp. 57–86 and *The South Wales Miners* (1967), pp. 174–273; E. W. Evans, *The Miners of South Wales* (1961), pp. 190–212; Sir N. Macready, *Annals of An Active Life* (2 vols., 1924), vol. 1, pp. 136–41.

111. Macready, *Annals of an Active Life*, pp. 136–7.

112. See Arnot's account, *Years of Struggle*, pp. 90–122; Askwith, *Industrial Problems and Disputes*, pp. 201–19; and R. Smillie, *My Life for Labour* (1924), p. 218.

113. Asquith's Cabinet Report to the King, 20 February 1912; Asquith Papers, vol. 6, fo. 113.

114. Herbert Lewis's diary, 18 February 1912; J. H. Lewis Papers, 10/130/102.

115. Samuel to his mother, 25 February 1912; Samuel Papers, A 156/400.
116. Arthur Murray's diary, 25 February; Elibank Papers, 8814, fo. 66.
117. Askwith, *Industrial Problems and Disputes*, p. 204. Sir Charles Macara, a leading cotton manufacturer on the Industrial Council, was equally scathing; *Recollections* (1921), pp. 173–5.
118. Ibid. p. 210.
119. The Government's proposals are reprinted in Arnot, *Years of Struggle*, pp. 99-100 and his *A History of the Scottish Miners* (1955), p. 123. The minutes of the meeting with the Miners' Federation on 29 February are in the Asquith Papers, vol. 93, fos. 6–21.
120. Herbert Lewis's diary, 3 March 1912; J. H. Lewis Papers, 10/130/104. Lloyd George similarly told Arthur Murray that 'the breakdown of the negotiations was in large part due to the fanatical obstinacy of Smillie'; Arthur Murray diary, 1 March 1912; Elibank Papers, 8814, fos. 67–8. Others felt the same about Smillie, see Edward Goulding to Bonar Law, 10 March 1912; Bonar Law Papers, 25/3/23.
121. Hopwood to Bonar Law, 15 March 1912; Bonar Law Papers, 25/3/36.
122. John Baird to Bonar Law, 12 March 1912; ibid. 25/3/22.
123. Steel-Maitland to Bonar Law, 13 March 1912; ibid. 25/3/27.
124. Arnot, *South Wales Miners*, p. 301.
125. Riddell, *More Pages*, p. 43.
126. Asquith to the King, 14 March 1912; Asquith Papers, vol. 6, fo. 117.
127. Asquith to Bonar Law, 15 March 1912; Bonar Law Papers, 25/3/38.
128. Askwith to Bonar Law, 15 March 1912; ibid. 25/3/37.
129. Riddell, *More Pages*, p. 38.
130. Ibid.
131. 23 March 1912; ibid. p. 47.
132. Asquith's Cabinet Report to the King, 16 March 1912; Asquith Papers, vol. 6, fo. 119.
133. Askwith to Bonar Law, 17 March 1912; Bonar Law Papers, 25/3/41.
134. Asquith's Cabinet Report to the King for 19 and 20 March 1912; Asquith Papers, vol. 6, fo. 121.
135. John Baird to Bonar Law, 15 March 1912; Bonar Law Papers, 25/3/34.
136. Emmott's diary entry for 29 March 1912; Emmott Papers, vol. 2, fos. 62–3.
137. Asquith's Cabinet Report to the King for 21 and 22 March 1912; Asquith Papers, vol. 6, fo. 121.
138. Arthur Murray's diary, 22 March 1912; Elibank Papers, 8814, fos. 71–3.

139. See Arthur Murray's diary, 22, 25 and 26 March 1912; ibid. fos. 71–7.
140. Cited in Jenkins, *Asquith*, p. 264. Keith Robbins in *Sir Edward Grey* (1971), p. 249 is mistaken in thinking that this proposal was the basis for ending the strike.
141. Asquith's Cabinet Report to the King, 26 March 1912; Asquith Papers, vol. 6, fo. 125.
142. Arthur Murray's diary, 26 March 1912; Elibank Papers, 8814, fos. 75–7.
143. See Herbert Lewis's diary, 26 March 1912; Herbert Lewis Papers, 10/131/103.
144. Some Ministers had expected it to do so. Samuel optimistically wrote to his mother on 17 March, 'It should pass this week, and the mines should start again next week'; Samuel Papers, A156.
145. Arthur Murray's description in his diary, 6 April 1912; Elibank Papers, 8814, fo. 79.
146. 26 March 1912; ibid. fo. 77.
147. See, for example, Loreburn's letter of 24 March 1912, on the threat of bread riots, McKenna Papers, McKn 4/4/15; cited in S. McKenna, *Reginald McKenna 1863–1943* (1948), p. 151.
148. Cited in Arnot, *Years of Struggle*, p. 108.
149. See for example Crawshaw's letter to Runciman of 2 April 1912; Runciman Papers, WR 63. Crawshaw wanted to be left to fight it out with his men, and observed, 'If you were not our M.P. I would not vote Liberal at the next election.'
150. Riddell's diary, 2 March 1912; *More Pages*, p. 42.
151. Ibid. 24 March 1912; ibid. p. 46.
152. Asquith's Cabinet Report to the King, 16 April 1912; Asquith Papers, vol. 6, fos. 131–2.
153. Riddell, *More Pages*, p. 53.
154. Riddell to Lloyd George, 25 April 1912; L.G. C/7/4/1.
155. For the details of this strike see Askwith, *Industrial Problems and Disputes*, pp. 220–33; Phelps Brown, *Growth of British Industrial Relations*, p. 329; Webbs, *Our Partnership*, pp. 501–2; H. Gosling, *Up and Down Stream* (1927), pp. 118–72; Dangerfield, *Strange Death of Liberal England*, pp. 300–5; J. C. Lovell, 'Trade Unionism in the Port of London 1870–1914' (London Ph.D., 1966), fos. 324–67; and G. A. Phillips, 'The National Transport Workers Federation 1910–27' (Oxford D.Phil., 1968), fos. 122–49.
156. Memorandum by Askwith, 17 May 1912; forwarded to Lloyd George by Buxton, 17 May 1912; L.G. C/3/10/2.
157. Lloyd George to Buxton, 20 May 1912; ibid. C/3/10/3. This disagreement over policy no doubt increased Askwith's contempt for ministerial interference in disputes.
158. Haldane to Lloyd George, 21 May 1912; enclosed a copy of a letter to Buxton of the same date; ibid. C/4/17/2. See also his letter to his mother of 22 May; Haldane Papers 5987, fos. 198–9;

cited in S. E. Koss, *Lord Haldane: Scapegoat for Liberalism* (1969), pp. 63–4.

159. Telegram, 22 May 1912; L.G. C/3/10/4.
160. Askwith, *Industrial Problems and Disputes*, p. 222.
161. Buxton to Lloyd George, 28 May 1912; L.G. C/3/10/5.
162. For their lengthy statement of their position to Buxton, of 31 May 1912, in response to his letter of the 28th, see L.G. C/3/2/1.
163. Askwith, *Industrial Problems and Disputes*, pp. 224–5.
164. *The Times*, 1 June 1912.
165. Asquith to Elibank, 5 June 1912; Elibank Papers, 8803, fo. 62.
166. Asquith's Cabinet Report to the King, 12 June 1912; Asquith Papers, vol. 6, fo. 143.
167. *The Times*, 1 June 1912. Samuel to Lloyd George, 13 June 1912; L.G. C/7/9/2. Samuel was still hoping such legislation would be introduced later in the month – see his letter to Lord Gladstone, 23 June 1912; Herbert Gladstone Papers, 45, 992, fo. 267.
168. Cabinet Report, 12 June 1912; Asquith Papers, vol. 6, fo. 143.
169. Asquith's Cabinet Report to the King, 13 June 1912; Asquith Papers, vol. 6, fo. 145. See also Askwith, *Industrial Problems and Disputes*, pp. 225–8.
170. That is other than supplying troops on the requisition of the Chief Constable of Essex to keep order in the docks when 'free labour' passed through. For army reports 14 July, see Mottistone Papers, vol. 19, fo. 141.
171. Askwith, *Industrial Problems and Disputes*, p. 228.
172. Ibid. p. 230.
173. The most useful discussion of this measure is in F. J. Bayliss, *British Wages Councils* (1962), pp. 1–12. See also Halévy, *Rule of Democracy*, pp. 251–3. For the working of the system see D. Sells, *The British Trade Boards System* (1923).
174. Sidney Buxton's Cabinet memorandum, 'Conciliation and the Board of Trade', 9 August 1911; CAB 37/107.
175. In the conclusion of the memorandum, 'The Present Unrest in the Labour World', June 1911; CAB 37/107.
176. Macara, *Recollections*, p. 165. For valuable assessments of the Industrial Council see Charles, *Development of Industrial Relations*, pp. 37–74; Askwith, *Industrial Problems and Disputes*, pp. 178–84 and Lord Amulree, *Industrial Arbitration in Great Britain* (1929), pp. 114–20.
177. Buxton to Asquith, 13 September 1911; Asquith Papers, vol. 24, fos. 51–4.
178. On 12 July 1912; *The Times*, 13 July 1912.
179. Riddell's diary entry, 1 July 1912; *More Pages*, p. 76.

IV *Lloyd George organises for victory*

1. Thus in his first major war speech at the Queen's Hall on 19 September 1914, he declared, 'We are not fighting the German

people. The German people are under the heel of this military caste, and it will be a day of rejoicing when the military caste is broken.' *Through Terror to Triumph* (1915), p. 12.

2. Samuel Papers, A 157/699. I am more impressed by Frances Stevenson's account of Lloyd George's hesitations at this time than her own view that his mind was made up from the outset; Frances Lloyd George, *The Years That Are Past* (1967), pp. 73–4.

3. *War Memories*, vol. I (1933), p. 130.

4. *Lord Riddell's War Diary*, pp. 35–6.

5. See Churchill's Minute, reporting Hankey's observations on the need of 'an Emergency Armament Multiplication Committee or Department', of 3 September 1914, MUN 5–6–170/21; also F. S. Oliver's cogent memorandum to Asquith of 16 November 1914; Asquith Papers, vol. 26, fos. 97–109.

6. Booth at the conference with employers from Manchester, 29 April 1915; MUN 5–7–171.

7. Asquith Papers, vol. 13, fo. 264.

8. Duncan Crow, *A Man of Push and Go* (1965), p. 69.

9. To Lord Riddell, 7 March 1915; *War Diary*, p. 65.

10. Speech at Liverpool, 14 June 1915; *Through Terror to Triumph*, p. 113.

11. *H.C.D.*, 5th series, vol. 71, col. 314; 21 April 1915.

12. *History of the Ministry of Munitions* (hereafter cited as *H.M.M.*), vol. 3, part 1, p. 2; though as this history points out, at other times he urged the Board of the Admiralty and the Army Council to secure the most economical contract terms.

13. *H.M.M.*, vol. 3, part 2, pp. 44–6 and part 3, pp. 1–30.

14. Ibid. p. 43.

15. Ibid. p. 9.

16. S. Pollard, *The Development of the British Economy 1914–67* (1969), p. 63.

17. Report of 6 March 1918; cited *H.M.M.*, vol. 3, part 2, p. 31.

18. Ibid. p. 29. It also noted, 'On the other hand, the matter is complicated by various factors tending to dislocate production, such as labour unrest, scarcity of material, and change of design.'

19. *H.C.D.*, 5th series, vol. 69, col. 899. After a similar question from the Labour M.P., W. C. Anderson, on 3 March, Lloyd George replied that he could 'rest assured that the profits he mentioned would be fully assessed', ibid. vol. 70, col. 780.

20. Ibid. vol. 71, cols. 1000–20. The question of an excess profits tax was passed to a committee of the Cabinet on 29 April and a special Cabinet meeting was held on the subject on 3 May 1915. Asquith and Crewe to the King, Asquith Papers, vol. 8, fo. 37 and fo. 156. But no immediate action was taken.

21. This is not to indicate McKenna was firmer on profits. In a memorandum on McKenna's negotiations with shipowners to limit their profits Olwen Smith commented, 'The shipowners seem to have squeezed Mr. McKenna pretty thoroughly'; a

viewpoint Llewellyn Smith endorsed – 'The Chancellor seems more squeezable than we were!' Memorandum, 6 December 1915; L.G. D/13/2/3.

22. The best study of the Government's financial policy is in E. V. Morgan, *Studies in British Financial Policy 1914–25* (1952), pp. 3–32. See also A. W. Kirkaldy (ed.), *British Finance During and After the War 1914–21* (1921); W. R. Lawson, *British War Finance 1914–15* (1915); F. Fairer Smith, *War Finance* (1936), which is a polemic against the various Governments' fiscal policies; and R. H. Brand, *War and National Finance* (1921), a collection of his essays in *The Round Table* between 1912–20.

23. Vol. 1, p. 62.

24. *Development of the British Economy*, p. 71.

25. See Balfour's comments on 23 May 1915 in *Lady Cynthia Asquith's Diaries 1915–18* (1968), p. 28 and similar comments in such sources as *Lord Riddell's War Diary*, pp. 55 and 57.

26. Sir J. Stamp, *Taxation During the War* (1932), p. 31.

27. *War Memoirs*, vol. 1, p. 74.

28. Lloyd George to Chiozza Money, 27 October 1915; L.G. D/3/2/14. In some respects his proposals were a very drastic forerunner of the Post-War Credits, introduced in 1941, and Pay-as-You-Earn (P.A.Y.E.) introduced in 1943.

29. Memorandum of 19 November 1915; L.G. D/13/2/3. For his first draft of a scheme, dated 13 December 1915, see L.G. D/13/1/1.

30. Vol. I, pp. 73–4.

31. J. R. Hicks, U.K. Hicks, L. Rostas, *The Taxation of War Wealth* (1941).

32. For example, after Allen Reith was asked by Macassey to procure a rate fixer, he wrote to James McKechnie, General Manager of Vickers at Barrow, and suggested he loaned one of his men 'because I think it would be very much to your advantage if the premium bonus system is spread as much as possible in other establishments, and, if it is to be so spread, that it should be worked on the right lines . . . in these days the disadvantage which will follow such a transfer will be more than outweighed by the assistance a general adoption of the bonus system would give to you in maintaining your present practice.' 2 January 1917: McKechnie Papers, 300, Vickers Historical Records, 119.

33. *H.C.D.*, 5th series, vol. 70, col. 1460; 10 March 1915.

V *Lloyd George's 'Charter for Labour': the Treasury conference*

1. *Manchester Guardian*, 8 October 1914. *The Board of Trade Gazette's* statistics of the percentage unemployed of insured workpeople (July 1914 as 100) show that by November the numbers had already returned to the July state: July 1914: 3·6%; August: 6·2%; September: 5·4%; October: 4·2%; November: 3·7%; December: 3·3%; January 1915: 2·6%; February: 2·0%; March:

1·4%; April: 1·1%; May: 0·9%; cited in G. D. H. Cole, *Labour in War Time* (1915), p. 70.

2. *H.M.M.*, vol. 1, part 1, pp. 115 and 125.

3. The negotiations are dealt with in detail in G. D. H. Cole, *Trade Unionism and Munitions* (1923), pp. 54–60, and critically discussed in his *Labour in War Time*, pp. 169–72.

4. *H.C.D.*, 5th series, vol. 69, col. 285; 8 February 1915.

5. Ibid. col. 666; 10 February 1915.

6. Later, at the Treasury conference with the A.S.E., Lloyd George, after explaining safeguards for the skilled men's position, was taken aback when one delegate asked, 'But could you devise ways and means of eliminating the skilled knowledge which the semi-skilled men will have acquired?' MUN 5–10–180–18.

7. MUN 5–8–171–29.

8. Askwith, *Industrial Problems and Disputes*, p. 365.

9. W. A. Orton, *Labour in Transition* (1921), p. 31.

10. Llewellyn Smith in February 1915 referred to employers' estimates that this would increase productivity by 25%; MUN 5–8–171–29. This was in response to a paper by Churchill which urged the trade union leaders' proposals as an alternative to entering 'the labyrinth of difficulties concerning the frontiers between different classes of trade union labour', 13 February 1915; MUN 5–10–180–38.

11. *H.M.M.*, vol. 1, part 2, pp. 37 and 43.

12. The Board of Trade figures for the first year of the war – percentage rise in retail cost of food over level of July 1914: September 1914: 10½%; October: 12%; November: 13%; December: 16%; January 1915: 18%; February: 22%; March and April: 24%; May: 26%; June: 32%; July: 34%; *H.M.M.*, vol. 5, part 1, p. 9.

13. The committee of enquiry's figures on London domestic coal are printed in Cole, *Labour in Wartime*, p. 127. For the history and significance of the former committee see Royden Harrison, 'The War Emergency Workers' National Committee 1914–20', in A. Briggs and J. Saville (eds.), *Essays in Labour History 1886–1923* (1971), pp. 211–59.

14. Detailed accounts in *H.M.M.*, vol. 4, part 2, pp. 36–40 and Cole, *Labour in War Time*, pp. 147–54.

15. For Lloyd George predicting that the war would last 'another two years', *The Political Diaries of C. P. Scott 1911–28*, p. 119.

16. *H.C.D.*, 5th series, vol. 70, col. 1833; 15 March 1915.

17. He thought better of using the word 'patriotism', which is crossed out, and substituted 'concern'. MacNamara to Lloyd George, 3 February 1915; L.G. C/3/16/22.

18. Askwith to Asquith, 10 March 1915; Asquith Papers, vol. 14, fo. 17.

19. Asquith Papers, vol. 8, fo. 13.

20. MUN 5–8–171–29; *H.M.M.*, vol. 1, part 2, pp. 63–4.

21. *H.C.D.*, 5th series, vol. 70, cols. 1271–97, 1453–94; 9 and 10 March 1915.
22. Tyson Wilson was the only M.P. to question the implications of it for Labour. In response to Lloyd George's reply that there was no compulsory transfer, he commented, 'It is practically compulsory if work is offered to a man by a Labour Exchange and he does not go, his unemployment insurance is stopped'; to which Lloyd George retorted, 'I am very glad to hear it'; ibid. col. 1459.
23. *War Diary*, p. 68.
24. *H.M.M.*, vol. 14, part 2, p. 39.
25. Askwith to Runciman, 4 February 1915; MUN 5–8–171–29.
26. Ibid. See Asquith's Cabinet Report to the King, 11 March 1915; Asquith Papers, vol. 8, fo. 19.
27. *H.M.M.*, vol. 1, part 2, pp. 146–54; Cole, *Trade Unionism and Munitions*, pp. 62–8.
28. *H.C.D.*, 5th series, vol. 70, p. 1832; 15 March 1915.
29. *H.M.M.*, vol. 1, part 2, p. 69.
30. Ibid. pp. 69–70.
31. When he met a deputation of the A.S.E., 29 December 1914; ibid. p. 38.
32. Acland to Bradbury, 14 March 1915 (passed on to Lloyd George the next day); L.G. C/1/3/10.
33. Runciman to Lloyd George, 15 March 1915; ibid. C/7/5/9.
34. Account of the negotiations, MUN 5–360–2; most points of which are summarised *H.M.M.*, vol. 1, part 2, pp. 74–7. See also Asquith's Cabinet Report to the King, 16 March 1915; Asquith Papers, vol. 8, fo. 21.
35. *House of Lords Debates*, vol. 18, cols. 721–4. This occasioned an adjournment in the Commons in which M.P.s called upon the Government to fulfil Kitchener's hopes 'that workmen who work regularly by keeping good time shall reap some of the benefits which the war automatically confers on the great companies'. *H.C.D.*, 5th series, vol. 71; 12 May 1915.
36. Lord Grey, most probably on Lloyd George's prompting, had found out the views of Sir Benjamin Browne (chairman of a leading Newcastle engineering firm) on how the Government should 'meet the industrial situation'. Browne urged that compulsion of employers would make the men 'submit to it more patiently'. Lord Grey to Lloyd George, 1 March 1915; L.G. C/11/3/10.
37. Askwith to Asquith, 10 March 1915; Asquith Papers, vol. 14, fo. 17.
38. Runciman to Lloyd George, 15 March 1915; L.G. C/7/5/9.
39. Memorandum of mid-June 1915; Professor W. G. S. Adams Papers, MUN 5–20–221.1/35.
40. Askwith to Asquith, 10 March 1915; Asquith Papers, vol. 14, fo. 17.

41. The full proceedings of the Treasury Conference, 17–19 March 1915, are in MUN 5–10–18017. *The Times* printed Lloyd George's initial address to the Conference and the Agreement. The Treasury Agreement is also reproduced in such books as Cole, *Labour in War Time*, pp. 185–8 and *Trade Unionism and Munitions*, pp. 72–3, and H. Wolfe, *Labour Supply and Regulation* (1923), pp. 361–3. The only account in any detail of the Conference is *H.M.M.*, vol. 1, part 2, pp. 81–8.

42. I.e. in Tennant's appeal to the parliamentary Labour Party to secure relaxation of trade practices.

43. Memorandum forwarded by Llewellyn Smith to Lloyd George, 16 March 1915; L.G. C/7/5/10.

44. Henderson to Asquith, 2 March 1915; L.G. C/6/11/35. Engineering Employers' Federation to Lloyd George, 18 March 1915; ibid. C/11/3/33.

45. Llewellyn Smith to Lloyd George, 16 March 1915; L.G. C/7/5/10. He also urged that arbitration should be restricted to war cases not old grievances ('*The present emergency is no time for reopening questions of acute controversy.* Sleeping dogs must be allowed to sleep during the war'). Llewellyn Smith to Lloyd George, 17 March 1915; ibid. C/7/5/11.

46. There had been a similar provision in the Shell and Fuses Agreement, which had also been formulated after the Clyde strike.

47. The full proceedings are in MUN 5–10–180–18. The written assurances required by the A.S.E. are in MUN 5–9–180–10. These are similarly dealt with in the books cited as sources for the main Treasury Conference.

48. The Admiralty were informed, after making suggestions to shorten opening hours in various ports, 'Mr. Lloyd George thinks it quite probable that after the interview (with Labour at the Treasury Conference) drastic action may be possible, but until that has taken place, he is strongly of opinion that nothing should be done.' Hamilton to Masterton-Smith, 12 March 1915; L.G. C/3/16/18.

49. See, for example, reports from Vickers Works, 11 April 1915; L.G. C/5/7/26. However there is a great deal of material suggesting that the role of drink was being exaggerated; see examples such as Sir Frederick Donaldson's report (Royal Arsenal, Woolwich), 1 April, a police report, 14 April and Booth's memorandum, April 1915; L.G. C/5/7/20, C/5/12/11 and MUN 5–8–172/4 respectively.

50. *The Times*, 30 March 1915.

51. Lloyd George to Stamfordham, 29 March 1915; L.G. C/5/6/11.

52. Lloyd George to Samuel, 19 April 1915; ibid. C/7/9/11. Earlier in March he said to Herbert Lewis, 'I wish I could do something to settle the drink question. I should die happy.' Herbert Lewis's diary, 2 March 1915; J. H. Lewis Papers, 10/131/113.

53. The drink debate always had moral overtones and was discussed

with passion; this was in marked contrast to the discussions about the problem of syphilis amongst the troops, which worried the Allied Cabinets in 1917–18, and which was treated dispassionately as a medical matter.

54. See Lansdowne, Austen Chamberlain, and Carson to Bonar Law, 1, 4 and 5 April respectively; Bonar Law Papers, 37/1/1, 37/1/7 and 37/1/11.

55. Bonar Law to Lloyd George, 7 April 1915; Bonar Law Papers, 37/5/15; cited in Robert Blake, *The Unknown Prime Minister* (1955), p. 239.

56. For the heated exchange between Lloyd George and Keir Hardie over the reports of a speech by the former at an I.L.P. meeting in Norwich of 4 April 1915, see L.G. C/11/3/45.

57. *H.C.D.*, 5th series, vol. 71, p. 1044; 4 May 1915.

VI *The Munitions of War Act*

1. Memorandum of 9 June 1915; MUN 5–57–320/1.

2. Thomas Shanks & Co. to Booth, 7 April 1915; MUN 5–6–170/5. They urged 'we consider more drastic steps ought to be taken at once'. Representatives of Government departments also complained of labour shortage and restrictions.

3. Orton, *Labour in Transition*, p. 44. Lloyd George told trade union leaders on 10 June, 'there are promises of deliveries in February which we have not yet had'; MUN 5–48–300/4.

4. Lloyd George's famous appeal, made during the introduction of the second D.O.R.A. Amendment on 9 March, was actually phrased: 'We are on the look-out for a good, strong businessman with some go in him who will be able to push the thing through.' *H.C.D.*, 5th series, vol. 70, col. 1277.

5. Apparently Sir Hugh Bell suggested area organisation to Booth; Crow, *A Man of Push and Go*, p. 88. The outline of his scheme is explained in a letter to Lloyd George, 8 April 1915; L.G. C/3/3/4 and cited Crow, *A Man of Push and Go*, p. 106.

6. *H.M.M.*, vol. 1, part 3, p. 14; Wolfe, *Labour Supply and Regulation*, p. 61.

7. To Rotherham and Barnsley employers on 27 April 1915; MUN 5–7–171/1; cited *H.M.M.*, vol. 1, part 3, p. 65.

8. Lloyd George to Balfour, 8 April 1915; L.G. C/3/3/4.

9. Balfour to Bonar Law, 3 April 1915; Balfour Papers, 49693, fos. 206–7.

10. Lloyd George to U. Wolfe, 15 May 1915; L.G. C/1/2/16. He appears to have used the existence of the committee to pressurise for a Ministry of Munitions. Crewe and Curzon were unsure whether it still existed in June 1915; their correspondence on this is in the Crewe Papers, M 13/14.

11. Llewellyn Smith wrote to him on 21 May 1915; 'Up to now we have . . . had to do our best to get along with a fundamentally

impossible situation. Now, however, the turn of events has made possible a really comprehensive reform which even a week ago seemed impossible. The all important matter now is not to let the opportunity slip, by failing to take all the necessary steps. I confess I am nervous about this . . .' L.G. C/7/5/21. For his letters on the administrative difficulties involved, see L.G. C/7/5 and Runciman Papers, box 2.

12. Memorandum on the meeting; L.G. D/3/3/1.
13. Lloyd George complained at a conference with trade union leaders on 10 June that 'the figure for one great works . . . showed about one-third to one-fourth of the men never turned up for the first quarter, and something like between 7% and 10% had not turned up all day. I am told that this applies . . . to a minority of the men, but it is rather an important minority in some districts.' MUN 5–48–300/4.
14. Both forms of tribunal consisted of persons nominated by the Minister of Munitions aided by one or more representatives of both employers and workmen.
15. MUN 5–10–180–33 and MUN 5–10–180–37 respectively.
16. MUN 5–20–221.1/23.
17. Memorandum 4 June 1915; MUN 5–20–221.1/17.
18. The records of these meetings are in MUN 5–7–171.
19. *Through Terror to Triumph*, p. 106.
20. *H.M.M.*, vol. 1, part 3, p. 96.
21. *H.M.M.*, vol. 1, part 4, p. 42.
22. *H.M.M.*, vol. 1, part 4, p. 44.
23. MUN 5–8–171/29.
24. Minutes of meeting with Birmingham employers, 20 April 1915; MUN 5–7–171/1.
25. 23 April 1915; *H.M.M.*, vol. 1, part 4, p. 39.
26. *Through Terror to Triumph*, p. 149; cited *H.M.M.*, vol. 1, part 4, p. 40.
27. W. H. Beveridge, *Power and Influence* (1953), p. 131.
28. Derby to Kitchener, 10 March 1915; Kitchener Papers, P.R.O. 30–57–73–WS.21.
29. Derby to Kitchener, 10 April 1915; ibid. P.R.O. 30–57–73–WS.22.
30. Derby to Runciman, 17 June 1915; Runciman Papers, box 4D. See also Derby's remarks cited in *Labour in War Time*, p. 211.
31. MUN 5–49–300/38; *H.M.M.*, vol. 1, part 4, p. 49. See also Beveridge Papers, vol. 2, fo. 14.
32. *Liverpool Daily Post*, 5 June 1915.
33. *Through Terror to Triumph*, pp 97–110.
34. In July Montagu joked about this. He suggested Lloyd George would fill in Walter Long's registration form's question, 'What other work could you undertake for which you are specially fitted?' with 'the work of a dictator'. 3 July 1915; Asquith Papers, vol. 14, fo. 82.
35. *Through Terror to Triumph*, p. 129.

36. MUN 5–9–180/7.
37. *H.M.M.*, vol. 1, part 4, p. 32.
38. MUN 5–22–242.1/2. In the following quotations the first italics are mine. The second piece was underlined by Lloyd George.
39. MUN 5–48–300/4.
40. Ibid.; cited *H.M.M.*, vol. 1, part 4, p. 33.
41. This section of the notes is headed 'suggestion of securing the support of organised labour for some form of compulsion in mobilising skilled workmen', 9 June 1915; MUN 5–57 0320/2.
42. Cabinet memorandum, 16 June 1915; CAB 37–130–9.
43. Ibid.
44. Cabinet memorandum by Lord Lansdowne, 12 June 1915; CAB 37–129–36.
45. Llewellyn Smith to Lloyd George, 12 June 1915; L.G. D/11/1/2.
46. MUN 5–20–221.1/24.
47. MUN 5–48–300/5.
48. Ibid.; mostly cited *H.M.M.*, vol. 1, part 4, p. 36. Lloyd George equally forcibly stated this to C. P. Scott before the meeting, and indicated that military discipline was at this stage still intended for controlled establishments. *The Political Diaries of C. P. Scott 1911–28*, pp. 127–8.
49. MUN 5–48–300/5.
50. *H.C.D.*, 5th series, vol. 72, cols. 1600–1.
51. *H.M.M.*, vol. 1, part 4, p. 1.
52. At a similar state of the Second World War (22 May 1940) the Excess Profits Tax was introduced at the rate of 100%. Henry Pelling, *Britain and the Second World War* (1970), p. 86.
53. MUN 5–20–221.1/35.
54. *H.C.D.*, 5th series, vol. 72, col. 1201.
55. Minutes of the N.A.C. (no. 17), 24 June 1915; MUN 5–22–242.1/180.

VII *The South Wales miners' strike, July 1915*

1. Runciman's Cabinet paper, 27 May 1915; copy in L.G. D/24/3/1. The best accounts of the South Wales miners' strike are in *H.M.M.*, vol. 4, part 2, pp. 5–9 and G. D. H. Cole, *Labour in the Coal Mining Industry* (1923), pp. 21–30.
2. *H.M.M.*, vol. 4, part 2, p. 6. It should be noted that the war situation had not prevented the owners lowering wage rates in Northumberland and Durham in the autumn of 1914 on the basis of the dislocated export trade.
3. MUN 5–48–300–6; MUN 5–48–300–7; and MUN 5–48–300–8.
4. 17 July 1915; Asquith Papers, vol. 14, fos. 113–16.
5. *Labour in the Coal Mining Industry*, p. 27.
6. *H.M.M.*, vol. 4, part 2, pp. 6–7.
7. The details of the dispute are summarised in the Appendix.
8. A point emphasised in a memorandum prepared for Steel-Mait-

land, dated 1 August 1915; Steel-Maitland Papers, G.D./193/73/6. Lloyd George extravagantly praised the coalowners in a telegram to Asquith (printed *H.M.M.*, vol. 4, part 2, p. 9) and received their gratitude (L.G. D/20/1/54); though in speaking to a mass meeting of the men, it was them on whom he lavished praise! (*The Times*, 22 July 1915).

9. TI–118040–16911.
10. L.G. D/11/1/6.
11. Ibid. D/11/1/7.
12. Riddell, *War Diary*, pp. 113–14.
13. Riddell to Lloyd George, 18 July 1915; L.G. D/18/7/2.
14. Asquith to the King, 19 July 1915; Asquith Papers, vol. 8, fos. 69–70.
15. Vaughan Nash to Runciman, 24 March 1915; Runciman Papers, WR 122.
16. Riddell to Lloyd George, 19 July 1915; L.G. D/18/7/3.
17. See Appendix.
18. *The Times*, 22 July 1915.
19. MUN 5–79–341/11.
20. Runciman to his wife, 26 August 1915; Runciman Papers, WR 303.
21. Ibid. 28 August 1915.
22. Ibid. 31 August 1915. Letters to his wife on 19, 27, and 29 also refer to the South Wales dispute.

VIII *Lloyd George and the trade union leaders in 1915*

1. Emmott's diary, 13 June 1915; Emmott Papers I, Diary 1911–15, fo. 197.
2. H. Pelling, *A History of British Trade Unionism* (1963), p. 261.
3. Jefferys, *The Story of the Engineers*, p. 191.
4. On 30 November 1915; *Manchester Guardian*, 1 December 1915.
5. Armament's Output Committee (A.O.C.) and Lincolnshire engineering employers, 21 April 1915; MUN 5–7–171, p. 35. Allan Smith, the Secretary of the Engineering Employers' Federation, worked for a time at the War Office and Ministry of Munitions. In the official history of the Engineering Employers' Federation it is stated that 'it was mainly through him that the Federation was able to exercise any influence on national policy'; E. Wigham, *The Power to Manage* (1973), p. 91.
6. A.O.C. and Birmingham engineering employers, 20 April 1915; MUN 5–7–171, p. 14.
7. A.O.C. and Lincolnshire employers, 21 April 1915; ibid. p. 39.
8. The range of their activities is revealed in the North East Coast Armaments Committee's minutes; MUN 5–9–173/5.
9. MacNamara to Lloyd George, 3 February 1915; L.G. C/3/16/22.
10. A.O.C. and Rotherham and Barnsley employers, 27 April 1915; MUN 5–7–171/1, p. 103.

11. Report of the Cabinet Committee on War Policy, 6 September 1915; CAB 24–1.
12. 'No system of tooth combing the country for volunteers or even compulsion is going to be any use, unless we dilute.' MUN 5–57–320–3.
13. *H.C.D.*, 5th series, vol. 72, col. 1201; 23 June 1915.
14. Lloyd George to Henderson, 21 June 1915; L.G. D/17/4/1.
15. The best account of the autumn 1915 Clyde unrest is *H.M.M.*, vol. 4, part 2, pp. 47–60.
16. 12 August 1915; MUN 5–48–300–9.
17. Ibid.
18. MUN 5–73–342/15/4.
19. A copy of their appeal to trade unionists on the men's behalf is in the Beveridge Papers, vol. 3, fos. 76–7.
20. *H.M.M.*, vol. 4, part 2, p. 55.
21. MUN 5–48–300/5. He told officials of the Ministry of Munitions on 13 September 1915, 'we substantially accepted the terms suggested by the Labour leaders . . . I did so because I did not want it said that if the experiment failed it failed because our terms were not sufficiently generous'; MUN 5–57–320/3.
22. Memorandum by Beveridge, 13 September 1915; L.G. D/1/3/8.
23. Rey to Lloyd George, 24 July 1915; L.G. D/11/3/1. The civil servants complained bitterly of the impracticality of the scheme; see the resolution of the committee of the Labour Supply Department to Lloyd George, 2 September 1915 (on the eve of the T.U.C.); L.G. D/1/3/4. So did Lloyd George, who called it 'a collossal failure', his Minute on the Labour Report 29 November 1915; copies in MUN 5–49–300/14 and L.G. D/3/2/23.
24. *H.M.M.*, vol. 4, part 1, p. 14.
25. *H.C.D.*, 5th series, vol. 77, col. 119.
26. *H.M.M.*, vol. 4, part 1, pp. 20–1.
27. Ibid. and p. 37.
28. MUN 5–70–324/1. She also called for equal rates for women on both piece work and time work; Lloyd George only agreed to the same piece rate and a fixed minimum hourly rate.
29. Beveridge's letter to the Treasury, 11 August 1915; MUN 5–70–324/26.
30. In a reference for Grace Roe (an associate of Mrs Pankhurst), whom he sent to France to investigate for him, 28 July 1915; L.G. D/19/6/5.
31. Amongst reports of such activities in the Lloyd George Papers is an amusing correspondence with Geoffrey Robinson of *The Times* on procuring the Bishop of Pretoria to be 'the Bishop of the Back' (D/18/1/21, 22, 24 and 25).
32. Conference with shipbuilding employers, 12 August 1915; MUN 5–48–300/9.
33. *H.M.M.*, vol. 4, part 1, pp. 33–6.
34. Addison to Lloyd George, 27 August 1915; L.G. D/1/1/5. N.A.C. Minutes (32), 31 August 1915; MUN 5–22–242.1/100.

35. Trade Union Congress, *Report 1915*, pp. 352–62. The N.A.C. were slow to arrange an invitation for him, raising the matter as late as the evening of 7 September; Minutes of the Parliamentary Committee of the T.U.C., 8 September 1915.

36. National Advisory Committee Minutes (34); MUN 5–22–242.1/ 100. The subcommittee consisted of Henderson, Brownlie and Mosses.

37. Minutes of the meeting; MUN 5–57–320/3.

38. Minutes of meeting with the A.S.E., 17 September 1915; MUN 5–57–320/4.

39. N.A.C. Minutes (35), MUN 5–22–242–1/100; cited *H.M.M.*, vol. 4, part 1, p. 50.

40. Minutes of the meeting with the A.S.E.; MUN 5–57–320/4. That the A.S.E. had a separate meeting was deplored by the other unions at their meeting – and they passed a resolution to that effect.

41. Brownlie and Kaylor (A.S.E.), Mosses (Patternmakers), Dawtry (Steam Engine Makers), Duncan (Workers Union) and Miss MacArthur (Women's Trade Union League).

42. The details of the formulation of these regulations are in *H.M.M.*, vol. 4, part 1, pp. 55–64.

43. *H.M.M.*, vol. 4, part 1, p. 68.

44. These recommendations were adopted as Circular L6, cited *H.M.M.*, vol. 4, part 1, p. 67; Cole, *Trade Unionism and Munitions*, p. 96; Wolfe, *Labour Supply and Regulation*, pp. 164–5.

45. This episode is dealt with in detail in *H.M.M.*, vol. 4, part 2, pp. 55–60; the ensuing brief summary of events is largely based on this account.

46. Report of the meeting; MUN 5–79–341/4.

47. *The Political Diaries of C. P. Scott*, p. 150.

48. At the conference with trade unionists on the Munitions of War Bill, 10 June 1915; MUN 5–48–300/4.

49. The rent agitation is dramatically recounted in Willie Gallacher, *Revolt On The Clyde* (1936), chapter 4. The episode is critically assessed in J. Hinton, *The First Shop Stewards' Movement* (1972), pp. 125–7.

50. *H.C.D.*, 5th series, vol. 76, col. 2484.

51. *H.M.M.*, vol. 4, part 2, p. 67.

52. The Clyde Enquiry Proceedings (commencing 4 November 1915); MUN 5–20–221.1/40.

53. Memorandum of December 1915; MUN 5–20–221.1/40.

54. MUN 5–20–221.1/40. For examples of Labour Party pressure see the memorandum by J.C.M. on the Bill of 17 November 1915; ibid.

55. *Manchester Guardian*, 1 December 1915.

56. However this control does not appear to have worried employers by this time. A memorandum of 2 December 1915, by the Labour Department points out, 'Employers who formerly were rather

shy of being controlled now often ask for this, as they say that they expect control will settle their labour difficulties'; MUN 5–49–300. Similar sentiments are expressed in a memorandum on the Amendment Bill; MUN 5–20–221.1/40.

57. *H.M.M.*, vol. 4, part 2, p. 70.
58. Memorandum, 1 December 1915; MUN 5–20–221.1/40.
59. *A.S.E. Journal*, December 1915; cited *H.M.M.*, vol. 4, part 1, pp. 76–8.
60. *H.C.D.*, 5th series, vol. 76, col. 2116 and vol. 77, col. 854.
61. B. Pribicevic in his *The Shop Steward's Movement and Workers' Control 1910–22* (1959), pp. 46–7, emphasises the employers' objections, whilst *H.M.M.* emphasises the disunity of the unions (vol. 4, part 1, pp. 80–2).
62. MUN 5–20–221.1/40.
63. Llewellyn Smith to Beveridge, 27 December 1915; MUN 5–20–221.1/40.
64. Llewellyn Smith to Lloyd George, 27 December 1915; ibid.
65. Minutes, 29 December 1915; MUN 5–70–324/3. 'Mr. Henderson thinks that as we are so much in the hands of the A.S.E. at present it would not be wise to refuse to see them . . . On the whole, the Minister agrees that he should see the deputation from the A.S.E.'
66. Memorandum with notes by Llewellyn Smith, MUN 5–70–324/3/1; also note by Llewellyn Smith for Lloyd George of 30 December, MUN 5–70–324/14/3.
67. Minutes of the meeting, MUN 5–70–324/3; cited *H.M.M.*, vol. 4, part 1, p. 85.
68. MUN 5–70–324/3.
69. Button was so enthusiastic that he declared, '. . . I do not mind saying that I intend after tonight to actively co-operate with the Ministry of Munitions on the scheme. The only reason why I refused to go further into it was because you failed to render legal and mandatory L3. Now that you propose to do that, you can have my body and soul for 24 hours a day'; ibid.

IX *Enforcing dilution on the Clyde*

1. *H.M.M.*, vol. 5, part 1, p. 69.
2. *H.C.D.*, 5th series, vol. 77, col. 10.
3. Ibid. col. 787; 4 January 1916.
4. A Minute approved by the Government in November 1915; *H.M.M.*, vol. 4, part 4, p. 128. Revealed to the Commons in a statement by Asquith, 20 January 1916; *H.C.D.*, 5th series, vol. 78, col. 626.
5. Montagu to Asquith, 3 July 1915; Asquith Papers, vol. 14, fo. 86. He urged amongst other economies that food consumption should be artificially lowered: the working classes 'must be made to feel the pinch of war'.

6. At the Central Hall, Westminster; *H.M.M.*, vol. 5, part 1, p. 70.
7. In many trades their actual earnings had gone up more than 10 per cent; but this was due to overtime, Sunday work, the removal of restrictions on output in piecework, greater regularity in employment and various bonuses and advances (such as 'time and a bit' and 'Hallelujah' rates). For the statistics see *H.M.M.*, vol. 4, part 4, p. 128.
8. Askwith to Beveridge, 29 September 1915; Beveridge Munitions Collection, vol. 3, fo. 66.
9. Beveridge Munitions Collection, vol. 3, fo. 54.
10. See W. Kendall's, *The Revolutionary Movement in Britain 1900–21* (1969), pp. 63–76 and 105–10; Helen R. Vernon, 'The Socialist Labour Party and the Working Class Movement on the Clyde 1903–21' (Leeds M.Phil., 1967), pp. 1–126; and R. K. Middlemas, *The Clydesiders* (1965), pp. 17–57.
11. Memorandum, 18 December 1915; MUN 5–70–324/4.
12. MUN 5–57–320/4.
13. MUN 5–70–324/3.
14. Lloyd George to Llewellyn Smith, 24 September 1915; L.G. D/3/2/7.
15. Lloyd George to Layton, 29 November 1915; ibid. D/3/2/23.
16. Minute on a memorandum on the Labour Department, 2 December 1915; MUN 5–49–300/15.
17. On the nature of it, see Kendall, *Revolutionary Movement in Britain*, pp. 116 ff.; W. R. Scott and J. Cunnison, *The Industries of the Clyde Valley during the War* (1924), p. 210.
18. 'Rank and File Militancy in the British Engineering Industry, 1914–18' (London Ph.D., 1969), p. 164. This is expressed less forcibly in his book, *The First Shop Stewards' Movement*, p. 125.
19. Copy in Beveridge Munitions Collection, vol. 3, fo. 95.
20. Paterson to Wolff, 22 November 1915; ibid. fo. 98.
21. Bartellot to the Third Sea Lord, 24 November 1915; ibid. fo. 94; cited Hinton, *The First Shop Stewards' Movement*, pp. 140–1.
22. Minutes of 6 December 1915; ibid. fo. 102.
23. Note of 5 January 1916; ibid. fo. 104. The Solicitor General for Scotland had reservations 'on political policy'. The Lord Advocate for Scotland emphasised that the leaflet did not specifically call for a strike though it did by inference; ibid. fo. 105.
24. *H.C.D.*, 5th series, vol. 77, col. 121; the italics are of a British Socialist Party leaflet, distributed at Lloyd George's Christmas Day Clyde meeting, which quotes these remarks (except the last phrase).
25. Henderson's letter of 22 October 1915; copy in Beveridge Munitions Collection, vol. 4, fo. 173. Kaylor's report of 7 December 1915; ibid. fo. 366.
26. Presumably by the Chief Labour Officer for the Tyne; MUN 5–73–324/15/2 (a folder of files removed from Lloyd George's Papers).

27. W. Gallacher, *Revolt on the Clyde*, p. 79.
28. *H.C.D.*, 5th series, vol. 77, col. 928; 4 January 1916. Gallacher's account differs from Kirkwood's, *My Life of Revolt* (1935), p. 103.
29. Paterson's Report, 18 December 1915; MUN 5-73-324/15/2. Lloyd George, *War Memoirs*, p. 314. In the Beveridge Munitions Collection (vol. 3, fo. 92) there is a letter to Duckham from an employer observing of the A.S.E., 'The leaders themselves are undoubtedly honest and sincere, but their authority is extremely limited.'
30. Official report in *The Times*, 23 December 1915.
31. Memorandum, 18 December 1915; MUN 5-73-324/15/1.
32. There are numerous accounts. See *H.M.M.*, vol. 4, part 4, pp. 101-9; Gallacher, *Revolt on the Clyde*, ch. 6; Kirkwood, *My Life of Revolt*, pp. 102-12; Pribicevic, *The Shop Stewards' Movement*, pp. 113-16; Kendall, *Revolutionary Movement in Britain*, p. 120; Hinton, *The First Shop Stewards' Movement*, pp. 134-5; Middlemas, *Clydesiders*, pp. 63-6; S. J. Hurwitz, *State Intervention in Great Britain* (1949), pp. 263-7.
33. He regretted thus causing bad feeling in the Commons on 4 January 1916; *H.C.D.*, 5th series, vol. 77, col. 927.
34. The *Forward's* account continues, 'My friends these are great Socialist factories (violent interruption).' This account also includes his characteristic plea before a Labour audience: 'I want to talk to you in all sincerity as a man brought up in a worker's home. I know as much about the life of the worker as any man here.'
35. Press notice, Serial D.335, 7.25 p.m., 24 December 1915; MUN 5-70-324/18.
36. *H.M.M.*, vol. 4, part 4, p. 111. That the request was not sent to *Forward* was deliberate press policy; a later memorandum noted: 'This was not sent to the *Forward* as the Press Bureau feel that they cannot safely send their confidential instructions to that paper.' Notes, 6 January 1916; MUN 5-70-324/18.
37. Lloyd George naturally denied in the Commons that the newspaper had been seized 'because a Minister's vanity has been offended', calling it 'a childish, fatuous, silly suggestion'. *H.C.D.*, 5th series, vol. 77, col. 1409; 10 January 1916. The policy of *Forward* and its suppression are discussed in an article by T. Brotherstone, 'The Suppression of the Forward', *Journal of the Scottish Labour History Society*, vol. 1 (1969), pp. 5-23. I do not agree with his 'more machiavellian interpretation' of the affair, p. 17 (Lloyd George was surely being too blatantly high-handed in public for this); or the view that the timing of the reappearance of the paper had any deep significance.
38. The Deputy Chief Constable for Glasgow endorsed this view. Notes from intelligence officer in Glasgow; MUN 5-70-324/18.
39. Notes on the suppression of *Forward*, 6 January 1916; MUN 5-70-324/18. *H.C.D.*, 5th series, vol. 77, col. 1417. The Intelli-

gence Department sent 'as promised' extracts from Scottish papers to Lloyd George on 6 January; MUN 5–70–324/18.

40. Notes on the suppression of *Forward*, 6 January 1916, MUN 5–70–324/18; cited Brotherstone, in *Journal of the Scottish Labour History Society*, vol. 1 (1969), p. 9.

41. MUN 5–70–324/18.

42. MUN 5–70–324/18. The italics indicate underlining by Lloyd George.

43. Memorandum by Beveridge, 9 January 1916; MUN 5–70–324/18.

44. Memorandum by Beveridge and intelligence officers' reports, both 6 January 1916; MUN 5–70–324/18.

45. Described, *H.M.M.*, vol. 4, part 4, p. 110.

46. Intelligence officers' report, 6 January 1906; MUN 5–70–324/18.

47. Quite possibly Lloyd George felt as Paterson did; the latter argued in a letter of 17 January that such action needed the support of public opinion, and, 'A very much clearer issue would be a strike against the enforcement of the dilution of labour, as the Government there would be in a position of asking the skilled men of the country to allow their skill to be used to the best advantage, and the public opinion would be overwhelmingly against the men. If, therefore, definite orders for the dilution of labour are to be given, I think it would be better to delay consideration of the question of removing any men out of the district.' Beveridge Papers, vol. 3, fo. 111; cited Hinton, *The First Shop Stewards' Movement*, p. 141.

48. Lloyd George to Elibank, 6 January 1916; Elibank Papers, 8804, fo. 1.

49. Lloyd George to Lady Murray, 18 January 1916; ibid. fo. 3.

50. *H.M.M.*, vol. 4, part 1, p. 69.

51. War Cabinet Minutes (45), July 1918; CAB 23–7–43. He made a similar comment to Riddell on 16 January 1916; *War Diary*, p. 150.

52. *H.C.D.*, 5th series, vol. 78, col. 765.

53. The beginning of Weir's memorandum; Beveridge Munitions Collection, vol. 3, fos. 229–31. There is a summary of it in W. J. Reader, *Architect of Air Power* (1968), pp. 51–2. The memorandum and the amendment to it are outlined in Hinton, *The First Shop Stewards' Movement*, pp. 143–4.

54. Printed paper, 'Dilution Campaign based on Mr. Weir's Memo', 20 January 1916; MUN 5–70–324/5. (In effect these proposals give teeth to Beveridge's view of the outcome of a widespread strike, memorandum, 6 January; MUN 5–70–324/18.)

55. Llewellyn Smith's Minute to Lloyd George, 7 February 1916; MUN 5–73–324/15/6.

56. Lynden Macassey's 'Report on the Progress of the Clyde Dilution Commission', 15 February 1916; ibid.

57. Kirkwood, *My Life of Revolt*, pp. 115–18; Gallagher, *Revolt on the Clyde*, pp. 102–5.

58. Beveridge Munitions Collection, vol. 3, fo. 353.

59. Beveridge's notes, 11 February 1916; MUN 5–73–324/15/8.

60. *H.M.M.*, vol. 4, part 4, pp. 119–23.

61. Paterson to Ministry of Munitions, 11 March 1916; MUN 5–79–341/8. He felt that if the local ratepayers had to meet the bill, 'there will be considerable trouble, which from what the Commissioners have been told, will without doubt, be ventilated in the House of Commons.'

62. Copies of the proceedings in MUN 5–70–324/6 and 324/44. The A.S.E. raised the matter again on 27 April 1916 with Addison; MUN 5–57–320/7.

63. Memorandum, 21 February 1916; Beveridge Munitions Collection, vol. 3, fos. 356–8.

64. Memorandum, 9 February 1916; MUN 5–73–324/15/7; the last sentence partly cited, Hinton, *The First Shop Stewards' Movement*, p. 146.

65. In fact it advocated syndicalism not an armed uprising. See Kendall, *Revolutionary Movement in Britain*, pp. 124–5, on this.

66. Glasgow report, 11 a.m. Memorandum by C. F. Rey, 7 February 1916; MUN 5–73–324/15/6.

67. Lloyd George to Elibank, 14 February 1916; Elibank Papers, 8804, fos. 8–9.

68. Papers on the 17 March strike, MUN 5–79–341/14. See also Addison's statement, 28 March 1916; *H.C.D.*, 5th series, vol. 81, col. 565.

69. Ibid. The A.S.E. Executive raised the treatment of the deportees with Addison on 27 April – but with little enthusiasm. Minutes of the meeting, MUN 5–57–320/7.

70. Asquith Papers, vol. 8, fos. 154–5.

71. Rey's memorandum on the Labour Supply Department, 8 August 1916; MUN 5–57–320/11. On the introduction of women as dilutees generally see M. B. Hammond, *British Labour Conditions and Legislation During The War* (1919), pp. 144–80. At a conference on 13 July 1916 Lloyd George publicly observed, 'Our main difficulties of organisation, construction, equipment, labour supply and readjustment have been solved'; *The Times*, 14 July 1916.

X *Conscription and manpower shortage, 1915–16*

1. *Labour Leader*, 28 January 1915; cited by M. I. Thomis, 'The Labour Movement in Great Britain and Compulsory Military Service 1914–16' (London M.A., 1966), fo. 43.

2. Memorandum, McKenna Papers; McKN 5/9/1–2; cited McKenna, *Reginald McKenna*, p. 255.

3. Runciman to his wife, 29 August 1915; Runciman Papers, WR 302. See also J. H. Thomas to Asquith, 20 August 1915; Asquith Papers, vol. 14, fo. 158.

4. Riddell, *More Pages*, p. 94.
5. From the summer of 1915 there are several letters to him from such prominent Tories as Derby and Curzon on the issue. By at least 11 August, Lloyd George was intriguing through F. E. Smith to achieve conscription; L.G. D/17/12/1.
6. Report by the Cabinet Committee of War Policy, 6 September 1915; CAB 24–1.
7. Thomis, 'The Labour Movement', fos. 52–3.
8. Report by the Cabinet Committee on War Policy, 6 September 1915, CAB 24–10. Henderson's views were soon passed on. See F. E. Smith to Lloyd George, 24 August 1915; L.G. D/16/4/1, and Selborne to Kitchener, 27 August 1915; Kitchener Papers, P.R.O. 30–57–80WV4.
9. Selborne to Kitchener, 27 August 1915; Kitchener Papers, P.R.O. 30–57–80WV4.
10. Forwarded with only the note, 'I enclose the memorandum I promised to let you have.' The report is dated 13 September 1915 and written by J. D. Irvine; L.G. D/16/19/5.
11. Asquith to Balfour, 18 September 1915; Balfour Papers, 4, 692, fos. 157–60; copy in Asquith Papers, vol. 28, fos. 162–6. There is also a memorandum on the conference in Asquith's Papers (vol. 29, fos. 208–9), which has the parts of Smillie's speech underlined in which he urges the need for national unity.
12. A detailed account of the Labour leaders' policy is given in Thomis, 'The Labour Movement', fos. 161–230.
13. Runciman to his wife, 28 December 1915; Runciman Papers, box 18.
14. Asquith Papers, vol. 16, fo. 18; cited Jenkins, *Asquith*, p. 437.
15. Asquith Papers, vol. 90, fos. 2–39 and vol. 30, fo. 114. As a member of the *Manchester Guardian* office informed C. P. Scott, Asquith carefully avoided giving a pledge that he 'would resign rather than consent to an extension of the Act to married men'; C. P. Scott Papers, 50, 908, fos. 189–90.
16. Memorandum by B. Wilson, 21 June 1916; MUN 5–57–320/8.
17. See Lloyd George to Llewellyn Smith, 8 March 1916 and Llewellyn Smith to Lloyd George, 24 April 1916; L.G. D/3/2/52 and D/11/1/18.
18. Lloyd George to Colonel Lee and to Llewellyn Smith, 13 May 1916; ibid. D/3/2/73. He saw employers and trade unionists in late May to arrange it; MUN 5–90–343.2/5.
19. Conference with Employers' Federation, 19 July 1916; MUN 5–90–343.2/7.
20. See Lloyd George to Geddes, 3 April 1916; he urged him 'to take steps to procure military labour, especially carpenters, for the rebuilding of the Filling Factory at Faversham'; L.G. D/3/2/66.
21. *Manchester Guardian*, 28 August 1916.
22. Derby to Lloyd George, 9 September 1916; L.G. E/1/1/5.
23. Esher to Haig, 17 August 1916; Haig Papers, vol. 214 f.

24. Montagu to Henderson, 6 November 1916 and Minute of 17 November 1916; MUN 5–79–328/1. For a similar approach to Henderson on Irish labour, MUN 5–58–320/44. Henderson's biographer wrongly implies Henderson was firmly against the scheme; M. A. Hamilton, *Arthur Henderson*, p. 114.

25. Memorandum, 26 August 1916; MUN 5–57–320/35. Report of conference of 30 August 1916; MUN 5–58–320/44.

26. *Dilution of Labour Bulletin*, November 1916; MUN 5–73–324/11.

27. In a deputation of the A.S.E., 27 April 1916; MUN 5–57–320/7.

28. Asquith to the King, 10 May 1916; Asquith Papers, vol. 8, fos. 163–4.

29. Minutes of the meeting, 27 September 1916; MUN 5–57–320/12.

30. MUN 5–57–320/16; copy in the Asquith Papers, vol. 91, fos. 128–55; cited in *H.M.M.*, vol. 6, part 1, pp. 15–16.

31. Ibid. p. 14.

32. Ibid. p. 49.

33. Ibid. pp. 27–30.

34. Hargreaves was a War Munitions Volunteer who had been transferred from Erith to Sheffield. When Hargreaves was called up an application from his firm for a badge had been resting at the Ministry of Munitions for nearly a month. The best account of the strike is *H.M.M.*, vol. 6, part 1. Developments in Sheffield are described in Bill Moore, 'Sheffield Shop Stewards in the First World War', in L. Munby (ed.), *The Luddites and Other Essays* (1971), pp. 245–61 and in S. Pollard, *A History of Labour in Sheffield* (1959), pp. 271–4.

35. W. C. Anderson raised in the Commons on 20 July the case of one Sheffield skilled fitter with a badge who was being sought after by the military authorities; *H.C.D.*, 5th series, vol. 34, col. 1214.

36. Proceedings of the conference, 15 November 1916; MUN 5–57–320/15. Apparently the Manpower Board prevented the Ministry of Munitions from issuing temporary badges of exemption from recruitment. Addison's diary, 22 November 1916; C. Addison, *Four and a Half Years* (1934), p. 262.

37. See his account of the dispute; J. T. Murphy, *Preparing for Power* (1934), pp. 127–32.

38. Proceedings of the conference, 15 November 1916; MUN 5–57–320/15.

39. *H.M.M.*, vol. 6, part 1, p. 38.

40. Copy in Austen Chamberlain Papers, AC/16/1/18; cited *H.M.M.*, vol. 6, part 1, p. 32.

41. Austen Chamberlain to Montagu, 10 November 1916; Austen Chamberlain Papers, AC/16/1/16.

42. Minutes of the meeting, 18 November 1916; MUN 5–57–320/17.

43. Addison's diary, 22 November 1916; Addison, *Four and a Half Years*, p. 263.

44. MUN 5–77–326/101; printed *H.M.M.*, vol. 6, part 1, pp. 39–40.

45. Office of the Labour Adviser to Barlow (Ministry of Munitions' official), 21 November 1916; MUN 5–57–320/16.
46. MUN 5–57–320/18. The outline scheme sent to Mosses is in MUN 5–57–320/16.
47. Addison's diary, 22 November 1916; Addison, *Four and a Half Years*, p. 263.
48. *H.M.M.*, vol. 6, part 1, p. 43.
49. CAB 23–1–21; cited *H.M.M.*, vol. 6, part 1, p. 44.
50. Ibid.

XI *Mounting discontent in the Labour Movement*

1. *Lord Riddell's Intimate Diary of the Peace Conference and After* (1933), p. 4.
2. G. D. H. Cole, *A History of the Labour Party from 1914* (1948), pp. 30–1. Lloyd George carefully outlined these terms to Curzon, Chamberlain, Cecil and Long; they are detailed in a memorandum sent to Bonar Law by Curzon, 10 December 1916; Bonar Law Papers, 81/1/36; largely reprinted in Beaverbrook, *Politicians and the War* (1960), pp. 520–7.
3. As Tom Jones observed, *Whitehall Diary*, vol. 1 (1969), p. 6.
4. Riddell, *War Diary*, p. 230.
5. *Beatrice Webb's Diaries, 1912–24* (1952), p. 73.
6. *The Political Diaries of C. P. Scott*, p. 242.
7. *Diaries, 1912–24*, p. 74.
8. A memorandum of 18 June 1917 admitted that the demarcation lines between the departments overlapped in practice though they could be defined in theory; MUN 5–79–340/2.
9. In her diary, 22 February 1917; *Diaries 1912–14*, p. 83.
10. 17 October 1916; *H.C.D.*, 5th series, vol. 86, col. 437.
11. 22 August 1916; ibid. vol. 75, col. 2513.
12. On behalf of the deputation of the parliamentary Committee of the T.U.C., 19 July 1916; copy of the Minutes of the meeting, Asquith Papers, vol. 91, fos. 81–104.
13. Crawford of Dalcarres (Minister of Agriculture) to Asquith, 8 November 1916; Asquith Papers, vol. 17, fo. 134. See also his letter of the 18th; ibid. fo. 150.
14. Riddell's diary, 26 November 1916; *War Diary*, p. 223.
15. For a summary of Milner's proposals see A. M. Gollin, *Proconsul in Politics* (1964), p. 289.
16. See for example, his letters to Arthur Lee and Lord Devonport, of 9 and 13 April 1917; L.G. F/31/2/3 and F/15/2/7. Kerr's letter to Maclay, 8 March 1917; Lothian Papers, G.D. 40–17–46, fo. 6. War Cabinet (97) Minutes, 15 March 1917; CAB 23–2–37.
17. War Cabinet Minutes (hereafter cited as W.C.) (71), 17 February 1917; CAB 23–1–242.
18. Appendix to W.C. (97), 15 March 1917; CAB 23–2–40.
19. See S. Pollard, 'The Foundation of the Co-operative Party', in

Briggs and Saville (eds.), *Essays in Labour History*, pp. 185–210, on this.

20. Barnes felt 'there was no person big enough for the job'. Barnes to Lloyd George, 15 September 1917; L.G. F/4/2/11. Barnes was writing to urge him to see a deputation, and listed their grievances. For a recent account of their particular grievances see T. F. Carberry, *Consumers in Politics* (1969), pp. 16–18.

21. As Bertrand Russell urged C. P. Trevelyan, 2 November 1917; C. P. Trevelyan Papers, box 17.

22. E. D. Morel to C. P. Trevelyan, 28 August 1916; C. P. Trevelyan Papers, box 19. For the role of the pacifist groups see Fenner Brockway, *Inside the Left* (1942), book 2 and M. Swartz, *The Union of Democratic Control in British Politics During the First World War* (1971).

23. At a conference, 12 August 1915; MUN 5–48–300/9. He was referring to George Davison. See Riddell's diary, 17 July 1913; *More Pages*, p. 169 and W. W. Craik, *The Central Labour College 1909–29* (1964), pp. 95–6.

24. Mrs Pankhurst to Lloyd George, 14 October 1915; L.G. D/11/2/24. He had similarly alarming letters on the situation on the Clyde and in Coventry from a friend of Riddell and the parliamentary Munitions Committee representative, 28 October and 25 September 1915; ibid. D/17/13/2 and D/11/1/9 respectively.

25. Lloyd George to Mrs Pankhurst, 15 October 1915; ibid. D/11/2/25.

26. Telephone message, 15 November 1916; MUN 5–57–320/16. He urged that 'some of the men might be dealt with in a similar manner to those on the Clyde'.

27. Sir A. Denny to the Board of Trade, 8 July 1916; Runciman Papers, box 4, folder D.

28. Notes on the Strike Movement by W.M.L., 15 December 1916; Milner Papers, vol. 128, fo. 6.

29. G. M. Young, reported that one Labour intellectual 'showed bitterness only on one point, the espionage and bribery which is being conducted by the War Office, Scotland Yard, and the Industrial Peace group, among trade unionists'. Forwarded to Lloyd George by Addison, 15 December 1917; L.G. F/1/4/5. The Ministry of Labour weekly reports (from May 1917) gave details of such developments.

30. The War Cabinet approved domestic propaganda after the May strikes, W.C. (142), 22 May 1917; CAB 23–2–179. See J. O. Stubbs, 'Lord Milner and Patriotic Labour 1914–18', *English Historical Review*, vol. 87 (1972), for another response.

31. Ministry of Labour report, 6 September 1917; CAB 24–25–302.

32. As noted with concern in appendix 2 of W.M.L.'s memorandum; Milner Papers, vol. 128, fos. 20–1.

33. Lloyd George's prime motive in starting the events that led to the overthrow of Asquith was the desire for effective control of

military strategy by a war council of three. See A. J. P. Taylor, *Beaverbrook* (1972), ch. 6 for a recent analysis.

34. Esher to Haig, 4 December 1916; Haig Papers, 214 f.

XII *The May engineering strike*

1. At a meeting with Addison, 12 December 1916; MUN 5–70–324/2/2.
2. *H.M.M.*, vol. 6, part 1, pp. 47–51.
3. Minutes of the meeting, 22 November 1916; MUN 5–70–324/9.
4. Minutes of the meeting, 12 December 1916; MUN 5–70–324/2/2.
5. *Four and a Half Years*, p. 283.
6. Minutes of the meeting, 18 December 1916; MUN 5–70–324/2/3.
7. *H.M.M.*, vol. 6, part 1, p. 54.
8. *Four and a Half Years*, p. 285. This impression is borne out, to a certain extent, by the Minutes of the meeting; MUN 5–70–324/2/3.
9. The N.A.C. discussed the measure with the Labour Party. See its Minutes (93 and 99), 18 April and 3 May 1917; MUN 5–22–242.1/100. For criticism of the measure in the debate on 27 April, see *H.C.D.*, 5th series, vol. 92, cols. 2753–64.
10. Walter Long to Austen Chamberlain, 22 January 1917; Austen Chamberlain Papers, 16/1/12.
11. MUN 5–63–322/33. The military felt that the main obstacle to their getting more men was the Government being 'afraid to tackle the trade unions'. Robertson to A. J. Murray, 13 February 1917; Murray/Robertson Papers, 52462.
12. 17 October 1916; *Four and a Half Years*, p. 256.
13. Memorandum, 21 November 1916; MUN 5–57–320/16.
14. These priorities were frankly put to the trade card unions by Robertson and Jellicoe on 2 April 1917; MUN 5–62–322/13.
15. Minutes of the conference, 3 April 1916; MUN 5–62–322/13.
16. 3 April 1917; *Four and a Half Years*, p. 350.
17. N.A.C. Minutes (93), 4 January 1917; MUN 5–22–242–1/100; memorandum by Addison, 21 February 1917; MUN 5–63–322/33; and letters by J. Hodge to Lloyd George, 31 March 1917; L.G. F/27/5/3.
18. Minutes of the conference, 4 April 1917; MUN 5–62–322/16.
19. Minutes of a conference, 23 April 1917; MUN 5–62–322/17.
20. Minutes of a conference, 10 April 1917; MUN 5–62–322/14.
21. Minutes of a conference, 23 April 1917; MUN 5–62–322/17.
22. Minutes of a conference, 10 May 1917; MUN 5–20–221.1/27.
23. Minutes, MUN 5–62–322/17 and 18.
24. W.C. (127), 27 April 1917; CAB 23–2–140. See also Derby to Lloyd George, 26 April 1917 on the problems of postponement; L.G. F/14/4/39.
25. W.C. (115), 6 April 1917; CAB 23–2–100.
26. Memorandum by W.M.L., late March 1917; Milner Papers, vol. 128, fos. 103–86.

27. The organisations mentioned included the Rank and File Movement, the Clyde Workers Committee, the British Socialist Party, the Industrial Workers of the World, the Socialist Labour Party, the Independent Labour Party, the No Conscription Fellowship and the Union of Democratic Control.
28. LAB 2–254–2189/8.
29. The best printed account is *H.M.M.*, vol. 6, part 1, pp. 102–20. A history of the strike was drawn up by the Intelligence and Record Section for the Ministry of Munitions, dated 29 August 1917; MUN 5–79–341/7. A critical commentary of this account was compiled by R. Chorley of the Ministry of Labour, dated 9 November 1917; LAB 2–254–2440/37. The Ministry of Labour officials were highly scathing of the Ministry of Munitions account. In a Minute Hope Simpson observed, 'The latter appears to some extent to have been framed as an apologia for, and explanation of, the action of the Ministry.'
30. MUN 5–62–322/19, 20 and 21; also 221.1/36.
31. *H.M.M.*, vol. 6, part 1, pp. 106–9.
32. Addison also stated that this was the main problem, without mentioning the extension of dilution, at the War Cabinet, W.C. (135), 9 May 1917; CAB 23–2–159.
33. Minutes of the conference with the A.S.E. Executive, 9 May 1917; MUN 5–20–221.1/26.
34. Minutes of the conference, 10 May 1917; MUN 5–20–221.1/27.
35. Entry for 10 May 1917; *Four and a Half Years*, p. 378.
36. Ibid. pp. 378, 379 and W.C. (136), 11 May 1917; CAB 23–2–162.
37. Minutes of the meeting (G.T. 742), 17 May 1917; CAB 24–13–162.
38. W.C. (139), 16 May 1917; CAB 23–2–170.
39. *H.C.D.*, 5th series, vol. 93, cols. 1896–907.
40. *H.M.M.*, vol. 6, part 1, pp. 115–16.
41. Minutes of the meeting, 19 May 1917; MUN 5–20–221.1/29. C. P. Scott noted in his diary for that day that Lloyd George was 'greatly occupied with engineers' strike and had deputation with him at the time'. C. P. Scott Papers, 50, 904, fos. 62–3. No doubt he was occupied with it, but there is no other evidence that he personally saw a deputation. Perhaps he wanted to avoid a further lengthy interview with Scott!
42. Addison to Lloyd George, 21 May 1917; L.G. F.1/3/20.
43. There was an unpleasant incident of a press release giving Lloyd George the credit for the negotiations. For Addison's resentment see *Four and a Half Years*, pp. 383–6; Addison felt it was the work of Montagu, and Lloyd George was not responsible for it; ibid. pp. 386, 393 and 395. Lloyd George made a statement in the Commons on 23 May ascribing the success to Addison.
44. LAB 2–254–2440/37.
45. Accounts of the conference are in: *Herald*, 9 June 1917; *What Happened at Leeds* (the conference's report); S. Graubard, *British Labour and the Russian Revolution* (1956), pp. 236–41; R. Miliband,

K*

Parliamentary Socialism (1961), pp. 55–7; Kendall, *Revolutionary Movement in Britain*, pp. 174–6.

46. *War Memoirs*, p. 1154. This refers to Milner in particular; see A. M. Gollin, *Proconsul in Politics*, pp. 548–50.

47. W.C. (147), 25 May 1917; CAB 23–2–195. After the conference they also censored press reports of the speeches. Colvin (*Morning Post*) to Milner, 4 June 1917; Milner Papers, vol. 144.

48. *War Memoirs*, p. 1154.

49. *Parliamentary Socialism*, pp. 56–7.

50. Copy of his notes (marked by him) for the meeting of the commissioners at 10 Downing Street, 12 June 1917; L.G. F/78/6/3.

51. Barnes's summary of the reports sent to Lloyd George on 17 July 1917; L.G. F/78/5/1. The reports were published with a summary (Cd. 8662–8669). For the problems of South Wales and the influence of 'the teaching of the Central College' see Barnes to Lloyd George, 20 August 1917; L.G. F/4/2/10.

52. This memorandum of 30 July 1917 gives details of the growth of the Rank and File Movement; L.G. F/78/5/1.

53. W.C. (159), 8 June 1917; CAB 23–3–15. The War Cabinet had earlier asked the Food Controller to consider it in view of restriction of imports which could lead to 'speculation and the creation of monopolies in articles that are arbitrarily reduced'. W.C. (70), 16 February 1917; CAB 23–1–240.

54. W.C. (171), 27 June 1917; CAB 23–3–54/5.

55. W.C. (188), 17 July 1917; CAB 23–3–114.

56. Undated Ministry of Food memorandum; MAF 60–159.

57. W.C. (190), 19 July 1917; CAB 23–3–117/8. 'Food Control and Labour Unrest', 10 October 1917; MAF 60–372.

58. Memorandum, mid-1918; MAF 60.469.

59. *Four and a Half Years*, p. 390.

60. W.C. (190 and 225), 19 July and 28 August 1917; CAB 23–3–118 and 242. The details of Government control of cereals during the war and up to the end of control are given in an undated memorandum; MAF 60–468.

61. Memorandum, 17 September 1918; MAF 60–159.

62. W.C. (188), 17 July 1917; CAB 23–3–114.

63. W.C. (192), 20 July 1917; CAB 23–3–125.

64. W.C. (169 and 170), 26 and 27 June 1917; CAB 23–3–48 and 51. It felt the men supplied by the army should not be discharged 'on the understanding it is temporary, until the question of industrial conscription is raised'. W.C. (184), 13 July 1917; CAB 23–3–103.

65. L.G. F/78/7/5.

66. W.C. (232) and (243), 13 September and 2 October 1917; CAB 23–4–45 and 75.

67. W.C. (194), 24 July 1917; CAB 23–3–129.

68. W.C. (217), 17 August 1917; CAB 23–3–216. See also W.C. (75), 20 February 1917 (where he first urged that 'a discontented

teaching class was a social danger'); CAB 23-1-249, and W.C. (268), 8 November 1917; CAB 23-4-161.

69. Minutes of the conference, 19 April 1917; LAB 2-254-2189/8.

70. Memorandum, 24 April 1917; LAB 2/254-2189/14. This gives an account of these events and reproduces the constitution.

71. Memorandum, 9 June 1917; LAB 2/254-2189/18.

72. 'The Growth of the Shop Steward Movement' (G.T. 897); CAB 24-14-424. He dubbed this policy 'giving Home Rule to industry' in a further memorandum on the subject. 'Industrial Unrest' (G.T. 1185) CAB 24-17-303.

73. For the Whitley proposals and the working of the committees see in particular Charles, *Development of Industrial Relations*, pp. 77–226; E. Halevy, *The Era of Tyrannies* (1967), pp. 82–122; Bayliss, *British Wages Councils*, pp. 13–16; H. Clay, *The Problem of Industrial Relations* (1929), pp. 143–84; and, less usefully, P. B. Johnson, *Land Fit For Heroes* (1968), pp. 156–64. It is difficult to judge whether the Ministries influenced the Whitley Committee's views or vice versa. It seems likeliest that the former was the case or that both arrived at this proposal separately; see the folders LAB 2-254-2189/8A and LAB 2-254-12475.

74. W.C. (157), 7 June 1917; CAB 23-3-11.

75. W.C. (165 and 247); CAB 23-3-35 and CAB 23-4-88.

76. Weekly Report on Labour Unrest, 9 August 1917; CAB 24-22-249.

77. As recognised in memoranda on the subject in August 1917; LAB 2-12475/2.

78. Memorandum, 9 June 1917; LAB 2/254-2189/18.

79. 'Attitude of Employers and Employed to the Whitley Report' (G.T. 2176) by G. H. Roberts; CAB 24-27.

80. Ministry of Munitions memorandum, 9 June 1917. The union leaders' doubts were well expressed by Dawtrey at a conference, 22 August 1917; MUN 5-71-324/31. One memorandum urged that 'the trade union officials should be brigaded with the Government and employers in recognising shop stewards committees (which has been done in the Coventry case)'; LAB 2/254-2440/37.

81. Addison to Lloyd George, 19 May 1917; L.G. F/1/3/19.

82. W.C. (157 and 165); CAB 23-3-11 and CAB 23-3-35.

83. As, for example, on the 25 November 1917 when Wilkie introduced a joint deputation from the shipbuilding industry; *The Times*, 26 November 1917.

84. Addison to Carson, 18 June 1917; Carson Papers, D 1507/4/99.

85. For the friction caused by its ending see the N.A.C. Minutes (105), 16 October 1917; MUN 5-22-242.1/100. The War Cabinet called for weekly reports on 11 May 1917. The Ministry of Labour's proposals to meet this request are in LAB 2-254-2189/11.

86. The negotiations took place between May and August. The records of the meeting are in the series MUN 5-20-221; MUN

5–69–322; MUN 5–71–324; and MUN 5–79–340. See also *H.M.M.*, vol. 6, part 2, pp. 1–16.

87. MUN 5–20–221.1/33.
88. MUN 5–71–324/30.
89. At a conference, 1 June 1917; MUN 5–20–221.1/30. For his committee's official view see their memorandum, 10 August 1917; MUN 5–20–221.42.
90. On 4 June 1917; *H.M.M.*, vol. 6, part 2, p. 2.
91. The view was Allan Smith's at a conference, 14 August 1917; MUN 5–79–340/6.
92. As Addison put it to the conference with the A.S.E., 13 June 1917.

XIII *The Stockholm conference*

1. J. H. Lewis's diary; H. J. Lewis Papers, 10/131/123. Herbert Lewis was the Junior Minister of Education at this time.
2. Henderson to Asquith, 26 July 1916; Asquith Papers, vol. 17, fos. 27–9; cited in Hamilton, *Henderson*, pp. 105–7.
3. Henderson to Asquith, 8 August 1916; Asquith Papers, vol. 17, fo. 45.
4. He specifically asked Lloyd George to allocate him 'man power in its broadest sense' and the Labour aspects of reconstruction as his special areas in the War Cabinet. Henderson to Lloyd George, 13 January 1917; L.G. F/27/3/6.
5. The Stockholm Conference is discussed in Hildamarie Meynell, 'The Stockholm Conference of 1917', *International Review of Social History*, vol. 5 (1960), pp. 1–25 and 202–25; D. Lloyd George, *War Memoirs*, ch. 58; P. Stansky (ed.), *The Left and the War*, which prints selections from various sources including the War Cabinet Minutes (though surprisingly not from the Top Secret Minutes, CAB 23–13); Graubard, *British Labour*, pp. 24–36; Arno J. Mayer, *Political Origins of the New Diplomacy*, pp. 191–241; J. Winter, *Socialism and the Challenge of War* (1974), pp. 253–9.
6. W.C. (104), 26 March 1917; CAB 23–2–69.
7. Rumbold to Balfour, 3 April 1917; F.O. 371–3010, fo. 5.
8. W.C. (135a), 9 May 1917; CAB 23–13–25.
9. W.C. (141), 21 May 1917; CAB 23–2–176.
10. W.C. (136), 11 May 1917; CAB 23–2–162.
11. Telegrams to Italian and French Governments, 15 May 1917; *War Memoirs*, p. 1120.
12. W.C. (139), 16 May 1917; CAB 23–2–170.
13. W.C. (141), 21 May 1917; CAB 23–2–176. Cecil spoke with Ramsay MacDonald on his attitude, and reported to Lloyd George that 'he regarded a separate peace with absolute horror', 29 May 1917; CAB 24–14–334/6.
14. Henderson's biographer implies that the telegram was Lloyd George's personal initiative, Hamilton, *Henderson*, p. 130. It was

drafted by Cecil and approved by Lloyd George, on the basis of the Cabinet discussion. This telegram of 22 May 1917 is printed, ibid. p. 131.

15. W.C. (201a), 1 August 1917; CAB 23–13–59.
16. W.C. (144); CAB 23–2–187. In the event the Sailors and Firemen's Union refused to let them sail.
17. Minutes of the Cabinet Committee on War Policy, 21 June 1917; copy in Milner Papers, vol. 125.
18. R. H. Bruce Lockhart, *Memoirs of a British Agent* (1932), p. 187; cited in Winter, *Socialism and the Challenge of War*, p. 252.
19. Henderson to Lloyd George, 4 June 1917; F.O. 371–3012, fo. 495.
20. Henderson to Lloyd George, 8 June and 1 July 1917; F.O. 371–3010 and 2997.
21. Henderson to Lloyd George, 15 June 1917; F.O. 371–3011, fo. 6. He declined to take over as ambassador as it 'would be regarded as a concession to popular clamour' in Russia. Henderson to Lloyd George, 14 June 1917; L.G. F/27/3/13.
22. *Report of the 17th Annual Conference of Labour Party*, 1918.
23. W.C. (202); CAB 23–3–149/50.
24. *War Memoirs*, p. 1127. For this phrase, see Addison on his return from breakfast with Lloyd George, 3 August 1917; *Four and a Half Years*, p. 416.
25. On his return in January 1917 from a socialist conference at Paris he reported this to the War Cabinet. W.C. (25), 2 January 1917; CAB 23–1–79.
26. *War Memoirs*, p. 1123.
27. W.C. (196a), 26 July 1917; CAB 23–13–37.
28. Printed, CAB 23–13–42.
29. W.C. (198a), 30 July 1917; CAB 23–13–44.
30. See Curzon's and Lloyd George's comments to C. P. Scott on 9 and 10 August; *The Political Diaries of C. P. Scott*, p. 297.
31. W.C. (213), 13 August 1917; CAB 23–3–181.
32. He emphasised it twice in the Commons debate of 13 August, *H.C.D.*, 5th series, vol. 97, cols. 909–32, and it was a regular theme in his observations on Russia during the war.
33. So Ponsonby wrote to Trevelyan on 28 August 1917 after lunching with MacDonald and Buckler. Trevelyan Papers, box 19.
34. W.C. (188), 17 July 1917; CAB 23–3–114.
35. W.C. (202), 1 August 1917; CAB 23–3–149/50.
36. W.C. Special Minutes (201a), 1 August 1917; CAB 23–13–58.
37. W.C. Special Minutes (199a), 30 July 1917; CAB 23–13–47/48.
38. This is a view which Henderson accepted; see P. U. Kellog and A. Gleason, *British Labour and The War* (1919), p. 12. Clemenceau took an even firmer line in France; D. R. Watson, *Georges Clemenceau* (1974), p. 286.
39. See Meynell, *International Review of Social History*, pp. 206–7.
40. Milner diary, 1 August 1917; Milner Papers, vol. 280.
41. Possibly Lloyd George saw Henderson on 7 August, and made it

clear he wanted Henderson to remain in the Cabinet. The only mention of this meeting is M. A. Hamilton, *Henderson,* and here it is muddled with the 1 August account in *War Memoirs.*

42. *War Memoirs*, p. 1129.

43. W.C. Special Minutes (201a), 1 August 1917; CAB 23-13-57. G. M. Young was firmly of the view that Henderson had seen the Labour Executive on his return quite regardless of Lloyd George's view on the matter; see the two notes by him. L.G. F/23/20 and 21.

44. Bonar Law to J. P. Croal, 3 August 1917; Bonar Law Papers, 84/6/99.

45. Lloyd George to Carson, 9 August 1917; L.G. F/6/2/45. This is borne out in the full Minutes of the Cabinet meeting of 8 August; L.G. G/250.

46. Lloyd George appears to have been genuinely very angry over Henderson when C. P. Scott saw him on 11 August; *The Political Diaries of C. P. Scott*, pp. 298-9. The full Minutes of the Cabinet meeting seem to support Lloyd George though early on in the meeting Henderson did urge that they take no decision until after the Labour Party Conference.

47. *H.C.D.*, 5th series, Vol. 97, cols. 909-32

48. *War Memoirs*, pp. 1133-4. Henderson felt that he had done enough in 'intimating [in his speech] that there had been a modification in the attitude of the new Government as compared with the old . . .' Henderson to Lloyd George, 10 August 1917; L.G. F/27/3/14.

49. He informed Lloyd George in advance that he would refer to nothing other than the Nabokoff telegram; L.G. F/27/3/19.

50. Arthur Murray's diary, 13 August 1917; Elibank Papers, 8815, fo. 31. This was the prime point in his letter of resignation to Lloyd George, 11 August 1917; L.G. F/27/3/15.

51. See Winter, *Socialism and the Challenge of War*, pp. 259-63 for a recent account.

52. Ponsonby to Trevelyan, 13 August 1917; Trevelyan Papers, box 19. Trevelyan was just as impressed, and observed, 'The Labour decision is so great an event that it may be better to let them make the running now.' Trevelyan to Ponsonby, 12 August 1917; Ponsonby Papers, box 1917-26.

53. Samuel to his wife, 14 August 1917; Samuel Papers, A157/894.

54. Lloyd George talking to Riddell on the evening of 11 August; *War Diary*, p. 264.

55. W.C. (212), 11 August 1917; CAB 23-3-178.

56. Samuel to his wife, 13 August 1917; Samuel Papers, A157/893.

57. The War Cabinet were optimistic that the T.U.C. when it met on 3 September might reject Stockholm, but felt this was too uncertain and too late for them to delay a decision on passports. W.C. (207), 8 August 1917; CAB 23-3-165.

58. Horace Rumbold to Balfour, 6 November 1917; F.O. 371-3102.

XIV *The manpower crisis, 1917–18*

1. See A. J. P. Taylor, *English History 1914–45* (1965), p. 87 on these statistics.

2. At the War Cabinet on 1 May Lloyd George gave the case against continuing the offensive in the West before American troops arrived and the alternative need for increasing shipbuilding; W.C. 'A' Minutes (128a), CAB 23–13–11. For a recent survey of the Government's doubts on Haig's offensive see P. Guinn, *British Strategy and Politics 1914–18* (1965), pp. 249–56. See also *War Memoirs*, pp. 1366 and 1468.

3. To Lord Riddell, 18 October 1917; *War Diary*, p. 283. He repeated this on the 21st; ibid. p. 286.

4. W.C. (330), 24 January 1918; CAB 23–5–63.

5. W.C. Secret Minutes (247b), 11 October 1917; CAB 23–13–101.

6. W.C. Secret Minutes (282a), 26 November 1917; CAB 23–13–149. The last point is the one Lloyd George put forward on 1 May. On 9 August, when accepting Neville Chamberlain's resignation, he observed that the War Cabinet were against conscription 'on a purely age basis, without reference to their occupation' ('the clean cut'), especially as 'the shipping and food problems have become more urgent'. L.G. F/7/1/14.

7. W.C. (289), 3 December 1917; CAB 23–4–222.

8. W.C. (293), 6 December 1917; CAB 23–4–234. At this meeting Churchill was most anxious to release more men from munitions; contrary to A. J. P. Taylor, *English History*, p. 97, f. 3.

9. Hankey's diary, 6 December 1917; Lord Hankey, *The Supreme Command 1914–18* (1961), p. 739 and S. Roskill, *Hankey: Man of Secrets*, vol. 1: *1877–1918* (1970), p. 469. For Lloyd George's bitter comments on the misleading nature of the army's estimates see *War Memoirs*, pp. 1569–76, and of their 'alarmist tone'. W.C. (295), 10 December 1917; CAB 23–4–239.

10. *H.C.D.*, 5th series, vol. 101, cols. 73–4.

11. There is a useful summary of the background to this measure in MUN 5–8–342/10. See also *H.M.M.*, vol. 5, part 1, ch. 6.

12. W.C. (248), 12 October 1917; CAB 23–4–92/3.

13. See Askwith's later comments in Askwith, *Industrial Problems and Disputes*, pp. 426–45.

14. For this decision, W.C. (49), 30 January 1917; CAB 23–1–161/2. Problems connected with the carrying out of this policy were referred to Henderson and Hodge, W.C. (95), 13 March 1917; CAB 23–2–32. For MacCassey's view of payment by results see his *Labour Policy: False and True* (1922), pp. 298–9. For Hodge's view see his *Workman's Cottage to Windsor Castle* (1931), pp. 193–5.

15. W.C. (252), 18 October 1917; CAB 23–4–106. See also W.C. (283, 285 and 286), 27, 28 and 29 November 1917 on the development of this; CAB 23–4–202, 209 and 213.

16. Via Hankey; L.G. F/23/1/28.
17. A. G. Anderson to Lloyd George, 24 November 1917; L.G. F/2/2/4.
18. W.C. (279); CAB 23–4–192. Milner had the Ministries of Munitions and Labour and the Admiralty discuss the concession, 19 November 1917; MUN 5–8–342/10. See also his diary, 24 November 1917; Milner Papers, vol. 280. Churchill saw such an extension as the chance 'for a rapproachement with labour'; memorandum (GT 2677), 17 November 1917; CAB 24–32–465.
19. Churchill to Lloyd George, 22 December 1917; L.G. F/8/1/21.
20. W.C. (310), 1 January 1918; CAB 23–5–4/6. Similarly Barnes urged, 'This situation was proving one of the main obstacles to the success of the negotiations of the Minister of National Service with the trade unionists.' W.C. (314), 4 January 1918; CAB 23–5–15.
21. W.C. (315), 5 January 1918; CAB 23–5–19/20.
22. W.C. (317), 7 January 1918; CAB 23–5–24/26.
23. W.C. (326), 21 January 1918; CAB 23–5–50.
24. Ibid. and W.C. (329), 23 January 1918; CAB 23–5–58.
25. Churchill to Lloyd George, 21 January 1918; enclosing a memorandum by members of his Ministry; L.G. F/8/2/4.
26. For a recent lucid account of war aims and peace proposals in 1917 see C. J. Lowe and M. L. Dockrill, *The Mirage of Power* (1972), pp. 256–70.
27. Barnes to Lloyd George, 29 October 1917; L.G. F/4/2/14.
28. L.G. F/27/3/20.
29. Lloyd George asked for elucidation on the motion, 19 December. Bowerman replied on the 20th, and Lloyd George made his reply on the 27th; L.G. F/327/3/21–3. The War Cabinet briefly discussed the first letter on the 19th, W.C. (302); CAB 23–4–266.
30. W.C. (308), 31 December 1917; CAB 23–4–282. It is interesting to note that later in the year Balfour took considerable interest in E. J. Phelan's views on 'Democracy and International Relations', which included the comment, 'It would probably be impossible *ceteris paribus* for our Government to make a peace greatly differing from the declared aims of the Labour Party.' F.O. 371–3442–64000.
31. As he said explicitly to C. P. Scott, 28 December 1917; *The Political Diaries of C. P. Scott*, p. 325, and on 3 January 1918 at the War Cabinet; W.C. (312); CAB 23–5–11.
32. To C. P. Scott; ibid. Hankey's diary, 23 and 29 December 1917; Roskill, *Hankey*, vol. I, pp. 471 and 474. T. Jones's diary, 7 January 1918; *Whitehall Diary*, vol. 1, p. 43.
33. At the War Cabinet, 3 January 1918; CAB 23–5–11.
34. The speech is reprinted in his *War Memoirs* as appendix 2 to ch. 70. The statement was drafted by Lloyd George, Cecil and Smuts, W.C. (308A), 31 December 1917; CAB 23–13, and W. K. Hancock and J. Van Der Poel, *Selections from the Smuts Papers*,

vol. 3 (1966), p. 590. Before delivering the speech Lloyd George consulted both the Labour and the Asquithian Liberal leaders; Swartz, *Union of Democratic Control*, pp. 197–8.

35. Beatrice Webb's diary, 1 March 1918; *Diaries 1912–14*, p. 112. Memorandum on an interview with Lloyd George, 27 June 1918; Ponsonby Papers, box 1917–26.

36. At the War Cabinet, 3 January 1918; CAB 23–5–11. Lloyd George emphasised this in his *War Memoirs*, p. 1491. This was the reason sent to President Wilson for not consulting him. W.C. (315), 5 January 1918; CAB 23–5–29.

37. W.C. (313), 5 p.m., 3 January 1918; CAB 23–5–12.

38. There is an account of the negotiations in the first half of 1918 in *H.M.M.*, vol. 6, part 2, pp. 39–63.

39. A. Geddes to Lloyd George, 16 January 1918; L.G. F/17/5/8.

40. There is an account of the meeting in *War Memoirs*, pp. 1593–7.

41. W.C. (324 and 326), 17 and 21 January 1918; CAB 23–5–45/6 and 50. On this latter occasion they warned that 'the rank and file did not yet understand what was proposed and were very angry'.

42. Substitution had been pressed on the unions in November 1916; Geddes stating 'that substitution would apply mainly to unskilled workers'. Minutes of the Parliamentary Committee of the T.U.C., 15 November 1916.

43. Similarly the policy of extending night shifts was modified as the scarcity of manpower and raw materials made the 'making full use of all plant and workshop capacity' a subsidiary consideration. MUN 5–72–324/100.

44. Though it had not been ruled out. W.C. (328), 22 January 1918; CAB 23–5–55. There is a memorandum on this position of roughly this date, L.G. F/4/2/16.

45. W.C. (336), 1 February 1918; CAB 23–5–79. On the 4th C. P. Scott urged Lloyd George to see the engineers, amongst other reasons 'to disassociate the extreme anti-war political movement of a small minority from the industrial issue'. *The Political Diaries of C. P. Scott*, p. 332.

46. W.C. (339), 5 February 1918; CAB 23–5–86. Their report (GT 3814) was approved on 13 March 1918; W.C. (365), CAB 23–5–159.

47. From figures in Jefferys, *The Story of the Engineers*, p. 186.

48. Barnes to Lloyd George, 20 February 1918; L.G. F/4/2/21, and W.C. (356), 28 February 1918; CAB 23–5–134/5.

49. W.C. (356); ibid.

50. *H.M.M.*, vol. 6, part 2, p. 47.

51. W.C. (364), 12 March 1918; CAB 23–5–155. The Secretary of State for Scotland seriously observed 'he was more or less a lunatic'.

52. W.C. (371), 23 March 1918; CAB 23–5–182.

53. *War Memoirs*, p. 1568.

54. Chamberlain for one failed to recognise the degree of opposition

in industry and in Ireland preventing them being done before. A. Chamberlain to Bonar Law, 5 April 1918; Austen Chamberlain Papers, AC/16/1/14. Lloyd George took the unusual step of summoning all top rank Ministers to the War Cabinet to explain the need for such drastic measures, 6 April 1918. W.C. (385); CAB 23-5-16.

55. W.C. (395 and 415), 19 April and 23 May 1918; CAB 23-6-46 and 119.
56. *H.M.M.*, vol. 6, part 2, p. 55.
57. GT 1498, 20 July 1917; CAB 24-20-440/2.
58. W.C. (359), 5 March 1918; CAB 23-5-141.
59. *The Times*, 23 March 1918. W.C. (370), 22 March 1918; CAB 23-5-177.
60. For the impact of this influenza epidemic see Sir R. A. Redmayne, *The British Coal Mining Industry During the War* (1923), p. 188 and Maclay to Lloyd George, 24 July 1918; L.G. F/35/2/69.
61. *The Times*, 11 August 1918.
62. The War Cabinet declined to take this step in early September after lengthy consideration. W.C. (468 and 470), 3 and 6 September 1918; CAB 23-7-96/8 and 101. For Milner's letter to Lloyd George opposing this, 3 September 1918; L.G. F/38/4/12.
63. *War Memoirs*, p. 1567.
64. Minutes of the conference, 16 April 1918; MUN 5-77-326/9.
65. W.C. (398), 24 April 1918; CAB 23-6-60.
66. The details of the scheme were approved 23 May 1918. W.C. (415); CAB 23-6-119.
67. *H.M.M.*, vol. 6, part 2, p. 60.
68. Munitions Council Committee, 21 June 1918; MUN 5-64-322/114.
69. A. Geddes to Lloyd George, 28 April 1918; L.G. F/17/5/18.
70. Munitions Council Committee, 6 May 1918; MUN 5-64-322/114.
71. Munitions Council Committee, 12 June 1918; ibid.
72. For an account of the strike see *H.M.M.*, vol. 6, part 2, pp. 63-9.
73. Conference of 3 April 1918; MUN 5-72-324/121.
74. W.C. (446), 16 July 1918; CAB 23-7-27/8.
75. W.C. (450), 22 July 1918; CAB 23-7-40.
76. W.C. (451), 24 July 1918; CAB 23-7-43/4.
77. Report of the conference, 25 July 1918; MUN 5-79-341/10.
78. A copy of the statement prepared on 26 July 1918, amended in Lloyd George's handwriting, is in L.G. F/79/4/31.
79. Ibid. This series of reports continued until 31 July.
80. Copy in Milner's Papers, vol. 117, fos. 114-31.

Conclusion

1. For details see C. J. Wrigley's 'Lloyd George the Labour Movement' (London Ph.D., 1973), fos. 350-448.
2. In Briggs and Saville (eds.), *Essays in Labour History*, p. 255.

3. A point MacNamara made to Riddell, 3 October 1920; *Peace Conference*, p. 240.
4. At the City Temple, 17 September 1919; *The Times*, 18 September 1919.
5. Riddell's diary, 20 September 1919; *Peace Conference*, p. 128.

Primary Sources

1. *Private Papers*

Asquith	Bodleian Library, Oxford
Balfour	British Museum
Beveridge	British Library of Political and Economic Science
Broadhurst	British Library of Political and Economic Science
Burns	(1) British Museum
	(2) Battersea Public Library
Campbell-Bannerman	British Museum
Carson	Northern Ireland Public Record Office
Robert Cecil	British Museum
Austen Chamberlain	Birmingham University Library
Crewe	Cambridge University Library
Curzon	India Office Library
W. H. Dawson	Birmingham University Library
Dilke	British Museum
Elibank	National Library of Scotland
T. Ellis	National Library of Wales
Emmott	Nuffield College Library, Oxford
H. A. L. Fisher	Bodleian Library, Oxford
Garvin	University of Texas Library (inspected on my behalf by Professor M. Fry)
Herbert Gladstone	British Museum
Grey	Public Record Office
Ellis Griffith	National Library of Wales
Haig	National Library of Scotland
Haldane	National Library of Scotland
J. L. Hammond	Bodleian Library, Oxford
Harcourt	Stanton Harcourt, Oxfordshire (courtesy of Viscount Harcourt)
Hardinge	Cambridge University Library
Kitchener	Public Record Office
Kitchener/Markham	British Museum
Lansbury	British Library of Political and Economic Science
Bonar Law	Beaverbrook Library

Lord Lee of Fareham   Beaverbrook Library
J. H. Lewis   National Library of Wales
Lloyd George   Beaverbrook Library
Lothian   Scottish Record Office
McKenna   Churchill College Library, Cambridge
Milner   (1) Bodleian Library, Oxford
    (2) Public Record Office
Morel   British Library of Political and Economic Science
Morley   India Office Library
Mottistone   Nuffield College Library, Oxford
Murray/Robertson   British Museum
A. Humphreys Owen   National Library of Wales
Passfield   British Library of Political and Economic Science
Ponsonby   Bodleian Library, Oxford
Rendel   National Library of Wales
Ripon   British Museum
Rosebery   National Library of Scotland
Runciman   Newcastle University Library
Russell   Canada (inspected on my behalf by Professor M. Fry)
Samuel   House of Lords Record Office
C. P. Scott   British Museum
G. B. Shaw   British Museum
Simon   Buckfastleigh, Devon (courtesy of Viscount Simon)
J. A. Spender   British Museum
Steel-Maitland   Scottish Record Office
St. Loe Strachey   Beaverbrook Library
C. P. Trevelyan   Newcastle University Library
Wargrave   Beaverbrook Library

Parliamentary Committee of the T.U.C. Minutes (available on microfilm)
Vickers Ltd   Millbank Tower, London

2. *Government Papers and Publications*

Cabinet   (CAB)
Foreign Office   (F.O.)
Ministry of Food   (MAF)
Ministry of Labour   (LAB)
Ministry of Munitions   (MUN)
Board of Trade   (B.T.)
Treasury   (T)

British Parliamentary Papers
Hansard
History of the Ministry of Munitions (*H.M.M.*)

Index